AMERICAN DREAMERS

The Wallaces and
READER'S DIGEST
An Insider's Story

PETER CANNING

SIMON & SCHUSTER

SIMON & SCHUSTER
Rockefeller Center
1230 Avenue of the Americas
New York, NY 10020

Copyright © 1996 by Peter Canning
All rights reserved, including the right of reproduction
in whole or in part in any form.

SIMON & SCHUSTER and colophon are registered trademarks
of Simon & Schuster Inc.

Designed by Kathryn Parise
Photo insert designed by Leslie Phillips

Manufactured in the United States of America

1   3   5   7   9   10   8   6   4   2

LIBRARY OF CONGRESS CATALOGING-IN-PUBLICATION DATA
Canning, Peter.
American dreamers: the Wallaces and Reader's digest:
an insider's story/Peter Canning.
p. cm.
Includes bibliographical references and index.
1. Reader's digest.   2. Wallace, DeWitt, 1889–1981.
3. Wallace, Lila Acheson, 1887–1984.
4. Publishers and publishing—United States—Biography.   I. Title.
PN4900.R3C36   1996
070.5′092273—dc20
[B]   96-21114   CIP
ISBN 0-684-80928-1

For Wally and Lila,
who would want the world to know.
And for Gaelen

Contents

"We have seen the best of our time. Now machinations, hollowness, treachery, and all ruinous disorders follow us disquietly to our graves."

—WILLIAM SHAKESPEARE, *King Lear*

In 1972, at a White House dinner in honor of the *Digest*'s fiftieth anniversary, President Richard Nixon awarded the Medal of Freedom to DeWitt and Lila. *(Wide World)*

Prologue: The White House
1972

At exactly 9:12 P.M., the President of the United States rose from his chair in the State Dining Room and waved his arms for silence. "This is a birthday party!" a smiling Richard Nixon announced to his guests. "The fiftieth anniversary of *Reader's Digest!* On such a birthday, I am sure everyone in this room . . . *and this is a very select group* . . . would like to say a word about Lila and DeWitt . . . or *Wally,* as some of us know him so well."

It was Friday evening, January 28, 1972—a cold, clear night in the nation's capital—and the occasion was a white-tie dinner in honor of the Founders of *Reader's Digest.* Over 150 guests were on hand at the White House, including Cabinet officers and their wives, Charles and Anne Lindbergh, Laurance and Mary Rockefeller, Billy Graham, Norman Vincent Peale, Bob Hope, James Michener, a variety of highly placed conservatives from the worlds of business, government and entertainment, and several tables of senior executives and editors from *Reader's Digest.*

"I was thinking about what the *Digest* stands for," Nixon continued, "that huge readership . . . a *hundred million* people! . . . a circulation of twenty-nine million . . . *it will be thirty million* by the time I finish! But when I think of what the *Digest* means, I suppose that its critics . . . and it has a few . . . as it has, of course, *enormous* supporters . . . would say in a deprecating way . . . *and I say it in a commending way* . . . that the *Digest* stands for God, for Country, and for the Joy of Life!"

Listening to this performance, *Digest* senior editor Jeremy Dole shook his head in wonder. From across the table, his wife winked as if to remind him of his vow not to let his antipathy for Nixon dampen their evening's excitement. This was DeWitt Wallace's moment in the sun, and Dole and his younger *Digest* colleagues considered the tribute well deserved and overdue. Although for most of them the legendary publisher remained a remote figure, they were genuinely fond of him—he was, after all, the provider of their substantial salaries, generous bonuses, lengthy vacations and plush offices.

But it was more than that. Elsewhere in Corporate America dramatic changes were taking place. The traditional cornerstones of the free-enterprise system—valued employees producing honest products for satisfied customers—were being replaced by something very different: *Maximum return to investors* was the new cry; *maximum rewards for management* its inevitable echo. And the gentler values of the past—community, fairness, loyalty— were disappearing in a whirlwind of greed.

But not at *Reader's Digest*. For sixty years, Wallace had run his business as a reflection of his own modest personality and those now-vanishing values, and he saw no reason to change. His publications were esteemed. His customers satisfied. His employees secure and content. That the enterprise remained highly profitable seemed almost incidental—he used the extra cash to expand the business, or to shower benefits on his colleagues. And his colleagues responded with affection, gratitude and loyalty.

At this point in the proceedings, the president proposed a toast to the Wallaces, and then the old man himself was rising to reply. For a long moment, while the applause faded and the guests settled back, he stood silently, a bemused smile creasing his handsome face. In truth, he had every reason to smile. The president of his beloved country stood at his side, and many of its most admired citizens had gathered in his honor. His publishing empire—which he believed to be a force for good throughout the world— had never been more influential or more profitable, and he had made what he felt were unshakable arrangements for its continuation in the Wallace mold "for five hundred years." His colleagues would be well rewarded, as always. But the bulk of the Wallace fortune would go to charity. "After all," he was fond of saying, "we take to our graves in our clutched fingers only what we have given away."

At eighty-two, he remained a tall, impressive figure, only slightly stooped, and when he moved, it was with the same easy grace he had displayed as an eighteen-year-old semipro second baseman. Beneath a high, balding forehead and wisps of close-cropped silver hair, his features were strong—large ears, high cheekbones, prominent nose—but regular and pleasant. There was an *aw-shucks* quality to him, a loose-limbed modesty that reminded people of Gary Cooper or Lou Gehrig. Standing alone in this crowd of the great and the near-great, he seemed entirely self-possessed and yet at the same time unmistakably aloof, his twinkling gray-blue eyes and shy, self-mocking grin hiding far more than they revealed.

He began slowly, almost apologetically, sounding not unlike a man who had anticipated a private evening at home only to discover—*surprise! surprise!*—that his sanctuary had been invaded by well-wishers: "Lila and I" —turning toward his wife, including her in the moment—"feel a debt of gratitude to you all for this wonderful evening, a debt we'll never be able to repay, that will grow and grow in the years ahead"—turning now toward Nixon—"sort of like the *public* debt, Mr. President!" The conservative crowd roared at this remark, and Wallace allowed himself a second smile. As always, the Founder of *Reader's Digest* kept his remarks brief. "These shenanigans are clearly premature," he pointed out. "The *Digest* is still in its infancy and I trust the baby will be with us for many years to come." He turned back to his wife: "I have always believed that age doesn't matter . . . and in support of that theory I offer to you all the blue-ribbon prize exhibit, my ever-loving, *eternal-springtime* wife, Lila *Acheson* Wallace!"

The crowd rose at this, applauding enthusiastically, and the diminutive woman who sat across from Wallace at the head table beamed. Lila *Acheson* Wallace (maiden name *always* emphasized), also listed as eighty-two but in fact two years older, was one of those women who age well, who radiate youthfulness even in their twilight years, and who, by combining strength with vulnerability, bring out the best in some men and the absolute worst in others. She was pretty—with delicate features, a halo of thinning auburn hair, her electric-blue eyes heightened by a heavy application of turquoise eye shadow—and that didn't hurt. But there was something more, something in the angle of her neck or the inflection of her voice, in her way of looking directly at people, of smiling, or not smiling, that conveyed an impression of real beauty and made her the center of attention wherever she was. She craved this attention, seemed almost to *demand* it, and when it was paid she could be very kind. But when it was not, when there was the slightest sign of fading interest, "she could cut your throat so fast," a former Digester recalls, "you wouldn't know you were bleeding."

As the applause continued, Lila waved gaily to her still-standing husband, and he waved gaily back. They had come a long way from the Greenwich Village storeroom where their little magazine had struggled to life on a borrowed shoestring. As sole owners of a publishing empire that extended around the globe, they had become very rich, richer than anyone suspected, richer than they themselves understood. After their deaths, a dozen years later, the world would discover that their magazine and its associated ventures had a market value in excess of six *billion* dollars. And all of it owned by these two aging Middle Americans.

Given that vast fortune, and the fact that the elderly Wallaces had no children and no close family members, it isn't surprising that serious maneuvering had already begun among their most senior associates. Wallace was aware of this. Several of the leading maneuverers were out there in the room tonight, smiling up at him: Hobart Lewis, his darkly handsome editor-in-chief; Walter Hitesman, his affable president; the crusty "money man" Dick Waters; the tangle-tongued Princeton lawyer Barnabas McHenry; the mysterious, sardonic Laurance Rockefeller. They were all out there, all his barons, dukes and advisers. And they all wanted what he had.

But it was *his* Kingdom, and he was in no hurry to give it up. Nor was he entirely convinced that these men deserved to have it. He had been thinking for the first time about bringing outsiders onto the Digest board and had discussed this possibility with his friend Harold Helm, the retired chairman of Chemical Bank. Helm had agreed to join the board, and had suggested that Wallace also ask Laurance Rockefeller, the powerful philanthropist. "Laurance is a fine person, Wally," Helm had said. "He will see that things are done the way you and Lila want them done, that *Reader's Digest* remains always in the Wallace mold."

That was the old man's real concern. The money had never been important. But his magazine was. He saw it as a vehicle for informing and inspiring people—for *teaching*—and with teaching as his goal had achieved an unprecedented success. Every month, his magazine was read by fifty million Americans, and around the world by fifty million more. Every month, while the nation's intellectuals gazed loftily in other directions, copies of "the *Reader's*" materialized in one of every four American mailboxes—eighteen million copies in all, with another twelve million sold abroad. Thirty-nine separate editions; fifteen different languages. No magazine had ever matched that. And no publication of any kind—not even the Bible—had ever informed so many human beings.

Nixon was back on his feet now, and Wallace, who had ended his remarks with a toast to the president's second term, was standing, too, leading a cheer for the President of the United States. When the room was quiet again, Nixon made a surprise announcement: "The highest honor a president can bestow on a civilian in this country is the Medal of Freedom. I have not often exercised this power. But tonight I am doing so, and I believe I have made two selections that millions of Americans will applaud."

The president read the citations—"Their magazine is a monthly university in print . . . teaching a hundred million readers . . . the wonders of common life . . . the joys of work"—and then the Wallaces came forward to receive their medals. Lila was ecstatic, and her unbounded pleasure clearly made DeWitt happy as well. For a long moment the two of them stood together, hand in hand between the president and the First Lady, and delighted in the richly deserved applause of their fellow Americans.

It did not occur to them, or to anyone else in that cheering assemblage, that this brief moment would mark the end of their rise to fame and fortune and the beginning of a shocking decline. Within a very short time, everything they had worked for—everything they were determined to preserve "for five hundred years"—would be swept away. Their magazine would be cheapened. Their employees mistreated. Their empire overrun by armies of salesmen and profiteers orchestrated by the philanthropist they themselves would ask to guard it as a "public trust."

By 1980, DeWitt and Lila would be prisoners in their own castle, ignored by the colleagues whose fortunes they had made, mistreated by the keepers those colleagues saw fit to provide, disoriented, malnourished, hopeless and alone. And they would come to understand—despite their isolation, despite their confusion, despite the pain that understanding brought—that all their careful plans for the future of *Reader's Digest* had turned to dust. That life in the Kingdom—where the bright dreams of their youth had come so gloriously true—had become after all a gray and pointless nightmare.

THE WALLACE YEARS

1889–1981

PART I

DeWitt

1889–1920

CHAPTER ONE

That he was different from their other children was immediately clear to both parents. Janet Wallace was enamored: "He is a baby of the first water," she wrote to her mother. "A prize, a premium, a paragon." James Wallace, A.B., M.A., Ph.D., LL.D., professor of Greek at tiny Macalester College in suburban St. Paul, Minnesota, was not so sure. "The child is a rogue, a rascal, a bandit, a thief," he wrote to his father-in-law, "without character or reputation, utterly lawless, wandering where he will . . ."

Their disagreement extended even to the newcomer's name. "I favor plain John Wallace," James wrote. "Since Janet doesn't endorse this—she favors James, or Harold, or Hubert—I guess we will call him Anonymous for a while."

"For a while" extended from the baby's birth, on November 12, 1889, until three days before Christmas, when his parents finally settled on a name that was anything but plain: William Roy was Janet's choice ("Roy for royal," she insisted. "Roy for *king!*"), while James held out for DeWitt, after a favorite cousin in Lafayette, Indiana. Thus did little Anonymous—part paragon, part rogue—become William Roy DeWitt Wallace.

Although delighted with her newest child, Janet Wallace reacted to the stress of his birth as she often reacted to physical crises: by becoming weak and melancholy. She and "Roy-Dee," as she began calling him, remained confined to her bedroom upstairs in the big frame house at 1596 Summit Avenue, across from the Macalester campus, until Christmas Day, when they joined the family downstairs for the first time. She doted on the child, holding him for hours at a time, dreaming of the great things he would achieve. But when she grew tired, the baby was quickly turned over to her sister, Miriam Maude, who had come to live with the family the year before.

As the New Year began, Macalester's financial status neared disaster. Basic running expenses could not be met, and the college sank deeply into debt. Faculty members left in despair, and the president was forced out. In early summer, with his salary months in arrears, James traveled one hundred miles north to become temporary preacher in the town of Fisher. The money he earned—at $10 a sermon—was needed to fend off creditors. While he was away, the family—including DeWitt's older brothers, Ben and Robert (known as Robin), and older sister Helen—summered with Janet's parents in Wooster, Ohio. It was not the first time this had happened, nor would it be the last.

In 1891, James Wallace was made dean of the college and also took on the administrative duties of president. For the next two years his family seldom saw him, so busy was he soliciting funds, administering the school, teaching and enlisting new students. In 1892, there was no graduating class because there were no seniors. In 1893, the country slipped into a deep depression that lasted for seven years. By 1894, it was clear to Macalester's trustees that the real bedrock of the college was James Wallace himself. They urged him to take over the presidency on a permanent basis, and on commencement day that year his election was announced. Now his troubles began in earnest, as he embarked on a seemingly endless trek in search of funds and students.

To ease the burdens on Janet, who was pregnant again, Ben and Robin were sent off once more to Wooster. In August, Janet gave birth to twins—named Janet and Miriam Maude—and again went into emotional decline. With James scheduled to go East on a lengthy fund-raising trip, it was decided that the rest of the family—Janet, Aunt Maude, Helen, DeWitt and the twin girls—would also seek temporary refuge in Ohio. But with the depression and the continuing crises at Mac, "temporary" stretched out for two years.

In August 1895, while James was canvassing for funds in southern Minnesota, baby Janet came down with dysentery. Although the child's temperature soared, her mother hesitated to call for help. Within a week, little Janet was dead, and now the ailing mother's depression became serious indeed. A hasty telegram was dispatched to James, reaching him at his hotel in the prairie town of Austin. "Janet's death is very sad and I think hearts of stone would weep at seeing such sweetness and innocency pass away," he wrote in reply. But the grieving father made no effort to return to his family. Macalester needed funds, and Macalester came first.

In the next town another letter from his in-laws was waiting. Little Janet's twin sister Miriam was now also sick, and his wife had once again lapsed into depression. Not that she was complaining. Though physically weak, Janet Wallace had a fierce will and if anything believed in her husband's quest more fervently than he himself. For both of them the college was the primary objective. They were patriots at heart, and each believed that democracy flourishes only where the citizens are educated. It was a belief with a long history in the Wallace family.

James Wallace's grandfather, also James, was born May 10, 1771, in Cookstown, a tiny village in the north of Tyrone County, Ulster, Ireland. The Wallace family had emigrated from Scotland earlier in the century during the "Highland Clearances" in which thousands of Scots were forced from their farms so that wealthy landlords might graze sheep. But tyranny was afoot in Ulster as well, chiefly in the form of exorbitant rents. James paid $800 a year for his forty acres, and however hard he worked, the reality of that sum was always staring him in the face.

In the fall of 1793, James Wallace and Mary Barefoot, each twenty-three, were married. Children came in a rush, and the extra mouths made the rent increasingly oppressive. James wanted more for his children. They would never have a better life, he knew, unless they had an education. And they would never get an education while he had to pay $800 to till a patch of rocks.

In 1810, the family emigrated to America, settling eventually on a small farm in eastern Pennsylvania. In 1824, Ben Wallace, the third child of James and Mary, married Ann Black, daughter of a neighboring farmer. Relatives had reported cheap land available in Wooster, Ohio, so the young couple piled their belongings onto a wagon and began a second migration.

During their first year in Ohio, Ben and Ann rented a farm of forty acres south of town. Ben split rails at the rate of one dollar for 300. For cradling grain, he was paid 62 cents a day. When his only horse died, he carried sacks of corn from field to barn on his own broad back. Within two years he had saved enough money—$800—to buy 160 acres southwest of the village of Jefferson. The young family (by now they had a daughter named Elizabeth) began to prosper.

But 1844 was a terrible year. Both mother and daughter died—Ann of pneumonia, Elizabeth after a fall from a horse. At the age of forty-four, Ben Wallace was a childless widower. He did not remain so for long. Twenty-one-year-old Janet Bruce, a recent immigrant from Scotland and a fellow member of the Wooster Presbyterian Church, soon caught his eye. The two were married in 1845, and over the next eighteen years Janet bore five sons: William, James, Robert, John and Benjamin; and two daughters: Margaret Janet and Mary Elizabeth.

Like his father before him, Ben Wallace believed in the value of higher learning. When the Presbyterians of Ohio determined to build a college at Wooster, Ben subscribed $500—the largest amount of any farmer in the county. Young James entered the new college on the day it opened in September 1870, and four years later graduated as valedictorian in a class of twenty-eight. After graduation, James was asked to become principal of Wooster's preparatory school and instructor of Greek in the college. One of his first students was Janet Davis, daughter of the Reverend T. K. Davis, university librarian. James was quickly taken with "Jennie" Davis. She was small, with delicate features and a lively personality, and her love for books and piety matched his own.

The two were married on September 2, 1878, in the Davis home on College Hill, and shortly thereafter babies began to arrive. In the spring of 1887, James resigned from Wooster to accept the professorships of Greek and Old English at Macalester College in St. Paul. He did this with trepidation. Wooster was an established institution with a bright future. Macalester was two years old, with a student body of eight sophomores and nine freshmen. Yet James and Janet didn't hesitate. Minnesota was pioneer territory, and other Christian denominations had already established colleges there. If the Presbyterians wanted to play a role on the expanding frontier, they too would need a college in which to educate their leaders.

After baby Janet died in that dismal Summer of 1895, Janet Wallace's mental health deteriorated sharply. Concerned about her "neurasthenia," and the effect it was having on the children, her parents made arrangements for her to go off to the famous sanitarium run by John Harvey Kellogg in Battle Creek, Michigan. Her absence did not sit well with six-year-old Roy DeWitt. His sister had died. His father was off canvassing. Now his mother had disappeared. Would she ever come back? Was her illness in some way *his* fault? He was full of questions, but no one in that overburdened household had time to hear him out.

That winter, after Janet had returned to Wooster, she wrote to James: "For more than a year the children and I have been homesick for Macalester, but we have held our peace. We cannot hold it much longer. Have you before God a right to utterly wear out your family for any cause?" The Wooster relatives, concerned about Janet's health, urged James to give up on Macalester. Even young Roy got into the act. During a session of religious instruction, he was asked if he understood what heaven was. "Yes," he answered. The teacher wondered if he wanted to go there. "No!" he replied. "I want to go to Macalester!"

In August 1896, when it appeared the college would somehow stumble through another year, James finally brought his family home. DeWitt entered school for the first time and quickly proved himself a precocious student, completing six years of elementary school in four years. He was a handsome lad, with an impish smile and an irrepressible spirit—the kind of boy few mothers can resist—and Janet became more convinced than ever that God had given her this son for a special purpose. In the afternoons, when she heard Roy's bicycle bell in the backyard, she always called him to her kitchen. They would sit there at the table, just the two of them, with a pitcher of milk and a plate of cookies. And Janet found she could confide in Roy DeWitt all the things she could not confide in James.

Although the family was together again, these were not easy years for the Wallace clan. The economic depression continued, and soon they found themselves living in penury. All three boys were expected to find jobs and contribute to the family finances. Ben and Robin dutifully turned over whatever they earned. But DeWitt always managed to hold back a portion. He worked very hard, mowing lawns, weeding gardens, raking leaves, shoveling snow. In his thirteenth year, he started a business raising chickens and selling eggs, and the daily "books" he kept displayed a talent for organization and detail that would later serve him well.

At Christmas in 1902, the Wallace family exchanged very modest presents. "Our gifts to each other are not expensive," James wrote to Janet's parents, "but they contain much good will." He did not mention that the presents given to all by young Roy DeWitt contained more than goodwill. The budding entrepreneur had used his nest egg to buy lavish presents for everyone.

However grim the Minnesota winters, the Wallace clan had something glorious to look forward to come summer. When Ben Wallace died, James had invested his small inheritance in four hundred acres of Wisconsin forest. In the middle of the forest was a body of water known as Lake Wapogasset, and jutting into the lake was a pine-covered peninsula the family called Wallace Island. Every summer, as soon as commencement was over, they headed for "Wappy."

James and his sons built a cabin on Wallace Island, and then a second cabin. They planted pine trees and orchards of apple and plum, and laid out a vegetable garden. The lake teemed with fish, the fields with wild berries. The children swam, canoed, fished and sailed. "Dear Mamma," DeWitt wrote from Wappy in June 1903:

> We are having a fine time, tho it is lonely and dry without you. . . . Tuesday breakfast: Cold rhubarb and fried potatoes. . . . What others are doing: Todd

—pickin' his teeth with a carpet tack. Clarence—Cleanin' his fingernails. . . . Sabbath Sermon was delivered by Mr. Howell. Subject: "The Sad, Sad Sorrow and Exceeding Sinfulness of Sin. Ugh!"

But there was another side to the fourteen-year-old comedian. That same summer he began filling a ledger with what he called "Camping Notes." And one could argue that the essence of what would later become *Reader's Digest* —useful information in condensed and organized form—was already stirring in the earnest adolescent:

> BLEEDING: May be stopped by an equal mixture of wheat flour and salt.
> COFFEE: Keep in a tight-covered can.
> FIRE, TO MAKE: Hold birch bark in hand. Shelter match. When bark catches, add more. Build up twig by twig.

His was a hard character to pin down: part cutup, part data-gatherer; part saver, part spender; part Mama's paragon, part Papa's rogue. Letters to his mother were signed "Roy." Letters to older siblings were signed "Willie" (or sometimes even "Little Willie"). When he wrote to James, he called himself "DeWitt." He seemed willing to give part of himself away, to take on whatever coloration was likeliest to please. But only part. Unlike his brothers and sisters, he kept a core of his personality very much hidden away.

James Wallace was the patriarch, and James's values—self-denial, penitence, hard work, frugality—pervaded the household. A large map of the United States hung on the wall in the family dining room. During meals, James would conduct history or geography lessons about one state or another, and woe to the child who wasn't prepared. The others went along with this program: Helen studied hard enough to graduate from Macalester with honors. Ben, the patriarch's favorite, would attend Oxford as Minnesota's first Rhodes scholar. Robert and Miriam succumbed to James as well, following exactly the paths he pointed them down.

But not DeWitt. Entering his teens, he discovered in the space cleared out for him by his obedient siblings a glorious opportunity to rebel. For most of his life he had contrived, more or less, to be his mother's "darling boy." But Janet was slipping deeper into her own confused world, so pleasing her had become more difficult. To his parents' dismay, DeWitt's grades plummeted, while his reputation as a prankster soared.

In the summer of 1906, James concluded that his errant son needed a dose of nonmaternal discipline. DeWitt was made to fill out an application to Mt. Hermon, a private boys' school in Northfield, Massachusetts, founded by the evangelist Dwight Moody and run on strict Calvinist lines. "I have not fully decided on my future life's work," sixteen-year-old DeWitt wrote on his application, "but I can say this, that whatever my occupation may be, I intend to do as much good in the world as possible." This declaration, despite his reputation as a hell-raiser, was persuasive enough to gain him admittance, with a full scholarship worth $90. Whether he wanted to go is another question. The idea of escaping Macalester was appealing. But the thought of what awaited him at Mt. Hermon—rich boys brought up in the "social swirl"—caused him great anxiety. "Just believe in yourself," Janet told him. "If you believe in yourself, you can do anything!"

"This place is a penitentiary," he wrote to his brothers that October, "governed by rules appropriate to any asylum for raving maniacs or murderous convicts." Writing to James, he was all business: "Your letters received, which interest me greatly. Macalester ought to be a better place from now on, especially if our house is repaired and you get your full salary." Only when he wrote to Janet did he reveal the real DeWitt:

> Since I probably won't be East again for years and years, it is my duty to see as much of this beautiful country as I can. The best way of doing this by all odds is a canoe trip. Charlie and I would do it, taking a train to a station on the Connecticut River 200 miles north of here and then canoeing all the way to Long Island Sound. . . . What do you think? Your good-for-nothing, Roy.

What do you think? Having shared his dream, he clearly worried that Janet would disapprove. He had come to see his real self—the dreaming risk-taker—as "good for nothing," whereas his other self (the self put forward for his family's approval) was expected to be "good-for-everything." During his first term at Mt. Hermon, in the same ledger once used for "Camping Notes," he began entering references to the interesting events of his daily life. On November 10, after complaining about his job in the school laundry, he balanced the entry by inserting the following "resolutions": "Read Bible more. Think of God oftener. Live a spotless life. . . ."

A spotless life? What healthy seventeen-year-old could approach such a standard? Certainly not young Roy-Dee Wallace. Whatever Janet thought of his canoe plan, the expedition never happened. Some time that spring, DeWitt and best friend Charlie Herriot, after playing major roles in a dormitory brawl against some "rich kids," were banished to separate rooms in remote corners of the campus. "My new cell is a scene of unadulterated barrenness," he wrote to James. "It isn't fair! Charlie and I are thinking of leaving school."

James was not impressed: "I hear your spinal column is weak; that you are run down at heels; that you *think* you have the blues; and a lot of folly of that kind. *You and Charlie don't know what trials are!* Brace up! . . . Write and tell us what you are doing. Your Father."

What they were doing—James's pleas notwithstanding—was escaping from the "penitentiary." Charlie had relatives in Boston, and the two unhappy exiles simply lit out for that city one morning two weeks before the end of the school year. In effect, this was DeWitt's declaration of independence. Blind obedience to James no longer made sense to him. James lived in his own world, with his own goals and values, and DeWitt was ready to risk living someplace else.

CHAPTER TWO

DeWitt and Charlie spent a week in Boston, reveling in their freedom, then traveled by steamboat down the coast to New York, where James Wallace was on sabbatical teaching Scripture at the Bible Seminary. After a whirlwind few days ("horse cars, zoo, Tiffany's," DeWitt wrote in his diary), the boys sat down for a serious talk with Dr. Wallace. What was said is not recorded. It is likely that James ranted and raved, and in the end subsided into confusion. It is known that he gave his wandering son enough money to cover a new suit, shoes, cap, train ticket to Los Angeles, and expenses. And then the boys were off. "Beautiful scenery through NY State," noted DeWitt. "Got drunk & scrapped w porter."

After a short stay in Los Angeles ("palm trees, ostrich farm, barrooms"), Charlie and DeWitt headed north for San Francisco. Charlie had other relatives living in Berkeley, and arrangements had been made for the boys to board there. Once they were settled in, they headed for San Francisco to sign on as construction hands. The Great Earthquake of 1906 was less than a year old, and armies of laborers were still at work removing rubble and rebuilding the city.

Years later, whenever San Francisco was mentioned, a dreamy look would come to Wallace's eyes. There had been something about his experience there that appealed to him—the freedom, the feeling of power, the knowledge that he was helping rebuild a great metropolis. Although he would describe it as "the greatest summer of my life," Janet Wallace obviously didn't share his enthusiasm. "I dislike hearing that you are worried about my being in San Francisco," DeWitt wrote to her in July. *"If I'm not old enuf to be turned loose in a city I suppose I had better go back to the cradle and milk and nipple.*"

The boys worked in San Francisco from May until the end of August. Charlie stayed in Berkeley to begin his freshman year at the university, while DeWitt returned to St. Paul to enroll at Macalester. It was not a festive homecoming. James had elected to spend another year in New York. Janet had retreated again to the sanitarium at Battle Creek; Miriam was living with Aunt Maude; Bob was boarding at Macalester; Ben was doing postgraduate work at the University of Wisconsin; and Helen was living with her minister-husband in Grand Rapids. So when DeWitt stepped off the train at the St. Paul station, there was no one there to greet him. He was on his own.

Yet his college career began on a high note. He was elected class president, found a job in the college bookstore and became a star on the football team. When they lost to archrival Hamline, he had no lack of excuses: "Our bunch scrapped from start to finish," he wrote to James. "We laid them up to a frazzle!" Some frazzle. The final score was 42 to 0.

DeWitt's cheery letters notwithstanding, it is clear that all was not well with the Wallace clan. Janet's emotional health continued on a steady downward course, and by November 1908 she was once again a patient at Battle Creek. She returned briefly to James in New York over Christmas, but by January was back in a sanitarium, this time upstate at Clifton Springs. "Was sorry to hear that our dear little mother wasn't feeling well," wrote DeWitt. "Bob and I are in the pink, feeling great, enjoying life. Soon we will have a grand family reunion at Wappy and we want you feeling pretty swell for such an auspicious occasion. Lovingly, DeWitt."

In the spring of his sophomore year, DeWitt's grades plummeted, mostly because of the effort he and his pals were putting into pranks. As the term ran down, DeWitt announced that he was through with Macalester. "I need two more years," he wrote his parents, "but would prefer to go away where I could take law or business."

After a rousing spring season as second baseman on Macalester's baseball team, DeWitt was offered a contract to play for a semipro team in Leeds, North Dakota. Dead set against this, James made arrangements for his errant son to work instead at his brother's lumber mill in Monte Vista, Colorado. But DeWitt held out. "I have signed my contract with Leeds," he wrote to James. "Mr. Wall has guaranteed a lumber yard job and $60 per month— which I think is pretty good. I will be rooming in a clean hotel with Fred Carson. . . . There is a library there and I expect to do some reading. . . ."

This, of course, was just the picture his parents needed—of a serious young man living a good clean life. Yet a different picture emerges from the sketchy phrases DeWitt entered that summer into his diary: "Playing pool— gambling at Leeds—country rubes and rape across tracks—Bloomer girls

—Blind Pigs," etc. This was the world he longed to live in, the *real* world, where he could be his real self. As for that "clean hotel," in later years he spoke often of his summer in Leeds, and of how to save money he had slept in the back of a truck at the lumberyard.

As the weeks passed, DeWitt began to worry about what would happen come fall. His father had decided to return to Macalester as head of the Bible Department, so there was considerable family pressure for the wandering athlete to return for a third year. But his own strong choice was to head west again to attend Berkeley. James was flat against this plan. "Can't understand why I haven't heard from Father," DeWitt wrote to Ben in mid-July. "I presume his teeming silence spells *s-t-u-n-g* as far as Berkeley is concerned."

Indeed it did. From New York, James had written to another brother in Colorado—Robert Bruce Wallace, owner of the Monte Vista bank—to arrange for DeWitt to spend the next year working there as a clerk. "Work in bank goes okay," a pensive DeWitt wrote to Aunt Maude in September. "Don't seem to be many fellows here to chum with. Guess they are all in school."

After St. Paul, Monte Vista seemed pretty dull to the fun-loving DeWitt, and he clearly found boardinghouse life lonely. To occupy long evenings alone, he began to read magazines. "Am reading a lot," he wrote to Miriam. "There are some good stories in the *Sat. Ev. Post.* I know Aunt M and Mother would disagree, but they are very clever, some of them, and show how other people live and act." Soon this reading became serious. "It is quite luxurious to sit in bed with an electric light overhead and read," he wrote to James in January. "I have subscribed to *The World's Work, The World Today* and *The Outlook.* Am very glad to get *The Literary Digest* from Helen. I also take the *American Magazine* and *System* and *The Chicago Tribune.*"

As the year went on he began to take notes on his reading, and he described this process in a remarkable letter to James:

> I have little cards and when I read a worthwhile article I index the subject, source, date and author. These I arrange alphabetically. On the cards I place an outline of the article—all the facts I wish to preserve or remember. At night, before going to sleep, I review what I have read during the day. . . . One reason so few men succeed is that they don't make a business of acquiring new ideas and *information of practical value.* I direct considerable reading toward this end.

Not bad for a homesick teenager. And not so great a leap from these "outlines of facts I wish to remember" to what would become the foundation of *Reader's Digest:* "Articles of lasting interest, condensed, in permanent booklet form." Still, the old yearning to join Charlie Herriot at Berkeley remained, and in March DeWitt's growing frustration burst forth in a letter to Aunt Maude: "Every time I hear the fellows here talking about college it makes me crazy to go to some good school myself. *If only I had money!* If only *Papa* had money, instead of having killed himself in that one-horse college!"

At this point, in an outburst so heartfelt he was forced to abandon typewriter and scrawl in pencil, DeWitt allowed himself to vent the anger that had been simmering inside him for years: *"Every church school in the country ought to be blown up with DYNAMITE! None of them are any good and as they don't even teach different doctrines, etc, what is the use of the blame things!!??"*

Later that spring, after receiving a letter from James that left him "in a solemn frame of mind," he reverted to gentler tones: "I can understand, Father, why you are not more enthusiastic about my going back to school after the record I made at Macalester. Realizing the life of self-sacrifice you have lived, I have concluded that I would prefer simply to ask you to loan me $250 for the coming year."

Whether James came through with the requested loan, or even responded to this letter, is not clear. What is clear is that on July 20, 1910—with a check from Aunt Maude in his vest pocket and the promise of a substantial loan from his Uncle Boyd (third of the Monte Vista brothers)—DeWitt headed west for the University of California. He enrolled as a freshman, and in later years would say he did so based on his belief that the first two years in college "are always the most productive." In truth, he had no choice, since Berkeley refused to credit his Macalester courses. He was initiated into Psi Upsilon and immediately set about becoming, as he would later admit, "The Playboy of the Western World."

On December 22, DeWitt and Barclay Acheson, an old Macalester friend then doing "pastor work" at a young men's seminary in San Rafael, boarded the SS *Watson,* an overnight steamer that would take them from San Francisco to Portland, Oregon. From Portland they took a train to Tacoma, where Barclay's family lived, arriving around eight on Christmas Eve. As they hurried up the walk to the parsonage at 4303 North Cheyenne (like James Wallace, Thomas Acheson was a Presbyterian minister), Barclay repeated what he had been telling DeWitt about his sisters: Jane was the prettiest, and unattached. She would be after him in a flash. Lila was the liveliest, but Lila was engaged. Marta Mae and Evangeline were too young.

While shedding their coats in the hall, DeWitt peered into the living room where guests had gathered for a Christmas celebration. At the far end of the room, standing by a blazing fire, was a lovely girl, petite and vivacious, with dark auburn hair, sparkling blue eyes, and a mischievous grin. He had never seen such a girl before, and in later years he often described this moment. . . .

> She was talking with several young men, but as I watched she turned her face in our direction. When she caught sight of Barclay, she broke into a grin and came rushing toward us. "Who is this?" I whispered to Barclay. "Oh," he said, "here comes Lila. Remember, DeWitt, Lila is engaged."
> "Lila is engaged," I repeated to myself. "Too bad." I felt self-conscious and awkward. But not for long. Lila was so confident, so full of laughter and fun. All I had to do was smile and go along. . . .

Whatever else happened during his two weeks in the Acheson household, it is clear that DeWitt never recovered from those first few seconds. He must have had a fine time squiring the Acheson girls around, because he spent every penny he had and managed to borrow (and spend) another $50 from the Bank of Monte Vista through a bank in Tacoma. "Haven't heard from Uncle Boyd in weeks," he wrote to James on February 1. "If I don't get money from him within three days, will you be able to send me some? That note is due in 6 days!"

There is no record of a reply from James. Nor is there throughout this period any sign of communication between DeWitt and his mother. She had lost her sympathetic "Roy-Boy"; he had grown up and grown away. So she stopped writing, and he stopped asking why. "Please write soon," he wrote to Aunt Maude in late April. "There is no one I am gladder to hear from—you and Father."

When exams were over in mid-May, DeWitt headed north by steamer for Oregon, where he planned to sell maps around Clatsop and Klamath counties in the southwestern corner of the state. "Sold 12 maps my first day," he wrote to James from Medford. "Three of the first four men I saw took one—a sign painter, a grocery man and the proprietor of a swimming pool. They cost $2.50 of which I keep $1.25. Think I can make big money all right. . . ."

Desperate to locate new customers, DeWitt eventually left the populated West Coast on a branch railroad that took him east to the isolated town of Dayville. "First place I looked into was a real estate office," he wrote to James. "And what should greet my eyes but SEVEN MAPS OF THE STATE OF OREGON! Have felt as down and out, blue, discouraged and homesick the past few days as ever in my life. Your good for nothing and superfluous son, DeWitt."

In the midst of his discouragement, he sat down one Sunday morning in the Dayville cafe and composed an extraordinary letter to Janet. He seemed to be trying to reconnect with her in the old way, to reassure her that their relationship was still intact and their future as bright as ever. "To the dearest little Mother who ever lived," his letter began:

Many times at night I lie awake for hours thinking of you and the rest of the family; of the happy home we had; of the many games of cricket, prisoner's base and hide and seek; of toboggan slides, waterfights, playing in the dark; of cozy winter evenings before the fire; of the stories you told us and the songs we sang. . . . The family has scattered physically, but in spirit we still cling to our Father and Mother. Not so old either but that they may live to see all their children well started in life, each of them making records in which their parents can take the greatest pride. Heaps of Love, Dewitt.

After his experience in Dayville, he gave up on selling maps, worked briefly in a lumberyard in Baker, got fired, worked one day as a carpenter's assistant, was laid off. He had $22 in his pocket, just enough to get him back to Berkeley by way of Tacoma. He wanted to stop by at the parsonage to thank Lila Acheson for forwarding his mail that summer. (In a letter to James, he had added this PS: "Must write now to Lila Acheson, who always adds a note to the letters she forwards. A dream of a girl!")

At this point he had no idea how he would support himself for a final year in college (the idea of actually graduating had been abandoned). It seems likely that James scratched up a little money, and also Aunt Maude, and that his uncles came through once again. However he got the funds, he was soon back at Berkeley. On his birthday that November he received a long letter from Aunt Maude bringing him up-to-date on the deteriorating situation in St. Paul:

The house is quiet, for all are out except Mama. She seems to enjoy the photo of you with your bicycle by the bay window. It is always in sight on her night table, and she studies it for hours on end. . . . Sometimes, when I look at her, my heart stands still. . . ."

CHAPTER THREE

DeWitt spent the summer of 1912 with the family at Wappy, then landed a clerical job with the Burnett County Abstract Company, a real estate brokerage in Grantsburg, Wisconsin. But working in a quiet office for another man was never going to appeal to DeWitt Wallace. The following spring an old St. Paul chum named Don Doty wrote to him about land opportunities in Montana. This set him to dreaming again—about open spaces, freedom, escape.

In June, the two boys headed west. On July 20, DeWitt wrote to James from Big Timber, Montana: "After a week of haying a man becomes appreciative of Sundays off. We are working on a ranch out along the Yellowstone River. Expect to quit tomorrow and head further west."

On his return to St. Paul, DeWitt listened for once to James's advice and took a position handling correspondence in the book division of the Webb Publishing Company, which put out farm magazines and textbooks used in agricultural schools. One of his chores was to wade through piles of pamphlets published by the U.S. Department of Agriculture. It was boring work —except that he discovered, hidden in the thousands of pages he read, nuggets of information that would clearly be of use to farmers. The trouble was, most farmers didn't know these pamphlets existed. And those who did know were kept from the useful information by a barrier of words—millions of words, more words than any farmer could possibly digest.

The secret, Wallace reasoned, would be to break through the barrier—to identify, organize and condense the information that was of truly lasting value. He began to make lists of pamphlet titles, together with short "digests" of the information they contained, and to organize the titles into groups. Under "Apple," for example, he listed twenty-six separate pamphlets, beginning with:

The Apple and How to Grow It. 1900. 32 pages. USDA Farm Bul. #113. "Propagation; locating the orchard; drainage, fertilizers; varieties for different states; pruning, protection and marketing."

He worked on his new project before breakfast each morning, during long evenings at home, whenever he found time. His real work at Webb—writing sales letters—gave him no satisfaction. He was looking for something to do on his own, something that would set him free. "Oh, that boy could write a fine sales letter," an associate at Webb recalled. "But he was restless—like a bird in a cage, always looking out. It was clear he wouldn't last."

He was living at home now, in a house James had rented at 1628 Laurel Avenue. It was not a happy time. James was as immersed as ever in the rigors of his calling. Miriam was there, finishing up college, and Aunt Maude came over on weekends. But a pall was cast over the household by the presence of Janet in her bedroom upstairs. It was hard to say precisely what ailed her. In addition to severe emotional problems (which had begun to resemble schizophrenia), she appeared to be angry—at James, at the demands her family made, at life itself for being unfair—and she expressed her anger in the only way she could: by becoming sick.

DeWitt visited her bedroom each evening on returning home from work. He told her about his day, about his plans for the future, about how he would make her proud. But the woman whose encouragement had sparked his earliest aspirations didn't seem to hear. He watched her fade away, unable to help. A part of him—the part that yearned for her approval—faded with her, and the process left him feeling small and weak, and very much alone.

In January of 1914, Janet lapsed into what appeared to be a coma, and was sent again to Battle Creek. When she responded to treatment, James made plans to send her to Florida along with her father and sister, to recuperate in the sunshine. But then James read about the segregation prevailing in Florida in those years, and his sense of morality was offended. "White teachers in Florida may not even *teach* the colored people!" he wrote to his father-in-law. He would not send his wife to such a place. So Janet remained in Minnesota, and on March 27, under the weight of a sadness she could not express, she passed away. She was fifty-six years old.

Though outwardly "bowed down," James Wallace was no more able to connect with his wife's death than he had been able to connect with her suffering. Within a year, missing not so much Janet as the presence of a wife to look after him, he began pushing Aunt Maude for her hand in marriage. Maude kept him waiting for six years.

There are no letters from DeWitt about Janet's death—he was living at home, after all—and thus no written indication of how it affected him. But of all the family he was the most like her and had clearly been her favorite. And she had held a terrible power over him: Wherever he wandered, whatever dreams he entertained, he had always sensed that Janet was nearby, her head nodding its approval or shaking its dissent. He didn't feel ready to go forward without her nod, and now it was gone forever.

But DeWitt Wallace was also in many ways like his father, and like his father was able to push painful feelings aside. In the weeks after Janet's death, he began to devote more and more time to his idea for a "digest" of farming articles, and to renewed efforts to get ahead at Webb. Throughout 1915, he observed the operation of the agricultural-books division, assembling a list of "inefficient" procedures he would recommend for change. At the end of the year, he showed this list to Albert Harmon, a managing partner. "This is an interesting document, DeWitt," Harmon said. "But we don't believe in this sort of thing at Webb. I'm sorry, but it means you're fired."

Word of DeWitt's other project had gotten around, so to soften the blow Harmon offered to extend a credit of $700 to help the young entrepreneur get started. Yet still DeWitt hesitated. He had been touting "schemes and stunts" for years—canoe trips, homesteading, banking, business, law—without getting past the talking stage. "It's all hot air anyway," he liked to say. "Just stuff I put in to fill the page." Now the page was full. It was time to act.

Within two months his pamphlet was ready for printing and he ordered 100,000 copies. He called it *Getting the Most Out of Farming*. It was 128 pages long, with every page containing references to hundreds of additional pages of valuable farming information available free of charge from the government. He promoted the bulletins with pithy sayings across the top of each page: "The hen is not strong," ran one, "yet many a flock has raised the mortgage on a farm."

He decided early on not to sell directly to farmers but rather to rural banks and feed stores for free distribution to their farmer customers. "These bulletins give information, in precise, understandable language, on any subject the farmer is interested in," said one of his promotional ads. "Millions of dollars—YOUR tax dollars—have been spent securing this information. But no one will *force* you to take advantage of it. IT IS YOUR MOVE!"

In March 1916, full of excitement, he and a cousin named Conrad Davis (whose plan was to sell spark plugs to service stations) set off by train for the hinterlands of Minnesota. Arriving at jerkwater stations along the way, DeWitt would head for the nearest bank or feed store carrying a satchel full of pamphlets. The books (and spark plugs) sold so well that soon he and Conrad were branching farther afield, crossing into North Dakota and Montana. On May 6, from Sioux Falls, Idaho, he wrote to James to announce his purchase of a secondhand Model T: "This auto is the greatest thing ever, no doubt about it! Everything is going smoother than silk, and it looks to me as tho the trip was a sure success!"

For the rest of 1916, he and Conrad crisscrossed the western states in Tin Lizzie, reveling in the freedom it gave them to go where and when they pleased, to meet people off the beaten track, to be thoroughly and completely on their own. They slept wherever nightfall found them, in orchards and graveyards, in barns and barnyards and sometimes, if they got lucky, in farmhouses. When it was cold, they raised Lizzie's leather top, dropped her isinglass side curtains and curled up on the seats. Breakfast and supper were often cooked over a campfire by the side of the road. The two of them were Tom and Huck, and Lizzie was the raft that turned the western plains into their very own Mississippi.

Although shy with strangers, DeWitt was prodded forward by his Scottish stubbornness and natural curiosity, and he soon discovered he was a pretty fair salesman. He liked people, liked learning about their lives, their interests, what they wanted from the world. The people he met as he bumped along from town to town were a simple, decent lot—farmers, ranchers, storekeepers, salesmen, bankers, laborers—imbued with a sense that with hard work, anything might be achieved. There were few college graduates among them, and even fewer intellectuals. But these were not ignorant people. Their minds were lively and their thirst for useful information boundless.

Wallace came to understand this. And something else: He saw that their lives were hard, and that there were no guarantees things would be better at the end of the year. So that while they yearned for knowledge, they yearned even more for what lay beyond knowledge: inspiration, encouragement, reasons to hope. The very act of seeking information—useful facts to apply to hard lives—was itself an expression of hope. Wallace saw this clearly. In his diary from this period, he wrote: "Among these people there is a strong undercurrent of desire for knowledge. Supply it and every dollar's worth of printed matter will come home to roost. . . ."

As the months went by and his stack of pamphlets dwindled, it dawned on him that his idea had worked. He had sensed a need, and figured out a way to fill it. "Cleaned up $62 this week!" he wrote to Miriam in November. "Should be home by December 24. Will spend the holidays working on my latest scheme." Even as he crisscrossed the Great Plains peddling farm booklets, he had been dreaming of a new venture. He wrote to James about this from Portland, Oregon:

> I have a list of the most important trade and business journals—magazines that publish examples of how successful merchants are forging to the front. I propose to get a large number of stores to sign up for a service I would provide. I am going to devote my entire time to reading all these journals in search of ideas of value to my clients. . . . Well, I hope you like my new stunt, and that it will go well so that in the course of time I may cease to be a parasite on society. Affectionately, DeWitt.

He worked hard on the new scheme over Christmas and into the new year. By March, he had his "digest" of trade journals assembled and was making the rounds of St. Paul businesses. He got nowhere, and it didn't take him long to figure out why. There were too few sourcebooks to condense from, and potential customers were already reading the ones aimed at their particular interest.

Discouraged, DeWitt reacted as he often did at such moments. When Mt. Hermon had become "penal," he and Charlie had run to Boston. When Macalester had begun to pinch, he had fled to Berkeley. After being fired by Webb, he had packed up his pamphlets and disappeared into the Great Northwest. Now he escaped his frustration by climbing aboard Lizzie and heading west again, just in time to catch another haying season. He was twenty-seven years old, with no degree, no job, no plan for the future. His father was a respected academic and the retired president of Macalester College, from which all of his siblings had graduated with honors. And what was he? A misfit. A dreamer. A flop.

He found the old ranch in Big Timber and soon was spending pleasant days pitching new-mown hay into cocks. In the evenings, around a potbelly stove in the bunkhouse, he listened to the tall tales of the other ranch hands

—"a motley bunch of good-hearted souls"—and pondered his future. Later still, lying on his cot, his thoughts returned to the notion that had been growing in him since he was a ten-year-old organizing "camping dope" out at Wappy. He was sure he was onto something, that there was a service to be provided in making knowledge accessible to people. The world was bursting with new information. Newspapers were flourishing. Books were being published. Libraries were springing up everywhere.

But magazines were where the action was hottest. Recognizing the importance of magazines as "national educators," Congress had given them second-class mailing privileges in 1879, and publishers had used this subsidy to spread their products across the country. Wallace was well aware of this. He had made it a habit to drop in at the local library wherever he found himself to catch up on the latest magazines. But he was often overwhelmed by the sheer quantity of publications, and by the fact that so much of what they contained was ephemeral. Too many articles, too many words, too much junk—with the end result an almost insurmountable barrier between readers hungry for information and the information itself.

Back in his Monte Vista days, reading magazines in his hotel room, he had overcome this problem by selecting the most worthwhile articles and then outlining "all the facts I wish to remember." He had done the same, more or less, with his farm pamphlets, and they had sold well. The retail version had gone nowhere because the field was too narrow. But what if he broadened the field? What if he took the idea that had come to him in Monte Vista and used it not just to educate himself, or farmers, or businessmen, but . . . *what the hell* . . . to educate everybody!

He thought about this new scheme from every angle. *Where were the flaws? The weaknesses?* He couldn't see any. People were thirsty for information. Yet information was exploding all around them. So there was demand, and there was a way to fill the demand. And *he* knew what it was.

For the next week, pitching hay in the sunshine, he could think of little else. When the haying was done, he returned to St. Paul and took a job as manager of correspondence in the mail-order department of Brown & Bigelow, a manufacturer of calendars and greeting cards. But, as always, office routine was more than he could bear, and within a few weeks he was looking again for escape.

It was not long in coming. Back in April the United States had joined the Great War going on in Europe, and soon calls for volunteers sounded across the country. Wallace saw the war as just the ticket—"a free pass to the greatest adventure of the day"—and became one of the first twenty-five men from the St. Paul area to join up. He was sent to Fort Dodge, Iowa, where after basic training he became a sergeant-instructor, impatiently teaching new recruits what he had only just learned himself. To get to France sooner, he asked for a reduction in rank to private. The move worked, and in March of 1918 he wrote home to announce his imminent departure:

> Dearest Family: We leave in a very few days, and all the dope says we're enroute to France. Am I down-hearted? Say! It would take all the King's horses and all the King's men to hold me back. . . . Lovingly, DeWitt.

Private Wallace ended up in France with the Thirty-fifth Infantry, slogging through a summer of brutal trench warfare. In September, the American Expeditionary Force launched an ambitious offensive along a line extending from the Meuse River to the Argonne Forest. Although this prodigious effort would end in a great victory and the Armistice of November 11, casualties were astronomical: 26,277 American dead, 95,786 wounded.

By the fifth day of the offensive, October 1, 1918, half the men in Wallace's outfit—"F" Company, 139th Infantry—were dead or wounded, and the entire Thirty-fifth Division was at the limits of its endurance. The German First Guards Division had hurled back the Thirty-fifth's final assault, and those who remained alive were hunkered down in soggy trenches, praying for orders to withdraw.

It was a terrible time: hours of waiting in the mud punctuated by spells of bursting shells and poison gas. But Wallace seemed able to disconnect from the danger, and would later describe the experience as exhilarating ("almost as much fun," he would say, "as the summer Charlie and I rebuilt San Francisco"). As in San Francisco, his underlying self—the seldom-seen *DeWitt*—was in the open on this occasion, and this self (which he typically described as "good-for-nothing") seemed suicidally casual about danger. . . .

> *Early that evening there was a lull in the shelling during which I visited the latrine. While I was there the shelling resumed, and the next thing I knew I was face down in the muck. When I came to I realized I was covered with blood, and that a large hole below my stomach required attention. I managed to crawl two miles through the mud and tumult, the sky above me flashing and roaring, until I found a dressing station. . . .*

Five days later, from a base hospital in Ponger-des-Eaux, he wrote to his sister Miriam:

> Things are wont to happen in superlative degree over here, and I hope that for all time to come the most miserable night I may ever spend will remain the one not long ago when we slept in mud and rain, wet to the skin, rolling in our holes in the wet mud clay. Around six o'clock . . . [Here there is a gap where censors have cut his description of actual fighting.] Now let me tell a little tale called "Pretty Lucky." When I reached the Aid Station the doc,

seeing a gaping wound the size of a fist just below my stomach, said, "Pretty Lucky! That's a mighty dangerous place!" At the field hospital, another doctor dressed the spot where a fragment of shell had made a non-stop trip thru a segment of my neck. "Whew!" said he. "Pretty Lucky! It came within an ace of your jugular!" Now another specialist spoke up: "Pretty Lucky! It just missed your larynx!" And I may add on my own account that I was "Pretty Lucky" that another fragment didn't stop in my lung rather than in the muscle of my diaphragm, where the X-rays showed it to be. . . .

Despite the letter's cheery tone, it is clear that Sergeant Wallace had come close to death. For the rest of his life his body reminded him of this: bits of shrapnel would work their way to the surface—of his shoulder, his neck, his nose—and require surgical removal. And one other thing: because of the "gaping wound" beneath his stomach, he would never be able to father children. (It may also be true—and aspects of his later behavior tend to bear this out—that the German shrapnel rendered him impotent as well.)

Comfortably bedded down in the hospital at Ponger-des-Eaux, he could return at last to the idea that had struck him in that Montana bunkhouse. The hospital was well supplied with magazines, and for once he had all the time he needed. The more he read, the surer he was that his idea would work. Two steps were involved: First, he would have to study every magazine he could lay his hands on—something the average person had no time to do —then select the few articles that were of more than passing interest, articles that spoke *directly* to readers about the real concerns of their lives. Then, because even these articles were often too long, he would have to cut away the nonessential to reveal the author's true intent.

In December, he described his progress to Aunt Maude:

> The family can't think highly of the changeableness of my career up to now. But I feel confident that a man's greatest success lies in work closest to his heart. And that is why I have faith in the stunt I have been working on here in the hospital. It's along lines that have been on my mind for years, but I never could think of the means of commercializing it. Now it seems to work out to a nicety. . . .

Three months later, discharged from the Army at Norfolk, Virginia, Wallace made a beeline for the library in Minneapolis, where Aunt Maude still reigned as head of the reference department. For the next six months—while his family looked on in silent dismay—he did nothing but read magazines and practice condensation. He worked swiftly, with the sure skills of a born editor and the unhesitating instincts of a true believer. Within six months, he was ready to assemble his best efforts into an actual magazine he had decided to call *The Reader's Digest.*

At this point he leaned on his brother Ben for $300, then turned to James for an equal amount. James hesitated, recalling how adept his youngest son had always been at "making the money fly." Besides, the very idea of dehydrating literature into pellets to be taken one a day was repellent to a man accustomed to conversing with colleagues in Greek or Latin. But DeWitt was adamant. "We are living in a fast-paced world, Father," he said. "People are anxious to get at the nub of things. I intend to search it out for them."

"Oh," said James, unhappily producing the $300. "The nub of things, is that it?"

With funds in hand, DeWitt placed a print order for two hundred copies of volume I, number I, of *The Reader's Digest.* This prototype issue, dated January 1920, was sixty-four pages long, bound in brown cover stock, with a green title logo set above a boxed statement of the editor's guiding principle: "31 articles each month from leading magazines. Each article of enduring value and interest. In condensed and permanent form." The cost per copy was 25 cents, or $3 for a year's subscription, and the topics covered ranged from sex ("Whatever Is New for Women Is Wrong" from *Ladies' Home Journal*) to ethics ("Is Honesty the Best Policy?" from *McClure's*) to self-help ("How to Open a Conversation" from *Vanity Fair*).

Seeing his dream in print, Wallace was elated. For once in his life he had brought a "stunt" to fruition. He was sure it was good, sure of its value to readers. And he had done it on his own, without permission from anyone.

He mailed copies to leading publishers around the country, offering his magazine to the highest bidder who would install him as its editor, then sat back to wait. He did not wait for long. Some of the replies he received were polite. Some were indifferent. But all were alike in one respect: They rejected his idea out of hand. The basic concept was called absurd, ridiculous, naïve. It was pointed out that magazine articles were meant to be "window dressing" for advertisements, and he *had* no advertisements. His articles were too serious, too *"educational."* And where was the fiction? "You can't publish a magazine without fiction," scoffed Gertrude Battles Lane, editor of the *Women's Home Companion.* Only William Randolph Hearst was even mildly encouraging. "Your publication might reach a circulation of 300,000," he wrote. "That's too small to interest us."

How could this be? He had been so sure of his idea, so convinced of its power. But he was wrong. DeWitt Wallace, Great Editor, was still only "Little Willie." He felt completely deflated, numb with discouragement. He was thirty years old, flat broke, with an unimpressive past, a dismal present, zero prospects for the future.

For a few months that spring, while his dream simmered on a back burner, he attempted to sell real estate. But his heart wasn't in it and he sold nothing. Then he hired on with a wholesale grocery outfit, slogging from market to market around St. Paul, pushing vegetables and canned goods. This was even worse. In March, his sister Miriam married her childhood sweetheart and moved to Pennsylvania. In August, James Wallace and Aunt Maude also tied the knot. Helen and her husband, John, were raising four youngsters in Indiana. Rob, with a degree in forestry from Yale, was working in Oregon. Ben had a position with Westinghouse in Pittsburgh.

Only DeWitt, who had boasted so often of how proud he would make his parents, had nothing to celebrate. He observed the others—that "Happy Tribe of Wallacites"—from what felt to him a great distance. They were inside the circle, it seemed, and he was outside.

In late September of that dismal year, making sales calls in downtown St. Paul, DeWitt ran into his old pal Barclay Acheson. The two men passed a pleasant hour together catching up on things over a few lagers at an open-air beer garden. Barclay had spent the war years working for the YMCA, and was now a Presbyterian minister attached to a foreign-relief organization. He had married, and already had a four-year-old daughter named Judy.

As they were parting, Barclay casually mentioned that his sister Lila was living in New York. "She never married, you know," he said. "The engagement broke up during the war. She's involved with social work now—improving the lot of the working girl. You ought to drop her a line. She lives on the West Side, at 35 Claremont Avenue."

After Barclay left, DeWitt sat alone for several minutes, sipping his beer and entertaining moody visions of blue-eyed Lila Acheson. *How helpful she had been that summer in Oregon. So efficient. So . . . determined. A dream of a girl. . . .*

When he finally left the beer garden, Wallace had forgotten about his next sales call. Instead, he wandered down Wabasha Street toward the Mississippi, idly glancing into shop windows, a thirty-year-old man with nowhere to go. He paused in front of a Western Union office, deep in thought. Then suddenly he smiled. *Why not?* he mused. *What harm would it do?* He opened the door and stepped inside.

The telegram he dispatched to New York that afternoon contained just eleven words. *It's only a lark,* he told himself. *Just another harmless stunt.* In fact, it was a desperate cry for help. And those eleven words would have consequences—for himself, for Lila Acheson, for the future of magazine publishing around the globe—that no one could have foreseen:

CONDITIONS AMONG WOMEN WORKERS IN ST. PAUL GHASTLY STOP URGE IMMEDI-ATE INVESTIGATION STOP DEWITT WALLACE.

PART II

Lila

1887–1922

CHAPTER FOUR

No one in the Acheson family was ever allowed to forget that her birth—on Christmas Day in 1887—had been marked by a special sign. The heralded event took place in a simple farmhouse on the bleak plains south of Virden, Manitoba. Those present for the occasion were the new baby's maternal grandparents, George and Mary Jane Huston, her father, Thomas Davis Acheson, her year-old brother, Barclay, a local doctor, and, of course, her mother Mary.

In the late afternoon, with the remains of the holiday meal put away and the last orange glow of the sun dying in the west, George Huston sat in an armchair in the living room reading his newspaper. To his left, a large fire was also slowly dying, while across the room the family's Christmas tree presided above a scattering of presents and baby toys. Little Barclay, tended by an Indian servant, was playing nearby.

Upstairs, the sound of women's voices rose and fell, and pacing footsteps caused the floorboards to creak with urgency. As the western windows turned completely dark, a chorus of low moans caused George Huston to look up in alarm. A few minutes later, Thomas Acheson, pale face creased by a broad smile, came charging downstairs. "It's here!" he shouted. "A *girl!*"

George Huston leaped to his feet and reached out to shake his son-in-law's hand. Little Barclay, resting in the maid's lap, watched in wonder as the two men laughed and cheered. And just then, as more steps could be heard coming down the stairs, a large blue ornament lost its grip on an upper branch of the Christmas tree and began to fall toward the floor below.

For a brief moment, everyone in the room watched the falling ornament in silence. It bounced once or twice on its journey through the branches, then slipped clear and struck the floor with a faint *splat*, shattering into several pieces. Grandfather George spoke first. "Well, well," he said, grinning in delight. "There's a sign if I ever saw one! We have a new girlchild, popped out of a blue ornament on the Birthday of Our Savior! *Hallelujah!*"

As often happens in families, the larger event—Lila Bell Acheson's arrival on earth—was never thereafter recalled without someone's also recalling the smaller event—the simultaneous fall of the bright blue ornament. The two became fused in the family history: Lila and the blue ball, Lila and the special sign. She grew up hearing that story—heard it every Christmas, every birthday, at every mention of the blueness of her eyes. In time, she came to believe it *was* a sign, that she was meant to *be* an ornament, shining, beautiful, the center of attention for all her years. Blue became her color, almost her theme, and blue was ever-present in her life: in her clothes, her jewelry, her makeup; in the paintings she bought and the rooms she preferred. Blue was the color that made her feel special, and feeling special—admired, envied, *unique*—became the way she liked to feel.

Looking back on the Acheson family history, Lila Bell found much to support this superior self-image. It all began with Alexander Acheson, a prosperous burgess during the days when Queen Mary ruled Scotland. Alexander's oldest son, Sir Archibald Acheson, became a successful solicitor during the first decades of the seventeenth century, and was eventually named solicitor general of Scotland.

After Sir Archibald's death in 1634, the Acheson family migrated to Ireland, where they acquired extensive estates and where the family today is represented in the Irish peerage by the earls of Gosford. Sir Archibald's great-great-grandson, Thomas Acheson, emigrated to Canada in 1837 at the age of seventeen. In 1841, at Mono Mills, Ontario, Thomas married Mary Mason of Lockport, New York, and Mary eventually bore Thomas five sons and two daughters.

In 1875, Thomas and Mary and their seven children packed all their belongings into a "prairie schooner" and headed farther west. When they reached the village of Virden, on the great plains in the southwest corner of Manitoba, they stopped. Thomas claimed a homestead south of town, and on those remote acres farmed until his death in 1884. His two oldest sons became Presbyterian ministers; his third son became a teacher; his fourth son a successful rancher. His fifth son, Thomas Davis Acheson, enrolled at the Manitoba College Theological School in Winnipeg in 1885, and in the same year married Mary Huston, whose parents homesteaded near the Achesons. In 1886, their first child, a son named Barclay, was born.

All these events reached a kind of culmination on that Christmas Day in 1887 when the blue ball fell and little Lila entered the world. For all the glory of the family history, it was a relatively poor and altogether middle-class world she found herself the center of. Her first years were passed in the farmhouse of her mother's parents while Thomas finished his training. In 1890, Thomas graduated from Manitoba College, and in 1891 he and his small family packed their belongings onto a wagon and headed south across the border into the United States, settling at the village of Pembina in the northeast corner of North Dakota. Later that year another girl, Jane, was born, and little Lila Bell—not yet three years old—would insist all her life that her earliest memory traced to this event. She recalled all the preparations for the birth, all the urgency surrounding it, and then the sudden feeling she had of being alone and abandoned. . . .

> *What I remember most of all is how Barclay came to my room that night to tell me the baby had arrived. The two of us whispered about this event, voicing our doubts and fears, and then Barclay took me by the hand and we crept upstairs to the room where Baby Jane lay in state. For a long moment we stared at our little sister in silence. I knew I was meant to be happy. But what I felt was not happiness at all. It seemed clear to me that one precious girl sufficed for any household. . . .*

In 1895, Thomas was ordained by the Presbytery of Pembina, and shortly thereafter the family began a period of wandering from church to church across the northern plains that lasted almost fifteen years, including stops at Hamilton, Cavalier, Bakoo and Park River in North Dakota; at East Grand Forks and Marshall in Minnesota; at Lewiston, Illinois, and finally at Tacoma, Washington. "We were like gypsies," Lila would later say, painting a romantic picture of a life that must have been traumatic, and that left her with an insatiable craving for a safe place to call her own.

Despite the nomadic existence, and the family's near poverty, Lila and her four siblings—Marta Mae joined the clan in 1893, and Evangeline in 1895—shared an agreeable childhood. At least that's the way Lila remembered it. "Whenever something went wrong in my young life," she claimed, "Daddy was always there. He would take me on his knee and we'd have a long talk. He never told me I couldn't do something. 'Let's talk it over,' he would say. 'I'll tell you what I think, and you tell me what you think. Then we'll decide.' "

Thomas Acheson was well connected in the Presbyterian Church, and each successive posting was to a larger pastorate. The various "manses" the family lived in were always comfortable, if not fancy, with a lawn and gardens to play in, and generally an Indian servant or two to help out around the place. "We always lived in small towns," Lila recalled, "and we never had much money. But my sisters and I didn't feel deprived. Every house we lived in had a stable, and so we always had horses to ride and pet and curry and feed.

"I remember one Sunday—I was about twelve—when my sisters and I went riding after the six A.M. service. This was in East Grand Forks, in northwestern Minnesota. I was on a white gelding named Sam, and my sisters were following behind me. As I came racing down the dirt track that ran past the church, I realized too late that the second service was already under way. Afterward, the church elders spoke to Daddy. 'Lila Bell should not ride on the Sabbath,' they said. 'And she should not ride so fast.' Daddy listened politely, but when he spoke his voice was firm. 'Lila can ride whenever she wants,' he told them. 'And as fast as her horse can go.'"

Mary Acheson was a quiet, reserved woman who performed her church-wife duties with impeccable if unenthusiastic decorum. What she loved was painting, and what she loved to paint were flowers. "However shabby the house we lived in," Lila recalled, "Mother would make it beautiful with paintings and flowers. She taught us that beautiful things—man-made or God-made, inside the home or outside in nature—were more important than money. I remember once coming home from school with a small pot of hyacinths in my hands. *Blue* hyacinths for which I had paid fifteen cents. When I gave them to Mother, she laughed with delight. 'So,' she said, 'you had no lunch today.' But I knew she was pleased."

While there never was much money in the Acheson household, it always seemed, somehow, to be enough. The secret lay in attitude. Every month the family gathered around the dining-room table for a budget meeting. Thomas explained how much money was available to cover the next four weeks, and then they discussed as a group how this sum would be divided. Each child got a small allowance, half to go to the collection plate and half to be spent however they wished. Chores were also divvied up—cooking, laundry, beds, barn work, gardens—so that when the meeting ended each member of the family understood that they would make it through another month. But there is more to life than making it through, and Thomas Acheson seems to have understood this as well.

Lila recalled how one day her father summoned his four daughters into his study. "Close your eyes," he said, "and hold out your hands." Then he produced a bag of coins—bright, shiny pennies, fresh from the mint, looking like gold—and began to pour them into the girls' outstretched palms. He poured and kept pouring, and soon their cupped hands were full and over-flowing. Pennies were everywhere, filling their hands, falling to the floor, tumbling across the sunlit room. "There," their father said at last. "Now you will never forget that at least once in your lives you had money, more money than you could hold in your own two hands."

Lila never did forget that moment, or the lesson that lay behind it. Money was important, and meant to be handled with respect. But when something more important than money came along—a bouquet of flowers, a gift for a friend—then money was meant to be spent with abandon, almost to be flung away.

In 1905, the family moved again, this time south to Lewiston, Illinois. Barclay graduated from Lewiston High School in 1906, and the following fall was sent off to a struggling Presbyterian college in St. Paul, Minnesota (where he soon befriended the president's son, a fun-loving young man named De-Witt Wallace). Lila graduated from Lewiston High the following year, number one in her class. Although few females went to college in those days, Thomas was determined that his girls would get the best education available in whatever part of the country suited their personalities. "Daddy and I talked this over at length," Lila recalled. "We finally agreed that I was meant to be a belle and therefore should head south."

Using funds from Mary Acheson's inheritance, Lila went off to fashionable Ward-Belmont College in Nashville, Tennessee. She was eighteen years old, with swept-back auburn hair, intense blue eyes set above a perky nose, and a determined smile. Small in stature—about five foot three and barely one hundred pounds—she attacked the world with a feisty self-confidence that made her seem larger than she was. Beneath this assured front, however, serious doubts persisted. Lila Acheson was on the verge of womanhood, and not at all sure she was ready for what lay ahead. As if to slow the process, she began to eat less—a tendency that would plague her for the rest of her life—and to worry about what she saw as an "overly fleshy" figure.

During her first year at Ward-Belmont, the Acheson family moved for a final time—to Tacoma, Washington, where Thomas was named vice president of Whitworth College. Two years later, Lila transferred to the School of Social Services at the University of Oregon. Her southern interlude had been pleasant, but she was twenty-one now and felt the time had come to learn some practical skills. Barclay was in training—like his father and uncles before him—to become a minister. Since Lila was not allowed to follow in their footsteps (which made her furious), a career in social service seemed the best way to accomplish some good in the world.

After graduation, Lila spent a boring summer doing nothing at the family home in Tacoma. Her fiancé, a wealthy Seattle man much admired by the family, was working in San Francisco, and her father had discouraged her from seeking employment herself. "Daddy was of the Old School," she later said, "strongly opposed to the idea of working women. I was meant to marry someone respectable, and settle down for life. I argued with him all summer about this. By September, he had given in."

But when Lila applied to the state superintendent of schools for a teaching position, he told her there were no openings for young women. She pressed him on this, and he finally admitted that there was one possibility. "But I'm afraid it wouldn't suit you," he concluded, peering at the pert young woman who sat before him. "It is on Fox Island in Puget Sound, a most desolate place. The Finnish immigrants on the island have been warring with the original settlers for years. There is a one-room schoolhouse serving grades one through eight. But so far no teacher has lasted out the year."

Lila accepted the position on the spot, and two weeks later found herself on a ferryboat chugging through the fog to tiny Fox Island. She took a room in a boardinghouse three miles from the school. Every day she walked through the woods to school, and every evening she walked back. Her students included several boys nearly as old as she was. They took one look at the "girlchild" sent to teach them and decided she would not last the week.

But they were wrong. On Lila's first day one of the largest boys had his lunch stolen. He went home and complained tearfully to his mama. The next morning, in the middle of the first period, mama came through the door of Lila's schoolhouse with fire in her eyes. But before she could get a word out, Lila told her firmly to sit down. "When class is over," she said, "we'll talk about your problem."

The astonished woman did as she was told, and after class the two women conferred in private. "Your son doesn't need sympathy," Lila explained. "What he needs is courage and discipline. I will help him with this. But you must help him, too."

Word of the new teacher spread around the island, and slowly the atmosphere in the little school began to change. Lila lasted on Fox Island for the entire year, and another year for good measure. During the summer of 1912, she was put in charge of a failing YWCA camp on the island, and by midsummer had it running at capacity. In 1913, she accepted a transfer to a junior high school in Puyallup, Washington. She taught at Puyallup for two years, at nearby Eatonville for two more, and then, with war breaking out around the world, her life as a rural schoolteacher ended forever. Because of the reputation she had made running the YWCA camp, she was recruited by the National Y to help out with the war effort.

For the first time in the nation's history, women were flocking into factories to take over jobs left behind by their departing menfolk. Unaccustomed to factory life, these girls suffered alarming turnover and accident rates, along with depression, boredom and loneliness. To keep the boys on the front lines supplied, something would have to be done for the working girls at home.

After training in New York City under a program sponsored by the YWCA and the U.S. Department of Labor, Lila was placed in charge of thirty social workers at a sprawling Du Pont munitions factory in Pompton Lakes, New Jersey. Working conditions were appalling: hot, noisy and dangerous. The first thing Lila did was to persuade the plant's managers to build a social center. Then she attacked the accident rate. To keep up with demand, the factory was operating around the clock, and this created problems. The night-shift girls worked from eight to midnight, got thirty minutes off for "lunch," then went back to work until 5:00 A.M. When the twelve-o'clock whistle blew, they would gulp down a cold sandwich, then look for a warm corner in which to grab a nap. Called back to their machines, hungry and half-asleep, they were sitting ducks for accidents. Lila changed all this overnight. Hot food was brought in, and steaming vats of coffee. Music was provided, and soon the girls were spending their breaks eating, drinking, dancing and singing. The accident rate plummeted.

Local residents were another problem. Pompton Lakes was a small town, and the sudden invasion of young women was causing considerable resentment. This made Lila furious. She spoke to every civic organization in the area, explaining that her girls were as important to the war effort as the boys overseas. "These women have come to your town to do a vital job—to make the bullets our boys are using against the enemy. They are lonely and scared. They need your *help*, not your anger."

Soon volunteers began to appear at the plant's social center—to teach, to counsel, to make friends. The girls were invited into local homes. Dances were held, and a Christmas pageant. The boredom faded, and the loneliness, and the turnover problem disappeared. Lila was on her own in all of this— the Y had no guidelines to offer, nor did the Labor Department—and she succeeded brilliantly.

When the Armistice was signed in 1918, the young miracle worker found herself in great demand. The YWCA had plans for her, as did the Labor Department. She went first to New Orleans for the Y. The cotton mills and tobacco factories there employed a largely female labor force, under conditions even more primitive than those at Pompton Lakes. Once again, Lila didn't wait for orders. Money was the first requirement. To get it, she walked straight into the inner sanctums of the most powerful bankers and mill owners in town—"into the lions' dens," as she put it—and inevitably emerged triumphant. She was young and pretty, and while undeniably a Yankee also so *southern* in an indefinable way that these smitten gentlemen could not resist. It was a game to her, and that was part of her secret. She enjoyed being the belle surrounded by the powerful men, telling them her needs, getting them to respond. It reminded her of childhood, of sitting on Daddy's knee and telling him the way she saw things, getting him to see things the same way. *Lila can ride as fast as she wants.* It was the same with these bankers. *Lila can have all the funds she needs.*

Having cleared that hurdle, the young social worker turned to her primary mission: The Girls. At first, the task seemed hopeless. They were dirt-poor, slatternly and defiant; many came from broken homes; many had backgrounds of alcohol and sexual abuse. Lila looked at them, and shook her head. They seemed so strange, so unladylike and, to tell the truth, so *ugly*. They looked at her—at this little *Yankee* girl, all prim and proper—and laughed in her face. It seemed, for a time, that war was inevitable.

But Lila won them over without a battle. She purchased a rundown mansion on Magazine Street in the French Quarter. After a top-to-bottom renovation, she persuaded the girls to help her furnish and decorate every room. When they were done, the place had a small restaurant, gracious living rooms where the girls could entertain friends, even a dance floor. And something many of the girls had never seen before—shower stalls.

Lila took her charges to the secondhand stores to buy dresses, nightgowns and other wonders. She taught them basic hygiene, showed them how to cook, how to walk, how to speak. Even how to pour tea! The girls began to change before her eyes, to care for themselves, to care for each other. Eventually, teachers were hired, and Lila organized classes in music, dance, homemaking, languages, even fine arts. At the end of her first summer in New Orleans, her girls organized a Great Ball to take place in the courtyard of the Magazine Street mansion. Lila never forgot that night.

> *I remember standing in the courtyard by myself, in the early evening, waiting for the first girls to appear. Suddenly, two of them came out of their rooms along the upper balcony. The sight took my breath away. They were so shiny-clean and proud and happy. It seemed like a miracle. I had created something beautiful out of something ugly, and it made me very proud. . . .*

With the New Orleans situation resolved, Lila chose to work next for the Presbyterian Church. Its Board of Home Missions had just established a social-service department, and Lila Acheson was asked to become national secretary. In fact, no one really knew what a "national secretary" was meant to do. "Just do what you've *been* doing," Lila was told. "You've been working miracles, and that's exactly what we want—more miracles."

Although based in New York, Lila quickly realized that her most useful role would be to spread the word—to tell other groups and organizations what she had learned about the problems of working women. So she began to travel, speaking to audiences on the San Francisco waterfront, up in the

Mesabi Range of northern Minnesota, back down in New Orleans, in Boston, at the Labor Temple in New York. In the spring of 1920, she was borrowed from the Presbyterians by the Inter-Church World Movement to work for a few months among the migrant families who followed the harvest from the Deep South north into New York State and New England. Lila was appalled by the conditions these families lived under, and did what she could in a short time to make their hard lives easier.

In the middle of that busy summer, Lila found time to write an article for the *Home Mission Monthly*. She described what she had learned during her months among the migrant families, and ended with an impassioned appeal to America's conscience:

> When you see the immigrants arriving at Ellis Island, their faces are happy and hopeful. "Here we are," they seem to say. "We have accepted your invitation and we are really here, at last, in The Land of Our Dreams. Aren't you glad to see us?" Alas, all too soon they learn it isn't *them* we want, but only their work. They come here hoping to enter into American life, hoping to educate their children, hoping for a chance in the world for their little ones. Instead, they are given the dirtiest work we have to do; the worst parts of our cities to live in, where the darkest ideals of American life surround them. And then we think it strange that they don't love America. . . .

This was written in New York in August 1920 by a young woman brimming over with life: confident, determined, on the rise and proud of her accomplishments, never doubting that better things lay ahead. She was serving three masters at once—the YWCA, the Board of Home Missions and the Inter-Church World Movement—and was sought after by still others. Where would she go next? How could she accomplish the most good?

It didn't occur to her, in the midst of these deliberations, that something might be missing from her life. She had gone into the world on her own, against her father's wishes, and taken full responsibility for her future. She had been on the go for nine years, proving herself, keeping up a frenetic pace, the very model of a modern working girl. But in all of this there had been little time for less serious things—recreation, adventure, romance— and no thought at all about the possibility of falling in love or raising a family. (She had long since thrown off her "respectable" Seattle man.) To the extent that such things entered her mind, she quickly pushed them away. All that can come later, she told herself. There will always be time for that.

But time was running out. She was thirty-two now, and the need to marry someone—*whatever* her fears—could be put off no longer. Only in marriage could she find real freedom. And only with a man to do her bidding—to be her agent in a world unfairly dominated by men—could she ever accomplish the truly great things she had in mind. But *what* man? Men in general she found disappointing—too foolish to take seriously and too coarse, too *manly*, to trust.

CHAPTER FIVE

One evening that September, Lila received a telegram that briefly gave her pause. It came from DeWitt Wallace out in St. Paul. She remembered him well. A tall, gentle boy, very handsome, very . . . *different.* And now, out of the blue, this telegram. What could he mean? CONDITIONS AMONG WORKING WOMEN IN ST. PAUL GHASTLY STOP URGE IMMEDIATE INVESTIGATION.

That sounded like him, all right. Mischievous and self-mocking. Barclay had mentioned something about a bad war experience. *How bad?* she wondered. But she had other things to think about just then. She set the telegram aside and pulled out her schedule book.

One week later, in one of those coincidences that make the birth of *Reader's Digest* seem foreordained, Lila Acheson was called into the Manhattan office of her superior on the National Board of the YWCA. A decision had been made to open an "industrial Y" for working women in Minneapolis. Would it be possible for Lila to go out and get things started? Of course. She had been planning a trip to California in any case; it would be easy to stop off for a week in Minneapolis on her way farther west. Only when she was leaving the man's office did she recall the telegram from DeWitt Wallace. *Well,* she thought, *things happen in strange ways.*

She called him from her hotel the night she arrived in Minneapolis. The next afternoon, he took a streetcar over from St. Paul and they met in front of the YWCA. He smiled shyly at her as he approached. He was thirty now, no longer a boy. But an air of boyishness persisted. He seemed sad and lonely, in need of a friend—*almost,* she mused, *in need of a mother.* They decided to take the trolley back to St. Paul. "We got to talking on that trolley," Lila would recall years later, "and we rode it back and forth for hours. We sat in the rear seat, just the two of us, and talked and talked. When we finally said good night, he looked at me for a long time. 'You are the most wonderful girl in the world,' he said at last. 'If I ask you to marry me, will you say yes?' I laughed. 'Don't ask me tonight,' I said. 'Tonight is too soon. Ask me tomorrow.' "

They met again the next day—October 15, 1920—and rode the trolley to the end of its line in the little town of Stillwater on the St. Croix River. They found a café there with a terrace set above the river, and stopped for lunch. Afterward, sitting together in the sun, DeWitt began to talk about a little magazine he had been working on. Lila listened quietly and asked encouraging questions, and eventually (as she later recalled it) the whole story came tumbling out. . . .

> *While DeWitt talked, he looked out over the river, away from where I sat, as if he were afraid to see my reaction. When he was done, he risked a glance in my direction. "What do you think?" he asked. I told him I thought it was a gorgeous idea. "It makes such perfect sense," I said. "It cannot fail."*
>
> *"Oh?" he said, offering that self-mocking smile of his. "That's good to hear, Lila. I appreciate it. But . . ." and here he pursed his lips and frowned . . . "there is a little problem. I've shown the thing to every publisher in the land, and so far you and I are the only living souls who think it's worth a hill of beans. . . ."*

He told her then about the rejections, about the nasty things the publishers had said. He had pretty much given up. It was time, he concluded, to forget his dream and get on with real life.

This time, Lila didn't listen. "I don't *care* what others think," she told him. "Your idea is perfect. All you have to do is stick with it. *Screw up your courage!*"

He looked at her in amazement. "So that's the secret, is it? Screw up my courage?" He smiled, obviously pleased. "Well," he said, "how's this for courage? I think you should marry me. Last night you promised me an answer. Have you got one now?"

Lila giggled. "My!" she said. "Talk about changing the subject. Why do you want to marry me? We hardly know each other."

"We've known each other for ten years. The night we met, that Christmas Eve, I knew right off that you were someone special. Special, hell! You're *wonderful!* I think you're the most wonderful girl in the world! So what do you say?"

She studied his face—firm jaw, high forehead, suddenly sober expression. And something else: seriousness of purpose, tenacity, even stubbornness. This man was destined to succeed, she was sure of it. She also felt that she could trust him, that unlike other men he would keep her safe. Beneath his serious exterior there was a quality—a kind of eager boyishness—that she found reassuring. "What do I say?" she repeated. "Why . . . I say *yes!*"

So that was that. A routine exchange, all in all. Yet beneath the words of courtship something deeper had taken place—an agreement that would cast its shadow over the rest of their lives.

"What do you think?" DeWitt had asked, seeking approval, seeking *per-*

mission. And Lila had given him the words he had to hear: "It is a gorgeous idea. It cannot fail!"

"Why do you want to marry me?" Lila had wondered, a leading question under any circumstances. "Because you're special," DeWitt had said. "Because you're wonderful—*the most wonderful girl in the world!"* For Lila Acheson, those words were needed, too.

Was something else discussed on that sunny terrace? DeWitt Wallace was incapable of dishonesty, so it is likely that he raised the subject of his war wounds and the problem with having children. And Lila must have said it didn't matter. "We'll be too busy for children," she might have said. Or "We can always adopt a child." And, in fact, it didn't matter. Lila Acheson wasn't seeking someone to father her children. Nor did she need a prince to make her whole. What she wanted was a *business* partner, a man with whom she could accomplish great things.

Five days later, her mission in Minneapolis completed, Lila continued her trip to the West Coast. She left behind a DeWitt Wallace suddenly eager to get on with life. He wrote to brother Ben in Pittsburgh. He needed a job, he said. He was getting married, needed money, and Pittsburgh—so much closer to New York—seemed as good a place as any to start. Ben asked around at Westinghouse and discovered an opening in the public-relations department. In December, DeWitt Wallace headed east.

He rented a room in a large Victorian house at 5710 Rippey Street in East Pittsburgh, and set about making a name for himself at Westinghouse. He hated it. Office routine had always bored him, and writing publicity handouts based on someone else's ideas was torture. In the evenings, in his little rented room, he pursued his plans for *Reader's Digest,* reading and condensing, pondering what steps to take next. He became friendly with a man at work who had experience in the mail-order business. One day, he showed this man a sample copy of the *Digest.* After reading the magazine, his friend was enthusiastic. "You don't need a publisher," he said. "Sell it through the mail. Be your *own* publisher."

DeWitt was intrigued. He had been thinking along those very lines himself. But there were problems, not the least of which was money. And how could he marry Lila if he quit his job?

When she wasn't traveling about the country, Lila came down to Pittsburgh on weekends, and the two of them wandered around town looking for a suitable apartment. In late February, on a Monday morning after they had finally found an affordable place, DeWitt's dilemma was solved when he was fired by Westinghouse. The post-war depression that hit the country in 1921 was gathering steam, and the head of his department had been asked to cut back. As the last man hired, DeWitt was the first let go. There was also the matter of the magazine he had been telling everyone about. "I'm sorry about this, Wallace," his boss told him. "But let's be frank. You've been dreaming about something else since the day you started here."

In a cold fury, Wallace returned to the Rippey Street apartment and phoned Lila in New York. There had been a change of plans, he told her. She'd better hang on to her job and her apartment. And she might want to rethink her future with him. Lila laughed. "This is the best thing that could happen!" she insisted. "Now you have no more excuses. *Let's get on with it!*"

He sat down that night and wrote a letter offering a provisional subscription to the *Digest*, emphasizing in straightforward language all the high points of his magazine and asking the recipient to join with him in a mutual effort —a "cooperative service"—to become better informed by reading every month a "diversified selection of significant articles from the leading magazines."

In the days that followed, he began to collect lists of potential subscribers —from teachers' associations, nurses' registries, church groups, professional and women's organizations, social-worker rosters, YWCAs. He worked late into each night, perfecting the basic message, typing up individual letters, stuffing and stamping envelopes. Most of these early letters went to women. "That is where your market is," Lila insisted. "The war has changed everything. Women are out of their homes for the first time, working, growing, curious about the world. They can even vote!"

Lila knew what women wanted, and she believed *Reader's Digest* could supply it. Wallace agreed with her. But he also felt his magazine would appeal to educated people of both sexes. He wrote to every college in the country, requesting catalogs. He compiled lists of faculty members and sent every one of them a letter. He kept at it all that summer, gathering new names, sending out fresh letters. The effort spread out of his own room into his landlady's living area. It covered her piano, her dining table, the floor of her library.

At first, returns were disappointing. But then the flow began to gather steam. He was astonished. People were actually betting $3 that he could deliver what he had promised! As fall came on, he had almost enough money to place an order for his first issue. It was time for the next step. On October 10, he left Rippey Street and headed for New York. Lila had found a tiny garden apartment at 76 MacDougal Street in Greenwich Village. On his first day there, they scouted around for office space, settling on a basement storeroom under a speakeasy at 1 Minetta Lane. Later that day, they visited Barclay Acheson and his wife, Pat, up on West 176th Street. Barclay took a photo of the young lovers "cuddling in a neighborhood snuggery," and later wrote to DeWitt about the "twin subjects" that had been on everyone's minds: the prospective birth of *Reader's Digest*, and the wedding that would unite "two compatible hearts."

Now things happened with bewildering speed. Wallace threw himself into preparations for a final mailing. On the fifteenth of October, he and Lila traveled forty miles north to the village of Pleasantville, where the summer before Lila had enjoyed a vacation away from her frantic schedule. They were married there in the Presbyterian Church, with Barclay Acheson presiding over a ceremony that was traditional in every detail except for one. Lila was happy to "love and honor," but she drew the line at "obey."

Back in New York, the newlyweds changed clothes, mailed off several bags of circulars, then raced to Penn Station to catch a train that would take them to the Pocono Mountains for a brief honeymoon. No descriptions of this trip survive, but one can imagine Wallace pacing the bridal chamber, worrying, brooding, pausing before the curtained windows to stare across the misty hills toward New York, wondering what the mails were bringing in, hoping that his future had arrived at last.

On their return, they found the little "mail drop" at Minetta Lane overflowing with letters—fifteen hundred in all, each with $3 enclosed. Lila was thrilled that so many had responded. DeWitt was distraught that so many had not. But even he had to admit that the last hurdle was cleared. With $5,000 in provisional subscriptions, and an additional $1,300 borrowed from James and Ben, he had sufficient funds to underwrite an order for the first five thousand copies of *Reader's Digest*. He called his printer in Pittsburgh and told him to go ahead. Then he and Lila went to a lawyer and made it official by forming The Reader's Digest Association, Inc. DeWitt was allotted 52 percent of the stock; Lila 48 percent. "I'm rich!" giggled Lila. "Co-owner of a seven-thousand-dollar debt!"

When the first five thousand copies arrived at Minetta Lane, late on a Friday afternoon in January 1922, the young co-editors were ready. Lila had persuaded a dozen girls from the community club down the street to hire on for an evening's work. When only half the expected number showed up, DeWitt wandered into the speakeasy above the storeroom and talked several of the barflies into sobering up for a few hours in return for some easy cash. By seven that evening, this unlikely group—his magazine's first subscription-fulfillment department—had crowded into the tiny basement room to wrap and address volume 1, number 1 of *Reader's Digest*.

By 6:00 A.M. the next morning, the job was done. The Wallaces treated their sleepy helpers to a breakfast of griddle cakes at a nearby Child's Restaurant, then crammed the bulging mail sacks into the trunk of a taxi and rushed off to the post office. The sun was well up when they returned to their apartment on MacDougal Street. They were exhausted, disheveled and elated. It was done.

When we got back to the apartment, Wally filled two glasses with bootlegged wine and we drank a toast to our success. Five thousand copies had gone out to subscribers. If we could build on that, nudge circulation up to ten thousand, we figured we could clear $5,000 a year. And that would be enough. At this point, I remember wandering over to the window that looked out on the courtyard behind our apartment. A group of kids had gathered there, immigrant boys dressed in rags. They were playing a kind of ball game in the early morning sun, laughing happily, shouting at each other in several languages. "Wally, come look," I called. For several minutes we leaned on the windowsill together, sipping wine while the laughing boys played ball in the sun. They seem so happy, *I remember thinking.* They have so little . . . nothing, really. Yet they seem so happy. We'll be happy, too. . . .

PART III

Bright Lives

1922–1950

CHAPTER SIX

They had talked of earning $5,000 a year, of actually living on the income produced by their little magazine. Were they crazy? Was this just another pipe dream? Lying on his bed that crisp January morning, still too excited to sleep, DeWitt Wallace thumbed idly through a copy of the first issue of *Reader's Digest*. He knew its contents by heart, had been laboring over its words and ideas for months. Was it any good? He could no longer tell. His readers—all those trusting souls who had risked $3 for a charter subscription —would have the last word on that.

There wasn't much to it. Just sixty-four pages, including front and back covers of the same plain white stock as the inside pages. No advertising. No illustrations. No color. No fiction. On the front cover, between the *Reader's Digest* logo and a slightly altered statement of principle ("Thirty-one articles each month from leading magazines. Each article of enduring value and interest, in condensed and compact form"), was a drawing of a woman writing on a scroll—an ornament they had selected from the printer's case in Pittsburgh because they were too broke to buy original artwork.

It was an appropriate touch, for Lila had convinced DeWitt that their magazine would appeal more to women—restless housewives and newly-liberated working girls—than to men. In fact, many of the articles in the first issue *were* aimed at a female audience ("Untying the Apron Strings," "Whatever Is New for Women is Wrong," "Wanted—Motives for Mother-hood"), and the masthead listed Lila Acheson, DeWitt Wallace, Louise Patte-son and Hazel Cubberly as its editors. Louise and Hazel were merely female window dressing—cousins of Lila's —and had nothing to do with the maga-zine.

All in all, that first issue was pretty plain stuff. Still, he had produced what his letters had promised: thirty-one articles condensed from the leading magazines. It wasn't slick, not compared with the popular magazines of the day. But there was an undeniable *solidity* to it. These were, for the most part, serious articles on serious subjects. His subscribers—fellow members of his "cooperative service"—could feel justifiably that they were a special group: curious, discriminating, even faintly intellectual. They were *learning* when they read *Reader's Digest,* and in the United States of 1922 there was an unending stream of new things to learn about.

In fact, the country was going crazy. Having won the war to end all wars, America was suddenly a world power and its citizens were hell-bent on enjoying the fact. Everything was changing—manners, morals, fashion, psy-chology—and fresh information seemed to be coming from every direction. New York City had *fifteen* newspapers. Radio had been born, and suddenly the whole nation was listening to prizefights and baseball games, murder trials and the latest song hits ("Yes, We Have No Bananas!"). Movies were all the rage, and names like Fairbanks, Pickford and Chaplin were on every-one's lips.

But magazines were where the "livest" action was, and magazines were everywhere, thousands of them, jammed with pulp fiction and trashy confes-sions, swollen with advertising. More magazines than anyone could read, with more coming every day. *Time* would appear in 1923, the *Saturday Review of Literature* and the *American Mercury* in 1924, the *New Yorker* in 1925.

This was the world—frenzied, sophisticated, unconventional—into which DeWitt Wallace's little "digest" had bravely tottered. No wonder the publish-ers had laughed. How could anything as plain and serious as *Reader's Digest* catch on in a world where everything else had become slick and chaotic? Yet it did. Its very plainness and durability—the way it made sense and sanity out of the wild ephemera of the times—seemed to appeal to early readers. "I love it!" wrote a subscriber from Pennsylvania. "Its contents shine like nuggets of gold!" "The French have a word for your magazine," gushed another admirer. "It's *magnifique!*"

As these early reactions trickled in, DeWitt worried and fretted. Every cent they owned or could borrow had been bet on the magazine. If it failed, *they* failed. To put food on the table, Lila kept her job with the YWCA, doing social work all day and helping DeWitt with the mail at night. To cut their rent bill, they sublet one of their four rooms to a young NYU instructor and his wife, also sharing kitchen and bath. Lila never complained. "Lila is a wonder!" DeWitt wrote to his family. "She is a fiend for reading & improving her mind, loves music, enjoys to keep house, is economical, never sick, easy to look at, thotful and affectionate. What more could a man want?"

Every morning, DeWitt rode uptown on the bus to the Public Library at Fifth Avenue and Forty-second Street. Current magazines were kept out on open shelves in the Periodical Room, and there he spent his days, hunched over a stack of magazines, painstakingly copying out condensations in long-hand. He worked with furious concentration, under conditions that would have discouraged a less-determined man. A depression was under way at the time, and a stream of jobless men poured into the Periodical Room to check the help-wanted columns. Harder to ignore were the winos and derelicts who wandered in from nearby Bryant Park.

Late in the afternoon, he took his stack of condensations to another room where a bank of typewriters was available. Banging away at an old Royal, he turned his handwritten notes into manuscripts suitable for the printer. When he returned to MacDougal Street in the evening, Lila would have dinner ready. They ate quickly, with the NYU couple waiting to use the kitchen, and after dinner settled down to go through the day's mail, balancing receipts against the costs of the next issue. For DeWitt, this was always an anxious time. If the stream of letters coming through the mail drop at Minetta Lane ever slowed, their dream would soon be over.

Inside the front cover of the second issue, for March 1922, a message from Lila happily announced that "*Reader's Digest* has been successful beyond all anticipations. On behalf of those who have felt that the fulfillment of our plan would fill a general need, we thank you." Yet still Wallace worried. The idea that had once seemed so foolproof now struck him as fraught with peril.

For one thing, he was entirely dependent on other editors for permission to use their material. Visiting them to gain this permission, actually entering their offices to explain himself and his magazine, made him sick with anxiety. It helped to take Lila along. While he was shy, diffident and polite, Lila sparkled with enthusiasm and charm. They made an effective team, and no one turned them down. Even George Horace Lorimer, the dictatorial editor of the all-powerful *Saturday Evening Post,* fell for the fresh-scrubbed young couple. The *Post* had a long-standing rule against quotations of their material longer than five-hundred words, no exceptions granted. Yet Lorimer made an exception for the Wallaces.

Only once that first summer did anything approaching a crisis loom. While they were working on the fifth issue, subscription receipts mysteriously slowed to a trickle. For a time it looked as if they would be unable to pay the printer's bill, and Wallace plunged into black despondency. Lila was horrified at the intensity of this mood, a combination of depression and anger so overwhelming he couldn't talk about it. "But then I decided he enjoyed worrying," she recalled later. "My answer was to laugh at his worries, to chide him out of his black cloud." A flood of new subscriptions also helped, and the crisis passed.

Discord loomed from another quarter later in the summer. Greenwich Village was hot and noisy, teeming with people and life, full of temptations and surprises. DeWitt loved it there, reveled in the excitement and the color. Lila felt otherwise. For her, the Village was *too* alluring. Her husband had a magazine to put out, and she was convinced he needed a quieter location. One Friday evening, leaving a local restaurant, she spotted an advertisement for a garage apartment in Westchester County. It sounded ideal, and when she saw the address—in Pleasantville, where they had been married—it seemed an omen they couldn't resist.

The next day, over DeWitt's objections, they took a train north to see what the place was like. The garage was on the hilltop estate of a public-relations executive named Pendleton Dudley. It was a two-story fieldstone structure, of Dutch Colonial design, with leaded casement windows and flower boxes overflowing with geraniums. To the right, beyond a split-rail fence heavy with roses, was a large vegetable garden; to the left, a stone-and-timber pony shed leaned against the garage, crowded by pink and white hollyhocks.

Finding no one at the main house, the Wallaces entered the garage and climbed to the second level. There, under an arched ceiling with exposed beams, they found a single long room with a huge fireplace at one end and a bath and small kitchen at the other. "Wally, it's perfect!" said Lila. He had to admit that it was.

They found Dudley playing golf at the nearby Nannahagen Club. When they told him they wanted to live and work in his garage—to publish a magazine there—he was astonished. But he decided they were attractive and honest, if somewhat naïve, and asked them to suggest a reasonable rent. The deal was agreed to for $25 a month.

Dudley never forgot that first meeting. "There was something about those two that held your attention," he later recalled. "They were enthusiastic and eager, but it was more than that. There was a seriousness about them. They were going to make it work, period."

The Wallaces moved their few possessions from the city the next day— two small beds, a chair or two, and boxes and boxes of letters, manuscripts and magazines. While Lila scoured and painted, DeWitt built shelves for the paperwork. Within three days, they were settled in and working as if the little garage had been their shop for years. DeWitt read and edited, wrote and addressed new circulars, carted sacks of mail to and from the Pleasantville post office. Lila helped out some with the reading, but mostly concerned herself with making their new home comfortable and efficient. In the evenings, Dudley often spied them strolling arm in arm through his garden, taking their first respite of the day. And when Dudley turned his own lights off, around eleven, it was always a good bet that the lights in his little garage would still be burning.

Within weeks, it was clear they needed more room—magazines and letters were spreading out from the working half of their quarters into the space meant for living. "I was unable to dress or undress," Lila would later say with a laugh. "There was no place to put anything. No place to *sit.*" Then Wallace bought himself an ancient desk, and that was the last straw. Lila spoke to Dudley, and he agreed to rent them the pony shed as well, for an additional $10 a month. All the paperwork was moved there, along with the desk, and for the next three years this tiny space—the former home of a single Shetland pony—served as national headquarters for *Reader's Digest.*

By the summer of 1923, the fledgling publishers had seven thousand subscribers. Feeling more confident, they began to get away for short working vacations, taking editorial material for the next issue and driving off to country inns in Connecticut or the Poconos. There they would put together an entire issue in a week to ten days before dashing back to Pleasantville to check the mail and attend to promotional efforts. These respites were important to DeWitt. He liked the idea of getting away, of being free and unfettered, in places where no one could find him. As he told his nephew Gordon Davies (son of his sister Helen), he found he always got more work done on such occasions. . . .

> *During our first Christmas in the country, Lila and I took adjoining rooms at the Inn in Ridgefield, over in Connecticut, and from there we put together the February issue. On Christmas Eve, while Lila wrapped presents in her room, I worked on a stack of manuscripts in mine. I managed to condense five articles that night—a record I never surpassed. In later years I would chide my colleagues about this. "How odd it is," I would say, "that I could cut five pieces in an evening while some of you take several days on a single manuscript. . . ."*

As new subscriptions rolled in, something happened that augured well for his little magazine. The first issues had been more tentative than he liked, almost experimental. He was trying something new and wasn't altogether sure what shape it should have. Lila had her own ideas, and at first he listened closely to what she said. But as readers responded, his confidence grew. He began to "know" what the public wanted, to feel it in his bones, and to an astonishing degree what they wanted turned out to be exactly what interested him. Once he understood this, he never looked back. He could read with ferocity, select material with confidence, condense with assurance. All the while staying true to his own likes and dislikes. What *he* liked, *they* liked. It was that simple.

What *did* he like? From the beginning, his political bias was conservative. His education, such as it was, came mostly from what he read, and what he read mostly was magazines. Since the magazines of the day were themselves mostly conservative in outlook—attacking big government, opposing social reforms, extolling self-reliance—it is not surprising that his political views developed along similar lines. But politics was never a primary concern for DeWitt Wallace. He wanted to *serve* people—to help them lead better, fuller lives. Toward that end, every article in his magazine would have to meet three criteria:

1. Is it *quotable?* Something people will remember and discuss?
2. Is it *applicable?* Does it come within the orbit of most people's interests and conversation? Will they find it useful?
3. Is it of *lasting interest?* Or is it too ephemeral, too perishable, to be of lively interest months or even years later?

Beyond these specific guidelines, there was one overarching principle: Nothing would be taboo in his magazine except despair and defeat. Wallace was himself profoundly pessimistic, always sensing disaster. He seemed to understand that his readers—the upwardly striving mass of average Americans—shared this tendency. They worried, as he did. They yearned for signs of progress, for reasons to hope. As he did. He determined to give it to them, just as he had struggled as a child to give it to his family. He sensed clearly the dark side of things, and this caused him to focus his magazine with religious intensity on the brighter side. He still listened to Lila's suggestions, but as time went by she found (as she later told her niece Judy Thompson) that she had less and less to say:

> *I watched these changes in Wally with interest and approval, and I was wise enough to understand that my time as his editorial sidekick was past. I continued to read magazines and to suggest articles, and I was never shy about expressing an opinion. But after our first year that was the extent of my editorial contribution. The seriousness I had sensed in him on that terrace above the St. Croix River was beginning to bloom. I felt its power and I understood where it could lead—even if he did not. . . .*

On a bright fall day in 1925, while DeWitt was standing outside the garage smoking a cigarette, a lanky young man strolled through a break in the hemlocks and introduced himself as Ralph Henderson. He had seen a copy of *Reader's Digest* at a friend's home the evening before—had stayed up late reading it—and since he was out of work had traveled to Pleasantville to see if the magazine was hiring. Wallace agreed to show the young man around.

In the pony shed, two girls were at work cutting and filing Elliot address stencils. Wallace had just bought a new rack—"big enough to hold 100,000 stencils," he said proudly, "though I doubt I'll ever need that many." The two men then strolled through the hemlocks to an adjoining property where a slate-roofed Normandy cottage was nearing completion. With circulation now above fifteen thousand and gross receipts over $45,000, the Wallaces had saved enough money to build their own dream house—part living space, part office/studio, as Wallace explained. While the men were exploring the studio, Lila Wallace appeared (Henderson would remember her as "blond, blue-eyed and charming") and after a pleasant chat Wallace invited his visitor to lunch at a restaurant in the village.

During the meal, Henderson described his background—Burmese upbringing, missionary parents, Harvard education—and expressed a willingness to help out around the *Digest* in any way that might be useful. Wallace suggested that Henderson read several popular magazines and send him a letter describing the articles he preferred. "The new office will be set up in a few weeks," he said. "Why don't you come back then and we'll see if something can be worked out."

Riding the train back to New York, Henderson was perplexed. Had he been hired? Given a runaround? He didn't know. Probably Wallace didn't know either. Sooner or later, if circulation kept rising, he would have to hire someone. Henderson seemed a decent chap; maybe he would do. But Wallace would think about it. This pattern—of allowing his instincts to work out their own solutions—would come to dominate his approach to every aspect of the business. All the facts might point one way, but if Wallace's instincts pointed elsewhere, that's where Wallace went.

On Henderson, his instincts said yes, and so in early September the young Harvard grad became the *Digest's* first full-time employee. He was paid $150 a month, and was expected to handle the mail, cut stencils and keep the place swept out—a routine broken one day a month when he climbed into his boss's Chevy roadster to deliver address wrappers to the printer in Long Island City. At the end of most days, after the typists had gone home, he and Wallace would shove two desks together so they could swat a Ping-Pong ball back and forth. Then he would grab his jacket and walk back down the long hill to town. For $5 a week, he had taken a room in a boarding house whose address—2 Sunnyside Avenue, Pleasantville, New York—caused his friends no end of amusement. "What's the rest of the address, Ralph?" they would giggle. "Cloud Nine, Paradise, U.S.A.?"

In fact, Pleasantville *was* that kind of town—sidewalks, trees, friendly people. At times, Henderson felt as if he had stepped into a dream, a mythological version of America the Beautiful, and the feeling persisted even during working hours. He sat at his desk in the studio, working his way through sacks of mail that seemed to grow bigger every day. To make room, "Wally" had moved his desk into the living room, where once again he and Lila were forced to share the same space. Wally sat at one end of the room, pounding away at his Corona. Lila sat at the other end, dwarfed by the grand piano she had acquired, tapping out the latest hit song. "The click of Wally's Corona and the hesitant notes of Lila playing 'Blue Room' would drift into the studio in the late afternoon," Henderson later recalled. "It was pleasant listening—an odd kind of love duet. Although at times I had to hold my breath while Lila went looking for a missed note."

It was also symbolic: DeWitt, flailing away at his typewriter with unmatched concentration, provided the effort, the sheer creative drive needed to shape a popular magazine; Lila provided the background, the ordered context against which the work could go forward. She tended her husband as she tended her roses, with patience and discipline. When he blossomed, as the roses did, she nodded her approval. In the evening, at an appointed hour, she would lead him from his desk into the "living" portion of the living room. They would sip cocktails, and she would ask about the problems of his day. Then dinner, and then, night after night, back to his desk. "You mind the magazine," she would murmur. "Leave the rest to me."

It was an extraordinary performance. Other magazines were coming to life in those years, but under very different circumstances. At *Time,* for example, Henry Luce had his friend and fellow Yaleman Britton Hadden to share the managerial load, plus a large staff, substantial financial backing and seventy shareholders. Wallace was alone—one man and a typewriter. His working days ended inevitably under great pressure, as he struggled to finish copy due the next morning at the printers. If he missed the 5:00 P.M. post office closing—a frequent occurrence—he would simply keep typing; then, after dinner, he'd hop into his roadster and drive the copy down to the Pleasantville station to meet the 9:22 mail train. In an unpublished memoir, Ralph Henderson recalled that scene:

The image of that solitary figure pacing the station platform under a single arc light remains as clear in my mind as an old film clip. Suddenly a powerful headlight rounds the curve and the 9:22 sweeps along the platform in a majesty of clanging steel and hissing steam. Wally has positioned himself precisely, and the engineer makes a game of doing it right. The half-door of the mail car pauses within Wally's reach as the postal clerk leans out to take the brown envelope from his outstretched hand. A burst of steam and sudden quiet as the big drivers begin to roll. A shouted "thanks!" and a returned salute. The lordly monster moves into the night, flinging back a single whistle as it rushes away toward the city, toward the printer, toward a success and a destiny beyond the far limits of his imagination. . . .

CHAPTER SEVEN

The circulation of *Reader's Digest* doubled in 1926, redoubled in 1927, and doubled yet again in 1928. By the end of 1929, the seven-year-old magazine had 290,000 subscribers and was bringing in $900,000 a year. The little venture the newlywed Wallaces had hoped might feed and clothe them had become a very big success.

With success came increased vulnerability, but Wallace seemed to sense each new threat before it gathered steam. In 1928, with money in the bank, he began to take his checkbook with him on visits to New York. The other publishers had so far been willing to let him reprint their stuff for nothing. ("Hell," one publisher later recalled, "back then we got a kick out of appearing in the *Digest*. It was like making All-American.") Now Wallace added to the kick by shyly offering checks for the material he reprinted. The publishers were glad to accept—why not? But they began to wonder about Wallace. Maybe there was more to him than they had figured.

Others reached the same conclusion, and toward the end of the decade imitation digests—same size, format, typography—began to appear on newsstands everywhere. Wallace immediately saw the danger. These imitators weren't real competition—their editorial content was trashy and their sales on the stands insignificant. But by pestering publishers for permission to reprint, or by reprinting *without* permission, they threatened to spoil the well for him.

Up to this point, he had resisted single-copy sales. The whole idea, after all, had been to offer a "reading service" to members of his exclusive "association." If he began selling on newsstands, his subscribers might be offended and cancel. Worse, he would be going head to head for the first time with the very magazines he depended on for reprints, and they might not be pleased. Tests in Cleveland and Los Angeles had already proved that the *Digest* would do well on the stands. But single-copy circulation was a rough business, with hundreds of magazines fighting for display, for more sales, for an edge on the competition. It would be a big gamble, and he didn't have a lot of cash to back it up. But it was a gamble he had to take.

In April 1929, using S-M News Company as his distributor, Wallace put

100,000 copies of the *Digest* on newsstands around the nation, and held his breath. Sixty-two thousand copies were sold—far higher than the normal ratio—and no subscribers canceled. But the other possibility—that his source magazines, sensing competition, might act against him—suddenly seemed very real. *Scribner's* refused to renew its agreement, claiming the *Digest* was stealing circulation. Then the *Atlantic* and *Forum* threatened to follow.

But Wallace was not without friends in the magazine world. His unfailing courtesy and clear honesty had impressed the other publishers, as had his insistence on paying them without being asked. A particular friend was Kenneth W. Payne, editor of *North American Review*. Payne convinced his fellow editors that the *Digest* actually added to their circulations by stimulating wider interest in quality magazine reading. With the fire temporarily under control, Wallace moved to extinguish it for good by offering generous contracts to the leading publishers for the right to reprint an article a month. Faced with what amounted to found money, the publishers were eager to sign up. By the end of that year, Wallace held exclusive contracts with the thirty-five top magazines in the country. He had cornered the reprint market, and he intended to keep it.

With Scottish canniness, he staggered the lengths of the reprint agreements so that in any given month no more than two or three would come up for renewal. And he never waited to be asked but always voluntarily increased his contract payments; indeed, as his own revenues grew he often increased his payments in the middle of a contract. He would simply appear in publishers' offices and in his *aw-shucks* manner lay down checks for thousands of dollars as advance payment on new contracts not set to begin for several months—and always at higher rates. For many magazines these payments spelled the difference between black ink and red, and for some they represented survival itself.

As the thirties began, Wallace could look back over eight frantic years and heave a sigh of relief. His magazine was now a clear success, with a growing army of loyal subscribers and an annual newsstand sale that exceeded 100,000. He had accomplished all this on his own, working out of his own home, on his own idea, with his own money. It seemed to him a miracle.

But the real miracle lay ahead. At the end of 1932, his circulation stood at 401,134; in 1934, it was 852,254; in 1936—the year *Fortune* magazine finally revealed to the world what was happening in Pleasantville—*Reader's Digest* was being mailed to an astounding 1,801,393 American households every month. Nothing like that had ever happened in the publishing world, and there didn't appear to be an end to the story. Most astonishing of all, it had taken place in the teeth of the Great Depression. When the writer of the

Fortune article stepped off his train at the Pleasantville station, he must have thought he had entered a different era:

> As you get off the train, any station lounger can direct you to the *Reader's Digest*, and will do so with an air, not improbably adding that his sister—or his cousin, or his aunt or his best friend—works "at the Reader's." If you want the business and circulation offices he points to the First National Bank Building on one corner. If you want the editorial office, he points to the Mt. Pleasant Bank & Trust Co. on the opposite corner. The latter building has a directory in the lobby with the names of three tenants—none of which is *Reader's Digest*. But you trudge up a flight of creaking wooden stairs and come to a door with a sign. It reads: "Please Keep This Door Closed." Beyond it are the *Digest's* editorial offices . . .

Elsewhere in the country, banks were failing. In Pleasantville, they were filling up with *Digest* employees. But all the banks in town couldn't house the magazine's growing staff. During the late twenties, Wallace hired the entire Plesantville Women's Club to cope with his mushrooming subscription list. By 1930, the good ladies were drowning in mail, so he hired two hundred full-time female clerks, with another three hundred on call for seasonal emergencies. The Pleasantville post office was expanded to handle *Digest* mail, and Wallace soon took over its basement and top floor. Other aspects of the business were located here and there about the town, so that at one time fourteen separate locations were involved.

By 1936, much to Wallace's bemusement, there were thirty-two people on his editorial staff alone—performing, he couldn't help but note, pretty much what he for several years had performed by himself. And a curious lot they were. Two had been clergymen, one a missionary. The others had done everything from selling linoleum to designing houses. Only two had previous magazine experience.

His managing editor was Ken Payne, who had come on board when the *North American Review* folded in 1931. One of the ex-clergymen was Harold Lynch, a W. C. Fields look-alike with a throaty laugh and an eye for figures. Lynch had been assistant rector at St. Mark's-in-the-Bouwerie in Manhattan, but had left after being caught in bed with the St. Mark's soprano. A friend had mentioned this to Wallace, who was immediately intrigued. Lynch was a churchman, which was good; he was also a scalawag, which was even better. Wallace sent for him, liked him, and hired him on the spot.

The other ex-clergyman was also the only other editorial employee with previous magazine experience. Charles Ferguson had been a circuit rider in Texas and Oklahoma after graduating from Southern Methodist. Tiring of the preacherly grind, he had turned to writing, contributing to Mencken's *Ameri-*

can Mercury and later producing three books on his own. He was head of a religious publishing house when Wallace discovered him.

Running things across the street in the business office was Arthur Griffiths, a lively Welshman who previously had handled promotional efforts at the *New York Journal of Commerce*. Griffiths was a neighbor who had wandered into the Wallaces' garage one evening during their first year in Pleasantville. The two men quickly became friends, and before long Wallace had persuaded "Griff" to leave the *Journal* and become the *Digest*'s full-time business manager.

With these four men as his chief assistants, Wallace debated his next gamble. Radio and movies were eating into the nation's reading habits, as was the increasing popularity of the automobile. With the Depression added to this mix, many of the *Digest*'s most productive sources had begun to disappear. *McClure's* and *Munsey's* ceased publication in 1929; *Century* in 1930; *Liberty* in 1931. While the magazines that remained were eager to let Wallace reprint whatever he wanted, he worried even so that he might run out of material. And there was something else: He had been corresponding with members of his "association" for almost a decade now, and was surer than ever about what mattered to them. If he couldn't find enough such material in other magazines, why not create it himself?

The very thought made him shake his head. From the beginning, the essential selling point of his magazine had been the service it provided: "It is the one periodical I read regularly," gushed an early testimonial, "knowing that in it I will get the best *sum and substance* of today's literary output." Wallace wondered about that. He had begun to sense that his magazine was, in fact, more than the "sum and substance" of others' work. Part of *his* personality went into the selection process, and another part into condensation. While the articles that resulted were undeniably reprints, they were also unmistakably *Digest* reprints, and he was sure his readers understood this. "We had a pretty clear sense what our growing readership expected," he recalled, "and we were confident we could produce such articles on our own better than anyone on the outside."

But still he moved slowly. The first *Digest* "original," published in April 1930, was unsigned. Called "Music and Work," it was described as "a special compilation." No reaction from readers. In June, Wallace took another step forward: "Music and Animals" was described as "a summary prepared by one of our editors." Still his readers didn't blink. And so it went. In February 1933, he finally put an actual author's name after a *Digest* article: "Insanity—The Modern Menace," by Henry Morton Robinson. When this proved the most popular piece in the issue, the gates were opened and original articles began appearing regularly. *Reader's Digest* was now a full-fledged magazine, speaking in every issue with its own clear voice. In August 1935, the volume of the voice rose several decibels.

The year before, feeling pinched in their Pleasantville cottage, Lila and DeWitt had invested in a country house in Pawling, New York, thirty miles north. A secret to all but their closest friends, the new hideaway soon became the scene of legendary parties. On a Friday in the fall of 1934, DeWitt and Arthur Griffiths were driving to the Pawling house at DeWitt's usual breakneck speed when an incident occurred that would go down in magazine history. As DeWitt recalled it:

> *Griff and I were chatting about something—who would be at the party or what was for dinner—and in the middle of this I bent forward to stub out my cigarette. When I looked up again the car was crossing the shoulder. We sailed over the ditch, crashed through a rail fence, and landed with a resounding bang in a cow pasture. The car was okay, but the left rear tire had blown. . . .*

The two men changed the tire and drove to a nearby garage to have the flat fixed. Noticing several wrecked cars on the premises, DeWitt asked the mechanic whether he had seen any of the accidents involved. *"I've seen everything,"* the man said. "People are being killed left and right. Or maimed for life. Nobody seems to understand how dangerous autos are." The man shrugged. "But what can you do? Just the way folks are, I guess."

Back on the highway, Wallace pondered what he had heard. The garageman was right, he decided. People were so crazy about automobiles that no one was paying attention to the growing slaughter. Back at the house, he called one of his writers, J. C. Furnas, and told him to stop what he was doing and get to work on a piece about automobile accidents. "Make it as bloody and horrible as the accidents themselves," he said. "Squealing brakes. Rending metal. Bodies torn apart. Describe it all second by second, horror by horror. Make readers feel they're *in* the accident. Make them *squirm.*"

Furnas did as he was told, producing an article that was deliberately brutal and grotesque (". . . the flopping, pointless efforts of the injured to stand; the queer grunting noises; the raw ends of bone protruding through flesh . . . " etc., etc.). Wallace added several final touches of butchery, and called the result ". . . And Sudden Death." Above the title, he offered the following warning:

> Like the horror of a bad auto accident itself, the realistic details of this article will nauseate some readers. Those who find themselves thus affected are cautioned against reading the article in its entirety.

Wallace showed the article to knowledgeable people in publishing. "Don't run it," was their universal reaction. Several insurance companies were given advance copies and offered a chance to issue free reprints. None would touch it. When he showed the article to Lila, she was horrified. "How can you *think* of publishing such rot," she said. "Our magazine is meant to inform and entertain people. This will make them *sick!*"

Wallace disagreed with all of them. Reluctantly, all too aware of Lila's disapproval, he followed his instincts and published ". . . And Sudden Death." It hit the country like a runaway truck. Thousands of newspapers reprinted it word for word. It was read on national radio, at Rotary and Kiwanis meetings, in traffic court and church. Reprints were passed out to motorists headed into New York's Holland Tunnel. Wyoming included a copy with every set of license plates. A movie was made of it, and a syndicated comic strip. Inside of three months, more than four million copies of ". . . And Sudden Death" had been supplied to businesses, clubs and civic groups, and demand showed no signs of slowing down. Six months after publication, the magazine was still receiving a thousand newspaper clippings a month that mentioned the article, and estimates were that at least thirty million Americans had read it.

No magazine article in history had ever had such impact. *Reader's Digest* received credit for performing a great public service. And its editor, heretofore ignored, was suddenly seen in a new light. "Those who had regarded Wallace as a scissors & paste man began to change their minds," reported *Time*. "They realized he had an extraordinarily common touch—a feeling for what the reading public wants and how they want it."

The attention sparked by "Sudden Death" brought in a flood of new readers, and the *Digest's* circulation soared closer to two million. With circulation came increased revenues, and with revenues came a challenge Wallace had never expected. For someone who had learned early and well that every penny must be accounted for and all personal extravagance shunned, prosperity was not an unmixed blessing. Even before "Sudden Death," he and Lila had found themselves in an odd situation: they had more money coming in than they knew what to do with. Since there was no way they could spend it on themselves, they began instead to spend it on others.

As the Depression deepened, DeWitt found himself providing full financial support for all the sisters and brothers who had once scoffed at his magazine idea. "What would become of Miriam and family and Helen and family were it not for you and Lila Bell?" wrote James in November 1931. "Their degrading poverty would have sent me to my grave broken-hearted."

In the winter of 1933, DeWitt persuaded James and Maude to take a vacation in the Southwest "on me." When they returned in the spring, DeWitt met them at the St. Paul station and drove them home. Not to the old barn they had rented on South Snelling, but to a lovely bungalow, shaded by maples and elms, at 112 Cambridge Street. James as always was grateful. "My Dear Lady Lila Bell," he wrote. "Lord and Lady Wallace are getting along most handsomely." Yet something about the gift grated. "Perhaps the final touch of aristocracy would be provided to our lives," the old boy added, "if we now purchased a dog and cat of the very latest breed and fashion."

The charity that began at home soon spread throughout the *Digest*. Near the end of 1934, with average Americans barely able to feed themselves, an article appeared in the *St. Paul Pioneer Press* listing the top executive salaries in the nation. James Wallace, who as president of Macalester had never earned more than $2,000 a year, was astonished to read that his once wayward son was paying his managing editor and his business manager $102,467 apiece. "Hey there, DeWitt!" he wrote in alarm. "Strange things we read! Can it possibly cost such fabulous salaries to get editors and managers for the R.D.? Looks like *madness* to me!"

It was possible, all right. As soon as he was able, Wallace routinely paid extraordinary salaries, even to the lowest clerks. Throughout the Depression, raises were annual events for Digest employees, as were sometimes-staggering Christmas bonuses. Wallace admitted to *Fortune* that "Digesters are paid more than employees elsewhere," and explained this much as he had earlier explained his voluntarily high reprint payments: "In our early years, we were not able to pay employees very much. And the magazines that helped us out were paid nothing at all. Now that we're doing better, I'm making up for that."

The real explanation is more complicated: for DeWitt Wallace, being generous was a way to make a point; in fact, he was *compelled* to share his wealth, just as he had been compelled to spend his childhood earnings on presents for every member of the family. In that hard-pressed clan, he had been the one who *ached* to make things right. "Just wait," had been his frequent promise. "When my grandest stunt comes through, then you'll see. . . ." And it had happened. His grandest stunt *had* come through, and now he was making things right, pushing back the dark for everyone.

CHAPTER EIGHT

Lila and DeWitt now appeared to have everything they had ever wanted. Their Normandy cottage had been transformed into a beautifully appointed mini-estate surrounded by tasteful landscaping and colorful gardens. They had a Japanese butler named Yama, a Russian wolfhound named Sorbin and a cocker spaniel named Topaze. With the office finally out of her home, Lila was free to concentrate on her own interests—flowers and painting, and planning for the even grander future she was sure awaited them.

DeWitt's routine was very different. Most days, he was at his corner office above the bank by 8:00 A.M. "He is 47, but looks five years younger," reported the *Fortune* reporter who found him there in 1936. "Seemingly ill-at-ease with strangers, he is shy, soft-voiced and speaks haltingly. Often he is absent in Manhattan, attending to magazine contracts or transacting editorial business in a publisher's office or over a leisurely scotch and soda in a good hotel bar. But mostly he is in Plesantville, running his editorial show, dispatching crisp memoranda to KWP, CWF, HAL and REH."

Around noon most days, Wallace would round up this group and two or three of their younger colleagues and head for the Maples, a simple frame building up the block where a private dining room was reserved upstairs. Meals cost 50 cents, and were paid for by whoever lost the daily game of odd man out. The same group met every week or two for poker, or a goofy version thereof in which any card, or two, or three, might be called wild and every pot was divided according to an arcane formula between winner and loser.

Once, on an impulse. Wallace rented a private railroad car and took the whole group out to Denver and back. They played poker, drank and slept all the way out; then turned around and did the same all the way back. Nearing New York City, one of Wallace's tipsy cronies risked the question that was on all their minds: "Do you realize, Wally, how much work could have been done during these days?" Wallace shook his head. "You don't understand," he said. "I got more from you people during this trip than I could in a decade at the office. I heard your ideas, learned about your problems, shared your thoughts. It was a great success. We should do it every year."

Perhaps that was the problem. Although he professed to enjoy his evenings with the boys, Wallace never seemed wholly relaxed; there was always something deliberate about his performance, something awkward and forced. "He loved those poker games," Ralph Henderson recalled. "But he never quite got . . . *loose* . . . like the rest of us. Back in there somewhere he was always still the Boss, and you had to meet him on those terms. He wanted desperately to be one of the boys, but it was not a role that came naturally to him."

Wallace was aware of his problem, and seemed to believe the answer lay in some kind of magic formula. In a series of notes from those years, headed "Strategies for Dealing with People," he struggled to find the key: "Don't show how clever and wise *you* are; draw out the other man so as to raise *his* ego. To have friends, one must be *friendly*." But he never mastered the formula. Just as he had existed outside his own family circle, so now he felt himself an outsider at his own magazine. The others—the men he longed to befriend—were "us." He was "them."

Then, of course, there was the matter of Lila. The struggle to make their Dream come true had been an exciting time—long days, hard work, deep satisfactions—and in all of this she had felt herself to be his equal partner. But now the Dream was real, and the equality was gone. He was the Star, surrounded by adoring colleagues. But who was *she?* What was *her* role to be?

"In the early thirties, Lila began to have grave doubts about her situation," recalls her niece Judy Thompson (Barclay Acheson's daughter). "She had no interest in raising a family. But after becoming DeWitt's partner, and achieving their huge success, she found herself with nothing to do—no family, no career, nothing to be the center of. And this began to drive her crazy."

In 1934, feeling unwanted and depressed, Lila became seriously ill with a thyroid condition. She was hospitalized at the Cleveland Clinic and remained bedridden for a year. "She came to stay with us in New York while she recovered," recalls Judy. "She was nearly helpless—unable even to dress herself. I was only sixteen at the time, and had always been afraid of my aunt. But in her weakened state, she seemed more human and really rather nice. She told me she was having problems with DeWitt—she became quite agitated when she spoke of this—and that she was determined to do something about it, to balance the scales one way or another."

In December 1935, DeWitt and Lila moved into New York's St. Regis Hotel for a few weeks of holiday theatergoing and socializing. It was an exciting time to be in the city. The darkest days of the economic crisis were over, and in the aftermath of Repeal (in December 1933) liberated men and women were thronging to restaurants and "cocktail lounges" to toss down legal martinis and manhattans. Several nights a week, the Wallaces invited friends in for dinner and whatever was scheduled afterward, and there was much drinking and laughter. Yet their Christmas that year was not a happy one. Lila was upset, and one evening she let DeWitt know exactly what was bothering her. After a long talk, he dutifully compiled a list of resolutions under a rather ominous heading: "LBW, 12/8/35, *Low Water Mark*":

1. Consult LB *always* before making dates with others.
2. Show affection, thotfulness—and *do so without fail when others are present.*
3. Take initiative re social life; suggest having friends in.
4. *Don't mention girls from past!*

It was only the beginning. On the day after Christmas, they sat together in the sitting room of their suite at the St. Regis and Lila spelled out a demand that had nothing to do with "thotfulness" or girls from his past. Her words made him furious and he stormed from the hotel to wander among the holiday crowds. When he returned, he sat at the desk in his bedroom and composed a note on a single sheet of hotel stationery: DECEMBER 26, 1935. TODAY PROMISED LB NEVER AGAIN TO GIVE SALARY INCREASE, OR ANY BONUS, WITHOUT FIRST GETTING HER COMPLETE APPROVAL AND CONSENT.

Lila was answering her own question. *Who was she?* For one thing, as big a Star as he was. And he—and all the others—would damn well treat her as such. She was also Co-Owner, and that made her Co-Boss. She intended to play that part as well. *Wife?* Of course. And there were aspects of the wife's role she cherished. DeWitt was as handsome and graceful as ever, and there was something about his whole approach—the shyness, the gentle self-mockery—that she still found irresistible.

Beyond these obvious traits, there was something indefinable—a kind of boyish independence—that she found at once attractive and challenging. From their first year together, she had understood that this quality, properly channeled, could take them far in life. "We have no children, quite deliberately," she announced at every opportunity and to all who asked (and frequently to those who did not). "I believe a woman can be a good wife or a good mother, but not both. My husband needs someone to believe in him, to be his partner in the business. That is my role."

It was also her part of the bargain they had made. She intended to keep her part, and she believed she could count on him to keep his. They trusted each other in this, for the most part, and it was this trust more than intimacy that made them close. In public, they held hands and kissed and said warm things. But this was all for show. Those who knew them best insisted they held hands on many occasions to keep from slugging one another. From the first year of their marriage, they had taken separate rooms at inns and hotels. When they moved from the garage to the Normandy cottage, Lila had had her room and DeWitt his. And so it remained for the rest of their lives. "Our sleeping habits are different," Lila explained to friends. "I go to bed early. He works all night."

But it was more than that. Sex had never been one of Lila Wallace's priorities. All her life, she had been attracted to men who were "controllable" and therefore safe: her father, Brother Barclay, the older man she had been engaged to. When she thought about herself, the image that came to mind was that of a sixteen-year-old girl, flirtatious, irresistible, on the verge of womanhood but not yet there, full of promise but . . . nothing more.

She would later fall in love with a Renoir painting of just such a girl, dressed all in blue, suffused with innocence and charm, unspoiled and virginal. She bought the painting in 1950 for $40,000 (it came to be worth millions) and hung it above the fireplace in her living room. "This beautiful creature is at the most marvelous stage of life," she would tell visitors. "She is no longer a girl but not yet a grown-up, occupying that in-between place where everything is possible but nothing demanded." *Jeune Fille en Bleu* became the centerpiece of her home—of her life, really—and guests who wandered into the living room were expected to pay their respects. DeWitt openly called the girl in the painting "Lila," and often blew faintly mocking kisses in her direction.

In fact, in many ways DeWitt had proved less controllable than the other men in Lila's life, and this tendency was compounded by the power balance at the office. His colleagues there still saw him as Boss, while she remained the Boss's Wife. And it was getting worse. As other magazines folded during the thirties, Wallace recruited their editors for the *Digest*. "Fritz" Dashiell came from *Scribner's*, Paul Palmer from the *American Mercury*, Fulton Oursler from *Liberty*. These men were experienced professionals, and they naturally lined up behind DeWitt. Feeling outnumbered, Lila decided to do some recruiting of her own.

The first soldier she enlisted was her brother. After college, Barclay Acheson had taught at the American University in Beirut, then served for nine years as director of overseas operations for Near East Relief. He returned to New York in 1930 to become executive secretary for the Near East Foundation, and from his West Side apartment observed the miraculous rise of *Reader's Digest* with considerable astonishment. But Barclay had no desire to work for his younger sister. He was a minister, and his calling was to help the downtrodden. Then his sister began to talk of making him general manager. She mentioned huge salaries and bonuses, foreign travel and country estates, and Barclay was sorely tempted. In 1935, he abandoned his preacher's role to become his sister's lieutenant.

With Barclay aboard, Lila cast her net a second time. She was captivated by the music of the big "swing" bands—Benny Goodman, Artie Shaw, Tommy Dorsey—and loved to dance at the hotels where they played. But her Presbyterian husband had never learned even the basic steps, so she signed them up for a series of lessons at an Arthur Murray studio in New York. On their first night, the instructor assigned to them was a handsome man named Harry Wilcox. Lila was entranced. Harry was a smooth dancer and a smooth dresser, but nothing about him was as smooth as his tongue. He was an "automotive engineer," Harry told them, and had been employed by General Motors until he'd been laid off during the Depression. (In fact, he had been a test driver for cars coming off the GM assembly line.) The Arthur Murray job, he claimed, was just something he had taken on until a better proposition came along.

The Wallaces danced with Harry for several weeks, and when the lessons ended Lila prevailed on him to come work for the *Digest*. No one remembers precisely what his first job was; something to do with shipping. But there was no confusion about Harry's power. From the day he arrived, it was clear that Harry Wilcox was Lila Wallace's surrogate. Also her hatchet man, flunky, spy and frequent companion. Harry was smart enough to grasp the situation at Reader's Digest in a single glance: lots of money coming in, and Lila Bell in charge. If he played his cards right, Harry saw, he could become rich, too.

When Lila wanted something done, she called Harry and Harry got it done. If she needed company, Harry was more than happy to oblige, and in no time rumors were flying everywhere. Harry used these rumors to advance his cause. But there was more to his relationship with Lila than rumor. Lila had always envied men. She didn't want to *be* a man—Heaven forbid!—but she longed to do the things that men could do. Now she had Harry to do them for her.

"Lila went wild after Harry was hired," recalls Judy Thompson. "She would go to football games with him. West Point. New Haven. She bought herself a bunch of fancy evening clothes and sailed alone to Bermuda. Naturally, everyone assumed Harry met her there. She was trying to build a new life for herself, an existence apart from Wally, and Harry was a major part of her plans." No one ever mentioned the fact that Harry already had a wife—"a pleasant woman named Rachel," recalls Judy. Rachel stayed in New York when Harry moved to Pleasantville, and eventually faded into history.

CHAPTER NINE

In the late twenties, when the Wallaces' fortunes first began to soar, they had scouted around for a site on which to build Lila's dream house, finally settling on 110 hilly acres high above Byram Lake near Mt. Kisco. It was a beautiful spot, and DeWitt loved to go there on weekends to tramp around his fields and woods. He wrote to James about the purchase—which cost them all of $20,000—and James replied with great enthusiasm: "We are eager to see your farm. Developing a piece of land can be a most interesting avocation."

Certainly it was to Lila, though not in the sense James had in mind. For several years—from the moment they completed their Normandy cottage in Pleasantville—she had dreamed of building something grander, something that would truly reflect their new status in the world. When they found their mountaintop, she was ecstatic. Standing atop a large boulder on the highest point of the property, she could see in her mind's eye exactly where everything would go—every garden, every pathway, every pool and lookout. She began meeting with architects and landscapers to work it all out. She had dozens of scrapbooks bursting with ideas—drawings and photos she had clipped from magazines and books over the years. She knew how she wanted the stone to look, what kind of wood would do, where the bedrooms would be located. One entire scrapbook was devoted to staircases; another to drapery treatments. Everything, inside and out, was to look as natural as possible, as if the Castle had risen from its craggy site through some prehistoric act of God. The walls would represent Earth; the roof would be Sky. She had taken sheets of silk in various shades of blue—azure, cobalt, indigo—and snipped them into tiny "tiles." These she had worked into a pattern, a kind of montage of blue, tiny piece by tiny piece. When the pattern was just right, real tiles were ordered from France to match it exactly. All in shades of "Lila blue."

This was to be *her* place, the home she had never had before, to make up for all the years of wandering across the northern plains. And she decided that her handsome dancing master, "Harry the Engineer," was just the man to build it for her. Acting as general contractor, Harry soon recruited a small army of workers—Italian stone masons, Portuguese landscapers, Swedish carpenters—and in 1936 construction began.

To help with the interior layout, Lila hired a designer named Delores Risley. Delores had a boyfriend named Roy Abbott, and when Lila met and liked Roy she wondered why the two didn't marry. "We can't afford to," said Delores. "Roy is a bank clerk in Stamford. He doesn't earn enough money." Lila solved that problem by hiring Roy herself. Before becoming a bank clerk, he had been a streetcar conductor and a movie projectionist. Now Lila put him in charge of paying her contractors' bills. When construction ended and Roy had nothing to do, Lila spoke to Wally. "He *is* wonderful with figures," she said. "Can't we find a place for him?" Eager to please his wife, Wally hired Roy Abbott—a perfectly decent fellow who in fact did have a way with a column of numbers—to be treasurer of Reader's Digest. And Roy and Delores got married.

Lila's Army was growing, and her troops were odder even than DeWitt's. She had hired her dance instructor to be business manager, her decorator's boyfriend to be treasurer, and her preacher/brother to be whatever it was Barclay was doing just then. These men remained in place for decades. Wilcox turned out to be surprisingly competent when sober, but also monumentally dishonest. Abbott was perfectly honest, but over his head; Lila decided the one thing he was good at was mixing drinks, and when she had parties in those days she always asked Roy to tend her bar. Barclay was well meaning but ineffectual, and would prove a pushover for the sharp Europeans lurking in his future. Yet so solid was the business her husband had created that it flourished despite the best efforts of these and all the other bumblers waiting down the line.

In the summer of 1938, when High Winds* was finally finished, James Wallace was invited east to see the "farm" his son had bought. (Aunt Maude was ailing and remained in St. Paul.) James's eyes widened as he and DeWitt drove through the main gate and up the long hill. When they reached the top and swept around to where he could see the mansion itself, he let out a gasp of astonishment. "My God!" he said. "What on earth do two people want with all of this?"

He meant it, too. And this quality in James—this unalloyed conviction that life was hard and extravagance sinful—was something DeWitt had struggled with for years. In truth, High Winds embarrassed him. But whenever he mentioned this to Lila, she laughed: "You don't have to like it. I'm paying for it, and *I* like it."

It was different for Lila. She had learned to respect money, but also to understand that being rich was a fine thing, was in fact a sign that God had smiled on you, that you were rich because you were also *good*. And that for certain things—a pot of pretty hyacinths, a splendid Castle in the Clouds— money might be flung away. When High Winds was finally done, Lila decided to have a movie made to show her mother and sisters just how fine her new home was. She wrote the script herself, in the form of a "Letter to My Mother":

> The opening scene shows me at my desk, writing, with Topey and Sorbin lying at my feet. The camera zooms in on the letter, and my first words become the title of the film: "DEAR MOTHER," it begins. "This is the story of my Fairy Castle. We call it . . . HIGH WINDS." The camera pans through the open doors of my sitting room. It shows the lawns and gardens. It shows the distant Lookout. It shows, beyond the Lookout, the wind-blown Lake. "We started out to buy ten acres," I write, "and we ended up buying a hundred and ten . . . !"

The remainder of the fifteen-minute script describes a world perfect in every respect—pristine and glorious—and clearly Lila wanted her mother and her sisters to understand this (her father had died in 1932). Yet there is also something sad about that script. For Lila Wallace was very much alone in her perfect world, whereas her sisters—middle-class housewives in middle-class homes—were surrounded by children and grandchildren. Lila would come to resent them their happy families, and they in turn would resent her for being rich. "Missus's family seldom came to High Winds,"

* The name was taken from an inscription on the imported mantel in DeWitt's tower office: "On High Hills, High Winds Blow."

recalls Gene Doherty, the Wallaces' longtime chauffeur. "In the thirty years I worked there I could count family visits on the fingers of one hand."

Even in DeWitt's family—that "Happy Tribe of Wallacites"—there were problems caused by money. In 1936, in a blatant attempt to solicit funds for Macalester, James arranged for DeWitt and Lila to receive honorary degrees. DeWitt was furious and refused even to attend the ceremony. His problems with brother Ben were worse. After reading the *Fortune* article, Ben couldn't resist taking a nasty dig at the kid brother who had made good: "That article certainly makes Pater & I out to be pikers—$300 each when you apparently needed $5,000. . . . Do you recall the days when we worried lest someone with capital sh'd grab your idea and run off with it?" Although Ben's $300 would be repaid many times over, he and his siblings never forgave DeWitt for not offering them shares in the Digest itself. Even the trust funds that were eventually established for every member of the family did not heal these wounds. For several years, Ben refused the income from his trust because taking it "would keep alive the memory of a painful experience."

In all the years they lived at High Winds, DeWitt referred to it as "Lila's place." "Lila's place showed its worst aberrations this winter," he wrote to a cousin in 1939. "With the wind blowing 40 mph, the temperature in my Tower remained at 48 degrees *with the furnace going full blast!*" Although he eventually came to terms with "Lila's place," for many years its grandeur grated on his Scottish soul. Yet he wasn't a miser. When the boyish part of him became excited, Wallace was willing to spend freely.

In the early thirties, he developed a passion for airplanes, and from that moment on thought nothing of grabbing a satchel of manuscripts and flying off to destinations all over the country. In 1935, he bought his own aircraft —a four-passenger Fairchild monoplane—and flew it himself out of an airport in nearby Armonk. Often he would disappear without telling anyone where he could be reached. "He liked to fly in and out of small towns in remote areas," recalls his old friend, the writer James Stewart-Gordon. "He might spend a day or two, incognito, trying to find out what was going on, what the people were thinking. He talked with everyone—car salesmen, barbers, clergymen, waitresses. These people were his readers and this was his way to keep in touch with them."

It was also a way to escape—from Lila, from rules and routines, from the expectations he always sensed in others. Eventually, he built his own airstrip in the little valley running along the north end of Lila's property. Now flying became a bigger passion than ever. Alone, high above the world, he would feel a satisfaction tinged with elation. This was the ticket! Sometimes, banking over his neighbors' estates, he could scarcely believe his good fortune.

—

As High Winds was nearing completion, the Wallaces had to face the prospect of putting up another building. All the banks in Pleasantville, all the floors in the post office, all the nooks and crannies the little town afforded, could no longer house their growing staff. DeWitt was inclined to return to New York. A move there would save money, provide a larger labor pool, and enable his editors to stay in tune with the "true pulse" of the nation. That it would further free him from Lila went unsaid, and thus no one was surprised when Lila said no. "Our readers live in towns like Pleasantville," she sniffed. "Not in places like New York. To stay in touch with them, we need to stay in touch with this."

As always on noneditorial matters, Wallace yielded to his wife. Soon thereafter he bought eighty acres of rolling farmland five miles north of Pleasantville, on the Mt. Kisco side of Chappaqua. "Put a building up," he said to Harry Wilcox. "When you're done, let us know." Lila had a few additional thoughts for Harry. Locating a major commercial enterprise in a suburban area of large estates was a pioneering concept in those days, and Lila Wallace was determined to do it right. Their building should fit in with the surroundings, she insisted. It should look like a large estate itself or, better yet, like a small college. She had been impressed with the buildings of Colonial Williamsburg, and now she sent a team of architects down to Virginia for a look around. They came back with a plan that combined features of the Governor's Palace and the Capitol, and Lila heartily approved. The building that resulted is a graceful, three-story Georgian structure, surmounted by a tall, white-pillared cupola, with lower-lying wings extending out on either side. It was completed in 1939 at a cost of $1.5 million.

As a crowning touch, chief architect John Mackenzie proposed decorating the cupola with four spread-winged eagles. Lila thought about this for several days. Then one night she awoke with a start. "I had been dreaming of Pegasus, the winged horse," she related later. "According to the legend, when Pegasus stamps his feet the sound is supposed to inspire men to write."

She explained all this to MacKenzie, who dutifully circled the cupola with the rising front quarters of four winged horses, thus providing the desired decorative effect while at the same time creating a new corporate symbol. Digesters immediately began taking bets as to whether the *rear* quarters of the animals were visible *inside* the tower, and a member of the art department went so far as to draw a large poster depicting how that might look. The poster was displayed on a wall inside the unfinished building, and when DeWitt passed it he is alleged to have exclaimed: "Why, look at that! All the vice presidents in one room!"

When the building was up, an army of landscapers was brought in to dress up the grounds. Their first efforts did not pass muster with Lila Wallace. Too bleak; too barren. She called Wilcox into her office and let him know exactly what she wanted, whatever the cost. And she wanted it *soon.* Harry nodded, and went to work. "When I went away that weekend, the view from my office was over an asphalt loading dock," recalls a woman who was a junior editor at the time. "When I came in on Monday the loading dock was gone, replaced by tulip beds, acres of green, a lovely brick walk and a life-sized statue of Pegasus rising above a reflecting pool." Barclay Acheson entered his office that same morning, looked out his window and exclaimed in surprise. Where before there had been nothing but a patch of grass, a gorgeous maple tree stood, fully grown, looking as if it had been there for years. "Now that's what God would do," murmured Reverend Acheson, "if God had money."

By the fall of 1939, Lila's winged horses looked out over eighty acres of landscaped fairyland: boxwood and rhododendron, dogwood walks and lilac groves, vast beds of perennials and annuals, sunken gardens and walled gardens, reflecting pools, secret courtyards, picnic tables and bubbling fountains. The parking lots were hidden behind stands of maple, pine, birch and oak. Bulbs were planted everywhere, so that in springtime the hillsides around the main building came alive with crocus and daffodils, hyacinths and tulips.

Lila was even more lavish inside. All the principal offices were furnished like rooms in a well-appointed English manor house: high ceilings, fine carpeting, polished antiques, wood paneling. Offices without exterior windows looked down instead on interior courtyards where birds sang, flowers grew and fountains murmured. Fresh flowers, arranged in a cutting room off the entrance rotunda by a full-time resident florist, were sent around to offices twice each week. But the most extraordinary touch of all—what made her offices truly special—Lila saved for last.

For some time, she had been collecting works of art that she found pleasing. Mostly her paintings were French, from the nineteenth and early twentieth centuries, and in time they would include works of all the great masters of that period—Van Gogh and Picasso, Monet and Matisse, Degas, Gauguin, Bonnard, Pissarro, Renoir and Vuillard. Like many newly rich collectors, Lila believed that owning fine art somehow made one *better* than other people. "All those fancy New Yorkers think of us as this tacky little magazine in the stupid suburbs," she confided to a friend. "*That's* why I buy these paintings—to show those snobs we're not so dumb." But it was more than that. Lila also understood that no one truly "owns" great art. In the early forties, she began moving the bulk of her collection from High Winds to Headquarters, hanging masterpieces worth millions along major corridors and in offices throughout the building. "Too many beautiful things are hidden away where only the privileged can see them," she said. "But art is not for the few. Art belongs to everyone."

When she was done, she had created a civilized oasis, a place of business that in every way reflected her own feminine taste and her own sense of how people ought to live. In effect, she had done for Digesters on a grand scale precisely what she had done years before for the factory girls in New Jersey and New Orleans. And Digesters appreciated this. "When you walked in there in those days," recalls an early member of the art department, "you knew you were someplace special. It had an air about it, a feeling of caring, of wholeness and civility. It wasn't like other offices, even other lavish offices. It was different, and it made all of us feel different, too—made us feel valued, important, *special.*"

For the most part, DeWitt was proud of Lila's achievement and pleased that his employees would be working in such pleasant surroundings. Yet, as with High Winds, doubts lingered. It was all so huge, so grand; there were so many offices, so many lights, such a monstrous heating plant. When he saw his own palatial office—a huge high-ceilinged room in the southwest corner of the first floor, with a fireplace and fine moldings and a private bathroom—he put his foot down. Lila and Delores Abbott had run wild with plush white-leather furniture and bright chintz drapes and pillows. It was lovely and airy, with a huge Chagall painting installed above the mantel, but far too lavish and frilly for James Wallace's son.

"Very nice," he said. "I imagine this stuff would go well at auction." It soon did, replaced with simple armchairs, an antique partners' desk and plain drapes. Over the years, the other offices at Headquarters were refurnished on a regular schedule—new drapes, carpeting, slipcovers—but no one ever dared suggest refurnishing Wally's office. When he finally stopped working there, thirty-five years later, his was the only room in the building with the original green carpeting still on the floor. And even at that he seldom used the place, preferring to work in his Tower or in the city. On more than one occasion in those early years, he was observed standing outside the main entrance, staring in wonder down the long drive that led to the huge building where thousands of people now worked for him.

When Lila Wallace considered the Kingdom she had created—its Castle crowning a ridge in Mt. Kisco, its Village spread across a Chappaqua plain —she was very happy. Her word in the Kingdom was final. No one else, not even her husband, dared interfere. She was a Star now, too, in some ways brighter than Wally himself. But the world she shone upon was far from perfect. In fact, as the thirties neared an end Lila Wallace felt herself beset on three sides at once.

Her first problem centered on the man who had become her husband's chief lieutenant. Between 1930 and 1938, the magazine's circulation had soared from 300,000 to more than 3,000,000—and the individual most responsible for this miracle wasn't even an employee. Albert Leslie Cole, the rock upon which the Digest's business operations grew, never finished high school. He was born in Chicago in 1894, and his family moved to Brooklyn while he was still a baby. When he was fifteen, his father died, and from that point on young Albert's mother looked to him to provide financial help.

During the summer of 1909, Albert applied for two positions advertised in the newspaper: one with the American Woolen Company and the other with Frank E. Munsey, a publishing company with several magazines (including the very popular *Munsey's*). "Al took the job with Munsey," says his widowed second wife Peggy. "His mother needed the money and the Munsey job began the next day, a Saturday, whereas the AWC job didn't begin until the following Monday. Times were that tough."

Cole liked working for Munsey so much he decided there was no point in returning to school when summer ended. He stayed with the firm for several years, learning the publishing business from the ground up. Still in his early twenties, he switched over to *Popular Science* as an ad salesman ("He loved selling ads more than anything," says Peggy Cole), and by 1929, at the age of thirty-four, he was president of the company.

In those years, *Popular Science* and *McCall's* were both distributed by a subsidiary called S-M News (for "Science-McCall's"). In 1929, when DeWitt Wallace decided he had to risk selling the *Digest* on newsstands, he went to S-M for help. He was introduced to Cole, and the two men—Wallace tall, shy, diffident; Cole handsome, burly, outgoing—immediately hit it off. Already regarded as one of the most astute circulation men in the business, Cole was intrigued by the problem Wallace brought to him. He agreed to help, and it was Cole who thereafter masterminded the first successful sale of *Reader's Digest* on the newsstands.

Impressed, Wallace tried to persuade Cole to work for him full-time. Cole refused—he was making plenty of money at *Popular Science* and was a substantial holder of its stock—but did agree to become an unofficial adviser to the fledgling *Digest*. In 1932, this agreement was made official by the signing of a contract under which Wallace would pay Cole $10,000 a year, plus 20 percent of any net increase in subscription profits. Under this arrangement, Cole was soon earning so much—$50,000 in 1934 alone, in the midst of the Depression—that Wallace cried for mercy. The agreement was rewritten so only 10 percent of the annual increase went to Cole. But so dramatically did circulation rise, and keep rising, that even under these terms Cole was taking more money from Wallace's business than Wallace was paying himself.

In 1937, the two men got down to hard bargaining. Wallace knew he needed Cole's experience full-time; he could no longer run both ends of the business himself, and while Arthur Griffiths was a gifted amateur it was clearly time to hire a professional. Cole was happy at *Popular Science*, but regarded the *Digest* as a better opportunity ("the greatest chance in publishing for fun and profit," he called it). Yet there were problems. Cole was a major stockholder in *Popular Science*. If he left the company without first obtaining a controlling position—thus losing his voice in its affairs—the stock he already owned might go down the drain. He needed a loan from Wallace of $300,000 to accomplish this. He also wanted, in addition to salary, an annual bonus based on increased profits. And he wanted this bonus paid "partly in cash and partly in Digest stock."

There was the rub. Wallace was agreeable to everything but the stock. The idea of permitting someone else to own a piece of his business—to have a right to ask nosy questions and to examine his books—was not something he wanted to consider. "But Wally," Cole argued, "if I become your general manager I'm going to know all that stuff anyway." Wallace regarded him coldly. No one—not Griffiths, not Wilcox, not even Lila—was privy to the innermost secrets of his business. He didn't see why that had to change.

The two men argued about the stock issue for almost two years. Finally, in the summer of 1938, Wallace invited Cole and his wife, Marguerite, to fly to Miami in the Fairchild with him and Lila. The women were left alone at the Roney-Plaza Hotel while Cole and Wallace walked for miles along the boardwalk, arguing over the stock question. Finally, Wallace gave in. The men returned to the hotel with this happy news only to find their wives not speaking. Marguerite Cole was a formidable woman, not the type to kowtow to anyone. Put off by Lila's queenly airs, she had taken to calling her "Lulu," and Lila was livid.

The plane ride back to New York was a quiet one, and Lila Wallace never did forgive Marguerite Cole. Or Al Cole either, for that matter. Lila didn't like people who got close to her husband, and she didn't like men who were masculine and strong. Cole refused to cater to her, and she didn't like that either. He was friendly and polite, but made it clear that his dealings were with DeWitt.

For Lila Wallace, the hiring of Al Cole as general manager constituted Round Two of a power struggle that was evolving between herself and DeWitt, a struggle that would fester over many years before exploding into open hostilities. Round One had been the hiring of Barclay Acheson and Harry Wilcox, and it had gone to Lila. When Cole was hired, Arthur Griffiths— also close to Lila—was retired. And Barclay Acheson, whose sister had promised to make *him* general manager, was forced from the business office into public relations. Round Two had gone to DeWitt. And Lila was furious.

Her second problem evolved from an ill-advised attempt to fill the single yawning void in her perfect world. By 1939, Judy Acheson had graduated from Vassar and was teaching school in New York. At twenty-three, Judy was an attractive young woman, bright and articulate, and both Wallaces were extremely fond of her. "Lila's interest in me became very intense during this period," recalls Judy. "She bought my clothes, sent me off for beauty treatments, even planned my social life. It was her idea that I should go to Ward-Belmont—I would never be a proper belle, she said, unless I learned the rules. She paid for that, and for Vassar as well. My parents were having problems with their marriage at the time, and Lila spoke to me about this on several occasions. 'You know,' she would say, 'your father has asked me to adopt you so he can leave your mother.' She never admitted she wouldn't take me—that the thought of having a younger woman around terrified her. It was just that *not* having a child—not *possessing* a child—affected her self-image."

So it was that Judy Acheson became for Lila and DeWitt the child they were unable to have for themselves—a perfect Princess for their perfect Fairy Castle. And it soon turned out that Lila had been busy creating a Prince as well. Fred Thompson was born in Texas and raised in Virginia, where his father worked for the YMCA. When Fred was fourteen, he earned a scholarship to attend summer classes at Lincoln School in New York (an experimental academy funded by the Rockefeller family, which purposely included a few poor students among its otherwise wealthy student body). Judy Acheson was also a student at Lincoln, and Judy and Fred soon became fast friends. Judy hoped that the handsome Fred would stay on as a boarder after that first summer, but Fred's family couldn't pay the tuition. Judy spoke to Lila about this—without telling Fred—and Lila saw to it that $1,000 was made available through a program for "worthy boys" run by the Riverside Church. After Lincoln, Fred went on to study at the American University in Beirut, where Barclay was a teacher, and at Columbia Law School, and Lila's money paid for all of this.

After Columbia, Fred and Judy became engaged, and Lila persuaded Al Cole to hire Fred as an ad salesman at *Popular Science*. In 1938, when Cole came over to the *Digest*, he asked Fred to come with him. The two men, each of them hard-driving, astute and jovial, had become very close. "I'll pay you $300 a month," said Cole. "I'll take it," said Fred, "but $300 is too much." "No, it's not," said Cole. "The job is worth that much, and so are you."

In May 1939, Fred and Judy were married. Not in church, or in the Acheson home, but at High Winds. By all accounts, it was a stunning affair, with a cast of several hundred, including the entire Digest family, horses and carriages, flowers and champagne, all unfolding against the gorgeous spring panorama of Lila's mountain-top in full bloom. The Queen herself was resplendent in a blue gown bedecked with shimmering ribbons (of a very special shade; the first versions had been rejected and Harry Wilcox had had to scour Manhattan for proper replacements). As the reception gathered steam, DeWitt suddenly appeared overhead, a King in a silver airplane, climbing and diving high above his celebrating subjects. Everyone waved and shouted, although Lila pretended to be furious. "I hope you all hear what a *noise* that damn thing makes," she shouted.

It was all very much a fairy tale: perfect, radiant, sun-blessed. Yet also sad and somehow ominous. Because the King and Queen were, in fact, childless. And the real parents of the Princess, the hapless Barclay and his caustic wife Pat, had been relegated to the sidelines.

"Oh, it was a slippery situation," says Judy Thompson. "Everybody looked at us and thought, *'How marvelous! The Prince and Princess! The new Wally and the new Lila!'* Well, fine. I wasn't completely free of such thoughts myself. But I also knew there was something odd about that vision—something dangerous. One minute Lila would act as if our "coronation' were inevitable. But the next minute she would say something very different, something that made you feel as if a shadow had fallen across your grave."

(On a table in a dark corner of Judy Thompson's library, there sits today a large album of wedding photos, including several pages of pictures taken of the rehearsal the day before the ceremony. Lila had decreed that Judy not appear at the rehearsal—"It would be bad luck," she insisted. Instead, the Queen played the role of bride herself, and is seen in several photos smiling in virginal excitement at everyone in sight. She and handsome Fred march down the "aisle" together—a path between perennial beds leading to the High Winds Lookout—stand together before the minister, say their vows together before all the world. In an enlarged photo filling an entire page, Lila is seen with her arms around Fred's neck, leaning backward in a classic version of "kissing the bride."

"I didn't know *that* was customary," murmurs Judy, shaking her head as she closes the album. "Fred *hated* the whole thing! In fact, he came to hate Lila herself.")

The third problem Lila faced in the late thirties—and the only one she was able to resolve to her satisfaction—had to do with DeWitt's airplane. From the beginning she had hated his flying, and especially his habit of buzzing High Winds. She saw the plane for precisely what it was: a vehicle that enabled the untamed part of her husband to be free and empowered. She began to lean on him about the plane. It was dangerous, she insisted, and irresponsible.

She had a point. Landing on the little High Winds airstrip was a tricky proposition, and on one occasion (and probably others) Wallace almost lost his life. Harry Wilcox happened to be at High Winds that day, in the summer of 1938, working on a project with Lila, and he later remembered thinking that the Fairchild's engine sounded funny as the plane approached. "Then there was an explosion," Harry liked to recall. "Wally had come in too fast, worrying about an engine problem, and he ran the damn thing off the end of the runway. When I reached the scene, the plane was on fire and Wally was trapped inside. I pulled him from the wreck." This, of course, was a lucky moment for both men. Wallace's life was saved, or so Harry claimed. And Harry, who already had Lila in the palm of his hand, thereafter had DeWitt as well.

The Fairchild was soon repaired and DeWitt back in the air again. But Lila's campaign to ground her husband only gathered steam, and as war blew across Europe she gained an ally. In January 1939, Ben Wallace, who was now on better terms with his brother, wrote to DeWitt to explain that his wife's long illness was nearing a sad end. No doubt prompted by Lila, Ben closed his letter with a plea: "I wish you'd sell your plane. With Pater so aged, and Mother Maude so frail, and Katherine leaving us, I don't like this business of feeling uncertain from day to day whether you will live or die. You are too important to the clan—and to the country, too."

In 1940, with the Battle of Britain raging, Wallace published an article called "Rush All Possible Aid to England!" Shortly thereafter, to Lila's intense satisfaction, he donated his beloved Fairchild to the Royal Canadian Air Force. Lila had won another round.

CHAPTER TEN

The miracle that had begun with the first issue of *Reader's Digest* gathered steam throughout the thirties. Although academics were already sneering, calling it "simplistic" and "naïve," Wallace's magazine was clearly reflecting something deep in the national psyche. With the Depression lingering, Americans were desperate for good news. Wallace provided it. Every issue of his magazine offered stories to laugh at or wonder over or be inspired by. Human-interest stories. Heroic profiles. Examples of ordinary people doing extraordinary things. And while other magazines tended to "talk down" to readers, *Reader's Digest* spoke without condescension or pretense, in straightforward language emphasizing clarity. This, too, became a source of mockery for sophisticates. Yet clarity was not an unsophisticated goal. Indeed, in his insistence on being clear—on publishing articles that were simple, short and comprehensible—Wallace was if anything ahead of his time.

In 1938, *RD*'s circulation stood at 3,000,000. By 1941, it was 4,000,000 and rising. And Lila and DeWitt Wallace, who had dreamed of surviving on

$5,000 a year, were becoming very rich. In 1939, their combined income was $600,000—unheard-of in those days—and could have been far higher. "A large income is apparently as depressing to Wallace as a long article," wrote author John Bainbridge in the *New Yorker*. "He must get rid of as much as he can of both to be happy. A tax man recently declared that Wallace's employees couldn't be worth as much as Wallace was paying them. But Wallace talked him down on that."

In fact, what he paid them had little relation to what they were worth. He and Lila took modest salaries out of whatever money was left after all other obligations were paid ($30,000 each in 1936), then divided the rest among their employees. Using this system, Wallace obviously paid them more than was necessary, with bonuses and other benefits to match, and his generosity lasted—in fact, it grew year after year—until well after his retirement in 1973. But the period old-time Digesters remember most fondly—the true "Camelot years"—stretched from the mid-thirties until the advent of advertising in the mid-fifties.

During these years, the core group in Chappaqua was relatively small— perhaps fifty people—and exceptionally congenial. Every one of them had been hired by DeWitt and Lila, and they tended to be well-mannered Ivy League types, bright, ambitious, eager to do the right thing. They lived like squires and ladies, in fine homes scattered throughout northern Westchester. They came to work wearing sport coats and casual dresses, worked for several leisurely hours, then returned to their homes or country clubs to enjoy the last hours of daylight. If the weather was nice and spring was in the air, Wally might decide to send everyone home at noon. One winter he took a large group to Florida, to finish an issue on the beach. Vacations were normally limited to four weeks, but this was often stretched to six, or even to two months if the vacation involved a trip abroad, which both Wallaces encouraged.

Even the "little people"—groundskeepers and cleaning ladies, clerks and cafeteria workers—were treated like family in those days. When the new cafeteria opened in 1942, Jennie Guignardi and several of her girlfriends were hired to work in the kitchen. "At that time, the buses dropped you off on the highway outside the Digest and you had to walk a half mile to the main building. My first day there this guy pulls up next to us in a little Chevy roadster. 'C'mon, girls!' he yells. 'I'll give you a ride!' So we got in. This happened several times. Then one day he asked us if we knew who he was. We said no. 'Well,' he says, 'I'm DeWitt Wallace.' We were amazed. We thought Mr. Wallace would be driven to work in a limousine.

"Once he rented a train and took the entire workforce into Manhattan for a party at the new Digest offices there. We all drank too much and had a swell time. He did the same thing whenever the circus came to town. And when he heard about a new movie that he thought we might like, he would arrange to have it shown at the Mt. Kisco Cinema before it opened in New York. He'd rent the whole theater and send us all down to see it. During working hours!"

Although he liked to do things for people, DeWitt worried at the same time that some might take advantage of his "softness" (as they surely did). He insisted, for example, that everyone arrive at work by 8:30. No exceptions. When a young editor named Jerry Ellison, who lived in Manhattan, found this difficult, Wallace sent him a frosty note: "Jerry: Can you think of a single reason why you can't be at your desk by 8:30 like everyone else? Wally." Ellison mulled this over for a while, then sent back a one-word reply: "Wally: No. Jerry." Wallace thought this a reasonable answer, and that was that.

In fact, he did not want what he called "greasy grinds" putting out his magazine. When the working day ended at 4:00 P.M., he would stride down the main hall past the offices of his chief subordinates. "Time to go home, Fritz!" he would shout. "Let's pack it in, Hobe. Family is waiting, Bun!" Everyone would shout back: "Right, Wally. Just finishing up!" And there would be a flurry of papers and briefcases. Someone would be posted at the window looking up the main drive. When the Boss's Chevy headed toward the exit, they all returned to their desks, unpacked and resumed their work.

Twice a year, the editors and their wives were invited up to High Winds for cocktails with the King and Queen. The rules for such occasions were simple: You parked your car at the foot of Lila's hill as near to the witching hour of 5:00 P.M. as possible, then waited to be driven "up top" by Wallace chauffeurs. Since no one wanted to be the first to arrive, early couples chatted nervously in the parking field until critical mass—at least ten people—was achieved. Then the whole group went up the hill at once.

After passing through the mansion, grabbing a cocktail on the way from the bar where loyal Roy Abbott did the mixing, the arriving couples stood on the Main Terrace and gazed in wonder at Lila's landscaped paradise. With all the awe of children visiting Santa Claus, the excited groups would work their way toward wherever on that vast lawn their queenly hostess had established her presence. Lila was always gracious and friendly—these, after all, were the moments she lived for—and the routine was simple enough. As cleverly as possible, you murmured the right words—"How lovely you look, Lila, how gorgeous your gardens, how nice of you to think of us"—and then moved on. Yet tensions at these soirees ran high, and gaffes were not uncommon. On one such occasion, a newly hired associate editor named Daniel O'Keefe approached his patroness, glass in hand, smile on face, to speak his piece. "My goodness!" exclaimed the tiny Lila. "Aren't you a tall one!" "Yes, ma'am!" replied O'Keefe, rising to the occasion. "Six feet two, when *fully erected!*" O'Keefe was so undone by his indiscretion that he quickly downed two glasses of gin and spent the evening under a rhododendron.

DeWitt himself endured these affairs with as much politeness as he could muster, for Lila's sake and because he knew his guests enjoyed being there. But his boredom was thinly disguised. At one party in the late thirties, he found himself sharing champagne and solemn conversation with several younger colleagues, including Jerry Ellison's long-legged wife, Frances. "Frances," he said suddenly, grabbing a tray of champagne from a passing waitress, "I'll bet you can't kick this champagne out of my hands." He held the tray at shoulder height, staring in admiration at Frances's shapely legs.

"Oh, I could do it, all right, Wally," said Frances. "But I won't."

"I didn't say you wouldn't," replied Wally. "I said you *couldn't.*"

Frances raised her dress and with a swift swing of her right leg sent the drinks flying. Lila closed the bar shortly thereafter.

When the time came to depart, the rules were as precise as those for arrival: locate the King and Queen, line up to say good-bye, be gone no later than seven. The Wallaces sat down to dinner at seven and any couple still hanging around was apt to look silly. But this never happened. Well before the magic hour, the limousines would begin transporting groups of happy Digesters back down Lila's hill. In the parking field, directions to local restaurants would be shouted back and forth, and doors would slam and expensive cars speed off into the night. Now the party could begin for real. Now they could let their hair down and really *enjoy* the evening that stretched ahead.

As the last groups departed, DeWitt was often seen standing outside his front entrance, one arm raised in a gesture of farewell, the granite walls behind him turning pink in the glow of the setting sun. There was something very sad about such moments. The party was ending and suddenly he seemed to regret this. His colleagues were vanishing into worlds he could only dream of, full of laughter and singing, friendships and family; where real people could be their real selves. And, once again, he was left behind.

As war clouds darkened over Europe, DeWitt Wallace found himself in a dilemma. Part of him believed that tyranny should be fought wherever it existed—"Fight the Hun to the hilt!," as his father had urged during the Great War. This part favored America's early entry into the battle for Europe. But another part of him had doubts. He knew too well what war was like, and that its horrors seldom solved anything. As in many things, his ambivalence closely reflected the way the American people felt. In May 1940, according to the Gallup Poll, 64 percent of Americans wanted to stay neutral, while 36 percent favored helping England. By December, it was 40 percent for staying home and 60 percent for war.

One year later—on December 7, 1941—the Japanese made such arguments moot. With most of the Pacific fleet destroyed at Pearl Harbor, America woke up to the fact that it was at war and that things were not going well. At the time of the Japanese attack, Lila and DeWitt were vacationing in Arizona. They returned home immediately, and when DeWitt saw early copies of the upcoming January issue he was not pleased. Too grim, he felt. Although the presses up in New Hampshire had already churned out several thousand copies, he decided to make some changes.

Five articles in the issue touched on the war in one way or another, and all made it sound like a losing proposition. Working through the night, Wallace chose five replacement articles that painted a more hopeful picture, did some cursory editing, and ordered the presses stopped. The gloomy pieces were yanked and Wallace's replacements, rushed to New Hampshire by car, inserted. "The only thing we have to fear is fear itself," Roosevelt had counseled during the Great Depression. Wallace believed this. And he believed that the role of his magazine was to emphasize hope.

What he did not then understand, and would later find hard to believe, was the effect the war would have on his own fortunes. In 1938, pressured by Al Cole and other executives, Wallace had agreed to publish *Reader's Digest* in Britain. He was never quite sure why he did this—his abiding interest in life was to serve readers in America. But the British public was appreciative, and circulation in England quickly rose to 300,000.

And that was just the beginning. During the early years of the war, Nazi propagandists were active throughout South America, and the U.S. State Department was desperately seeking ways to counter their efforts. Because of *RD*'s success in England—and because the *Digest* offered such an upbeat picture of life in the United States—the government asked Wallace if he would consider translating his magazine into Spanish for distribution in Latin America.

Al Cole and Marvin Lowes, a thirty-five-year-old Williams graduate who had been in charge of the British edition, went to South America to check out the possibilities. They came back discouraged. "There aren't enough people down there with 25 cents to spare," said Cole. "The only answer is to sell the magazine for a dime and take advertising. But even with ads we would face an annual deficit of at least $50,000." Wallace thought this over. Covering the deficit was no problem. But the prospect of advertising, with the attendant loss of independence and the possibility of stirring trouble among his source magazines, worried him. Still, if his government thought publication would help the war effort, and if by taking ads he could spread his message to millions of South Americans, he was willing.

A maximum sale of 50,000 copies had been predicted, but a first printing three times that size was sold out in two days. The circulation of *Selecciones del Reader's Digest** quickly rose to 800,000 copies—four times larger than any magazine ever printed in the Spanish language. An edition in Portuguese for distribution in Brazil followed within a year, and it too was soon breaking records, selling more than 300,000 copies a month.

In the spring of 1942, the government approached Wallace again, this time seeking a deal under which the Office of War Information (OWI) would subsidize distribution of the *Digest* in Sweden. The thought of surrendering control to the government's propaganda branch horrified Wallace, and he turned them down. But he did promise to look into publishing in Sweden himself. And here he made a fateful decision. Barclay Acheson had been confined to PR work since the arrival of Al Cole. Now Lila suggested that Barclay might be the man to handle the Swedish assignment. Without giving it much thought, DeWitt agreed, and in June 1942 Barclay, Marvin Lowes and Hobart Lewis, a young Princeton grad rising rapidly on the editorial side, set out for Stockholm.

The first person they met was Albert Bonnier, the largest publisher in Sweden. Bonnier told them they couldn't possibly sell more than 20,000 copies a month. Undeterred, the *Digest* team ordered a first printing of 75,000 copies. To their delight, it disappeared from newsstands in less than five days. Within six months, circulation had risen to 300,000 and the *Digest* was the largest-selling magazine in Sweden.

While breakfasting at his Stockholm hotel one morning in 1944, Hobe Lewis was handed a telephone by his waiter. "Here is Eljas Erkko from Helsinki," said a voice. "I wish please to speak with Dr. Acheson." Erkko was an important Finnish publisher and he invited the *Digest* group to come to Helsinki to discuss a Finnish edition. At the time, Finland was essentially a Russian outpost, unrecognized by the United States, and no one knew how Moscow would react to a Finnish *Digest*. After a personal meeting with the president of Finland, Acheson decided to go ahead. "The first printing of fifty thousand copies was gone within days," recalls Lewis. "The next printing was upped to one hundred thousand. Same result. And the Russians never blinked."

Meanwhile, in another part of the world, Al Cole and Fred Thompson were having a more difficult time. Turkey was another key neutral country where German propagandists had been active, so OWI asked the *Digest* to open an

---

* The foreign editions typically consisted of "selections from" the U.S. edition, with emphasis on material of international interest.

edition there. Private citizens weren't allowed to travel to that part of the world during wartime, so Cole and Thompson were recruited by OWI as "publishing agents" (the first of what would become a long-standing series of relationships between U.S. intelligence and Reader's Digest). "It took us three weeks to get there," recalled Thompson. "We flew to Brazil and then to the Gold Coast of Africa in Pan American planes. A military plane took us from there to Cairo. From Cairo we took a train to Istanbul."

After six weeks in Turkey, they decided the situation was hopeless. Germany controlled the shipment of paper into Turkey and the Nazis threatened to cut off all supplies if the *Digest* opened for business. Back in Cairo, they worked to salvage something from their arduous trip. Several Arabs had suggested launching an Arabic-language edition for distribution throughout the Middle East—in Egypt, Syria, Lebanon, Jordan, Iraq and Saudi Arabia. After studying the situation, Cole sent Wallace an enthusiastic cable: THERE ARE 50 MILLION PEOPLE IN THE AREA, INCLUDING MORE THAN 5 MILLION WHO ARE LITERATE. AMERICA IS POPULAR HERE, AND THERE IS GREAT INTEREST IN READING ABOUT THINGS AMERICAN. WE COULD PROVIDE A REAL SERVICE. Wallace liked this argument, and plans were made to go ahead.

The first issue of *Al Mukhtar min Reader's Digest* went on sale September 2, 1943, two weeks after Cole and Thompson had returned to the States. On September 4, the Cairo office sent this cable:

ARABIC EDITION SOLD OUT IN TWO DAYS STOP NEWSBOYS BEGGING FOR MORE COPIES STOP REGRET ONLY ABLE PRINT 60,000 OCTOBER ISSUE AS INDICATIONS PROVE 100,000 SALE POSSIBLE.

The launch of the Japanese edition was the most improbable of all. Dennis McEvoy was the son of one of Wallace's favorite roving editors, J. P. McEvoy. At sixteen, on a trip to the Far East with his father, Dennis was dropped off at a YMCA in Tokyo to spend several months learning Japanese. In 1940, he published an article in the *Digest* called "Japan's 'Patriotic' Gangsters," exposing the fascism of the political system. Thrown out of the country, he served during the war as an agent for the Office of Naval Intelligence in Southeast Asia. Right after VE Day, Dennis McEvoy showed up in Pleasantville.

"We've got to open a Japanese edition," he told Wallace. Why would the Japanese want to read an American magazine? Wallace wondered. "Because they are realists," McEvoy argued. "They believed themselves unbeatable. Now that we are beating them they will want to read all about this strange democracy that has accomplished the impossible."

When victory came, McEvoy was in Tokyo before the Armistice was signed. By February 1946, he had established the feasibility of a Japanese edition and obtained permission to go ahead from Supreme Commander

Douglas MacArthur. (He had also enlisted Mateo Okini, chief of intelligence for the Japanese Navy, to be managing director.) When the first press run of 120,000 copies appeared on newsstands, the Japanese lined up for blocks and the entire run was sold out within hours. Circulation eventually climbed above a million copies.

With the war over, Barclay Acheson set up shop in Paris to contemplate the inevitable spread of the *Digest* into countries that had been off-limits during hostilities. In Paris, he ran into a handsome young brigadier named Paul Thompson, who had been involved in the *Stars and Stripes* newspaper operation during the war. Thompson was looking for work, and since he already had *Digest* experience (*Stars and Stripes* having published weekly supplements consisting of *Digest* articles) Acheson took him under his wing. Huddled over calculating machines in smoke-filled hotel rooms, surrounded by Europeans eager to tap into the Digest treasury, Acheson and Thompson worked out deal after deal. A French edition was established in 1946, followed quickly by editions in Germany, Austria, Belgium, Holland, Switzerland and Italy.

As had been the case elsewhere during the war, sales in these countries were phenomenal from the start, and soon other countries were demanding their own editions. By 1950, *Reader's Digest* was being published in eleven languages for distribution in over fifty countries. "It is read in foxholes in Korea, in the cockpits of transatlantic planes, by Swedish farmers, Brazilian housewives, Japanese coal miners, Igorots in G strings," reported *Time*. "In France and Belgium, *Selection du Reader's Digest* is the biggest of all monthlies. In Sweden, *Det Basta ur Reader's Digest* is the biggest monthly, as *Selezione dal Reader's Digest* is in Italy and *Valitut Palat koonnut Reader's Digest* is in Finland. The Portuguese and Spanish-language *Digest* are tops all over South America, and the Japanese edition, with a circulation nearing 700,000, is the biggest monthly in Japan. Based on global circulation, De-Witt Wallace, the *Digest*'s founder, owner and boss, is the most successful editor in history."

How did this editing colossus feel about his international success? He was proud, astonished, even a little embarrassed. He pointed out that his government had come to him, and that he had considered establishment of the foreign editions a patriotic duty. "We believed the *Digest* could be an effective interpreter of the United States to those living in other countries," he said, "and that this would promote an alliance of interests in the cause of peace."

But what really pleased him about the *Digest*'s extraordinary international growth was the discovery that readers everywhere "like what I like." Readership surveys in every country showed that the most popular articles in the U.S. edition were also those highest-rated around the world. "In the long run," concluded *Time*, "Wallace's greatest contribution may be found in the cumulative impact of his overseas editions. The *Digest's* articles—depicting the innate decency, kindness and simple virtues of ordinary Americans—have done more than all the government's propagandists combined to allay the fears, prejudices and misconceptions of the U.S. in other lands." *

This ability to mirror "America's goodness" made the *Digest* popular in Washington as well—especially at the State Department and within the newly formed Central Intelligence Agency. In 1947, when Barclay Acheson complained to State about the money RD was losing because of its inability to transfer foreign currencies out of the countries where it published, the government offered to cover the difference itself, or to buy the blocked currency in U.S. dollars. Anxious to avoid the appearance of a direct subsidy (because detractors were already calling the *Digest* a government puppet), Acheson chose the latter course—and insisted that funds used to buy the blocked currency come from the budgets of "existing U.S. agencies, such as the U.S. Information Service."

The CIA, concerned that influential publications in Europe and elsewhere were coming under Communist control, also had its eye on the *Digest,* offering in 1949 to finance several "news bureaus" at strategic locations around the globe. Although Wallace again refused to surrender any form of control ("accepting financial assistance from the government would compromise our integrity"), the Agency was not long deterred. Several top RD executives, including two of its most senior editors, had served in the OSS (precursor of the CIA) during the war; as intelligence alumni, they were willing to do what they could for the cause. In addition to Dennis McEvoy in Japan, other early Digesters with intelligence connections included: Terence Harmon, a British agent who became managing director of the Italian edition in 1947 (Harmon had been liaison to the OSS during the war; critics have charged that he used *Selezione* to spread CIA disinformation during the Italian elections of 1948); Eduardo Cardenas, RD's first managing director in South America, who had run a CIA propaganda outlet called Editor's Press Service; Adrian Berwick, who managed OWI's Overseas News and Features Bureau before becoming *RD's* international editor; André Visson, an alumnus of Radio Liberty (another OSS/CIA propaganda branch), who began writing "political analyses" out of the *Digest's* new Washington bureau in 1948; Alain deLyrot, European bureau chief for Copley News Service (a CIA-run cover for Agency operatives), who later became editor of the French *Reader's Digest*; and John Dimitri ("Dimi") Panitza, a Bulgarian-born aristocrat who became the *Digest's* European editor in 1952.

---

* *RD's* spread around the world was greatly aided by the U.S. government. Other magazines, for example, had to wait years for "authorization to publish." The *Digest* seldom waited longer than two weeks. And while paper supplies were severely rationed throughout Europe, the *Digest* somehow always got the paper it needed.

Despite all this international activity, Wallace's own interest in operations outside the United States remained minimal. His goal had always been to establish a thriving magazine with which to keep Americans informed. All the rest of it—the foreign editions, and the book clubs, record albums and videos waiting in the future—essentially bored him. And there was another problem. He had gone along with expansion overseas because it seemed like the right thing to do. He had allowed Lila to put her brother in charge because he had seen these editions as a wartime phenomenon; if Lila wanted to give this temporary plum to Barclay, why not? Now international circulation was approaching six million. It was a big business—more than half the size of the U.S. operation. But Barclay was in charge, and that mean Lila was the real boss.

Before long, rumors were inundating Pleasantville about corruption and graft in Europe and South America. Hands in the till. Political payoffs and astronomical expense accounts. Wallace was aware of the rumors, but not greatly troubled. He wasn't looking for money from these businesses. As far as he was concerned, profits earned abroad were best kept abroad and used to build circulation or to improve the individual magazines.

Other RD executives weren't so sure about this. In fact, Al Cole was livid about the way things were going overseas. As general manager of Reader's Digest, he had established certain procedures that had proved extremely profitable in the United States. Now Barclay Acheson was running things overseas very differently, and his actions were costing the company millions. Cole had confronted him on this, but Barclay, sure of his sister's support, had refused to back down. In January 1953, Cole had written a memo to Wallace listing Barclay's failures and asking that he be replaced for the good of the company. It was not a memo Wallace was happy to receive. "Barclay is in charge overseas," he wrote to Cole. "You stay out of it."

The next morning, when he reached his desk at Headquarters, Wallace was not surprised to find a letter of resignation from Cole staring him in the face. He picked up his phone. "Al," he said, "have you got a minute?" Cole appeared shortly thereafter, and silently took a seat opposite his boss. For a moment, the two men looked at one another across the leather top of Wallace's huge desk. The letter lay by itself in the center of the desk. To accept it, Wallace knew, would be disastrous for his company. On the other hand, to accede to Cole's wishes would bring the wrath of Lila onto all their heads.

"Al," he said, "as you well know, Lila is co-owner of this business." He paused to let the weight of his obvious remark sink in. "And Barclay Acheson is Lila's brother." He paused again. "Lila wants Barclay running International. I understand your arguments against this. I agree with most of them. But they don't change the situation. So couldn't we"—he reached forward to nudge the letter a little closer to Cole—"couldn't we just . . . *forget* this?"

Cole leveled a hard look at his employer. But when he spoke, a faint smile creased his handsome face. "Okay, Wally," he said, reaching for the letter. He was not a whiner, and he still had plans for the further expansion of Reader's Digest. But as he rose to leave, he could not help wondering how a man like DeWitt Wallace came to be so cowed by a five-foot-three-inch woman with a bad temper and an ill-concealed weakness for the likes of Barclay Acheson and Harry Wilcox. But whatever else she was, Cole thought, Lila Wallace was tough. She had won Round Three on every card.

CHAPTER ELEVEN

In December 1948, the *Digest's* editorial staff showed its appreciation for all the blessings rained on them by the Wallaces by staging *The RD Follies of '48,* a collection of mildly risque skits in which they poked fun at themselves and their fairy-tale Pleasantville existence. One skit involved an article "condensation" in the form of a striptease; another focused on the unplanned meeting of three *RD* roving editors on assignment in the Gobi Desert. The opening chorus, sung to the tune of *Mañana, Mañana,* ended with a friendly warning:

> A jolly, jolly family, good friends when all is said,
> We are the Scots and Scottesses *wha' hae wi' Wallace bled,*
> So if you'll bear with us tonight, we'll dish it from the top
> And when you think you've had enough, you'd better holler STOP!!
> > *Chorus:* Dear Lila—Dear Wally
> > Perhaps right now you'd better holler STOP!!

The Wallaces loved the skits and the evening was a great success. Yet there was an unintended irony in the suggestion that they "holler STOP." For close to thirty years, they had labored without pause to create their Kingdom. Now, finally, they were able to step back and consider what they had wrought, and what they saw filled them with pride, wonder and frustration. Their little magazine was reaching sixteen million homes around the world—was being read now by fifty *million* people! At the same time, the "family" they had assembled to produce it—their "Scots and Scottesses"—had grown so large and far-flung that all real resemblance to a family was disappearing. "Wally and I had our happiest time when we started the Digest," Lila began telling friends. "Now it is all so big, and there are so many problems. People problems, mostly. Greedy people. Jealous people." DeWitt agreed with this. "From 1950 on," says his longtime secretary Betty St. John, "it was clear that the thrill was gone for him. At least once a week he would say to me, 'Oh, Betty, I'd like to junk the whole thing and start over.' "

The difference, of course, is that DeWitt understood what he was saying and meant every word. Lila was incapable of seeing that the "people problems" she complained about were often her own doing.

During the last years of the war, *Reader's Digest* had been bitterly critical of the Roosevelt administration, and as a result the magazine had become the target of a concentrated smear campaign launched by Democrats and left-wing commentators. Worried about this, Wallace had sought counsel from his old friend Norman Cousins, the liberal editor of the *Saturday Review of Literature*. "The problem is not insoluble," Cousins advised. "As captain of your own ship, you are in a position to correct what might be described as a list to the extreme Right. Your own political position is far closer to the Center than the impression created by the *Digest* itself, and some of its editors, and ought to serve as a good stabilizer."

The trouble was, Wallace didn't seem to care anymore about politics. Right, left, center—whatever his position was, he wasn't particularly interested in reasserting it. In its 1951 cover story, *Time* seemed to sense this: "On the broader questions of politics, Wallace describes himself as left of center, whereas he feels most people are middle-of-the-roaders. . . . He thinks the Democrats' Big Government is dangerous, but admits he would be critical of Government no matter which party was in power."

This was true, at least in part. But there was more to it. The secret of his magazine lay in talking to people about the everyday problems of their lives. "Big Issues"—of politics, government, international affairs—weren't what interested his readers, and they weren't what interested him. A Guesthouse luncheon at the Digest in the summer of 1948, described by Dennis McEvoy in an unpublished memoir, is indicative of this trait:

> It was a most impressive gathering: besides several of the *Digest*'s top editors, there was a general with wide experience in Asia, several high-ranking government officials, and a professor who was a world-famous expert on Japanese and Chinese affairs. The talk was on a high level: Asian geopolitics, estimates of decisions which chiefs of state might make, suggestions about American political and military strategy.
>
> DeWitt Wallace, normally very quiet anyway, was quieter than usual this day, and I, being the most junior guest, kept my mouth shut during the entire conversation. Suddenly, Wallace cleared his throat. The table fell silent. To my surprise, his question was addressed to me:

"Dennis, tell me, is it true that in Japan babies don't cry?"

I was stunned, and so were the others. "Well, come to think of it, Wally," I stammered, "I don't remember hearing them cry very often, if at all."

"Why?"

"Well, *um*, possibly because they are breast-fed longer than Western babies. Or because they are carried about on the backs of their mothers. But, Wally, these are only guesses. If I could study the matter, I could give you a fuller report."

"I wish you would," he said. "I think *that* might make a good article."

The talk of geopolitics gradually resumed. Wallace listened attentively, as usual, but spoke up immediately after coffee to remind our guests that there was just time to catch the 1:25 train to New York.

The truth was, Wallace was bored. Bored by arguments over "issues" and bored even more by the growing lack of challenge in his life, by the fact that his magazine was now largely in the hands of others, steaming along with little interference on his part. He still read everything that appeared in the *Digest,* and occasionally—when an article struck him as too long or a headline seemed overwritten, or when someone mistook passing fashion for "lasting interest"—voiced his mild objections. But this was fiddling, and he knew it. He was still the editor of *Reader's Digest.* But the real work was being done by others—by Ken Payne and Paul Palmer in editorial, by Al Cole and Fred Thompson in the business office, by scores of eager younger men throughout the company.

Wallace was also troubled by the lifestyle that had overtaken him—the endless parties, the flirting, the drinking, the inescapable fawning, the pretense and softness of it all. He had always longed to know how the story of his life would turn out, whether he would be its hero. Now he knew. His story exceeded every childhood dream. He *was* its hero. And that was precisely the problem. He began to spend more time in his Tower, pondering these thoughts with the help of his ever-present three-by-five cards:

> Many faculties vital to primitive man are still dormant within us, but because they are unused we suffer in health, in energy. But if we use them we can be flooded with power. Two hints on how to begin:
>
> 1. When you feel drowsy at night, *fight it off.* Make up the sleep at a later time.
> 2. Skip a meal now and then. Say to yourself one evening a week: *"No dinner tonight!"* Such behavior leads toward the toughened ascetic life, not so different from that of our primitive forebears.

During this period, he began to build a system of roads connecting various locations on Lila's estate. It was brutal work, with pick and shovel, saw and ax. But it became the one thing that made him feel alive. Wearing boots, chinos and an old Yankee cap, he would drive his Jeep to wherever he had left off the day before, strip to the waist and have at it. Sometimes he finished several feet in a day; sometimes only a foot. When he had a section cleared, he would dump in barrow-loads of sand, then carry stones from crumbling walls in the surrounding woods and set them into the sand. He had gardener Joe Guignardi fetch used oil from the Digest garage. He would pour this oil around the stones to harden the sand. "Those roads were built to last," recalls Guignardi. "They became like macadam."

Wallace began this project in the late forties and kept at it, whenever he had a few spare hours, until he was ninety years old. There was something about it that appealed to him: the solitude of the forest; the opportunity for quiet reflection; the fact that it had no beginning and no end. The process reminded him of his recently deceased father, and of how James Wallace had regarded death itself as an opportunity to "circle back" in search of new opportunities for "spiritually profitable" activity. He thought also of Grandfather Ben Wallace endlessly carrying sacks of corn from field to barn on his own broad shoulders, because he had no money for a horse. Thoughts of Ben and James made him feel ashamed of his own profligate life, and that's when he looked for his Yankee cap and headed into the woods.

But he knew there had to be a better answer to his problem than building roads. As the half-century mark approached, he found himself in his Tower later than ever, thinking deeper into the night. A plan was forming. Yet, something held him back. He was frequently depressed during this period, and not sure why. One night, he pulled a sheet of paper from his desk and addressed this issue:

> Why do I get depressed? First, think of the effort you spend on fear. *Refuse to spend it so wastefully.* Substitute for fear the thought that you are trying to do good, that there can be no penalty for this. With yr mind flooded with this thot, there can be no fear. . . .

Except, of course, there was. Success had come so quickly, with such overwhelming force, that he had lost his way. Now he was contemplating a new direction—a way to go forward again—and the prospect of taking even a single step filled him with dread. Could he do it? Was it the right thing? *Would Lila approve?*

After James Wallace's death, Macalester professor Edwin Kagin wrote a biography in honor of the "Old Roman's" struggle to preserve the college. Before publication, a copy was sent to DeWitt with a request that he supply a foreword. As he immersed himself in his father's story, DeWitt became aware of another struggle, and his heart sank in recognition. He wrote of this in his foreword:

As I read this manuscript I was profoundly shocked—for this is a saga essentially of suffering, acute and prolonged. Its reader cannot help but ask, as I have done: *Why did my father do this?* Why did he contine through those dark and hopeless years? Why did he subject himself, his wife, and his children to such hardship. I do not know. . . .

In the Kagin manuscript, Wallace saw his childhood clearly for the first time. It had been, in its essence, "a saga of suffering." But what of the other version? "To the dearest little Mother who ever lived," he had written from that Oregon café. "I lie awake at night thinking of our happy home, of our joyous, idyllic existence. . . ."

Which version was true? He saw now that his letters to Janet were mostly bunk—the well-intended efforts of a lonely boy to comfort a troubled mother (and to induce that troubled mother to admire her wandering son). That had been his role in the family—to focus on the bright side—and he had performed it faithfully ("All to the merry!" "In the pink!" "Couldn't be better!") for many years. Only rarely—as in that single angry letter to Aunt Maude—had he allowed himself to confront the darker side. To do so terrified him because it always seemed somehow that *he* ("your good-for-nothing son") had caused it all.

Now, alone in his Tower, he contemplated the painful truth. The family myth ("our happy home," "our joyous life") was only that . . . a myth. It would have to be abandoned. It may also be true (and the proposal he was about to make to Lila supports this view) that he had reached a similar conclusion about his magazine. That he saw it now—in its focus on the bright side, in its belief that simple answers existed for the darkest, most complex problems of human life—as no more than a reworked version of the old family myth, the well-intended (sometimes necessary, sometimes *precious*) effort of a lonely man to comfort fifty million troubled readers.

But however ready he was to abandon the myth itself, the demands that went *with* the myth—his compulsion to do good, to hold back the dark, to be his mother's "royal boy"—remained. His great success had provided him with power—to please Lila, to support family, friends and employees, to reassure readers—and he had used this power with faith and dedication. He had not failed anyone. Yet the same success had isolated him (*imprisoned* him) inside his old, conforming self. Now he wanted to go forward again, to "do good" in a new way, on his own terms. But he was afraid. And he worried that his *real* self—the maverick, the dreamer, the golden boy yearning for the open road—had been lost forever.

PART IV

Fading Dreams

1950–1973

CHAPTER TWELVE

On a soft June evening in 1950, DeWitt Wallace stood behind his chair in the dining room at High Winds. Across the table, partially obscured by a halo of light rising above the candelabra, Lila Wallace glared at a dish of strawberries. There was no one else present, and it was clear that DeWitt had been speaking about something so important he had felt it necessary to rise from the table.

The two of them ate together every night when they were in residence at High Winds, and every night the ritual was the same. Whatever had happened during the day, Lila insisted that her husband join her for cocktails in the Game Room at 6:30 sharp. She always wore an evening gown on these occasions, and she expected him to appear in a dinner jacket, freshly shaved, bearing amusing gossip to brighten their brief time together. She allowed few exceptions to this ritual. One night when DeWitt arrived home at 6:25 after a long day in New York, he suggested they go straight to the Game Room. "No, Wally," Lila had said, "You go up and bathe and change. I'll wait here in the rotunda. *Then* we'll go down."

Despite its name, the Game Room was an elegant space with Italian murals on the walls, antique rattan and canvas furniture, and polished, wide-board floors. The Wallaces would sit there on a chaise and sip their cocktails—vodka martini for her, Wild Turkey on the rocks for him—before a huge fireplace in which oak logs blazed three seasons a year. ("Even when the house is empty," Lila often said, "I'm never lonely as long as there's a fire.") When they were properly relaxed, they always danced together for fifteen minutes before going up to dinner. Once in the dining room, DeWitt ate his meal with a strong appetite, while Lila chattered on about this or that, and toyed with hers. When the meal was over, they took their coffee in the library. After a few polite sips, DeWitt inevitably excused himself to head for his Tower. Lila liked to linger alone, sipping her coffee and enjoying a final glass or two of wine before retiring to her bedchamber.

On this evening, Wallace was wearing the red dinner jacket Lila had picked out for him at Knize's in New York. Although he was himself indifferent to clothes, he knew this jacket was Lila's favorite and had purposely chosen it on this occasion to please her. Standing there in the dim light, with his slender form and military bearing, he looked younger than his sixty years. And there was something in his expression, an earnest, pleading quality, that added to the impression of youth.

"I know you think I'm crazy," he was saying, "but this plan is important to me, and I believe it could be important to you as well." Lila's frown deepened, and it was evident that his words to this point had not met with her approval. At sixty-two, she too conveyed an impression of youthful vigor. She had been riding that afternoon on a favorite mare named Red Sails, and the exercise had done her spirits a world of good. But her elevated mood was fast disappearing.

"Our magazine is a great success," DeWitt continued. "The company is operating smoothly and the money is pouring in. But the thing is . . . it can work just as well without me. Ken Payne can manage editorial. Al is a better businessman than I will ever be. Besides, I'm *bored* with it. I need to get out, to get back into the world, to *do* things . . . "

He was ready, he said, to move on to something new, something that had always been important to him: "America isn't paying sufficient attention to its classrooms. I would like to do something about that. My father and my grandfather were devoted to education and they each did something that made a difference. But I can do more. I have the good fortune . . . thanks mostly to my wife . . . to be a wealthy man. So I should be able to make a bigger difference."

Lila was glaring at him as if he had lost his mind. He looked away. The room itself and everything in it—Regency cabinets, George III sconces, Monets and Bonnards on every wall—seemed to mock his thoughts. He continued: "I think we should sell the *Digest*. And perhaps—" he risked a glance in her direction—"perhaps we should sell High Winds." Lila's face remained impassive. "Anyway," he concluded, "that's what *I* think. What about you?"

When Lila spoke, after a long pause, her voice was cold as steel. "You can sell your half of the *Digest, sweetie,*" she said, "and go wherever you please. But I am holding onto mine. In fact, if you're looking for a buyer, here I am. As for selling High Winds" . . . she paused, shaking her head . . . "you must be mad. We have everything here we ever wanted. How can you even *think* of giving it up?"

DeWitt's jaw hardened and for a fleeting moment something close to fury filled his eyes. But no answer came to him, and after a long silence he pulled his chair back and sat down. The plan he was contemplating affected both of them—was, in fact, a breaking of the deal they had made thirty years before —so it was only fair that she should have her own opinion. He didn't feel he could challenge her in any case, since he wasn't sure himself the plan made sense.

But the matter didn't end there. For several months, he raised and reraised the issue, searching for the right words, for a way to make clear to her how important this move was for him. But the more he persisted, the more Lila found his plan amusing. "Wally wants to escape," she began telling others, rolling her eyes in derision. "He's planning to run away from home."

He had encountered an obstacle that felt very familiar. *Sweetie,* she had called him, and he had no answer for that. He didn't run away, or sell his half of the Digest, and after that year he never raised the subject again. He yielded, as he had been trained to yield as a child. For thirty years he had placed his trust in Lila, just as he had placed it earlier in Janet Wallace. When he had chafed at Janet's control—her "Darling Dee" scoffing at "cradle and nipple"—she had dropped him cold. Now Lila was threatening to drop her "sweetie," and the threat alone was enough to fill him with panic. Without Lila, what would he be? *A misfit? A flop? "Little Willie" after all?*

But the anger this aroused in him didn't go away. Outwardly, he remained the "good boy" the world (and Lila) seemed to require. But another part of him, the part that might have turned the good boy into an empowered man, ran off and hid (as it had so often in the past). And from its hiding spot— angry but impotent—this part fretted and fumed and stamped its feet.

"What he yearned for were the early days of struggle," says his friend James Stewart-Gordon. "It wasn't so much that success made him uncomfortable as that it deprived him of challenge. Lila got from the Digest precisely what she wanted. Wally wanted something else, something he no longer found at the Digest. He had a new plan, and he desperately wanted to follow it. But Lila said no."

Blocked from pursuit of this new dream, Wallace looked to others to pursue it for him. Paul Davis had served as vice president of Columbia University during Dwight Eisenhower's tenure there as president, and Wallace had come to know him during negotiations over several articles Ike had written for the Digest. In certain ways, the tall, Presbyterian-raised Davis was a mirror image of Wallace: he had flown De Havilland biplanes during World War I, then wing-walked his way through Stanford University; before coming to Columbia, he had overseen San Francisco's Depression-era relief programs, managed a utility company in Brazil and become a sought-after consultant on college financing and administration.

But what really attracted Wallace were the convictions the two men shared about what was wrong with America. Wallace distrusted the rising tide of technology—the new machinery, the exploding sciences, the spread of giant corporations. Something vital in America was threatened, he felt, and Davis agreed. "Our very success has become our undoing," Davis was fond of saying. "We have been so captured by the materialistic ethic that we've lost sight of the qualities of character that brought us our high standard of living in the first place. In our early history, when we were struggling, our efforts and attitudes were high, and we succeeded. But with affluence we became arrogant, and so we began to go down."

The two men agreed that leadership was needed to turn the country around, and that the search for leaders had to begin with an overhaul of the U.S. educational system. "We need to place emphasis where none now exists," said Wallace. "We have concentrated on science and technology, and our technological growth has been impressive. But the old values once taught in home, church and school—ethics, morals, *integrity*—are no longer taught effectively anywhere. *That's* where we need to concentrate."

In 1951, Wallace hired Davis to serve as his personal "education adviser." Davis began to travel about the country, interviewing prominent people in the field, studying educational alternatives, identifying promising schools and talented students. At first he focused on Macalester, seeking ideas and innovations to further James Wallace's dream of turning the little school into an "Amherst of the West." But as time went on the effort was broadened to encompass dozens of colleges and hundreds of independent schools.

The program brought Wallace great satisfaction, but also considerable frustration. He understood that the effort was his in name only; others were doing the real work—creating, imagining, planning. He provided money and encouragement, but otherwise remained tied to the Digest and to Lila. Only when Davis came East to report to him in person did he feel truly involved. "When Paul was in town, he and Wally talked for hours at a time," recalls nephew Gordon Davies. "From the early fifties on, those conversations were the one thing that really stimulated him."

During the first year of this collaboration, Davis always came directly to

High Winds and stayed there overnight. But eventually Lila became jealous of his rapport with DeWitt. The three of them would sit at dinner and inevitably the conversation would turn to education. Since Lila knew little about the theories the men discussed, she quickly became bored. "All right, you boys," she would say, "let's talk about something else." Sometimes this worked; more often it did not. When it failed, Lila would excuse herself and go upstairs. When this happened three or four times, she decided that henceforth Davis would be more comfortable in the Guesthouse.

Even down at Headquarters, Wallace felt himself increasingly removed from the real workings of his business. When the Condensed Book Club was launched in 1950, Wallace was barely involved. The idea of selling condensed fiction had been kicking around for years. Wallace had included a condensed *non*fiction book in the magazine's second issue—Arnold Bennett's *How to Live on Twenty-four Hours a Day*—and when Ralph Henderson was hired Wallace put him in charge of finding suitable books for every issue. But Henderson was frustrated by this task. Many of the best books he read were fiction, and Wallace didn't feel fiction belonged in his magazine. "*RD* is about *facts,*" he insisted. "Our goal is to provide readers with factual information they can use to improve their lives."

So Henderson began to dream about a separate use for books—a whole new publication, in magazine format, that would contain condensed fiction and sell for the same price as the *Digest*. For several years Wallace ignored him. But Henderson persisted. In 1938, he and a writer named Gordon Carroll put together several paper-covered books consisting of four condensations of popular fiction and designed to sell on newsstands for $3 each. Wallace thought that was a bad value, and again the idea was shelved.

But Henderson remained convinced. In 1945, he approached Al Cole about the possibility of starting a book club. Cole liked the idea, but decided that bound volumes—"with the look and feel of *real* books"—made more sense. Henderson put together several prototypes and a mailing price was sent out to *RD* subscribers offering four volumes a year, each containing four condensed books, for $10. Although this clearly *was* a good value—sixteen hardcover books for 62 cents apiece—the test failed. Readers had never seen a "condensed" book and weren't eager to shell out $10 merely on the *Digest*'s promise that condensed fiction could be as enjoyable as the real thing.

The concept lay dormant for four more years. Then, at a 1949 lunch attended by Cole, Henderson and circulation chief Frank Herbert, the notion of a book club came up again, and this time Herbert had a bright idea. "People need to *see* this product," he said. "Why not offer a condensed book free of charge to all subscribers? Those who like it can sign up for additional books, one each quarter. Those who don't have no further obligation." Cole and Henderson looked at each other. "That's it!" said Cole. "Let's go see Wally."

Before their visit to Wallace's office, the two men prepared themselves for every question the Boss might ask. "I was to state the editorial appeal," recalled Henderson. "Al was to back me up with cost figures. But before I had opened my mouth, Wally looked from me to Al and back to me. 'If you two agree on this book-club idea,' he said, 'why don't you go ahead?' And that was that. Before we knew it we were out in the hall clutching what I vastly underestimated to be a million-dollar go-ahead."

As the fifties progressed, a more serious decision loomed, and once again Wallace played a largely passive role. For more than thirty years, *Reader's Digest* had been selling for 25 cents a copy and $3 a year, and even at those low rates—with no advertising revenues—profits had rolled in. But now expenses were rising dramatically, for paper, printing, postage, distribution, even editorial, and it began to look as if the money machine might go into the red. "Al Cole came to me in 1953," Wallace recalled later, "and he had some figures which showed that the U.S. magazine would start losing as much as a million a year unless we charged more per copy. Or we could take advertising. It was that simple."

Except that it wasn't simple at all. For one thing, Wallace himself had always had mixed feelings about ads. One side of him strongly disapproved. To allow ads in the *Digest* seemed to this side a violation of the pact he had made with charter members of his reading service. "Their" magazine was meant to be pure—a serious compendium of facts and ideas rather than a sideshow for the huckstering of toothpaste and cereal. Then there was the question of control. If he went along with advertising, power would shift inevitably toward Cole and his associates. This was worrisome, especially to Lila. *"Don't do it!"* was her advice.

But on this crucial issue DeWitt didn't listen. He was beginning to perceive that the power struggle between himself and Lila had somehow evolved into a power struggle between Lila and Al Cole, with himself in the middle. Lila's Side had been winning in recent years, but in the debate over advertising, the devil in DeWitt Wallace sensed an opportunity to score some points for Al's Side.

His goal had always been to give readers the best possible magazine at the lowest possible price. Now he asked Cole to poll readers on whether they preferred a higher price or a magazine with ads. To no one's surprise, 81 percent of those surveyed expressed a strong preference for the 25-cent version with ads.

"So there's your answer, Wally!" Cole crowed. "If we raise the price, circulation will go down something fierce. Our only choice is to take ads." Yet still Wallace hesitated. "He just didn't seem interested," Cole recalled.

"Then one day several of us were in his office talking about this or that—everything *but* advertising—when out of the blue he turned to me. 'By the way, Al,' he said, 'if you still think we should take advertising, I suppose the first thing to do is tell the other magazines. They may not go for it, you know. They may cancel our reprint rights.' "

That was his real worry—that in becoming an advertising competitor the *Digest* would risk its franchise as a reprint magazine. But Cole was prepared for this. "I'll handle it, Wally," he said. "If we raise what we pay for reprints, I think they'll go along."

Cole handled this assignment as shrewdly as he had handled the subscriber survey. At the time, the *Digest's* two biggest sources were Curtis Publishing (with the *Saturday Evening Post, Ladies' Home Journal, Country Gentleman* and *Holiday)* and Time, Inc. (with *Time, Life* and *Fortune).* If he could convince the two giants, Cole figured, bringing the other publishers into line would be a cinch.

He went first to Curtis, which was already sliding into hopeless financial straits. On Friday, November 6, 1953, he met with Walter Fuller, the Curtis chairman, and offered to double the *Digest's* reprint fee (from $100,000 a year to $200,000) if Curtis would accept the *Digest's* advertising decision. Without blinking an eye, Fuller agreed. (A costly decision: Within five years, *RD* was subtracting traceable *millions* from Curtis ad revenues.)

After leaving Fuller's office, Cole hurried north to Manhattan to offer Roy Larsen, president of Time, Inc., a similar deal—except that now he could preface his offer by pointing out that Curtis had already been informed and had not balked. After conferring with Andrew Heiskell, publisher of *Life,* and James Linen, publisher of *Time,* Larsen also gave Cole a go-ahead.

With the big boys lined up, Cole turned to the telephone. "Now that we've decided to take ads, John [or Ed, or Bill, or whoever]," he would say, "we've worked out a new reprint arrangement, a very generous one. The folks at Curtis and Time are on board, and I'm sure you'll want to be, too. Here's the deal. . . ."

No one refused Cole's offer, and "deal" is what it was—for the *Digest.* In return for doubled reprint fees— a drop in the bucket compared to the ad revenues they would soon be losing—every major publisher welcomed a powerful new competitor into the advertising sweepstakes. Back in Pleasantville, Cole announced the good news to his Boss. Still uneasy, Wallace gave him a reluctant go-ahead to solicit no more than thirty-two advertising pages per issue. Cole had already tabbed Fred Thompson to be his ad director. Now, with great excitement, he told Thompson to prepare an announcement to run as a full-page ad in the *New York Times* on the following Tuesday.

"We knew there would be tremendous interest," Thompson recalled later, "so to be fair we wanted to put our story before every advertiser and agency at the same time." To ensure security—because he worried that New York printers might have friends in the ad business—Thompson spent the weekend having the announcement set in type at a print shop in Bridgeport, Connecticut.

He might have saved himself the trouble: "When I reached the office on Monday morning, the phone was ringing off the hook. The *Wall Street Journal* had broken the story, and orders for ads were pouring in at a frightening rate. With more business than we could handle, our announcement had become pointless. I tore it up and began answering the phone. One agency exec placed a frantic order for twelve full-color pages. At thirty-one thousand dollars per page—the highest page rate ever—that came to three hundred and seventy-two thousand dollars. But he never even asked the price! "

And so it went, day after day. By the end of two weeks, the *Digest* had received orders for 1,107 pages of ads, three times the number it could accept for the entire first year. Yet a nagging question remained. How had their security been broken? Who had leaked, causing the chaos? The *Journal*'s article was fuzzy on this point. "The Digest made no formal announcement," it said. "But DeWitt Wallace indicated the decision was revealed through a spokesman in answer to a query from this newspaper." In fact, as Lila later told Judy Thompson, it was she who had forced the issue . . .

> *When I realized that advertising was coming to* Reader's Digest *whether I liked it or not, I was furious. And it only made me madder to see what a good time Al and Fred were having with that silly announcement business. So I told Wally that any such announcement should come from the owners. I suggested he call the* Journal *himself, over that weekend. And he did what he was told . . .*

During his sixteen-year Digest career, Fred Thompson had gained wide experience in circulation, production and advertising. On every assignment, he had performed brilliantly, and his genial manner and obvious honesty had made him a favorite throughout the company. Everyone understood that Cole was grooming him to be the next general manager, and it was also widely assumed that one day the Wallaces would ask Fred to rule over the Kingdom itself.

There was only one thing standing in his way. Lila Wallace was sixty-seven in 1955, and while she had aged with extraordinary grace, it was getting harder for her to see herself as the *Jeune Fille* in the Renoir painting. The harder it got, the more she demanded assurances from the princes of her realm. Those who were adept at this—veterans like Harry Wilcox and Brother Barclay; handsome younger stars like Paul Thompson and Hobart Lewis—were well rewarded. Those who did not were destroyed.

For a number of years, Lila had had her sights on Fred Thompson. He was tall and handsome, and that was part of his appeal. But there was something else Fred had that Lila coveted. She expected her world to be perfect; that it was not, that imperfection had crept in, including the absence of offspring and onrushing old age, was more than she could bear. She *wanted* proper heirs for the Kingdom (without having to conceive them herself) and she *wanted* to live forever, and to accomplish these miracles she decided to appropriate certain aspects of her niece's life: Judy's perfect husband would become *her* perfect husband; Judy's manly sons would become *her* manly sons. And Judy herself—with all her promise and all her potential—would become her own promise and her own potential.

"I was nearly swallowed alive by Lila in those years," Judy says today. "I dressed the way she dressed, acted the way she acted. I even found myself buying certain clothes for my children because I thought Lila would approve. *This is ridiculous!* I kept telling myself. *These are* your *children. This is* your *life. You've got to forget her!* But it wasn't easy. The situation was very complex."

Understandably confused, Judy sought to please her aunt in any way she could. But Fred Thompson was too straightforward for the goofy games Lila had in mind. In the mid fifties, after a High Winds soiree during which his "unresponsive" behavior had left the Queen in a foul temper, the would-be Prince was pulled aside by Lois Monahan, the *Digest*'s first female roving editor and something of a sage in the Wallace Court. "Fred," she said, "why don't you just make love to this woman?" When Fred stared at her in disbelief, Monahan smiled sadly. "Look," she said, "I'm from Georgia, so I know about these things. If you won't make love to her, can't you at least be a little nicer? A little . . . warmer? That's all she wants."

But Fred could not. He was respectful and attentive, but it wasn't in him to play the lover game. "Fred was too honest for that," says Judy. "Lois was giving him good advice. Had he followed it—had he been *half* as ardent as Lila's other suitors—everything that followed might have been different. But he couldn't do it. He thought Lila was beyond the pale."

CHAPTER THIRTEEN

One morning during this period—spring 1955—Judy Thompson received a phone call at her apartment on West Twenty-third Street in New York's

Chelsea district. Her Uncle DeWitt was on the line: "I will be down on Twenty-third Street, in front of the delicatessen on the corner, at eleven-thirty. Meet me there." Before she could protest, he hung up.

When she speaks of this today, Judy's voice fills with sadness. "What was I supposed to do?" she asks. "Leave him standing on the sidewalk like an idiot? I *had* to go down. There were too many people in my family whose lives depended on DeWitt Wallace."

From the time she was a child, Judy and her uncle had had a special relationship. "When I was small," she says, "he would hold me in his arms and carry me about the house. 'This is my baby,' he would tell everyone. 'Isn't she adorable?' He kept a photo of me on his bureau—the only picture I ever saw there. He never said so—he wasn't good at expressing feelings—but I think he missed having his own children."

Until the early fifties, Judy's relationship with her uncle remained friendly and comfortable. In those days, the atmosphere at the Digest, and especially at High Winds affairs, was blatantly flirtatious. DeWitt was the worst of the lot, and it behooved Digest wives, including Judy, to be responsive. But all of this was kept within limits—"just good fun," according to many who were around at the time. Except that at several parties the "flirting" between DeWitt and his niece went farther. "We would get a little drunk and start behaving like kids," says Judy. "It all seemed innocent to me. But on one occasion, in the middle of the silliness, an odd thing happened. DeWitt announced—referring to his genitals—that he would never allow anyone to see or touch him there. I thought: *Who, me? I haven't the slightest desire to see your genitals!*"

In 1948, Fred became managing director of RD's Canadian company and the Thompsons moved their young family to Montreal for five years. When they returned in 1953, something had changed. "It is hard to say just when I woke up to this," says Judy. "DeWitt had always been there in my life, so when things between us began to go awry I suppose I blocked it out. He kept pushing the situation farther and farther, and I kept pretending harder and harder that all was well. Then that call came, and after that I couldn't pretend any longer.

"We went to a bar on Third Avenue and took a booth in the back. We drank a lot and after a while he became . . . *voracious.* I could have slapped him in the face and walked away, I suppose. But there were so many others to think about—my father, my husband, my children. *Be careful!* I said to myself. *There are too many hostages.*

"That night I went to Fred and I said, 'I have this terrible problem with my uncle.' I told him everything. He said, 'Do you want me to do something about it?' I thought about this, then told him no. 'I can handle it,' I said. 'It's probably better that way.' *I was wrong!*"

The calls from DeWitt persisted, sometimes coming two or three times a week. "I'm still not sure exactly what he was after or where he thought it would end. It seemed to me at times that he was pursuing a fantasy, trying somehow to resurrect his youth. We began going to little bars down in Greenwich Village, near where he and Lila had lived when they were first married. We would sit in the back and drink and drink. Never *ate* a thing. He fed me so much liquor I don't know how I survived. I played little games with him, anything to keep him occupied. I held his hand, pretending to be a swami, and read his fortune. I told him stories and jokes. But no matter what I did, those boozy afternoons always dissolved finally into kissing and necking and . . . rummaging about in my skirts. It was *exhausting*.

"After a while, he grew tired of the Village spots and we began going up to the West Side. This was even farther in the past. Lila had lived up there when he was courting her—on Claremont Avenue, near Riverside Church— and now he began to take me to their old hangouts. He was like a kid, a lonely, self-destructive kid searching for something, What he needed, I suppose, was a mother—someone to give him a hug and tell him he was okay and to behave himself. But I couldn't be his mother. I was his *niece!*"

A year went by, and then two, and still the calls came. "I thought he'd get it out of his system," says Judy. "That it would stop and we would still be friends." But it didn't stop, and Judy began to grow frantic. She spoke again to her husband, and also to Al Cole. But by now both men had concluded that Wallace was just "being Wally"—that he didn't mean anything by his attentions and that if Judy kidded him along the problem would go away. "They didn't want to make waves," says Judy. "Complaining to Wally about his behavior toward me—exposing him as a dirty old man—would have destroyed his image. And very likely Fred's and Al's careers as well."

DeWitt Wallace had hoped that his Great Success, with all it enabled him to do for others, would bring him love and acceptance. In fact, it only further isolated him from everyone—family, friends, his own real self. And any attempt to break free from this isolation was quickly blocked by Lila. "It is important to remember," says Judy, "that he was at heart a very decent, very *giving* man. A lot of his crazy behavior—acting like a sex maniac half the time, for example—was just a pose. Part of him was driven to do good things. But when doing good things became tiresome—because he wasn't doing the good things he *wanted* to be doing—he felt compelled to balance the equation by doing *bad* things. He had always admired scalawags, as he put it, and he wanted desperately to be a real scalawag himself. He just didn't know how."

Wallace's inability to be a "real" scalawag was evident in several areas. His "flirtations," limited for the most part to employees or wives of employees, are the most obvious example. He liked to reach under tables and fondle knees and legs. Some women, terrified by these gropings, suffered in silence. Others reacted angrily, and Wallace was slugged more than once. "He was at our home one night," remembers Peggy Cole, "and he tried that stuff with me. 'If he ever does that again,' I told Al later, 'I will slit his throat.' "

The famous Wallace poker games are another example. These sessions began in the early thirties and continued until Wallace's eyesight dimmed around 1976. The men involved always claimed to have great fun, but it is hard to credit this since in their way the poker games were as phony as DeWitt's sophomoric gropings. "We played wild games for very low stakes," recalls Jim Stewart-Gordon. "But Wally wanted to feel like a real gambler, so he insisted we *pretend* the stakes were high. 'I'll raise you two hundred' really meant 'I'll raise you two dollars.' "

The pretense extended even to the consumption of alcohol. "Come on, fellows!" Wallace was always urging. "Let's drink up!" The "fellows" were always happy to oblige, but Wallace himself inevitably nursed his second drink for hours on end. He *wanted* to get drunk, just as he wanted to be a big-time gambler. (Just as he no doubt longed for a *real* sexual affair.) But he couldn't do it.

Why not? What could such a man—successful, wealthy, admired around the world—be afraid of? In his own words (but ringing with the admonitions of Janet Wallace), he was afraid of himself, of what he might lose by "being himself." In an extended note "On Fear," he wrote: "I must pay and pay, in fear and uneasiness of mind, for every ignoble thot, for every unkind act, for every hurt I give my fellow man." Yet it is also true that he understood the dangers of being someone *other* than himself: "The timid person, dissatisfied with his own real self, is unhappy because he is never *natural*. To thine own self be true is still the law of life."

On a summer Thursday in 1954, Lila Wallace peered down from the upstairs window above the main entrance into High Winds to see if her limousine had arrived for the weekly pilgrimage to New York. It had not, and she frowned with displeasure. Two gardeners—Peter Scalla and Rossario Cutri —were weeding the rhododendron beds just below the window. In a loud voice, Scalla was bragging about the birth of his fifth child. "I got five already, Rossi, and I'm ten years younger than you. My old lady wants a new kid every year. I'm tellin' you, she . . ."

"That's *enough!*" Lila's voice brought both men to attention.

"Sorry, Mrs. Wallace," mumbled Scalla.

"I pay you to *work*, not make noise," Lila snapped. The limousine arrived a few minutes later, and Lila descended. As she entered the car she growled to Doherty: "That *stupid fool*"—nodding in Scalla's direction—"all he knows how to do is make babies . . ."

In the fifties life suddenly went downhill for the Queen of High Winds. The glories of her Castle began to pale and her days there followed one after the other in empty perfection. She rose late most mornings and after a breakfast of coffee and toast busied herself with desk work related to her charitable affairs. After lunch, she liked to putter in her gardens, and then she took a nap in the Teahouse down by the Lake Outlook. There was an antique four-poster installed there, shrouded in gauzy curtains, and she would lie in this elegant bed and dream of who she had been in the past and who she might become in the future. The high point of the day arrived when DeWitt returned in the evening, and after their brief time together—drinks, dancing and dinner—she retired to her bedroom to read until sleep came.

But she seldom slept for long. Around three o'clock most mornings she came wide awake, and that was when she felt her lowest. To fight off the oncoming depression, she would rise and wander about the Castle, stopping here and there to admire a painting or adjust a flower arrangement. These expeditions inevitably ended in the living room, where she would sit in her favorite chair, alone among the familiar shadows, and gaze at the illuminated *Jeune Fille* on the wall above the fireplace. *That* was what she wanted. To be young again and full of promise. To have hope. To be . . . perfect.

According to Judy Thompson, her aunt was terribly conflicted over not having children. "She brought this subject up at the drop of a hat," says Judy. "You couldn't be around her and not hear about it: *'We never had children because we had the Digest. We couldn't do justice to both.'* It was obvious she protested *too* much."

Conversations about children tended to upset Lila. Once, when she and DeWitt visited their neighbors for tea, they were treated to thirty minutes of slides featuring grandchildren. On the ride back to High Winds, Lila was beside herself. "Can you imagine the nerve of some people," she snapped. "Who wants to look at stupid grandchildren?" When chauffeur Gene Doherty and his wife, Ilse, moved into a High Winds cottage in 1960, Lila made one rule crystal-clear: *"Keep your children out of sight. I do not want to see or hear them."*

DeWitt's feelings on the subject were similarly confused, but touched with a deeper sadness. One evening in 1959, the Wallaces invited Digest senior editor Tony Oursler (Fulton's son) and his wife, Noel, on one of their weekly forays into New York. In the car on the way from Trader Vic's to the theater, DeWitt suddenly turned to Noel: *"Umm,* uh, Noel, how many children do you and Tony have?"

"Well, Wally, we have three—a girl and two boys."

"Is that so? Are you planning to have more?"

"Oh, yes. I guess we'll have a few more."

"Ummm . . . well . . ." Wallace seemed to ponder her answer. Then he

smiled and said: "Lila and I feel that you should have as many children as
you want. It's very fortunate that you *can* have them, and . . . um . . . raise
them. Because, you see, Lila and I have had long *discussions* about this, and
we have decided that . . . that you and Tony should go ahead and have *our*
children for us!"

Inevitably, the absence of children in the Wallace marriage (along with
the separate suites and disparate schedules) raised questions about their sex
life, and Lila was well aware of this. Over the years, DeWitt had done his
best to establish a reputation as a rake—all the silly feely stuff, the boyish
games and flirtations. Lila put up with this, to a point, because it was
harmless and seemed to make him feel better. And, of course, she kept the
scales balanced through her relationship with Harry Wilcox.

No one knew—no one will *ever* know—the real truth about Harry. He told
everyone he was sleeping with Lila, but Harry was such a liar that his claims
were largely disbelieved. Yet Lila was not above adding to the rumors herself.
"When the Wallaces had their New York quarters at Hampshire House, back
in the forties, I went up there one day to drop in on Lila," recalls Judy. "She
was in a very gay mood. She told me she had brought 'Mr. Wilcox' home with
her. 'When we came through the door,' she said, 'I took all my clothes off
and we had some drinks and'—I forget exactly how she put it—'and then
we had a gay old time,' something like that. Later I asked her about this.
'Oh, no,' she said. 'There was nothing like that.' So that story was either a
fantasy or the truth. My guess is she made it up."

Like most narcissists, Lila Wallace appeared to have little real interest in
sex. ("Sex is okay, I guess," she confided to James Stewart-Gordon. "But
those positions are *ridiculous!*") Yet it was important to create an *illusion* of
sexual success, and thus all the acting out with Harry. By the late fifties,
however, the illusion was becoming harder to maintain. She needed more—
more success, more adulation—and wasn't sure where to find it. The business side of the Kingdom—*Al Cole's* Side—was growing more powerful every
day, and that meant that Prince Fred was prospering as well. At the same
time, *Her* Side, represented chiefly by Barclay and Harry, had come on hard
times. Harry was aging poorly—drinking too much, putting on weight. As
for Barclay—well, to put it mildly, Barclay was a disappointment. For the
first time, scraps of criticism began getting through to Lila. Criticism with
undertones of mockery. People were *laughing* at Barclay, and that meant
they were laughing at her. And it made her furious.

Then there was the matter of her husband and her niece, a situation she
had been aware of from the beginning. Judy had confided in her Aunt Marta
(Lila's sister), and Marta had taken this desperate confidence directly to Lila.
For a time (while she was making her own play for Fred), Lila had chosen to

ignore it. But the situation had gotten out of hand. Wally had his "new Lila" to pal around with, while she had no one since Fred refused to play.

Toward the end of 1956, during one of Fred Thompson's many trips abroad, Judy was asked to spend the weekend at High Winds with her aunt and uncle. And something happened that Saturday night that Judy will never forget. After they had all gone to bed, DeWitt got up and began to wander around. Lila heard him go down to the kitchen (as she later told Judy), and heard him come back upstairs. At the top of the stairs he paused, and then she heard him enter the guest suite—what they called the Pink Room— occupied by Judy.

"I was wide awake when this happened," says Judy today. "DeWitt settled into the armchair next to my bed. For fifteen minutes, he sat there watching me, while I pretended to sleep. Then he got up and stood by my bed, and then he left the room and went down the long hallway to his own room. I was terrified, but also very sad. He seemed like such a lonely boy, in need of something Lila couldn't give him. Something no one could give him. Lila eventually spoke to me about this visit. She was quite upset. . . ."

> *After Wally's little trip to Judy's room, I knew I would have to do something. On the following Sunday, we visited Judy and the boys in Central Valley. While we were there Wally went off driving in the Jeep with Geoffrey and Jonathon and Cameron. I sat with Judy on the terrace. When Wally and the boys drove past, I watched Judy's expression change. Then I told her what I knew about that midnight visit, and I gave her fair warning: "Do not go to bed with him," I said. "It would be a grave mistake. . . ."*
>
> *When the boys returned from their Jeep ride they were laughing and happy. "Well," I said to Wally, "haven't you been having fun." And he said something then that froze my blood. "I always have fun here. It's so much pleasanter here than at High Winds. . . ."*

CHAPTER FOURTEEN

On March 25, 1957, Lila Wallace was brought by ambulance to Northern Westchester Hospital with a severely fractured right hip and leg bone. A bulletin distributed to Digest employees explained that she had fallen in the front hall at High Winds. In fact, she had suffered a terrible accident while riding Red Sails that morning. According to groom Pat Miggins, the horse had stepped into a woodchuck hole and fallen. Lila was thrown clear, but the panic-stricken animal had rolled across her body, crushing her right side. Miggins somehow got her back to High Winds, and from there an ambulance took her to Northern Westchester. The official announcement was fudged because Lila—who boasted that in sixty years of riding she had never once been thrown—wanted no one to know that a horse had gotten the best of her.

Her fractured hip was extremely serious, and would eventually make necessary a total hip replacement. There was also considerable internal bleeding, and much of this blood soon filled her lungs. For a time her life was in danger, and she lingered in critical condition for several weeks. When her lungs finally cleared, she was transferred to Columbia-Presbyterian Hospital in New York City, and there Dr. Frank Stinchfield performed the hip operation. On the 14th of June, DeWitt sent the following announcement to all Digesters:

> Mrs. Wallace is home at last. Her spirits will be buoyed for years to come by memories of the hundreds of messages and countless bouquets she received. Her doctors said they had never seen such an outpouring of sympathetic affection. . . .

In 1934, when Lila's perfect life had seemed about to come apart, a thyroid attack had sent her to bed for most of the year. Now, at a similar juncture, she found herself once again in bed, and once again at the absolute center of everyone's concern. And as she had before, she took the opportunity to plan some changes.

Her first move focused on Barclay. For more than twenty years, Lila had stood firmly behind every move her brother made. When Barclay spoke, he spoke for her, and everyone knew it. But maintaining Barclay's power had not been easy. Al Cole was a forceful figure at Reader's Digest, and when Al gave orders—even to foreign executives who reported to Barclay—they were followed. This had produced considerable tension within the company, so in May 1953 the Wallaces had sent the following memo to senior members of the International (RDIE) and U.S. (USRD) offices:

> Al Cole is General Business Manager of USRD. Barclay Acheson is General Business Manager of RDIE. Both are subject only to directives from DW and LBW. *But all final RDIE directives are issued by Barclay Acheson.*

Over the years, Barclay had grown fond of the lifestyle that went with his position, and he had been assiduous in expressing his appreciation to those who made it possible. In the mid-fifties, as he sensed his grip on power slipping, these efforts increased. "Dear DW and LBW," he wrote in the spring of 1956:

> Making the ten-percent bonus part of my fixed salary is yet another gener-ous act that leaves me wordless. First there was the profit-sharing bonus, then the special bonus, and on top of all that the two-months vacation you insisted I take. I should also mention the lovely office that gives me a constant lift.

In June 1957, while on business in West Germany, Barclay received word of Lila's successful hip operation. He cabled her immediately: "Look forward to progressive improvement and praying for your return to co-leadership with King Wally. Hoping to embrace you soon and look into your courageous eyes and hear again a well-done from your smiling lips. Love and kisses, Barclay."

Alas, it was all for naught. Paul Thompson (whose courtship of Lila was at least on a par with Barclay's) was summoned home from Europe that spring, ostensibly to take over as head of international operations. But Bar-clay refused to give up without a fight, so for a time the younger man occupied a small office next to Barclay's, and waited impatiently for someone to break the impasse.

Later that summer, on a Monday morning after a long weekend, Barclay returned to "the lovely office that gives me a constant lift" only to find that his furniture and files had been removed. A crew of painters was at work, and when he asked what was going on they said the office was being redeco-rated for a new man—"What we hear," they said, "is that Paul Thompson is moving in." Sure enough, an announcement went out to "All Concerned" later that same day: "Paul Thompson is now General Manager of Interna-tional. Barclay Acheson will fill a new post, undertaking important missions in the realm of national and international political and public relations. His office will be at 230 Park Avenue in New York City."

"That's how she got rid of him," says Judy Thompson. "Daddy was horri-fied. He had forgiven her for many things over the years—had literally sold his soul to her—but he never forgave her for this. But that's the way she *always* did things. No warning. No confrontation. Just . . . *zzzap*. It broke Daddy's heart."

Barclay eventually reported to his new office in the city, and for a time did his best to figure out what was meant by "national and international political and public relations." But the meaning of the phrase eluded him, and as fall turned to winter his days in New York became shorter and shorter. On December 5, while shoveling snow at his home in Briarcliff, he suddenly slumped to the ground. Three hours later, a doctor pronounced him dead of a cerebral hemorrhage.

The following Saturday, in accordance with Lila's instructions, her brother's body was taken from the undertaker's parlor in Pleasantville to lie in state on a long table in the center of the Digest's editorial library. Viewing hours were held all that day and the next, and every employee—more than three thousand in all—was expected to show up. "The whole process was ludicrous," says Judy Thompson. "You'd have thought some head of state had died."

When the funeral was over, Lila began telling everyone that her brother would still be alive had it not been for his wife. "Pat Acheson made his life miserable," she insisted. "Barclay stayed with her for Judy's sake—for *all* our sakes—but the pressure of the relationship finally wore him down. And now, poor dear, he's gone."

The truth, of course, is somewhat different. "Lila killed him," says Judy Thompson flatly. "She lured him from his natural calling as a minister into a complex business position way above his head. He knew this. But he tried anyway. Then, at his most vulnerable moment, she threw him out. And he never recovered."

On a summer afternoon in 1958, Harry Wilcox sat on the terrace of the Bird & Bottle Inn in Garrison, New York, high above the nearby Hudson River, enjoying an early cocktail with a woman named Connie Stearns, the inn's proprietor. Stearns was filling Harry in on the latest gossip about Boscobel, the historic residence designed by famed Scottish architect Robert Adam and built by Staats Dyckman in the early 1800s. Called by some the most beautiful home in America, Boscobel had been saved from the wrecker's ball in the early fifties when the Veterans Administration commandeered its original site for a new hospital. Local history buffs bought the building, dismantled it piece by piece, and stored it away in barns and garages up and down the Hudson Valley. Now these same concerned citizens were looking for a new site on which to reconstruct the historic house. "A beautiful piece of waterfront property has just come on the market," Stearns told Wilcox. "Right up the road from here. If we could persuade the Boscobel group to rebuild the mansion there, it would do wonders for this restaurant. But the problem is money. The restoration group is broke."

Harry thought about this. "Why don't I mention it to Lila Wallace," he said finally. "She has a thing about houses, and she's bored stiff these days. Maybe we can get her involved."

Within a week, Harry, Lila and Ben Frazier, head of the Putnam County Historical Society, were tramping about the property. As it turned out, only sixteen of the thirty-eight acres were immediately available, and Lila quickly agreed to buy them for $20,000. The other twenty-two acres had been purchased just the day before by a group of local investors (no doubt including Harry Wilcox). These investors were willing to resell, at a stiff premium.

Word of Lila's interest had obviously spread, and now everyone wanted a piece of the action. Ben Frazier had already persuaded his colleagues in the Boscobel group to offer him, "out of whatever funds might become available," a manager's stipend of $25,000 a year. Connie Stearns was talking about opening a new restaurant. A woman on Long Island who had bought some of the original façade was willing to sell it back "for a consideration."

"Lila quickly saw which way the wind was blowing, and she said 'Nuts to this,' " recalls Fred Stanyer, a senior editor in the *Digest* art department who later became Boscobel's administrator. "If I'm going to be involved,' she insisted, 'I will do it *my* way, period.' She set up something called Boscobel Restoration, Inc., with a board that consisted of herself and several friends, including Harry Wilcox and Fred and Judy Thompson. From then on, she was in total command. Boscobel gave her something to do at a time when she needed it, and her feelings for the place became very intense. It was like a second home to her—almost a second High Winds."

While the bits and pieces of the house were being unearthed and brought to the site, Lila asked Judy to study the Dyckman family history. "This was typical," says Judy. "Lila had no capacity for absorbing documents herself, and no interest in trying. No interest, really, in what they might reveal. She wanted to be in charge of the project, to use her money to create something beautiful. But I was to do the work."

While Lila was thus involved with Boscobel and Judy, DeWitt was launching a project of his own—something outwardly very different, yet at its core very much the same. It began in June 1959, when he found himself lunching at the Sky Club atop the Pan Am Building in midtown Manhattan with a fresh-faced young man named Harry Morgan. Morgan was a Westerner— from Salinas, California. After high school, he had lasted one unhappy semester in junior college before quitting to go to work in a sugar mill. The summer he was nineteen, he read about a disastrous flood in Holland and just like that (just like another teenager had once headed west for San Francisco) Morgan packed a bag and headed east for Amsterdam. When he showed up at the Friends' Center there, officials were incredulous that an unaffiliated American would come so far simply to help out. But help Harry did. His story spread, and soon he was famous all over Holland.

Back in the United States, Harry joined the Air Force and was stationed at Wright-Patterson Field in Dayton. But he could not forget his experience in Holland. He raised $1,500 from Dayton businessmen and used it to bring two of his Dutch friends to America. He wanted them to see for themselves what this country was like. His venture was given considerable press coverage, and soon Harry began receiving contributions through the mail. He formed something called "Ambassadors for Friendship" and invited Americans to buy "shares" in his project for $1 apiece. With funds thus generated, he brought over a second group of Europeans and press coverage of this second visit led to a February 1958 article in *Reader's Digest.*

Harry was discharged in 1958 and entered Rutgers University. But the *Digest* piece generated so much mail—and so many small contributions—that he was able to continue Ambassadors for Friendship from his college dormitory. The following summer, an intrigued DeWitt Wallace invited him to lunch at the Sky Club.

As Morgan rattled on about his experiences, Wallace found himself impressed. Like himself, Morgan had nurtured a dream focused on the goodness of America, and had worked to make it happen. He was young and innocent, but beneath the innocence Wallace sensed a stubborn toughness.

"What are your plans for after graduation?" Wallace asked when his guest paused to take a bite of food.

"I'm not sure," said Harry. "Maybe I'll try to land something with the United Nations. Or perhaps the State Department."

"What about Ambassadors? You're not going to drop it?"

"No, sir," said Harry. "Ambassadors is my first love. Whatever I do, I'll keep it going on the side, as a hobby."

"In my experience, men do best when they pursue their real interests. What if someone *paid* you to run Ambassadors? Would you be interested?"

"Of course, but. . . ."

"Then you're hired. I have a plan in mind."

During the fifties, encouraged by educational adviser Paul Davis, Wallace's long-simmering interest in Macalester College had turned into an obsession. His gifts to the school, already approaching $30 million, increased, and he found himself supporting every aspect of Macalester's budget, from endowing professorships to buying uniforms for the marching band. Now he wanted Harry Morgan to go to Macalester, to serve there as his eyes and ears—as a kind of surrogate self. Arrangements were made for Harry to become assistant to the president and director of the college's international programs. A substantial house was purchased—less than a block from the house DeWitt grew up in—and the upper floor was converted into a comfortable apartment for Harry and his bride, a recent Smith College graduate named Catherine Johnson. The lower floors would serve as a home-away-from-home for Macalester students from abroad, and also as headquarters for Harry's Ambassadors for Friendship. "I want you to think big," Wallace told his protégé. "I have plenty of money. What I need . . . what I want *you* to provide . . . is ideas. New ways to educate and inspire. New ways to spread the word about America. You're a dreamer, Harry. I want to help you make your dreams come true."

Harry Morgan could scarcely believe his luck. He had a new wife, a new house, a new job—and one of America's richest men standing behind him.

Wallace called him every day—to ask how he was doing, how the programs were going—and Harry quickly perceived that his elderly employer regarded him as more than just a hired hand. *Hang in there,* he told himself. *You're going to get it all.*

The entire upper echelon at Digest Headquarters also sensed this possibility, and it made them furious. During a trip to Macalester (where he served on the board), Al Cole made a point of visiting Harry's office at what was now called International House. "How's it going, Harry?" Cole asked suspiciously. "Where are all these great ideas you're supposed to be producing?"

When Harry hesitated, claiming he had something promising in mind that needed work, Cole suggested they return together to Chappaqua the next day. "You need to touch home base, Harry," he said. "I'm sure Wally would like to hear about this idea in person."

To his credit, when Harry met with Wallace and Cole at a Guesthouse lunch two days later, he did have an idea, and it *was* promising. "I propose that we invite fifteen foreign journalists, from fifteen different countries, to come to America every year. For three months they would reside at Macalester, taking courses in American social, political and economic traditions. Then they would serve three-month internships with newspapers or radio and television stations. Finally, they would embark on a grass-roots tour of the U.S., riding in station wagons, visiting ordinary American families, seeing what this country is really like."

Wallace beamed. This was just the ticket—a simple idea with leverage, just like his own simple idea for *Reader's Digest.* If the plan worked as Harry promised, its advantages were clear: It would enhance Macalester's reputation, improve international understanding, maybe even serve as a way to recruit writers and editors for the *Digest's* foreign editions. Most importantly, by impressing a small group of influential journalists it would help spread America's real story to hundreds of thousands, maybe even millions, of foreigners. In that sense, it was like an extension of the *Digest* itself—a new way to spread The Word.

They decided on the spot to call Harry's venture the World Press Institute, and a delighted Wallace agreed to provide $750,000 to get things started. Harry was named executive director and sent back to Macalester with the praises of his benefactor ringing in his ears. It did not hurt when he was subsequently named one of America's "ten outstanding young men" by the Chamber of Commerce.

In June 1959, shortly after DeWitt's initial meeting with Harry Morgan, Lila Wallace held a party for all her favorite people. She had a new friend, she announced, and wanted everyone to meet him. Bill Kennedy had entered Lila's life through the auspices of society decorator Syrie Maugham, widow of British author Somerset Maugham. Syrie had achieved a major success in her field, working in the United States for such prominent ladies as Bunny Mellon and Babe Paley, in addition to serving as Lila Wallace's decorator in Chappaqua and Mt. Kisco. As Syrie aged, she took Bill Kennedy under her wing, and when she died Bill took over many of her rich clients. In 1959, the young decorator came to see Lila Wallace at High Winds bearing a letter from Syrie praising his many talents.

Kennedy arrived at Lila's front door in a taxi. But the meeting went so well that when he left Lila insisted he take DeWitt's 1940 Cadillac convertible (a birthday gift that had never been used because DeWitt considered it "ostentatious"). In fact, Bill Kennedy was everything Lila Wallace craved in a confidant—tall and handsome, with a light touch, a disarming sense of humor and the wisdom to keep secret things secret. That he was also quite talented, with a lively sense of color and an intuitive feeling for what Lila liked—in paintings, furniture, clothing, conversation—was frosting on the cake. And all of this was topped by the fact that Bill was homosexual. Lila had preferred effeminate males, straight or gay, all her life. She seemed to feel safer in their company, and of course with such men the irksome issue of sex did not arise.

When Kennedy arrived at High Winds on the evening of Lila's fete, he had a friend of his own in tow—a dancer with the Robin Gregory company named Ben Garbor. As the two men entered the living room, all the women gasped. They looked like a pair of movie stars—slim, debonair, incredibly handsome—and moved with a graceful assurance that made the other males present feel suddenly clumsy. Lila was beside herself with excitement. At the first opportunity, she pulled her niece aside. "Well, Judy? What do you think?"

"What do you mean?" Judy asked. "Are they handsome? Of course they are. Why do you ask?"

"Well," said Lila, hesitating, "you realize of course that both of them are homosexual?"

Judy laughed. "No, I didn't. But what of it? They aren't here for *breeding*, are they?"

Lila covered a giggle, and began to relax. She was very proud of her new find, and she wanted the evening to be perfect.

For Lila Wallace, Bill Kennedy could not have arrived at a more auspicious time. The restoration of Boscobel was nearing completion, and now she asked Bill to undertake the formidable task of furnishing her historic mansion as accurately as possible. With his friend Ben in tow, Bill traveled all over England and Scotland, looking through country houses, attending antique shows, searching for things that were unmistakably English, vaguely associated with the Adam tradition and—most important—pleasing to Bill and Ben. The result was impressive—"Boscobel's carefully selected antiques tastefully reflect the grace and refinement of the architecture," reported the *New York Times*—but also fabulously expensive. Lila Wallace poured a total of $8 million into Boscobel, much of it passing through the hands of Bill Kennedy. And from whatever passed through Bill's hands, a substantial percentage always found its way into his own pockets. Soon Bill was driving a bronze Bentley and filling his new country house (a gift from Lila) with fabulous antiques and paintings.

"Bill was a great one for graft, no doubt about it," says Dick Waters, the hardnosed executive who served as RD treasurer during the Kennedy era. "An ordinary decorator gets a small percent from the seller. Not Bill. He always built it in up front. If a certain antique settee cost twenty grand, for example, Bill would simply add several thousand on top of that for himself. And we always paid it."

Yet Kennedy had his defenders. "Despite what everyone said, Bill was not an outright thief," says Fred Stanyer, who as a confidant of both Kennedy and Lila Wallace was in a good position to know. "Bill and Ben lived a high life, it's true, and much of their support came from Lila. But they were in business, they were good at what they did, and they were paid by commission. If Lila went into town with them and they picked out some jewelry for her, they got a commission. Nothing wrong with that. Bill and Ben did it for several rich ladies, and it made them very rich themselves.

"Now, Lila may not have understood this. I think she did, but with her you never knew. If you went to lunch with her at the River Club and she had a second martini, well, you might end up owning the Empire State Building. Once, when we were walking down Fifty-fifth Street, she stopped me and said, 'Oh, Fred, I love your jacket! I want it for Wally! I'll give you two thousand dollars!' Well, what do you do? You laugh. 'I *like* my jacket, Lila,' I said. 'I want to keep it.'

"But others, you see, didn't laugh. Lila might go gallery hopping with Bill and if they came across a painting he admired—a nice little Corot, say—she might very well announce, 'Fine, I'll buy it for you.' And Bill would take it. Does that make him a thief? Many people thought so. I didn't.

"The thing is, despite everything, Bill *cared* about Lila. He knew her better than anybody, well enough to be able to say to her, 'You've got your stockings on crooked, Lila,' or 'There's a spot on your dress, Lila,' or 'Don't wear *that*, Lila, that's all wrong,' and not let her go out looking foolish. Nobody else could do this. Certainly Wally couldn't. Harry Wilcox couldn't. And that's what she needed. Someone to put a little *life* into her life. To be her *friend*.

"From the fifties on, most of her days were pretty bleak. But not the ones she spent with Bill. They might go to Mainbocher in the morning for a fitting.

Bill would be there at her side, telling her what looked right, what did not, reassuring her. After lunch at the River Club, they might go to a gallery to look over some paintings. Or perhaps to Olga Tritt's to have some shoes made up. Whatever she had to do.

"And it wasn't just weekdays. Bill might show up at High Winds on a Saturday morning and say, 'C'mon, Lila, we're going to do this today' or 'Let's do that,' or whatever . . . go to a festival or an antique show or a recital. *Anything*. Just to *do* something. I mean, she was a very rich lady, yet she spent half her days waiting for something to happen. She needed to get away from those grasping Digest types. They were such *wimpy* people, always crying for her attention. *Do this, Lila! Do that, Lila!* The wives would *fawn* over her, and she would turn into a guillotine. *Zzaap!* She would cut them off. She was very good at cutting people off, and that's partly why she ended up the way she did. When trouble finally caught up with Bill, there was no one left to take his place. Then she really was alone."

On May 21, 1961, a grand opening party was held for Boscobel. It was a glorious evening, with music and fireworks, and everyone was in attendance from Governor Nelson Rockefeller (who called Lila's place "the most beautiful home in America") to the workmen who had helped with the restoration to every key member of Lila's Court: Bill Kennedy and Ben Garbor (happily accepting congratulations for their "gorgeous" furnishings), Paul Thompson, Harry Wilcox, Judy and Fred Thompson, Hobe and Edie Lewis, and a man named Harry Rudick who had been the Wallaces' personal lawyer and close friend for decades. The Wallaces had come to rely on Rudick's advice in many areas, and Lila had persuaded him to serve on the Boscobel board. Rudick was a senior partner at the New York firm that handled the Digest's legal business, Lord, Day & Lord, and in 1961, as he prepared for retirement, he had begun to delegate portions of the firm's Digest work to a young Columbia Law grad named Barnabas McHenry. McHenry wasn't present for Boscobel's grand opening, but it was the last such affair he would miss for many years.

Several months after the Boscobel opening, Al Cole and Digest treasurer Dick Waters had a discussion about the Digest's legal bills. Lord, Day was costing the company over $500,000 a year, and Waters was convinced the time had come to hire an in-house counsel. In 1959, when Cole was negotiating with RCA over setting up the Digest's record club, he had asked Herb Brownell, managing partner at Lord, Day, to loan him a lawyer to iron out some contracts—"a junior guy, someone who comes cheap"—and Brownell had sent him McHenry. "Barney was a generalist," Waters points out, "whereas the other young lawyers at Lord, Day were specialists. So Barney was the guy we usually talked to and that made him a logical choice."

When Waters approached McHenry about the possibility of moving to the

Digest, McHenry was receptive. An appointment was set up for the young attorney to meet with Wallace over lunch at Delmonico's Restaurant, and during lunch the deal was worked out. Afterward, driving the two men from Delmonico's to the Pinnacle Club, Gene Doherty was impressed by McHenry's enthusiasm: "He kept going over the details of the arrangement—how it would work to their mutual benefit, how much money the Digest would save, and so on. He was very happy. He had made his move, and the Boss had gone for it."

Even so, McHenry was kept on a short leash for an extended period, confined to a small office in the Pan Am Building and given routine corporate work to handle. "Barney had nothing to do with the Wallaces during his early years at RD," says Betty St. John, DeWitt's secretary. "But he kept his head down and his eyes open. He was like a shadow. No one noticed him at first, but the shadow grew and grew until eventually it cast a cloud over everything."

CHAPTER FIFTEEN

"It dispenses more medical advice than the *AMA Journal,* more jokes than Joe Miller, more animal tales than Uncle Remus, more truth than Oral Roberts. It is published in 13 languages and 40 editions, not to mention one for school children and two (Braille and recorded) for the blind. It is read in more than 100 countries, and outsells all other monthly magazines in Argentina, Belgium, Canada, Colombia, Finland, Italy, Mexico, Peru, South Africa, Spain, Sweden, Uruguay, Venezuela and, of course, the U.S. Last week, *Reader's Digest*—circulation *23 million*— proudly observed its 40th birthday with an anniversary issue 300 pages long."

So began an article in the February 2, 1962, issue of *Time* magazine. The miracle that had begun to unfold on Minetta Lane in 1922 was still unfolding, still spreading, growing bigger and richer every year. *Everyone* was reading the *Digest:* young and old, male and female, rich and poor. The notion that had come to Wallace in that long-forgotten Montana hayfield—of a magazine for *everyone*—had become a glorious, unimaginable reality.

But even as the miracle grew, vast change was coming to Pleasantville. In 1962, for the first time, revenues from ad pages—$65 million—exceeded the $60 million earned from circulation. Other products were also thriving: Condensed Books was bringing in $20 million a year, and a newly launched record club additional millions. Total revenues were $160 million, and rising fast, and were about to get a huge additional boost from something called Reader's Digest Sweepstakes.

"I got the idea from the lucky-number contests automobile companies were running in the early sixties," says Gordon Grossman, a young VP in charge of Digest marketing at the time. "We had been mailing a 'yes-no' option to our list for several years. If you placed a token in the 'yes' box you got the *Digest*. If you used the 'no' box you got nothing. This worked surprisingly well—having a 'no' box seemed to increase the number of 'yes' responses. But when we added a sweepstakes, with the implication that a 'yes' response increased your chances of winning, the response doubled."

The *Digest*'s U.S. circulation had leveled off at twelve million in the early sixties, but started up again with the advent of Sweepstakes. By the end of 1965 it was nearing seventeen million, and Grossman was bragging that the sky was the limit. "Just tell me where you want to stop," he crowed to the Digest board. "Forty million? Fifty million? Just tell me, and give me the funds, and I'll get you there."

In the early seventies, with circulation above eighteen million, Grossman demanded a seat on the Digest's executive committee. "I made this company what it is today," he insisted. "I deserve it." The Wallaces decided he deserved something else, and his career thereafter hit a frustrating plateau. He left in 1974, when it became clear that his road to the presidency was blocked.

Not surprisingly, the Digest Sweepstakes (which eventually revolutionized direct-mail promotion for all magazines) came in for criticism. "The *Digest* no longer sells itself as an editorial product, but as a chance in a national lottery," cried one publisher. "This is *journalism?*" There were editors at the magazine who felt the same way. "Taking ads was always considered the great divisional point in *Digest* history," recalls Tony Oursler. "But to many of us the Sweeps were worse. We were really beginning to sell our souls."

The problem was, Sweepstakes worked, and this was very frustrating for DeWitt Wallace. He professed to hate the whole idea, calling it sleazy and dishonest. *"Reader's Digest* has always sold itself," he complained. "Now we're *tricking* people into buying!" On another occasion, riding up Park Avenue with Al Cole and James Stewart-Gordon, Wallace expressed a deeper concern. "Do you know anyone who ever *won* the thing, Al?" he asked. "No!" said Cole. *"Neither do I,"* said Wallace. To Stewart-Gordon, it appeared that the Founder of *Reader's Digest* and his general manager were pondering the very question that millions of skeptical Americans had also pondered: *Could the whole damn Sweeps thing be a hoax?*

For as long as he lived, Wallace rode herd over the Sweeps operation, slashing at copy he felt was deceptive, double-checking that every prize was awarded. In the early years, he even went down to Headquarters on Saturday mornings to do some fence-mending on his own. A secretary in the circulation department would leave a file of Sweeps complaints on her desk, and Wallace would sit there all morning dialing numbers and listening to angry subscribers—people he still regarded as members of his "cooperative society." And he made sure that the steps he agreed to during those telethons were followed up. But he never ended the operation because whatever its faults, Sweepstakes undeniably helped to spread the reach of *Reader's Digest*.

As the RD miracle gathered steam during the early sixties, Wallace came under increasing pressure to make some form of ownership available to his top people. He had thought about this himself, and about the whole issue of who would own the company when he and Lila were gone, without reaching any firm conclusions. The notion that he and Lila would eventually turn the company over to Fred and Judy had come under a shadow, and was in any case a subject he preferred to ignore. Part of him wanted to reward his loyal colleagues, and there was talk of a gradual transfer of ownership along the lines David Lawrence was beginning to implement at *U.S. News & World Report*. But another part of him hesitated. The thought of ceding control over any portion of his company worried him, and worried Lila, too, and deep down he wasn't altogether sure his key executives merited such generosity.

While Wallace hesitated, Al Cole fumed. "Al and I and Harry Rudick worked on various stock plans for years," recalls Dick Waters. "Al would take the latest version up to High Winds, and Wally . . . well, he would kind of *finger* 'em to death. Just didn't want to face the issue. So Al would back off. Then we'd go at it again in a different way. Finally, we came up with something that Rudick swore was as fair as possible, and Al more or less gave Wally an ultimatum. 'Look, dammit,' he said, 'you've got good people working for you. If you want to keep them you better let us have this thing.'

"Wally went along, but not because of Al's ultimatum. He trusted Harry Rudick, and Harry had made clear to him the tax advantages of the scheme. But for Wally the real selling point was the fact that the shares made available to key employees would have no voting rights. Thus he could be generous and still retain total control."

The Wallaces had cause to be suspicious. Their only child had grown very large—was, in fact, many children, each of them spoiled and demanding— and controlling this clamorous family was becoming difficult. They worried about many things: about complacency and greed. About the ever-growing power of the business side. About how to assure a Wallace future for the Kingdom.

Lila dealt with her worries by giving her trust only to those whose loyalties she had purchased (who invariably proved unworthy). DeWitt pursued a different course, striving even in his seventies to retain control by keeping everyone else off balance. He had spies everywhere, and wherever he was—High Winds, Arizona, Europe, Hawaii—he always seemed to know what was going on. "Wally likes to upset the apple cart," Lila often said. And it was true. But all of this was a far cry from the happy family that had once put together the Wallace reading service. Camelot was disappearing—blowing away in a whirlwind of advertisements, sweepstakes and record clubs—and both Wallaces were painfully aware of the difference. "I walk around these corridors," DeWitt complained one day, "and I don't know what all those people *do.* In the old days, I did it all myself."

He was troubled by these changes, and most of all by his inability to understand which of his top people were friends and which enemies. He had never been good at this, and as the level of sycophancy rose around him, he became confused and hesitant, creating a vacuum Lila was all too willing to fill. And with Lila in control, those who were clever and dishonest began to prosper, while the real people in their lives, one by one, began to disappear.

Paul Palmer was the first to fall. For twenty-five years he had been a major presence at the Digest and was thought by all to be Wallace's natural successor as editor. He was also one of the few Digest executives able to cross the Wally/Lila line. "Lila liked Paul because he was handsome and charming," says James Stewart-Gordon. "Wally liked him because he was clever and able."

By the late fifties, Palmer was eager to take charge. But Wallace put him off, and only those high in the Wallace Court understood that once again Lila was at work. It was acceptable for "her boys" to marry once, or in special cases even twice. But after that she felt they owed their allegiance to her. So Palmer's third, fourth and fifth marriages had cost him Lila's favor.

In 1960, when Palmer suffered an apparent heart attack, Wallace's reaction dumbfounded everyone. A lifelong hypochondriac, Palmer decided that the strains of running the magazine would be too much for his weakened system. So Wallace arranged for his old friend to live and work in Paris. But not as elegantly as Palmer had envisioned. His first paycheck under the new arrangement showed a drop in annual salary from $125,000 to $25,000.

Next came Ken Payne. For thirty-one years, Payne had been Wallace's right-hand man—the only editor trusted to run things when the Boss himself was away. As the sixties began, Payne was still a major force at the *Digest.* But he was tired and in ill health, and on several occasions had sought to retire. Wallace wouldn't hear of it. "We *need* you, Ken," he insisted. "There's no one else who can do what you do." So the loyal Payne held on.

His reward for this was not pretty. Beneath the happy surface, Lila Wallace had long resented Payne. "Ken had some opinions of his own," explains Judy Thompson, "and a balanced view of the world that did not sit well with Lila."

In January 1962, the Wallaces asked several colleagues to join them on a Hawaiian holiday. Ken and Ruth Payne were included, and chose to travel to the islands by ship. Lila's sister Jane Tollefson and her husband were on the same vessel, and on the second night out the Tollefsons and Paynes were part of a group dining at the captain's table. A man sitting next to Ruth asked her about the *Digest* and about Ken's job there, and Ruth filled him in. "My," said the man, "sounds like he runs the place." "Oh, yes," said Ruth. "The *Digest* wouldn't be the *Digest* without Ken."

This was a mistake. Jane Tollefson made note of Ruth's remark, and upon arrival in Hawaii could not resist passing it along to her sister. "Lila was not amused," says Judy Thompson. "She was insanely jealous of anyone even *hinting* they had played a role in the *Digest*'s success." By the time Lila returned to High Winds, she was in a rage. "He has to go!" she ordered DeWitt. And that was that. As described by Ralph Henderson: "Ken Payne had a notice of dismissal so abrupt he was barred from further use of his own office."

One of those who came closest to the top—who seemed for a time to have the Crown clutched in both hands—was Hobe Lewis. By the mid-sixties, with Palmer in Europe, it was apparent to everyone that Lewis would eventually succeed Wallace as editor, and that this would be a popular choice. At the same time, Al Cole was still in charge on the business side, and Cole had made it clear that he intended to stay around for several years. So the only question was who would run the overall show when the Wallaces retired. Lewis was an able editor, but his experience in business matters was nil. Cole had run the business operations of the Digest for more than twenty-five years. When he first joined forces with Wallace, in 1929, circulation had stood at 290,000. Now it was twenty-five million, and for this miraculous growth much of the credit had to go to Cole.

Nevertheless, anyone betting on Al Cole for the top job didn't know Lila Wallace very well. Hobe Lewis's dark good looks and effortless charm had attracted her from the beginning, and he had courted her for years with shameless dedication. During Christmas week of 1964, with no advance warning to anyone (including Lewis and Cole), the Wallaces suddenly announced that they were creating the new office of president of Reader's Digest, and that Hobe Lewis would fill the position. "Neither Lewis nor anyone else at the Digest expects the Wallaces to let their concern for the magazine or their control of the company diminish," wrote *Time* magazine. "But the baby does continue to grow, and its parents are getting older. Help was needed at the top, and *Digest* editors are unanimous in their relief that the chosen foster parent comes not from the business side, but from the editorial hierarchy."

That was the basic message: Hobe Lewis was the second-ranking editor, after Wallace himself, yet now he was president. Al Cole was number one on the business side, yet he remained vice president. But there was also a secondary message: "Making Hobe president was Wallace's way of affirming the importance of editorial," says Peggy Cole. "But it was also a way, through his control of Lewis, to remain the real boss himself. Al was *too* strong. The thought of making Al president scared Wallace. And it scared Lila even more."

CHAPTER SIXTEEN

As spring came to High Winds in 1962, DeWitt's "affair" with his niece approached its seventh anniversary. Nothing much had changed. He still called her once or twice a week, and they still wandered sadly from bar to bar in search of whatever it was he had in mind. But one day that spring something did change at last. The furtive pair emerged from a saloon on Third Avenue and began to walk silently through the arcade of the New Westin Hotel, from Fifty-seventh Street to Fifty-sixth. Halfway through the arcade, as they approached an entrance into the hotel, DeWitt grabbed Judy's elbow. They stopped walking and she looked at him questioningly.

"I . . . could get us a room here," he said. "We could go upstairs?" There was so little conviction in his voice that Judy found it easy, after all the years of pretending, to reply with steady conviction in her own. "No," she said. "I'm not going to do that."

"Well," he said, "then I guess this . . . *thing* . . . between us isn't going any further?"

"No," said Judy. "I guess it's not."

He continued to call her after that day, but only infrequently and never again to suggest meeting in a bar. And the physical business ended for good. He had found the courage (if that's what it was) to have an "affair." And Judy had found the courage to tell him no. Now it was over and they could each breathe a sigh of relief.

Wallace's other interest during this period was the progress of his surrogate out at Macalester. The World Press Institute was flourishing, and Wallace was pouring huge sums into it and into Harry Morgan's other endeavors at International House. In 1965, the old man decided it was time to bring Harry and his wife to Chappaqua. "You will do well financially," he wrote. "Even second-string Digest editors are handsomely paid, and I see no reason why you shouldn't become a star. But if editing is not your choice, I'm sure we can set something up in advertising or circulation or public relations. Whatever you want."

Whatever I want, thought Morgan. *The Digest world on a platter.* Wallace's letter went on to describe Harry's salary and benefits, and ended with yet another display of paternal concern. By this point the Morgans had two young sons (their firstborn was named Howard DeWitt, and called DeWitt), and Wallace now assured Harry that he need never worry about the costs of their higher education: "These confidential agreements between us should enable you to devote a full and exciting lifetime of service to your fellow man. In the meantime, DON'T WORRY ABOUT ANYTHING!!"

Harry Morgan's arrival at Headquarters provoked no hosannas in the editorial department. "We had never seen anyone like him," recalls Tony Oursler. "He seemed to have sprung from some Botticelli shell. The Birth of Harry, the Divine Twentieth-Century Man. I tell you, his arrival in our midst, so carefully coiffed and cologned, with his antique desk and his oriental rugs and his simpering self-assurance, was a moment that wonderfully concentrated the mind. *Who was he? What was he up to?* We had no idea. And the fact that he reported directly to Wally did not help."

"Harry wanted to become involved editorially," says Cappy Morgan, who became the new man's secretary/assistant (and eventually, after his divorce from Catherine, his second wife). "But the other editors resisted him at every turn. He'd invite guests to editorial lunches, and no one would come. He'd send ideas around, and no one would respond. But Wally didn't want him in editorial in any case. He wanted Harry to be *him*—to be his surrogate in dispensing money to the educational world. Wally wanted his money to go to new people with new ideas, to help *leverage* these new ideas into reality. But identifying such people was difficult, and Wally needed help. That was to be Harry's role."

Harry got off to a bad start. On a Friday shortly after his arrival in Chappaqua, he got a call from Lila Wallace. DeWitt was out of town, but she wanted Harry to come for dinner on Saturday night. Just the two of them. She wanted to get to know him. Harry said yes, of course, and immediately began to worry. DeWitt he could handle. But he wasn't sure where he stood with Lila. So in the hour before driving off to High Winds that Saturday he managed to down three scotch-and-sodas. As a result, when he strolled through Lila's grand entrance he was feeling pretty good.

At nine o'clock that evening, playing poker down at the Mt. Kisco firehouse, Gene Doherty got a call from his wife. Mrs. Wallace was looking for him. She had a guest who had become too drunk to drive home. "When I got to High Winds," Doherty recalls, "Harry was sitting half-asleep on the little bench in the rotunda. Veikko Kotalainen, the Wallaces' butler, was standing beside him, holding him up. Missus had gone to bed. I got Harry into the car and drove him home. *Well,* I thought, *that's the end of you, kid."*

Lila's affairs during this period were no happier than DeWitt's. Fred Stanyer was doing exciting things at Boscobel—creating a Gatehouse and an Orangerie, bringing the original Springhouse up from its former site—and overseeing his efforts had come to occupy more and more of her time. But she was incensed over the "history" of the mansion being prepared by her niece. Judy had come into possession of some Dyckman letters that raised questions about the patriotism of Boscobel's original owner. "In fact, Staats Dyckman had served the king throughout the Revolution," says Judy. "This made Lila furious. She didn't want to hear that her glorious *American* house had been built for an English loyalist."

Lila demanded that Judy turn over the Dyckman letters. Judy refused. "I was writing a book about the place," she says, "and I was afraid if I gave the letters to Lila that she would burn them." The deteriorating situation between aunt and niece was not helped by the events of March 1964. Pat Acheson cracked a vertebra and was laid up at Northern Westchester Hospital for several weeks. According to Judy, during this period Lila routinely tormented her mother. "She would send *dead* flowers to the hospital," Judy claims. "Or *rotten* candy. Mother was scared to death. She begged me to keep Lila away."

Later that spring, apparently suffering a nervous breakdown, Pat Acheson began to babble odd accusations about the Wallaces, and to demand the return of Barclay's personal papers (which were held under lock and key at High Winds). Lila suggested to Judy that it might be wise, under the circumstances, to remove Pat to a sanitarium. Not willing to risk a final break with her powerful aunt, Judy went along with this. Pat was transferred to a mental hospital in Upstate New York and kept there until her death a year later. When neither Wallace came to the funeral, something finally snapped in Judy. A week later, Gene Doherty got a call from Lila. "Come up, Gene," she said. "I have a job for you."

"She took me to the Handball Court above the garage," says Doherty. "The Boss had played there in the early days, but for decades they had used it as a storage area. Lined along one wall were a dozen transfer files. 'These are Barclay Acheson's personal papers,' Mrs. Wallace told me. 'I want you to take them to that *bitch* in Central Valley.' I was astonished. Missus had never used such language around me before, certainly not about Judy. I got a truck and the next day made the delivery. The day after that, a Thursday, I was driving Missus into the city. 'What happened in Central Valley?' she asked. 'What did Judy say?' I told her I hadn't seen Judy. Then I asked her why Judy wanted all those papers. She didn't answer. Then, after a long silence, she suddenly blurted out, *'Those papers belong to me!'* She was real agitated.

'Judy threatened to drag our name through the mud unless I turned them over!' "

"Of course, that is sheer nonsense," says Judy today. "I never asked for those papers nor did I ever want them. They have been in my barn for thirty-two years and I have never opened a single file."

Whatever the truth of the matter, by June of 1965 relations between aunt and niece had reached a new low. "After Mrs. Acheson died," says Veikko Kotalainen, "Mrs. Wallace no longer took Judy's calls. 'Tell her I am resting,' she would say. 'Tell her I'm asleep.' "

Every year for two decades it had been Al Cole's pleasure to host a Guesthouse luncheon for Digest senior management on the Friday before Christmas. These were always convivial affairs, since every year there were happy figures to celebrate—greater circulation, higher profits, bountiful new bonuses. Among the group attending the 1965 lunch—which included Cole and his assistant, Paul Thompson, Hobe Lewis, Fred Thompson, Dick Waters, Walter Hitesman (in charge of books and records), Ralph Henderson (director of Condensed Books) and production manager Kent Rhodes—two in particular looked forward to the proceedings. Hobe Lewis was listed as president on the editorial side of the *Digest* masthead, but not on the business side, raising questions as to the full extent of his authority. Now he believed something new might be coming his way. Fred Thompson understood that he was in line for Cole's job. And he wondered—with Al approaching seventy-two—if this would be the year. Probably not. Al had talked of hanging on for another year, or maybe two, and that was fine with Fred. A memo had been prepared—Cole had shown Fred a copy—listing possible successors to the general manager's job. Fred was at the top of the list and Paul Thompson at the bottom. But that was Cole's list, based on merit and common sense. Lila Wallace had her own list, based on something very different.

Just as Cole began a toast, there was a knock on the door and then the door opened. And there, resplendent in holiday finery, were Lila and DeWitt. "Wally!" cried Cole. "Lila! What a surprise! Come in, come in!" The others all leaped to their feet and the room rang with holiday greetings. Cole especially—whatever problems Lila may have caused him over the years—seemed genuinely pleased to see his employers. "Sit down! Sit down!" he called. "Let's get you a drink!"

After a fresh round of cocktails before the fire in the sitting area, the group rose and reassembled around the long dining table in the adjoining room. DeWitt sat at one end, with Al Cole to his left and Walter Hitesman to his right. Lila sat at the other end, between Hobe Lewis and Paul Thompson. DeWitt seemed preoccupied during the meal. Lila, on the other hand, exuded excitement.

When dessert was served, DeWitt suddenly cleared his throat and rose. "Well," he said, "since we are all here together in these delightful surroundings, celebrating another successful year, Lila and I thought it would be a good time to make some announcements." He looked around the room, smiling coldly at each of his colleagues. "Al Cole has run our business operations so successfully for so many years that we feel he is owed a well-deserved retirement. As of January first"—Fred Thompson leaned forward at this point, sensing that his life was about to change—"*Paul* Thompson will become the new general manager of Reader's Digest."

Cole, whose face had turned beet red at Wallace's first statement, now rose spluttering to his feet. "You can't mean that, Wally," he said. "That makes no sense. Why . . . I . . . I . . ." He stared helplessly at his employer, unable to speak. Wallace met his stare, betraying no emotion, and for several seconds waited for Cole to sit down. But Cole remained standing. He looked once at Lila, and once back at DeWitt, then stormed from the room.

Now a chorus of protests rose from the table. Walter Hitesman stood. "Wally," he said, "with all due respect, I think a mistake is being made . . ." But Wallace raised his hand for silence. "Sit down, Walter," he said. "I haven't finished." To his credit, Hitesman didn't sit. He glared at Wallace, then followed Cole out the door. Now Dick Waters also rose, put down his napkin and headed for the exit. The others remained at their places, and the room again grew quiet.

"Fred," said Wallace, turning to his stunned advertising director, "I have something new for you as well. The Australian company has been foundering. I want you to go out to Sydney and take over as managing director. I know you'll do a fine job." Thompson popped a tablet into his mouth—nitroglycerin for a heart problem—then rose from the table and followed the others out the door.

Wallace began to speak again. "Hobart," he said, "you've been listed as president on the editorial masthead. Now we want to drop the other shoe. Beginning January first, you are in overall charge of the company, president of editorial *and* business. Which makes you our chosen successor for the years to come. Congratulations!"

Lewis murmured his thanks, and after a few moments of further confusion the luncheon disintegrated. Lila and DeWitt were whisked off to High Winds, while their dazed executives wandered back to Headquarters. "The Christmas Massacre," as that historic lunch was thereafter known, had come out of the blue, and it left them all, Lewis and Paul Thompson included, feeling shocked and incredulous.

Several things happened in the immediate aftermath of the Massacre that are worth recording. Walter Hitesman and Dick Waters wrote out resignations (but refrained from delivering them). Harry Wilcox celebrated with Paul

Thompson. Cole, Hitesman and Fred Thompson drove to a nearby bistro called Nino's and proceeded to get drunk. Hobe Lewis called his wife. "I got it all, Edie!" he crowed. "I got it all!" And Lila Wallace, her blue eyes registering sweet innocence, immediately began spreading a story to cover her plot. "We couldn't give the top job to Fred," she assured everyone. "Fred has a bad heart. The pressure would have killed him."

As the days passed, other decisions were made. Waters and Hitesman tore up their resignations. Instead of a pension, Cole worked out an agreement with Wallace under which he would serve as a paid consultant for thirty years. And Judy Thompson called her Aunt Lila to tell her what she thought of the whole proceeding.

"You have done a terrible thing," she said. "A foolish, rash, cruel and ill-considered thing." According to Lila's will, Judy was meant to inherit High Winds. Now she told her aunt she didn't want it. "I would have been pleased to become . . . *custodian* . . . of your Castle," she said. "Under these circumstances, however, I want nothing to do with it. Or with you either, for that matter. And since you don't appreciate their father, I insist that you stay away from his children. We'll go to Australia, if we must, but that's the end of it."

Fred and Judy did go to Australia and served there in exile for two years. "The whole thing happened so suddenly," Fred would later say, "that it took me that long to figure out I'd been fired." When the truth finally did sink in, the Thompsons returned to Chappaqua and Fred met with Wallace to inquire about a position at Headquarters. Wallace was not optimistic. "There may be something in Mexico," he said. "Other than that, *umm . . .*" Fred indicated that Mexico was out of the question. "We want to be in Pleasantville," he said, "so our boys can attend a U.S. school." Wallace said he'd have to think it over.

"That meant going to High Winds to confer with Lila," says Judy. "And Lila laughed in his face. The whole idea, after all, had been to get us out of the way. To punish Fred for being less than ardent. To punish me for her own husband's sad transgressions. It was a crazy situation. Totally insane. Lila longed to be Queen of Reader's Digest forever. When this proved impossible, she set out to destroy us all."

None of these private events, of course, had any immediate impact on the continuing success of *Reader's Digest*. Indeed, in the spring following the Massacre a story in the *Wall Street Journal* hailed the *Digest* as "the top publishing success since the Bible." In the four years since its fortieth anniversary, the *Digest*'s worldwide circulation had risen from twenty-three million to twenty-seven million and its annual sales from $160 million to $300 million. "How long can the *Digest* keep this up?" asked the *Journal*. "As a sort of Mama and Papa business on a colossal scale, it might seem vulnerable to any loss of vigor by the Wallaces. But there is no sign of this whatever. DeWitt controls his magazine as tightly as ever, is still alert and straight-bodied, still greets visitors with a bone-crushing handshake. And he seems to have imbued subordinates with the *Digest*'s editorial formula so thoroughly they could carry it on without a break."

CHAPTER SEVENTEEN

On the evening of November 3, 1968, Wallace and several of his editors gathered in the Game Room at High Winds to celebrate the election of Richard Nixon as President of the United States. Their confidence turned out to be premature, however, and when the party broke up after midnight Nixon and Hubert Humphrey were still neck and neck. It was not until the following morning that Nixon's narrow triumph became apparent.

That night the President-elect entertained Republican bigwigs at a special reception in New York. Since the Wallaces' apartment at the Pierre Hotel was just around the corner from Nixon's residence on Sixty-second Street, arrangements had been made for the two couples to drive to the party together. When Dick and Pat Nixon came down from their apartment that evening, surrounded by Secret Service agents, they found the Wallace limousine already parked outside. Spying the Nixons, DeWitt came over to offer them a lift. After a short conference, he returned to Lila.

"Lila," he said, "the Nixons want us to ride in their car."

"No!" huffed Lila. "I'm in this car already. They can come with us."

"But . . ."

"*Tell them to come with us.* This car is perfectly fine."

Back went DeWitt. After another conference, he returned. "Lila," he said, "Mr. Nixon is President-elect of the United States. He *has* to travel in that car, with the agents and the communications gear and all. He can't ride in our car."

"Oh, for God's sake," growled Lila, not at all convinced that a Queen should take orders from a politician. "I don't *need* this! We should have driven to the party alone."

But she finally did get out, and she and DeWitt rode with the Nixons. And no doubt before the night was over they were made to feel that the money they had given to the Nixon campaign was well spent. Wallace remained loyal to Nixon deep into Watergate, and the Nixons came to High Winds more than once during their presidential years. But the real Nixon connection at Reader's Digest would never be DeWitt Wallace. There was something about Nixon that put Wallace off, a forced geniality that made his own natural diffidence more pronounced. If Nixon were going to have a friend at Reader's Digest, it would have to be someone else.

During the last dozen years of their lives, when their labors should have sustained a rewarding retirement, disappointment after disappointment piled up for Lila and DeWitt Wallace. Perhaps the bitterest centered on the man they had chosen to lead the Kingdom into the next generation. Although Hobe Lewis had seemed a natural choice, actually taking the step—turning their child over to someone else—had not been easy. Listed on the masthead as chief executive officer, Lewis quickly discovered that the *Journal* writer's prediction had been accurate. He managed the day-to-day affairs of the company, and ran the monthly board meetings. But the *real* board meetings, where the real decisions were made, still took place up at High Winds.

To a great extent, Lewis was able to delegate responsibility for the magazine to executive editor Harry Harper and managing editor Walter Mahony. But the Wallaces had put Lewis in charge of the business side as well, and this was proving onerous. Lewis had little business experience, and his associates on the business side, aware of this, quickly sought to fence him out. Frustrated by this arrangement, resenting the fact that after all these years he was still under Wallace's thumb, Lewis began to look beyond the Digest for opportunities to make his mark in life.

One of the first places he looked was the Nixon White House. In fact, Lewis's connection to Nixon went back to 1965, when he and Al Cole were part of a small group that plotted and financed Nixon's comeback from political oblivion. According to Maurice Stans (Nixon's commerce secretary and campaign finance chairman, later convicted of Watergate crimes), Cole and Lewis were especially effective "at tapping certain wealthy people that they knew."

During these years, Nixon contributed several articles to the *Digest,* and on several occasions lunched with *Digest* editors at the Guesthouse. Once in office, he showed his appreciation by inviting Lewis to the White House on several occasions, and even to Camp David, and twice the president arrived by helicopter at Lewis's estate in Bedford Village. At the same time, the *Digest*'s tepid support for the war in Vietnam—a war Nixon was intensifying —suddenly became impassioned. Article followed article, many of them written with staffers at the White House. The lead in the December 1969 issue—"No Surrender in Vietnam!"—called on the nation to rededicate itself to the struggle. Although signed by "The Editors," it turned out to be a thinly disguised version of an upcoming Nixon speech. This fact, and the hawkish tone of the article itself, caused several of Lewis's liberal editors to protest. But Lewis stood firm. A few phrases were softened and the credit line changed to "An Editorial." Otherwise, the article ran as written.

Two months later came "From Hanoi—With Thanks," a compilation of speeches and reports from North Vietnam, prepared with help from Nixon's State Department, that purported to show how antiwar demonstrators were "giving aid and comfort to the enemy." Although *Digest* articles normally circulated among the editors before publication, with comments encouraged, "From Hanoi" was shown only to those considered "politically reliable." When others finally did see copies, on the verge of publication, there were further protests and much talk about mass resignation.

In the end, however, only three editors left. And *Digest* support for the war, and for every other aspect of Nixonian policy, only gathered steam: "Stand Firm in Vietnam!"; "A Time for Toughness in America!"; "America on the Brighter Side"; even "Spiro Agnew—Vice President Extraordinary." The Agnew piece provoked more laughter in the ranks than dissension, and in some ways this was worse. Wallace had always seen his magazine as a serious vehicle for helping others. Now Lewis appeared to be using it to further his own personal ambitions, even to the extent of praising Spiro Agnew.*

Wallace's role in the Vietnam controversy was largely passive. He supported the war, as he had always supported every effort to contain Communism, but not without doubts. The pro-war/pro-Nixon articles flowing up from the White House were Hobe Lewis's doing, not his, and by early 1972 (despite the performance staged by Nixon at the Freedom Medal Dinner that January) he had seen enough. He ordered a reduction in the number of such articles, and shortly thereafter surprised everyone by suggesting that the *Digest* publish an editorial from *Life* magazine calling for a negotiated peace.

Written by former defense secretary Clark Clifford, the editorial represented the collective wisdom of the nation's political and business elites, who had concluded that the war was unwinnable and no longer worth its escalating costs. Although Nixon essentially agreed with this view, he also believed that his political interest lay in postponing a settlement until after the November elections (to avoid the appearance of a sellout). Under intense pressure from the White House, Lewis persuaded Wallace that Clifford was "unreliable" and that publishing his peace arguments in *Reader's Digest* would constitute a "betrayal of the President." The article was withdrawn.

---

* Lewis's efforts were apparently rewarded. In early August 1971, he astonished his business colleagues by suddenly ordering an across-the-board rise in RD prices. "We never raised prices without testing," recalls sales promotion director Tom Bundrick. "But Hobe was adamant. No tests. Just raise the prices. So we did. And one week later Nixon put price controls on everything sold in America."

Nixon won overwhelmingly in November, and thereafter unleashed his infamous "Christmas bombing" of Hanoi and Haiphong. The war dragged on for two more years, with the loss of hundreds of thousands of additional lives. The U.S. media remained astonishingly supportive of Nixon's hawkish policies during these years, and thus bear a heavy responsibility for the devastation. But no medium was as supportive as *Reader's Digest* under Hobart Lewis, and none bears more responsibility.

Lewis's next target was Hollywood. "We know better than anyone what Americans like to read," he reasoned. "Why shouldn't we be equally successful at deciding what they like to *see?*" He enlisted Tony Oursler to be his "creative assistant" and Dick Waters to be his money man. The effort began modestly, with the establishment of a "mini-department" to produce TV shows. Initial results—several animated fairy tales and a medical series based on *Digest* articles—were critically acclaimed but had trouble finding sponsors.

But Lewis had the Hollywood bug, and nothing was going to stop him. After chatting with producer David Brown at a New York cocktail party, he decided RD should collaborate with United Artists on a musical version of *Tom Sawyer*. Although this involved sailing into a sea he knew nothing about, full of sharks and barracudas, Lewis eagerly presented his plan to Wallace. "Wally had grave reservations about Hollywood," recalls Dick Waters. "But he knew Hobe was frustrated in Pleasantville and figured if we could have a little fun making a picture or two, why not."

As it turned out, Lewis had bigger ideas, and it didn't help when *Tom* astonished everyone by becoming a huge success. "Everybody loved it," recalls Tony Oursler. "And after that, Hobe began to think he knew more about making movies than anyone."

In the afterglow of *Tom,* Lewis made a deal with UA chairman Arthur Krim to make *Huck Finn.* But Krim convinced him to "cross-collateralize" the two pictures, so the money the Digest should have made from *Tom* went into *Huck,* and *Huck* was a disaster. Undeterred, Lewis set up an entity called Reader's Digest Films (on the theory that only an independent producer could make money), and a string of box-office disasters *(Quilp, Sarah, All Things Bright and Beautiful)* ensued. "But that was it," recalls Dick Waters. "We made five pictures, and then we shut it down. Perhaps if we'd done it right—spent more money in better places—we might have succeeded. But we were amateurs, and star-struck at that. Because, I mean, it *was* a glamorous life. I got caught up in it, and Hobe was even worse. He was in it up to his eyeballs."

In fact, Lewis's life was becoming complicated on several fronts. On June 14, 1972, forty female Digesters filed a complaint with the EEOC charging the Digest with discrimination in hiring, promotion and pay policies. News of this action hit Headquarters like a bombshell. The Wallaces had always treated all employees—male *and* female—like family. In every area of employment practice—working conditions, pay scales, benefits, vacations, medical care—the Digest had been ahead of its time. How could such a large group of women feel so unhappy (and be so *disloyal)* as to file a lawsuit?

It turned out that the problem was far from new. The previous November, a women's committee had discussed the problem with members of the Digest personnel staff. The discussion went nowhere. In January, leaders of the committee had met with Hobe Lewis in his office. Nothing came of this either. On March 17, a formal "white paper" proposing changes in working conditions, signed by 112 female employees, was delivered to the Digest executive committee, chaired by Lewis. It, too, was ignored, seemingly on the theory that the women, being women, would get bored and go away.

But they didn't go away. Two months after the white paper was ignored, the women filed their complaint. "We tried as gently as we could to persuade management to reexamine its double standards," said one female employee. "They laughed in our faces."

The EEOC complaint eventually became a class-action suit, representing twenty-six hundred female Digesters, and worked its way through the court system until November 1976, when plaintiffs and the Digest finally reached agreement. "In one of the biggest settlements to date of a sex-discrimination lawsuit," reported the *New York Times,* "Reader's Digest agreed yesterday to pay more than $1.5 million to 2,600 current and former female employees."

"That lawsuit was my fault," admits Lewis today. "I simply didn't understand there was a problem. And even when it was brought to my attention, I ignored it. Counting legal fees, it cost us four million dollars."

Nor were the women the end of Lewis's troubles. Just three days after they filed their complaint—on June 17, 1972—five burglars were discovered inside the Democratic National Committee's offices in the Watergate apartment complex, setting off political shock waves that reverberated louder and louder until eventually they drove Richard Nixon from office. In the months after the break-in, the men around Nixon became involved in a massive effort to contain the scandal. Money had to be raised to pay the burglars' legal expenses and to buy their silence. "How much will it cost?" Nixon asked White House counsel John Dean (as recorded on the famous tapes). When Dean replied that it might take a million dollars, Nixon had shrugged: "That's no problem. And you could get it in cash. I . . . I know where it could be gotten. . . . It doesn't come outta me."

Republican fund-raisers had been very successful that year, and Party coffers bulged with money (more than $10 million). Rose Mary Woods, the president's secretary, kept a secret list of donors who had given $100,000 or more ("Rose Mary's Baby," they called it). DeWitt Wallace's name was on the list. Now, with Watergate expenses mounting, the White House apparently asked Lewis to see if his boss would help out one more time, and Wallace apparently agreed to provide an additional $100,000. But there was a problem: under the recently passed Federal Election Campaign Act, after April 7, 1972, all political gifts above $100 had to be recorded publicly. So a way had to be found to disguise Wallace's new gift. Lewis assured him this could be done. (Earlier, at Lewis's urging, Wallace had donated substantial sums to several GOP "shadow committees"—phony groups created to evade campaign-giving rules. After an IRS investigation, the Founder of *Reader's Digest* had been made to pay a substantial tax penalty.)

Some time in early 1973—just before the Senate hearings on Watergate began in May—Lewis concluded that his life was spinning out of control. For several weeks, the Digest chairman disappeared from sight. Rumor had him in Washington helping Nixon; or having a prostate operation; or going to jail. Only later was it learned that he had checked himself into a posh clinic in Switzerland to rest and recuperate from nervous exhaustion. While at the clinic, he became friendly with an Englishwoman named Adele Dillingham, and when he returned to Pleasantville that summer he seemed much happier. For a time, the rumors subsided. But not for long. In July, Lewis dispatched a memo to all editors announcing the hiring of Ms. Dillingham, described in the memo as "a former *Time* researcher, now living in London, with a wealth of ideas for the *Digest.*"

Dillingham showed up at Headquarters shortly thereafter to discuss her ideas over lunch with Lewis and Tony Oursler. It was an occasion Oursler has never forgotten: "The first thing that struck me was her perfume— overwhelming and seductive. She was slim, dark-haired, intense; not pretty, really, but stylish and dressy. She was full of criticisms about the *Digest,* crazy ideas about what was needed to make it livelier. She kept talking about women's lib—batting her eyes at Hobe—and insisting that only by being *freed* could women become truly submissive."

After this lunch, Adele Dillingham's ideas, which were uniformly terrible, began to rain on Pleasantville. Soon the corridors were buzzing with questions: "Who *is* Adele Dillingham? What's going on between her and Hobe?" And inevitably these questions found their way up to the Tower at High Winds.

These were not happy years for DeWitt Wallace, and the travails of his designated successor were only part of the problem. His most reliable colleagues—Paul Palmer, Ken Payne, Al Cole, Fred Thompson, who had told the truth—were gone, banished from the Kingdom for failing in their attentions to the Queen. Those who replaced them—men like Hobe Lewis, Paul Thompson, Harry Morgan, Barney McHenry—were a different breed, willing to do or say whatever was required in order to get ahead. Wallace found this confusing.

Meanwhile, money continued to pour in, and this only added to his problems. For Wallace, giving away money was a serious business, and as he aged it became more and more of a burden. Some of the work was handled by the company, and some by the Reader's Digest Foundation (a company-sponsored charity set up in the early fifties for public-relations purposes). But the bulk of DeWitt's and Lila's giving remained private. That was how they wanted it: to give quietly and anonymously, when and how they pleased. For help in this endeavor, Wallace turned increasingly to a small group of people who were as close to family as he could get: his nephew Gordon Davies, his education adviser, Paul Davis, and, more and more, to Harry Morgan and Harry's efficient secretary.

"The situation was out of control," recalls Cappy Morgan. "We had file drawers all over our office filled with projects Wally was supporting. Hundreds of schools. Thousands of scholarships. And he insisted on knowing how every project and every scholarship kid was doing. He read stacks and stacks of reports and letters, read through half the night. The process had taken over his life.

"At one point in 1970, Wally called me to his office. 'I'm having trouble keeping track of my commitments,' he said. 'Sometimes at lunch I can't remember what I've promised, and this makes it difficult to decide what I can do for the guest.' He asked me to condense all of this information onto a single card—'something I can keep in my pocket. Then, if I get confused, I can excuse myself and go to the bathroom and check the list.'

"So I went through everything we had—all his ongoing gifts, all the projected gifts, how many millions were committed to this fund, how many years to that grant—and somehow got the basics onto a single sheet of paper. But, you know, this was ludicrous! I was a twenty-seven-year-old secretary who barely understood the process. He had dozens of employees better able to handle it. Lawyers. Accountants. Barney McHenry and his staff. The Foundation. Why weren't *they* helping him? The answer is that he didn't trust them.

"Wally knew that Harry and I would do what we were told and keep our mouths shut. So more and more of the money began to flow through our office, and as it did Harry became surer and surer that he was going to control the whole thing. He had been blocked in editorial and shut out on the business side. Now he sensed that his path to the top ran through Wally's philanthropic funds, and through the Foundation. But an elderly retainer named Sterling Fisher was still running the Foundation, so something had to be done about him.

"At the time, I was handling a lot of Wally's correspondence, so I had a stack of his stationery locked away in my desk. One day, Harry took a sheet of this and wrote a note to Sterling suggesting that it was time to retire. Then he mentioned to the Wallaces how excited he was at the prospect of taking over the Foundation. 'That's right,' Wally said. 'Sterling is getting too old. It's time for a change. And how nice that Cappy will be there to help you run things.'

"Well, that was a problem. Because Sterling already had an assistant named Adele Gmelin, who clearly intended to be around another twenty years. But Harry never hesitated. If I was to be part of the deal at the Foundation, then Adele had to go. He went to Paul Thompson and told him Wally wanted Adele fired. Hearing those words, and knowing how close Harry was to Wally, Paul fired Adele. Then everything blew up. Adele called Sterling in hysterics. Sterling called the Wallaces, and the Wallaces called Paul. Paul denied firing Adele, and suddenly the knives that had always been out for Harry were flying all over. Harry went up to High Winds to confer with Wally about the Foundation. 'I'm afraid it's out of the question,' Wally told him. 'In fact, I think you'd better leave the Digest altogether.'

"So that was that. Harry showed up at my place the night he got fired. I was furious at him for obvious reasons, but when I saw the state he was in—sobbing, distraught, nearly hysterical—I had to feel sympathy. All his dreams had vanished. His marriage was over. His job was gone. And the Wallaces—who had virtually crowned him as their son and heir—cut him off with a one-year severance."

During the early seventies, even the "other Harry," Lila's once-untouchable dancing master, came under fire. Dick Waters had been made senior vice president as well as treasurer, and in this new capacity had nominal supervision over Wilcox. Everyone had known for years about Harry's scams and kickbacks, but now the no-nonsense Waters set out to prove a case: "I went to every supplier and contractor we had. 'Look, Frank,' I would say—or Bill, or Bob, or whoever, there were dozens of them—'it's your ass or Harry's ass. Either you give me an affidavit about what's been goin' on all these years or you'll never get another nickel of Digest business.'"

Armed with the affidavits, Waters was able to convince the Wallaces that Harry had been robbing them for decades. Yet still they didn't turn totally against him. No charges were brought, and as Harry's health deteriorated arrangements were made for retirement on a disability claim. "They could have sent him away on tax-evasion charges alone," says Waters. "But Harry had an ex-wife somewhere, and the Wallaces didn't want to make trouble." When outsiders inquired about her missing business manager, Lila dismissed the subject as if Wilcox had never existed. "Wilcox?" she would say. *"Harry* Wilcox? Oh, yes. He was a drunk. We got rid of him."

With Wilcox gone, a sizable vacuum developed at High Winds. For several decades, Harry had taken care of the Wallaces' most intimate needs—everything from fixing DeWitt's speeding tickets to unraveling Lila's financial transactions. *Who will take over Harry's role?* everyone wondered. It was like a game of musical chairs. When the music stopped—when the King and Queen breathed their last—who would be poised above the empty throne?

The early favorites—Fred and Judy Thompson, and later Harry Morgan —had fallen by the wayside. Bill Kennedy was available, at least to care for Lila, but Bill was on a collision course with Barney McHenry. Many believed Dick Waters was the best choice. He had handled aspects of the Wallaces' financial affairs for years, and both Wallaces trusted him. But Waters was a rising star at Headquarters, with responsibilities there that precluded full-time duty at High Winds. So in the end the field was left to Barney McHenry.

"Barney started weaselin' his way in up there more and more in the early seventies," recalls Waters. "He convinced the Wallaces that I was too busy to handle their personal affairs—which was largely true—and that therefore he should take over. This was okay with me. It was legal work, most of it, and the tax returns could always be done down at Lord, Day. So I backed out of it and Barney moved in."

"It was all a matter of timing," says another Digester, a veteran who at the time toiled in McHenry's own legal department. "The opportunity opened up and no one down at Headquarters felt strong enough to keep Barney out. And the sad thing is that neither Wallace liked him. Lila was always on the verge of firing him. But he would bring her things—candy, cookies, flowers —and she would change her mind. Wally more or less ignored him. After Wilcox and Kennedy, he may have found Barney a relief."

So the ambitious attorney kept his place at Court. And the longer he was there, the more he learned about the Wallaces' personal affairs. "Eventually," says Fred Stanyer, "Barney knew *too* much. Not that the Wallaces had terrible things to hide. They were just extremely *private* people. Lila didn't want anyone to know anything personal about her life—from what she paid for a dress, to how much she had given to some charity. But now Barney was privy to such information, and this gave him a measure of immunity.

"After I had been at Boscobel for several years I called Barney one day about my salary. 'I need a raise, Barney,' I said. 'It's been six years.' He asked me how much I wanted, and I told him. Then he called Lila and told her I had demanded an increase in my *bonus*. This was typical. In Barney's view, I was too close to the Wallaces, and this was his way to get rid of me. Lila called me on the phone, so angry the receiver almost flew off the hook. 'What *is* the matter, Lila?' I asked. *'Money,'* she snapped. 'Do you understand *money?'* I asked if I could come over. When I got there, we sat in the living room—Wally was also present—and I explained what had happened. 'I never asked for a bigger bonus,' I said. 'Just for a raise. You're a business-woman. You should understand that.' Lila thought about this, then began saying horrible things about Barney.

" 'Well, Lila,' said Wally. 'If you really feel that way, here's your chance to get rid of him.' So she called to Veikko to bring her the phone. 'Are you sure about this?' I asked. She pondered my question for several minutes, sitting there with the phone in her lap. Then she shook her head. It was too risky."

CHAPTER EIGHTEEN

As the seventies advanced, DeWitt Wallace increasingly withdrew from day-to-day supervision of his Empire. He watched over his executives and editors, made occasional suggestions, sometimes came down hard in one area or another. But the business of Reader's Digest was proceeding as it always had, one record year following another, so there was little to complain about. Except for one thing: Try as he might, he could not make his executives understand that they weren't in the magazine business to maximize profits. "Reader's Digest is a *service*," he repeated over and over. "We have to charge money to make the enterprise possible. But *over*charging won't be tolerated. It is morally wrong. In the long run, it will ruin our business. And what is the point? All the extra profit ends up in *my* bank account, and then *I* have to think up ways to give it back."

The message didn't sink in. Every day, it seemed, one of his lieutenants came up with a new scheme to make money. When the Spanish edition encountered difficulties in the early seventies, for example, his colleagues urged him to shut it down. Wallace listened to their arguments, and for a time seemed on the verge of agreeing. "But then he would start talking about the people who worked there," recalls John Allen, an assistant managing editor who later ran the company's public-affairs department. "The money saved by killing the Spanish company would flow directly into his hands—*he* would become richer at their expense—and he couldn't deal with this. You could literally sense the questions he asked himself: *I have all the money I need. How can I accept more when I know it comes from families who will be out of work, who do need it?* He could not put the equation in business terms. It had to be personal."

On the home front, Wallace's battle against excessive profit was even more frustrating. His primary interest remained the magazine, because the magazine could be used to help people. He had been willing to accept Condensed Books, sort of, because it was a natural extension of the magazine and encouraged reading. His enthusiasm for the record club was cooler. He was persuaded that it brought fine music to millions of customers, at low cost, and that apparently was enough. But then Al Cole discovered that customers who would buy low-cost records would also buy low-cost record players and radios. Around 1970, the company began importing cheap components from Taiwan and Korea and marketing the assembled units through the mail and door-to-door to millions of Digest customers.

Now Wallace *did* draw the line. The executive in charge was summoned to his office. "Why should a Digest customer buy a record player or radio from us when they can go to any discount store and buy the same thing for less?" he asked.

"But, Wally," countered the executive, "our radios and record players are an excellent value."

"Oh?" said Wallace. He pointed to a clock/radio sitting on his desk. "How much are we charging for this?"

"It goes for thirty-nine ninety-five."

"Well," said Wallace, "I have just seen an identical product in Caldor's for twenty-nine ninety-five. We are using RD's reputation, backed by misleading advertising, *just to make money!"*

In a later memo to all involved, Wallace made his position clear:

> The only purpose of this clock-radio promotion is to make money. *But should the desire to make money ever come first in our calculations?* I don't think so. Should you wish to proceed with the current mailing, I won't object. *But no more!* DW

Nowhere was Wallace's frustration greater during this period than at Macalester. By 1967, his gifts to the college topped $40 million. "Old Main," the single Victorian edifice James Wallace had found in the center of a wind-blown cornfield, was now surrounded by a tree-shaded campus of stately brick buildings spreading across a hundred acres. The little denominational college on Summit Avenue had been transformed into a first-class liberal-arts institution.

Most of this was DeWitt Wallace's doing, and he was eager to do more. When Macalester's aging president, Harvey Rice, announced his retirement, Wallace himself volunteered to recruit a replacement. His heart was set on Arthur Flemming, then serving as president of the University of Oregon. But Flemming came with a stiff price tag. He wanted a million dollars for Oregon to complete a project he had begun there, and another $7 million to underwrite a program of expanded liberal arts courses at Macalester. Wallace happily paid it all, then sat back to watch developments.

He was not pleased with what he saw. Something was happening at Macalester in those days (and on campuses all over the country) that Wallace was singularly unprepared to accept. There were antiwar demonstrations—violent affairs, with teargas and police dogs—right on the campus. He saw photos of students in ragged clothing, with long hair and arrogant expressions, bearing posters attacking the college administration, the war in Vietnam, the president of the United States, even the United States itself. Al Cole represented him on the board at Macalester, and Cole reported to Wallace that during a visit to the school the flag in the center of the campus had been flown upside down. Despite all he had done for Macalester—perhaps *because* of what he had done—his father's college was splitting apart.

For several decades, going back to his original gift in 1939, Wallace had automatically covered Macalester's annual deficit. But when Flemming got his $7 million in 1967, the new president assured his benefactor that deficits were a thing of the past. In the summer of 1970, however, Flemming wrote to Wallace to explain that once again a large deficit loomed, and would it be convenient to send $4 million as soon as possible. Now Wallace's patience ended. His reply to Flemming (a one-sentence letter containing "too many bad words," as he later admitted) made it brutally clear that he was through with Macalester. They were on their own.

Wallace's decision hit the college like a thunderbolt, and prompted the Minneapolis/St. Paul newspapers to wonder what had gone wrong. Wallace remained unavailable to the press, but through Paul Davis explained his decision this way: "It appears to me that Macalester has become *too* affluent and that the school would benefit from an extended period of austerity."

In fact, Wallace had come to believe the whole *country* was too affluent. At a Guesthouse lunch with several key editors the following spring, he suddenly raised this subject. "I think we're all making too much money," he suggested. "Don't you agree?" One of the editors took this as a joke. "I can't speak for you, Wally," he said, "but as for me, right now, the answer is no. Now, maybe in the future, maybe sometime very *soon* . . . " The others laughed at this blatant hint. But the point is, Wallace meant what he said. Affluence had undermined his own life, and his father's college, and many of his closest colleagues. And he believed that affluence was beginning to undermine the country. The "toughened ascetic life" of his ancestors was disappearing under a flood of vanity and greed, and nowhere was this more true than in the Kingdom.

And so it was that the scalawag in him, the bad boy who liked to stamp his feet, began to appear more often. One Friday that spring, Wallace suddenly phoned several of his top executives, including CEO Lewis. "Lila and I were down at the Mt. Kisco railroad station the other day," he told each one. "We were dismayed at the litter on the tracks. I think we should do something about it and I want you to meet me on the station platform tomorrow at eight. Can you do it?"

As always, *Wally wants* had its mesmerizing effect: golf games were canceled, picnics postponed, gardens deserted. Lewis and the other executives appeared on the station platform the next morning at eight sharp. Wallace met them there, handed out garbage bags and spiked sticks and pointed at the tracks. "There's the enemy, gentlemen," he said. "Let's get to it!"

For the next three hours, what was surely the highest-priced garbage squad in history scoured the Mt. Kisco railroad tracks, grubbing out litter that had accumulated over decades. Although there was much quiet grumbling, Wallace himself appeared to be having a fine time. When one of his younger associates discovered a $5 bill on the tracks, the old man laughed with pleasure. "We ought to do this every week, Peter," he chortled. "We'd get rich!"

Wallace took his compulsion to "upset the apple cart," as Lila put it, several steps further during a dinner party that summer at the Bird & Bottle Inn, after a ceremony of some sort at Boscobel. It was the kind of evening he had come to dread: speeches in praise of Lila; speeches in praise of him. By the time their little group reached the restaurant, Wallace was clearly in a gloomy mood.

But during the soup course, he interrupted the general conversation to tell an off-color story—something outrageously sophomoric about how the size of a woman's vagina can be predicted by the size of her mouth. The others laughed politely, and this only seemed to egg him on. "Have I ever told you all about *Lila's* vagina?" he asked. He paused while his companions choked on their soup, then went on. "Well . . . you see . . . Lila has what I am sure is the most *extraordinary* vagina in the world. I mean, I cannot *imagine* . . . "

"Oh, Wally," said Lila, rolling her eyes. "Knock it off. Be a good boy." For Wallace, the evening had become a success. He had been good for as long as he could stand it. And then he had been bad.

Lila's own reaction to these years of disappointment was simply to become more herself, to become Lila *intensified.* Those who made her feel safe and adored were treated with queenly benevolence. Those who did not were in danger. Jeremy Dole recalls a summer day in 1975 when he and a group of male editors were briefly in very great danger indeed:

"I had been invited to lunch with Mrs. Wallace and a 'special guest' who turned out to be Miss America. Our beauty queen that year was a student at Macalester, and in view of the Wallace legacy it was only natural that she should come to Pleasantville to pay her respects. Lila had asked that a small group of male editors be assembled for the occasion.

"When we gathered at noon in the Guesthouse, Lila was already in place in her favorite wing chair by the fireplace. Miss America hadn't arrived, so as drinks were brought out we men circled around Lila and babbled inanely as we always did in her presence. Then our guests arrived—an older chaperon and a stunning Nordic creature who was a dead ringer for Brigitte Bardot.

"Introductions were made, chairs assigned, more drinks brought out. We all sat down—Lila at one end of the small room and Miss America and her chaperon at the other. And in between five stupefied males who should have known better. Lila had ordered her usual vodka martini, and a small dish of hors d'oeuvres had been placed at her right side. As the odd ritual unfolded, the chairs of all five men seemed to gravitate toward the lovely Brigitte.

" 'JOHN!' Our heads snapped in the direction of this unexpected sound. Lila Wallace was staring daggers at John Allen. Her martini glass was empty. The hors d'oeuvres had disappeared and the little dish was gripped in her right hand. And just that fast she sent it sailing across the room at Allen's head. He reached up and somehow caught the dish. He stared at it, and then at her. 'Why, Lila,' he said, searching for the right word. 'What a lovely . . . *toss!* Would you . . . *um* . . . care for more hors d'oeuvres? Another drink?'

"As he spoke his chair turned—all our chairs turned—and what had been a semicircle facing Miss America became a semicircle facing Lila Wallace. We all began to speak at once, and as we did Lila settled back with a satisfied smile. She was eighty-seven years old. Her eye makeup, excessive as it was in those days, made her look like a raccoon. But her point had been made: There was only one Miss America in that room, and now, by God, we were looking at her."

CHAPTER NINETEEN

As control of his corporate world inevitably slipped away from him, Wallace struggled harder and harder to retain a semblance of control over his personal affairs. As owner of Reader's Digest, he was accustomed to transferring tens of millions here and there, and back again. But business transactions, handled by armies of lawyers and accountants, had never seemed real to him. It was different with personal matters—buying clothes, the expenses of High Winds, the salaries paid to servants. This was *real* money, and real money could not be wasted.

In December 1971, after the Wallaces had made their seasonal move into the Pierre apartment, DeWitt began to fret about all the tipping that lay ahead. Tipping had always troubled him, and men who *over*tipped left him fuming. ("How can a man of means upset the system that way?" he muttered to Doherty after emerging from lunch with a famous industrialist who had given the hatcheck girl $5. "I'll *never* lunch with him again, I promise you that.") Now he decided to try a new tack. Rather than slip $10 into every hand, he asked the Pierre management for a list of service people who might rightfully expect a modest gift. Management responded with a list of *thirty-six* names, and suggested gifts ranging from $10 to $100. Wallace was outraged. He gave everyone on the list $10, and sank into a holiday funk. And in January he persuaded Lila to put the Pierre apartment on the market.

Nowhere was Wallace's frugality more apparent than in matters of personal wardrobe. He liked his things old and worn, and Lila had to threaten hellfire to get him to buy anything new. He even balked at dry cleaning. When Veikko ironed his employer's pants, he kept a handkerchief over his nose because they smelled. But he was under orders to stay away from the cleaner's. When he complained to Mrs. Wallace, she would tell him to take the pants anyway. Then DeWitt would have a fit: "Who gave you the right to take my pants and run up a bill?" Relying on the fact that it was Gene Doherty who actually delivered the pants to the cleaner's, Veikko would insist that he was innocent. "Then who *is* guilty?" By now Wallace would be shouting. "You are *responsible* for my things! You must know who. . . . "

At this point, from somewhere in the mansion, Lila was sure to interrupt. "*I* sent your pants to the cleaner's, Wally!" she would shout. "Because they *stank!*"

He was even worse about footwear. His dress shoes, which Veikko polished every night, were old and cracked, and the boots he wore to work on his roads looked as if they had survived both world wars. When he finally wore a large hole through the sole of the right boot, he swallowed his pride and asked Veikko to get the hole repaired. But the shoemaker wouldn't do it. "I don't fix *holes,*" he said. "New half-soles on *both* boots will cost eighteen dollars." When Veikko reported this news, Wallace was appalled. "What a waste of good material," he said, shaking his head. He stuffed more cardboard into the boot and went on using it for several years.

Although Wallace's frugality was often colorful, there was one time when it produced a sad result. Veikko and Aino Kotalainen had arrived at High Winds in 1959, and had served the Wallaces with skill and grace for twelve happy years. Only one disagreement marred the relationship. Veikko had been employed on several estates before coming to High Winds, and at each place had been allowed to take free gas from the estate pump on his day off. He continued this practice when he arrived at High Winds. But then DeWitt found out about it, and was troubled. "It isn't right, Veikko," he would growl. "I pay you enough. You can buy your own gas."

"The gas is part of my pay, Mr. Wallace," Veikko would say. "Part of our arrangement."

For several years the two men agreed to disagree. But as DeWitt's frugality became more pronounced in the early seventies, he began to grouse again about the gas. One night, just as Veikko was maneuvering a portion of chocolate mousse around his employer's elbow, the old man's anxiety about the gas got the better of him. "I want you to stop taking the gas, Veikko," he said. "It's not right."

"As you wish, Mr. Wallace," said Veikko, releasing the mousse with a clunk. The next day, Veikko and Aino gave notice. They would stay on until suitable replacements could be found. Then they were moving to Florida. A few weeks later, John and Ann Tichi arrived at High Winds, and the Kotalainens disappeared. And from then on life in Lila's mansion slid downhill. Not that there was anything wrong with the Tichis. John was an affable little guy, soft-spoken and skillful. Ann was intelligent and articulate; her chief interest was playing bridge, and she was very good at it. But there was a vast difference between the Tichis and the Kotalainens. For Veikko and Aino, serving the Wallaces had been a calling. For John and Ann, it was a job, and they quickly set out to make it as easy as possible.

Early on, sensing a potential friend in Ann, or perhaps because she had grown tired of eating alone with DeWitt, Lila suggested that the Tichis might take their evening meal with the Wallaces. "That's very kind of you, Mrs. Wallace," said Ann. "But we eat early and our schedules would be thrown off." In fact, the Tichis had arranged their schedules so each could pursue a personal interest. After the noon meal, John generally spent his afternoons in the back room of a local liquor store, returning in time to serve the evening meal with polite if unsteady aplomb. Ann spent her afternoons preparing dinner, and as soon as John showed up hustled off to a bridge game. To defend this setup, the Tichis had turned down an invitation to dine with the King and Queen. It was a sign of things to come.

In their own way, of course—despite their wealth, despite the airs Lila put on for her subjects—there had always been something touchingly modest about the two of them, and as they grew older this quality also produced a raft of stories.

In the summer of 1970, at Lila's suggestion, a Flemish carillon was installed in the tower at Headquarters. The idea was to inspire Digesters by playing lively tunes from 8:15 until the workday began at 8:30, and again for fifteen minutes at noon, and again at the end of the day. Lila and DeWitt drove down from High Winds to hear the initial concert. But when they parked in front of the building, a security guard—obviously new at the job —hustled over to shoo them away.

"But we came down to hear the bells," explained DeWitt. "We'll just sit here in the car until the concert is over. Then we'll leave."

"I'm sorry," said the guard, as the first notes of "Indian Love Call" pealed forth. "You can't park here. It's the rule." And he directed them to the visitors' lot. When they got back, on foot, the concert was over. "Well"— DeWitt shrugged—"there's always next time."

It wasn't in them to pull rank, and they were not pleased when senior colleagues did. In the mid-sixties, after Hobe Lewis was named president, twenty parking slots nearest the main building were suddenly "reserved" for top management, with little signs bearing the names of the chosen few planted in the ground at the head of each slot. The signs didn't last for long. On a winter's afternoon in 1966, DeWitt parked his '53 Oldsmobile in the most distant lot (no one had dared offer *him* a reserved place) and began the long hike to Headquarters. Along the way, he caught up with Jim McCracken, an editor whose promising career had been sidetracked into administrative duties. The two men walked along together until they reached the row of reserved slots. Wallace stopped and grabbed McCracken's arm. "Tell me, Jim," he asked, "which of these places is yours?"

"Well, Wally," said McCracken, "I don't have one."

"But how can that be? You've been here for years."

"Twenty-five, all together, Wally."

Wallace pursed his lips. "You know, Jim," he said. "It seems to me if *you* don't have a slot . . . after twenty-five years . . . then nobody should." By noon the next day, all the little signs were gone.

Around Pleasantville, the Wallaces' aversion to special treatment was generally well known, and Digesters did their best to accommodate it. But the Digest Empire now extended around the world, and in its foreign offices, in places seldom visited by King and Queen, the Wallace name evoked images of mystery and power, and special treatment was hard to avoid.

In 1967, Lila and DeWitt drove themselves north to Montreal to visit the World Exposition. When they reached Montreal, they discovered that news of their impending visit had preceded them. They were compelled to attend a luncheon organized by Paul Zimmerman, managing director of the Canadian company, at a fancy downtown restaurant. When lunch was over, Zimmerman announced that a limousine was waiting.

"What limousine?" asked Wallace.

"Well, Mr. Wallace, the limo we've arranged to take you to Expo."

"Oh," said Wallace. "We don't want a limo."

"But it is all arranged. And when you get to Expo, you will have VIP treatment at every one of the exhibits. It is all taken care of."

"But we don't *want* special treatment," insisted Wallace. "We want to go as just plain people."

In the end, the offer of the limo was rebuffed and Lila and DeWitt traveled by subway to the island where Expo was taking place. And when they got there, they waited in line with the ordinary people.

The Wallaces' modesty extended even to the process of giving away money. "Lila and I discovered long ago," DeWitt was fond of saying, "that there are better uses for money than its mere accumulation." Lila for once was more to the point. "Wally and I have composed a new, one-sentence will," she announced to a suddenly attentive dinner gathering in 1970. "Being of sound mind and body, *we are giving it all away!*"

Certainly they tried. By the mid-seventies, their philanthropy totaled an estimated $150 million. They gave when and how they pleased, refused to be bound by formal guidelines and only occasionally called on others for help in the task. Above all, they did everything possible to keep their giving secret. As they aged, the whimsical nature of their generosity would lead them into trouble. But for a number of years the Wallace giving was characterized by a spontaneity unique in the history of philanthropy.

When Digest senior editor Andrew Jones arrived at his office one February morning in 1969, his phone was already ringing. "Andy," said a reedy voice, "this is Wally. I've just read John Hubbell's piece about Outward Bound. Very interesting. And this fellow Josh Miner sounds like a decent sort. Do you suppose I could meet him?"

The Outward Bound program, in which young people are confronted with strenuous outdoor challenges in order to gain self-confidence, had just traveled across the Atlantic from Scotland, where it had been a great success for years. Josh Miner was in charge of the U.S. operation, which in 1969 was struggling to get started on a small island off the Maine coast.

"No problem, Wally," replied Jones. "Josh is an old Princeton pal of mine. I can set up lunch whenever you want."

One week later, Wallace and Miner met for lunch at the Sky Club. Wallace asked quiet questions, probing for information about Outward Bound, trying to gauge whether the experiment was as promising as the *Digest* had made it sound. Miner did most of the talking, spinning out tales of the hard life on Hurricane Island, while the aging publisher stared at the clouds passing by outside. Miner worried that his host was bored. In truth, Wallace was thinking that Outward Bound was based on everything he had always admired: freedom, challenge, the "toughened ascetic life" of his forebears.

When lunch was over, Wallace asked Miner where he was staying. "At the

Princeton Club, Mr. Wallace," said Miner. "Then, first thing tomorrow, back to Maine."

"Well," said Wallace, "I want to be sure you and Mrs. Miner enjoy your visit." He went on to explain that dinner and theater reservations had been made for the Miners. Then, almost as an afterthought, he extended a well-worn envelope. "When you get back to the club, you might want to glance at this. I think Outward Bound is doing a splendid job and I hope this helps to keep it alive."

Miner stuffed the envelope into his pocket, said his thank-yous and rushed off to another appointment. Only when he got back to his room at the Princeton Club did he remember Wallace's envelope. Andy Jones had explained about the old man's generosity, so Miner hoped that a sizable check might be involved, perhaps as much as $5,000. But what he pulled from Wallace's used envelope was a check for *one million dollars!* He sat heavily on his bed, then reached for the phone and dialed his friend Jones in Pleasantville. "Andy," he asked, "is this guy Wallace for real?"

"Sure he is, Josh. Why?"

"He has just given me a check for a *million* bucks! Do you suppose it's good? Can I cash it?"

"Listen, Josh," said Jones, laughing happily. "Do me a favor. Don't light your cigar with it!"

One year later, still liking what he saw, Wallace gave Outward Bound another million, and he continued to provide regular support for years to come. There was a pattern to DeWitt's giving: discovering a worthwhile cause in some serendipitous way, providing seed money, "leveraging" this money by offering matching grants, encouraging other groups to get involved. He wasn't interested in established institutions or bricks-and-mortar. He liked giving to *people,* especially young people who were learning, growing, trying new ideas. He sought always to get in at the beginning, to get others involved, to get the biggest bang for every dollar he gave.

But for those who knew him best, it was Wallace's personal giving—small daily gestures of kindness and concern—that remained most memorable. He kept little lists of those he knew to be in need, compiled with the assistance of secretary Betty St. John, and every night placed a call or two to see what he could do. "Joe," he might say to a writer laid up with a bad back, "this is Wally. I hear your lumbar region is acting up. I can get you an appointment with the best back man in New York on a moment's notice." Or speaking to a junior editor: "David, this is Wally. I'm sorry to learn your wife is ill. The work you're doing for the *Digest* is too important to have you distracted by money worries. I want you to bring the bills directly to Betty." Or to a father who had just sent his third son to an Ivy League college: "Dan, no one can afford such tuitions three times over. Consequently, you've just been awarded a DeWitt Wallace Scholarship for your youngest son. Congratulations."

Small gestures, perhaps. But for those thus helped—an astonishingly high percentage of the RD population—the sound of that high-pitched "This is Wally" would never be forgotten.

His generosity toward individual Digesters was often expressed toward Digesters as a group. In fact, it was nearly impossible for him to experience something good, something he personally found exciting and worthwhile, without wanting to share it with his corporate family. Colonial Williamsburg had been a favorite Wallace vacation destination since the late forties, and DeWitt especially was fond of strolling along the historic streets where the foundations of American democracy had been established. In 1970, he launched what he called his "Employees to Williamsburg" project. Every month for the next decade he sent eight Digesters down to Williamsburg on the corporate jet for a weekend stay, all expenses paid. He showed up at Westchester Airport himself to see them off, always bringing with him eight envelopes each containing five crisp new $10 bills. Later in the decade, he was so thrilled by a whitewater raft trip down Utah's Green River that he began sending small groups of colleagues on similar trips. Even the experience of giving itself was something he felt compelled to share. Starting in the mid-sixties—to the dismay of budget-conscious senior executives—Digesters were given the opportunity to allocate annual cash amounts ranging from $450 to $4,000 (depending on salary) to their favorite charities.

Lila's giving was just as adventurous and even more spontaneous. In the spring of 1964, for example, she received a phone call from a woman at the YWCA in nearby White Plains, New York. "We're starting a fund drive to underwrite construction of a new residence," said the caller. "We hoped—in view of your long interest in the needs of working women—that we could call on you." The next day, three women arrived at High Winds for tea. Lila received them graciously and listened while they described their plans. "We need one million dollars," they explained, adding that they had already raised $6,000.

Lila almost choked. "You have a long way to go," she pointed out. "Do you really think you can reach a million?"

"Oh, yes," insisted the women. "All we need is a major gift to get the ball rolling."

"How much?" asked Lila.

"Well," said the group's spokeswoman, eyeing her companions, "we were hoping you might be willing to consider . . . one hundred thousand dollars."

Lila asked for a week to think it over. The next day, she sent two Digest executives down to White Plains to do some investigating. Everyone they questioned—store owners, business managers, Chamber of Commerce leaders—gave them the same answer: The White Plains YWCA was doing a splendid job, but it had no chance of raising the dreamed-of $1 million.

When the women returned to High Winds, Lila greeted them with a worried expression. "I couldn't sleep last night," she told them. "I kept thinking about your problem. And it seemed to me, quite frankly, that giving you one hundred thousand wouldn't help very much."

The women's faces fell.

"But then I remembered something—a little nest egg I put away a few years ago for a rainy day. Early this morning, I decided it wasn't ever going to rain again. So I won't need the nest egg and I want you to have it." Smiling happily, Lila presented her visitors with a check for the full $1 million.

Lila was equally happy when she helped her friend, the soprano Risë Stevens, out of a similar jam in 1967. After attending a Sunday performance of the Metropolitan Opera, the two women went across the street to have chocolate sundaes at O'Neals' Baloon. Stevens seemed glum, and Lila asked why. "Mr. Bing has put me in charge of our touring company," explained the singer, referring to Rudolf Bing, the Metropolitan's imperious managing director. "My dream is to take the company on an extended trip around America. Millions of people in the smaller cities and towns never get a chance to experience live opera, and I thought this would be a way to make up for that. But I am far behind in raising funds—more than a million dollars, in fact. So, unless some angel should appear, some very *generous* angel"—Stevens smiled apologetically—"I am afraid the tour will never take place."

Lila didn't hesitate. "It may take me a day or two," she said, "but you will get your million. That's a promise."

When Stevens reported this news to Bing, the great man was unexpectedly cold. "Such a large gift to an unimportant subsidiary might confuse those who are contemplating giving to the Met itself," he told Stevens. "We cannot allow it." A few days later, Bing summoned Lila to his office. "Really, Mrs. Wallace," he said. "One million dollars for a *road* company, to support a tour of the *provinces?* How would that look when Mother Met herself, right here in New York, so badly needs funds? Perhaps you'd reconsider?"

Lila glared at him. "There's no need to reconsider, Mr. Bing," she said, rising to her feet. "You see, I happen to *come* from the provinces. And I know there are people out there who enjoy opera as avidly as anyone here in New York. I think those people—those *provincials*—should have a chance, too, don't you?"

Although the Wallaces did everything possible to keep their benefactions secret, rumors about their generosity inevitably spread. Requests for money, for an audience, for a chance to explain "a unique opportunity to make a difference" began to flow in from all sides during the sixties and seventies. Many of these requests were turned aside before reaching the Wallaces, but many got through to them and to each of these they gave honest consideration. If they were impressed, they frequently arranged to meet with representatives of the proposed cause over lunch at the Guesthouse. A lot of money was given away between the main course and dessert on those occasions, most of it to worthy causes, some to causes not so worthy. And some to causes neither Wallace cared about.

Over the years, to ensure agreement on such gifts, the Wallaces had developed a system of hand signals: Lila might pull on her left ear if she were inclined to favor a particular guest; DeWitt might scratch the top of his head if he disapproved. The problem was, sometimes Lila confused left with right, and sometimes DeWitt scratched because he itched.

In 1972, Pete Kriendler, co-owner of New York's "21" Club, decided to approach the Wallaces for a donation to the Buffalo Bill Museum in Cody, Wyoming, a project begun by his father. A lunch at the Guesthouse was arranged, with the Wallaces, Hobe Lewis and John Allen in attendance. During lunch, Kriendler told several hilarious speakeasy jokes, and Dewitt and the other men laughed with pleasure. But not Lila. To Lila Wallace, Pete Kriendler was a perfect example of the macho world she so abhorred.

Over dessert, Kriendler made his pitch about the museum. "Well, Pete," asked Wallace, "how much money do you need?" Kriendler began to add it all up—so much for this, so much for that—and as he did DeWitt glanced at Lila, who was furiously tugging her right ear. When Kriendler announced finally that $4 million was needed, Wallace was ready. "Okay, Pete," he said, "if you can raise three million by April, Lila and I will provide the fourth million."

Later, down at Headquarters, Lewis expressed surprise at this decision. "You didn't seem that impressed with the Buffalo Bill Museum, Wally," he said. "And I thought Lila was bored stiff."

"Oh, I know," replied Wallace. "It's a terrible thing! Lila was pulling her right ear when she meant to pull her left. Or maybe it was the other way around. Anyway, we agreed to give a million so we're stuck with it."

There are many such stories, and they are fondly repeated whenever Digest old-timers get together. Yet beneath the amusement runs an undertone of sadness. For as the Wallaces entered their last decade they began to lose control of the situation. They were old (DeWitt was eighty-one in 1970, and Lila eighty-three) and they were rich. So it is not surprising that signals got crossed or that those they believed to be friends sometimes behaved in unfriendly ways. The unraveling began slowly, beginning in the early seventies. But the potential for exploitation can be seen as early as the late sixties, and in the course of benefactions that were otherwise joyful and satisfying.

In 1966, Bill Kennedy and Ben Garbor, Lila's pet decorators, fell in love with modern dancer Martha Graham. As a result of their friendship with Lila, the two had become financially independent, and now they began to shower Graham with expensive gifts and other attentions. They bought her clothes, took over her personal appearance, even persuaded her to undergo several face-lifts.

But Graham's real need at this stage in her career was money. Her customary patron, Bethsabee de Rothschild, had supported the Graham company for years. But Bethsabee had become disenchanted. Graham was seventy in 1966, and no longer able to dance as she once had. Yet the thought of stopping made her frantic and she refused to give in. She also began to drink too much. As Bethsabee's support ebbed away, the future of the Graham company seemed at risk.

Now enter Bill and Ben. They plied Lila with stories about Graham, praising her greatness and courage. Lila attended several performances and eventually was introduced to Graham herself. Most women bored Lila. But *famous* women—women who had achieved great things on their own—were different. Lila quickly agreed to become the company's new benefactress. "What do you need most of all?" she asked. Graham replied that it would be nice if she could buy the building the company used for rehearsals. The cost: $1 million. "Fine," said Lila. "Consider it done." A Martha Graham Foundation was set up, with Barney McHenry as chairman, and soon Lila's money was flowing in a new direction. ("Lila had *zero* interest in modern dance," admits McHenry today. "But Martha Graham was fiercely independent, and Lila admired that.")

Although the Graham interlude cost Lila several millions, it was not in the same league with a connection that began inauspiciously on a rainy afternoon in February 1969. Lila was in her limousine, driving down Fifth Avenue past the Metropolitan Museum, when suddenly she asked Doherty to pull over. An elderly woman, umbrella in one hand and cane in the other, was struggling to climb the museum's high-rising front steps. "Look at that," said Lila. "Isn't it terrible? The entrance to a great museum should *welcome* passersby, not rise above them like a wall."

As it happened, Met director Thomas Hoving was also worried about the museum's entrance just then, and about several other things as well. Hoving had come to the Met in 1968 after a stint as New York City's parks commissioner. Among his early efforts to bring a sense of relevance to the staid Metropolitan was an ambitious photographic exhibition called "Harlem on My Mind." Many aspects of the show disturbed traditionalists, but the real bombshell was an essay in the show's catalog, composed by a Harlem schoolgirl, that contained anti-Semitic remarks. In the uproar that followed, the museum's trustees began to contemplate the need for a new director. "You need to come up with a stunning coup to survive," Hoving was told. "And you had better do it *soon.*"

The beleaguered director's only trump card was a master plan for renovating the Met—in his own words, "a total refitting of the structure, with the building of three new wings, a doubling of the interior space and redesign of the front façade." The façade troubled him more than anything, in particular the same stairs that had offended Lila Wallace. "They were downright dangerous," he admitted in *Making the Mummies Dance,* his best-seller about the Met. "The steep, narrow stairs ended not with a majestic Roman portal, but with a dingy door dubbed The Doghouse by employees."

Hoving had hired architect Kevin Roche to produce a design for his master plan, and in March 1969 Roche completed the early models. Hoving was thrilled: "The most beautiful part of Kevin's plan was the luminous Great Hall and the spacious exterior plaza with its tree-filled parklets and inviting stairs." If he could pull off this portion of the plan quickly, Hoving believed, he might survive. But several million dollars were needed, and this sum had produced "stony faces" among the museum's wealthy trustees.

Out of the blue, Hoving received a phone call from someone whose name he remembered from prep-school days. The man identified himself as a lawyer "with one client." This client, he said, had an interest in the Met that Hoving might find "deeply sympathetic." The man's name was Barnabas McHenry. Hoving invited McHenry to come in first thing the following morning.

As described by Hoving: "Barney McHenry was a suave, soft-spoken man who had a way of looking at one slightly askance. He would punctuate his conversation with an occasional low chuckle that suggested he was revealing a profound secret. We started off chatting about school days, but I was too curious about his single client. McHenry chuckled. 'She's Lila Acheson Wallace,' he said."

Although Hoving seemed to recall that his curator of Egyptology had once mentioned a Mrs. Wallace, he insisted that the name meant nothing to him. "Mrs. Wallace is co-founder of *Reader's Digest,*" McHenry explained, chuckling again.

"Oh," said Hoving. "Of, course." *

McHenry then described Lila Wallace's great wealth, and indicated that she was interested in making a gift to the museum. "Lila thinks the Metropolitan is *grungy,*" said the lawyer. "She feels the institution is too great to have

---

* Hoving was being sly. In fact, he had known Lila for years, having courted her with notable success while running the Cloisters and as parks commissioner. And Lila had earlier contributed generously to the Met's campaign to rescue the temples at Abu Simbel from the waters rising behind the Aswan Dam.

such a shitty-looking façade, and is convinced that the entrance hall you've got here is filthy and sad."

Hoving could scarcely believe his ears. "Why," he said, struggling to conceal his excitement, "it just so happens that our architects have come up with a spectacular design for the façade *and* the entrance hall. We have just finished the models."

The two men discussed when Lila Wallace might see these models, and a date was set for lunch the following week. "And on a sunny day in May," writes Hoving, "Lila Acheson Wallace came to 'have a glance,' as Barney put it. She was a strikingly beautiful woman in her seventies [she was actually eighty at the time], all in blue—dress, hair, eye shadow. Lunch was chatty and lighthearted. Lila talked of her affection for my father [the founder of Tiffany's] and for Billy Graham."

After lunch, Hoving and McHenry brought Lila to the gallery where Kevin Roche was waiting. Roche presented his models and explained the philosophy behind the project. Although the heralded young architect spoke with intensity and brilliance, Lila appeared unimpressed.

"What will the plaza and hall cost?" she asked.

"Around seven million," said Hoving.

"Do you mind if I suggest a change?" Roche stiffened, wondering what sacrilege this elderly Middle American was about to wreak upon his elegant design. "Think of having two *shops* opposite the entrance, instead of these coat rooms. A pair of shops might earn each year an income equivalent to that from a ten-million-dollar endowment. Anyway, I love your plans. Just send the bills."

At that point, writes Hoving, "Lila Wallace got up, thanked us for the lunch and our time, and apologized for staying so long. I escorted her down the steep old steps to her car, and returned to the gallery.

" 'What was *that* all about?' Roche asked. 'What did that remark about "the bills" mean?'

" 'I've no idea,' said Hoving."

The matter was clarified the next morning when McHenry called. "What a swell presentation!" he said. "I'll send you initially one million. But we won't hold you to the seven million you mentioned yesterday. Looks to me like it's going to be a bit more. And Lila will be good for all of it." And Lila *was* good for all of it. With her lawyer handling the arrangements, she agreed to pay $7.5 million for the reconstruction of the plaza and the Great Hall, plus an additional endowment of $4 million in Digest stock to cover maintenance of the Hall and the façade in perpetuity.

Nor does the story end there. When the restoration of the Hall was completed in April 1970, Lila took one look at its vast marbled space—cold, imposing, splendid—and decreed that flowers were needed to lend it warmth. She transferred to the Met another $4 million in Digest stock, to provide an annual income of $100,000, and soon huge tubs of flowers were blooming throughout the Great Hall. In gratitude, the Met's trustees presented her with a four-thousand-year-old gold chalice said to have belonged to Queen Nefertiti. Lila was ecstatic, and from that day on insisted on taking her evening martini from the precious cup. She had been meditating in recent months, in her stone Teahouse, and was beginning to entertain a belief in reincarnation. Sipping from the gold cup made her feel special and prompted her to wonder whether in some former life she had been one of history's grandest ladies—Empress Theodora, perhaps, or better yet Queen Nefertiti herself.

Earlier in the sixties, through her friend Frederick Osborn, Lila had become involved in efforts to improve the Bronx Zoo. Osborn owned a large estate near Boscobel and for a time had served on Boscobel's board. His family had given the land the zoo sits on, and for many years his cousin Fairfield Osborn had served as president of the zoo's trustees. When the zoo decided to build its "World of Birds" around 1966, Fair Osborn turned to Lila Wallace for help. Their discussions eventually included Laurance Rockefeller, who had succeeded Osborn as zoo president.

Between them, the two men persuaded Lila to underwrite the entire cost of the aviary. As a reward, Rockefeller gave her an exotic blue-and-green "peacock" brooch set with jade and lapus lazuli and studded with diamonds. She was thrilled, and in later years spoke of this brooch almost as often as she spoke of Nefertiti's cup. "That wonderful Laurance Rockefeller was strolling down Fifth Avenue," she liked to tell people, "and there in Van Cleef's window was this lovely bird. 'Take me along, take me along,' the bird was chirping. And Laurance did. And he brought the bird to me."

CHAPTER TWENTY

In many ways, they were a perfect match. Laurance Rockefeller is a man whose chief calling in recent decades has been to identify people with great wealth and no offspring, and then—summoning the legendary Rockefeller charm—to arrange matters so that as much of this wealth as possible ends up supporting causes he and his associates believe to be "in the public interest." In the late sixties, when Laurance entered her life, Lila Wallace was a childless woman with vast sums of money, vulnerable to charm and boundlessly determined to see only the best in those who paid her court.

From her earliest years in the wilds of North Dakota, she had been starstruck by the notion of Rockefellers. She believed them to be America's own royal family, and that to mix with Rockefellers would be to become herself a part of their royal world. *And it had happened!* Here was Lila Acheson, daughter of a country preacher often too broke to buy a new suit, calling on Rockefellers, dining at their estates, becoming *friends*. She wasn't completely innocent in this. She knew the Rockefeller history, and no doubt also understood in some degree what Laurance was up to. But she chose to ignore the murky side of their relationship and to focus instead on the aspects of Laurance Rockefeller that made her feel good about herself. ("Lila could be naïve about some things," points out Barney McHenry. "Over the years, she filled several scrapbooks with photos and articles about the duke and duchess of Windsor. The two *worst* people one can imagine! And yet . . . because they were celebrities, *royal* celebrities . . . Lila was enthralled.")

DeWitt had his own childhood memories of the Rockefeller family. During the bitterest years of the struggle to keep Macalester afloat, James Wallace had managed to secure an audience with old John D. himself, and from that meeting Macalester had realized a modest bequest from the Rockefeller General Education Board. James never forgot this. Nor did DeWitt. He grew up believing that the Rockefeller philanthropies were a model for all rich men to follow. "Wally thoroughly admired the Rockefellers," says James Stewart-Gordon. "He couldn't see the dark side of that family. Just didn't get it."

In the late sixties, the Wallaces began to see more and more of Laurance and Mary Rockefeller. On several occasions, they were invited to lunch or dinner at the Rockefeller estate in Pocantico Hills, and they responded with several dinner parties at High Winds. In 1967, Laurance invited the Wallaces to stay at his ranch in Wyoming. During this visit, one morning after the Wallaces had come in from a boat ride on Jenny Lake, Lila went upstairs to change and Laurance invited DeWitt into his study for a chat. Laurance had recently become chairman of New York's Memorial Sloan-Kettering Cancer Center, and for the next half hour he regaled DeWitt with stories of the advances the center's experts were making against cancer. There was no talk of money, or any suggestion that the *Digest* might support the hospital editorially. This was groundwork, pure and simple, and it would later prove extremely effective.

It helps, of course, to have at one's disposal the kind of resources a Rockefeller can command. "Laurance has always been a slick salesman," says Ed Thompson (who succeeded Hobe Lewis as *Digest* editor in chief in 1976). "He was forever flying the Wallaces somewhere on a Rockefeller jet —Colonial Williamsburg, Caneel Bay, Hawaii—and putting them up in spectacular Rockefeller homes. They were thrilled by this, and very grateful. Laurance always knows *exactly* what he wants, but sometimes he has trouble expressing it. This can make him seem apologetic, even deferential, when, of course, he is not deferential at all. In fact, his awkwardness hides a pronounced underlying arrogance. He has chosen not to fix it because it works. Certainly it worked on the Wallaces."

Fred Stanyer, who for many years was as close to the Wallaces as anyone, is even blunter: "When Laurance Rockefeller went up to High Winds he went with his hat in his hand, like everyone else. And the myth about them being bosom buddies is a lot of baloney. Laurance gave the Wallaces something they wanted. And in the end he took from them a great deal of what *he* wanted."

In 1971, Laurance did something for Lila that she talked about until her dying day. On April Fools' Day that year, a gang of thieves that had been plaguing estates all over Westchester County struck at High Winds. While Veikko was serving the Wallaces their evening meal, someone climbed the magnolia tree outside Lila's bedroom, broke through a window, and absconded with a small fortune in jewelry, including the diamond-encrusted peacock Laurance had found in Van Cleef's window. Although heartbroken by this loss, Lila decided not to replace the stolen items. "I have had my pleasure from those jewels," she said. "I can live without them." Instead, she gave the insurance money to an organization that sends children from Harlem to summer camp. "Money is an obligation," she pointed out. "One way or another, you must give it back to the people."

But Lila didn't have to live without her peacock for very long. Hearing of her loss, Laurance commissioned Van Cleef's to create an exact replica. Lila never got over this. She wore the new brooch everywhere, and told everyone who would listen how it had come to be hers. That a Rockefeller should buy her such a gift was wonderful. That the same Rockefeller should do it *twice* was beyond wonder, was, in fact, a childhood dream come true.

Early in 1972, DeWitt and Harold Helm, chairman of Chemical Bank, had a long talk about the future of Reader's Digest. Chemical had been the Digest bank for twenty years, and during most of that time Helm had been the Wallace's personal banker as well. "What will happen to the Digest if something happens to you?" Helm asked. "Is there someone around who can succeed you?"

Wallace shook his head. "I look around the shop," he said sadly, "and all I see are mediocrities."

Helm had a suggestion. "Why don't you pick a few broad-minded friends —outsiders to the Digest—and make them the voting trustees of your stock? That way, your desire to keep the Digest private will be honored."

Wallace asked if Helm would sit on such a trust, and Helm said yes. Then the banker put forth the name of Laurance Rockefeller. "I'm a businessman, Wally," he said, "a dollar-for-dollar guy. Laurance Rockefeller is a people person, someone who will ensure that the Digest remains in the Wallace mode. I've discussed this with him and I believe he will take it on. He sees it as a public trust."

Wallace asked for time to think this over—which, as always, meant time to present the matter to his wife. Lila thought it was a fine idea, primarily because Laurance was involved. Now they would be more than friends. Laurance would be her *personal adviser,* the latest in a line of Shining Knights going back to Barclay and Harry Wilcox, and including Bill Kennedy, Paul Thompson, Hobe Lewis and a host of others. But Laurance Rockefeller was clearly head and shoulders above the rest. Laurance had everything—celebrity, power, *charisma.* "Oh, *yes,* Wally!" said Lila. "Making Laurance a trustee is a *gorgeous* idea!"

Others weren't so sure. When Dick Waters told Wallace he'd have to pay the outsiders, the old man snorted. "Jeesus, Dick," he said, "these guys make enough money as it is." Then he discussed the plan with Al Cole, and Cole (seeing in Laurance less the Shining Knight and more the Great White Shark) was dead set against it. So DeWitt was back in a familiar position, caught between Lila and Al. As always, he sided with Lila.

But there were reasons for this that went beyond pleasing his wife. Wallace thought he saw in Laurance Rockefeller the answer to the Digest's future. All the others who had reached for the Throne—Fred Thompson, Al Cole, Hobe Lewis, even Harry Morgan—had wanted something for themselves: money or power or prestige. But these were things Laurance Rockefeller had in abundance, far beyond any conceivable need for more. Laurance was a philanthropist, a *conservationist.* He would *give* to the Digest, Wallace believed, not take away. He told Helm he wanted to proceed.

"Al had introduced Harold Helm to the Wallaces," says Peggy Cole, "and Harold was very fond of Al. But he was *enamored* of Laurance Rockefeller. It was Harold who suggested that Laurance would be willing to serve as a trustee, that he would see it as a public service. In Al's opinion, that was bunk. Laurance knew what he was doing from the beginning. He had figured out how much money was hiding in the Digest, and he was very patient about going after it."

On December 4, 1972, a first codicil to the Wallaces' wills was executed. The original wills, signed in 1969, had made the Digest's top three executives —Hobe Lewis, Paul Thompson and Walter Hitesman—the voting trustees of the Wallace estate. (The Wallaces owned all of the voting stock. In the event of their deaths, the trustees would vote this stock and thus control the company.) But Thompson had proved a disaster as the Digest's business head and had been forced into early retirement at the end of 1971. Now he was removed from the trust as well, and three new men were added: Al Cole, Harold Helm and Laurance Rockefeller. Just eight months later, in August 1973, a second codicil eliminated Cole from the trust (another round for Lila), and added the names of Kent Rhodes and Dick Waters. And at the same time, Helm and Rockefeller were named as the first outside directors in Reader's Digest history. (Inside directors were essentially rubber stamps for whatever DeWitt and Lila decided up at High Winds; the outsiders—and some saw this as an ominous development—were clearly expected to provide independent advice and counsel.)

Laurance Rockefeller's position in the Wallace Kingdom had suddenly become extremely powerful. He and his friend Helm were now the sole outside directors of the Wallaces' company, as well as the sole outside trustees of their estate. The four inside trustees, as Digest executives, could be terminated at any time. Rockefeller and Helm could be terminated only by a change in the Wallace wills.

So it is fair to say that as of August 1973 the first phase of what would become the inexorable encirclement of the Wallace Kingdom was over. And Laurance had barely needed to lift a finger. "My life has been Zenlike," he is fond of saying. "You know . . . finding without seeking." It is a remark that recalls his famous grandfather. "When it's raining porridge," Senior's sister Lucy used to say, "you'll always find John's bowl right side up."

In Reader's Digest, Laurance Rockefeller had found himself a *very* large bowl of porridge, larger even than he understood at the time. Later on, when he discovered (as he had suspected all along) that the company's real value was *many* times its listed value—was in fact greater than the fabled Rockefeller fortune itself—he must have allowed himself a satisfied smile. And when he considered the other contenders—men like Hobe Lewis, Walter Hitesman and Dick Waters, who had struggled for too long in Wallace's shadow, and relative newcomers like Jack O'Hara and Ed Thompson—his smile must have broadened into a happy grin. Laurance enjoyed a reputation for tinkering with people, as he had tinkered with machines in his youth, to see how they worked. For a man who had prospered in the Byzantine bureaucracy of the military-industrial complex after World War II, tinkering with the unsuspecting squires of Pleasantville was going to be easy work.

Later that month, Wallace had his new trustees up to High Winds for dinner. "He seemed very happy that night," recalls Dick Waters. "I think he was pleased with the six of us and pleased that everything was finally settled, that he could relax at last. After dinner he put us through a little ceremony, a swearing of fealty to the Wallace Digest and the Wallace Way of running things. . . . "

I told the trustees that night what my hopes were for Reader's Digest: To provide the greatest possible service to our customers. To secure happy, fulfilling lives for our employees. To spread the word of freedom around the world. I asked them to swear an oath to these principles. And to swear as well that they would never take the Digest public. "Money is not the goal, gentlemen," I said. "The goal is to preserve Reader's Digest exactly as it is today for 500 years." And they swore to this, every one of them. . . .

PART V

Nightmare

1974–1981

CHAPTER TWENTY-ONE

On an evening in late January 1976, DeWitt and Lila Wallace were eating a quiet dinner together in the breakfast room at High Winds when butler John Tichi suddenly appeared from the kitchen. "I'm sorry to interrupt, Mr. Wallace," Tichi said. "There's a phone call for you. It seems to be the White House." Wallace glanced at his wife, then excused himself and rose to follow Tichi from the room. Normally, for privacy, he would have used the telephone in a small closet off the front hall. But at eighty-six he was becoming forgetful, and so walked past the nearer phone and followed Tichi into the kitchen. The butler left him there and rejoined Gene Doherty in the pantry, where the two men had been chatting over an evening coffee.

Now, while their Boss spoke on the phone, Tichi and Doherty said nothing, their ears straining to pick up the conversation in the next room. "Yes?" said Wallace. "This is DeWitt Wallace." For several seconds the old man listened in silence. When he spoke again, his voice was quivering with rage. "Promises were made to me!" he said. "I was told no one would learn about that money!" There was more silence as he listened further, then he slammed the receiver down and strode from the room.

Doherty and Tichi looked at each other. "What was *that* about?" Doherty whispered. Tichi shook his head. Then they heard Wallace's voice again as he explained the call to Lila. "That was the White House"—the old man was pacing back and forth, spitting out his words—"they tell me that news about the money has leaked. There will be a story in the *Washington Post*. It will mention Hobe. It *may* mention me." He shook his head in frustration. "They promised me this could *never* happen!"

The story subsequently bannered across the front page of the *Post* (FOUR YEARS AFTER WATERGATE, MONEY QUESTIONS LINGER) was very strange. Written by star reporter Bob Woodward, it attempted to summarize various "loose financial ends" remaining after the Watergate hearings. One of the loosest involved substantial amounts of cash allegedly given to Nixon by Dwayne Andreas, the commodity tycoon and chairman of Archer-Daniels-Midland Corporation (who remains today one of the most controversial political givers in the country). Part of this money—in the form of a $25,000 cashier's check made out to Nixon fund-raiser Kenneth Dahlberg—had ended up (after a detour through a Mexican bank) in the Miami bank account of Bernard Barker, one of the Watergate burglars, thus providing investigators with their first concrete link between the hapless culprits and the Nixon campaign. But the rest of the "Andreas" money—$100,000 in cash given to Nixon in 1972 —remained in a safe at the White House. Partly out of fear that an FBI probe of the $25,000 would lead to Andreas, and from Andreas straight to the White House safe, Nixon ordered the CIA to tell the FBI that an Agency operation was involved, and that the Bureau should "stay the hell out of this." This order—delivered by CIA deputy director Vernon Walters to FBI acting director Patrick Gray on June 23, just a week after the break-in— launched the cover-up that led to the burgeoning scandal that in August of 1974 drove Nixon from the White House in disgrace.

Several questions about that secret $100,000 baffled Woodward. Rose Mary Woods, the president's secretary, kept a list of every campaign donor who had given $100,000. But Andreas's $100,000 wasn't on the list, and, in fact, had not been used during the '72 campaign. So why had it been collected in the first place? When Andreas gave the money, claimed Woodward's sources, he did so with the help of "golfing companion Hobart Lewis, chairman of Reader's Digest and close personal friend of Nixon." Lewis, wrote Woodward, "put Andreas in contact with Woods, and the $100,000 was soon delivered personally by Andreas to the White House." But in June 1973, when a nervous Nixon decided to return the money, Woods contacted Hobe Lewis—*not* Andreas—and asked Lewis to come to the White House. Why she called Lewis, wrote Woodward, "is not clear." Lewis flew to Washington, and Woods gave him $100,000 in cash. Lewis then asked Woods to inform Andreas that the money had been returned. But Lewis didn't give the money to Andreas. Instead, according to an account he himself later confirmed, he borrowed it from Andreas "to pay off personal loans."

The *Post* made no mention of Wallace, and only hinted at illegality in these strange goings-on. And there the story died. Except that anyone reading it closely had to be puzzled. Why would the chairman of Archer-Daniels require the services of the chairman of Reader's Digest in order to make a gift to the White House? Why, when the money was returned, would Andreas need Lewis to be his personal delivery boy? Why would a man as well off as Lewis suddenly need to borrow $100,000? What was going on?

Lewis's own recollection of these events doesn't help: "I had lunch with Andreas in Washington one day in 1971. After lunch he said he wanted to give Nixon $100,000. He had the cash right there with him, in a briefcase. But he was in a hurry to leave Washington, so he asked if I would take the money to Rose Mary Woods. And I did. Two years later, Rose Mary called me to say they still had the money and would I like to return it to Andreas. The next time I was in Washington, I picked up the briefcase. I then called Andreas and said I had the money and could I borrow it. He said sure. And I later paid it back. End of story."

But not the end of the questions. To Digest insiders, only one explanation covered them all: that the secret $100,000 hadn't come from Dwayne Andreas, but from DeWitt Wallace. According to this theory, Lewis persuaded Wallace to contribute the money to Nixon (whose aides at the time were desperately soliciting funds with which to buy the burglars' silence). Then— because Wallace had already given his limit—arrangements were made for the gift to be registered under Andreas's name.* When Woodward broke the story, the business about "borrowing" the money suddenly surfaced. What finally happened to the $100,000? Did Lewis keep it for himself? As the *Post*'s headline asserted: MONEY QUESTIONS LINGER.

All in all, 1975 had been a bad year for the beleaguered Digest chairman. The war in Vietnam was lost. His Hollywood adventure had subsided into a sea of red ink. His White House friend had become the first president in U.S. history to resign under a cloud, and the lawsuit brought against the Digest by its female employees, largely because of his own failure to pay attention, was looking like a sure winner. And now this fiasco over the Watergate donation.

No one could blame Lewis for staying away from the office for increasingly longer periods. Yet he was CEO of a major publishing company. Someone had to fill the gap left by his frequent absences, and for this role there were many candidates. Dick Waters had already more or less taken control over-

---

* H. R. Haldeman, Nixon's chief of staff, wrote in his diary on August 4, 1972, that "Dwayne Andreas has agreed to come up with a public statement saying he was the one who gave the $25,000 they're trying to track down in connection with Watergate."

seas. But the situation was murkier on the home front. After Paul Thompson's departure in 1971, a bitter battle to succeed him as business head of the company had developed between Walter Hitesman and Kent Rhodes. Hitesman was bright, articulate and hard-driving, but also intense and emotional. He wanted to be president of Reader's Digest in the worst way, and his obvious lust for the title gave Wallace second thoughts. Rhodes, on the other hand, was a calm, quiet voice of experience, well liked by his colleagues and respected throughout the magazine world. But Hitesman's wife, Betty—an attractive southern lady who had gained a high position in the Queen's Court —was favored by Lila, and in the end (as so often in the past) Lila's favor proved decisive.

In the summer of 1973, while Hitesman was recovering from a ruptured ulcer in a New York hospital, Wallace suddenly announced his elevation to the presidency. Later, when Wallace visited the hospital, Hitesman could barely contain his gratitude. "It's a great honor," he burbled. "I won't disappoint you, Wally."

"Don't take it so seriously, Walter," said Wallace dryly. "It's really not that big a deal."

It was, however, a big deal at Headquarters, where an already shaky command structure was suddenly shakier still. Many of Hitesman's key executives, still loyal to First Vice President Rhodes, were bitter that their man had lost. Those who *were* loyal to Hitesman had to keep an eye on Chairman Lewis, who was known to be jealous of Hitesman's new title. Then there was Executive Vice President Waters, happily running the international companies while waiting for a chance to make his move on the home front.

Behind these four was the mysterious Laurance Rockefeller. "I drove Laurance a lot in those days," recalls Gene Doherty. "It always amazed me how different he was with different people—charming and bubbly with Missus, serious and dignified around the Boss. But with the executives down at RD, a cold-blooded shark. If I drove him to the Guesthouse with Walter Hitesman, he was always talking about how Rhodes was after Hitesman's job. If I drove him someplace with Hobe Lewis, he would talk about the ambitions of Ed Thompson. That was the way he was. Always playing the game."

Overseeing this wrestling match, at eighty-five retired in name only, was the still-compelling presence of DeWitt Wallace. When the old man wrote a note on one of his yellow pads, up in his Tower at High Winds, those few scribbled words took precedence over every decision made by "the boys down at the shop," and the boys knew it. If Waters worried that Rhodes might disallow some initiative, he could mention it to the old man and thus ensure its passage. If Lewis felt that Hitesman was becoming too powerful, he could whisper something into Lila's ear that she would whisper into DeWitt's ear that would eventually bring the new president down a peg.

On several occasions, convinced the others were undermining him, Hitesman threatened to resign. Each time, Wallace persuaded him to calm down. But Wallace grew tired of this routine. In the summer of 1974, before a board meeting at which Hitesman was to make a major presentation, the beleaguered executive requested key financial data from Executive VP Waters. Waters and Lewis conferred about the numbers, and for some reason decided to withhold them. Without the numbers, Hitesman's presentation was a flop. Furious, Hitesman called Al Cole to complain. "Something has to be done," he said. "Otherwise, I will resign." When Cole called Wallace to report about this latest Hitesman threat, the old man was in no mood for conciliation. "Okay," he said, "that's it. Walter's out. Hobe is chairman and CEO, and Kent can become president."

Although the editorial end of the operation had always remained relatively insulated from corporate infighting, the situation that had evolved there under Lewis was just as murky and if anything more unpleasant than the situation on the business side. After several years as editor-in-chief, Lewis had persuaded himself that the magazine—given a few dedicated pencil pushers, with someone in charge to see that schedules were met—more or less put itself together. So he began to devote his limited company time to the business side, and to leave executive editor Walter Mahony in charge of seeing that "schedules were met."

"Bun" Mahony was a dedicated professional, hardworking, meticulous, insistent that every element in the magazine be "up to RD standards." He also believed that one day he would become editor-in-chief, and in this he was sadly misled. For as much as Wallace admired Mahony's dedication, he deplored the man's rigidity and narrow-mindedness. Accordingly, when Wallace made Lewis editor-in-chief he also created four new assistant managing editors. By 1975, it was clear to everyone but Mahony that one of this younger group—Ed Thompson, Tony Oursler, Ken Gilmore or Roy Herbert —would eventually succeed Lewis in the top job.

A brilliant pencil editor, Tony Oursler was the early favorite. His father, Fulton Oursler, Sr., was a long-time RD editor and Wallace crony (and author of *The Greatest Story Ever Told*), and Wallace liked the idea of continuity. But Oursler was an outspoken conservative—farther to the right than the magazine itself—and it didn't help that he was so closely identified with Lewis's ill-fated foray into Hollywood. Gilmore, newly arrived in Pleasantville after running RD's Washington bureau for several years, was an unknown quantity. But those who had dealt with him were dubious. "A hardworking straight arrow," they said, "but spineless and dim." Herbert by this time had fallen behind the others—because of personal problems and a general disinclination to run things—and so had more or less taken himself from the race.

That left Ed Thompson, and unlike the others Thompson was actively pushing for change. He had always been impatient. After graduating from MIT in 1949, he worked for an oil company on the Texas Gold Coast before signing on with a McGraw-Hill magazine called *Chemical Engineering*. "I thought the magazine experience would make clear to me what other opportunities were open in the field," he says. "I discovered that I liked being a journalist."

For a time he was managing editor of another McGraw-Hill publication, *Chemical Week,* and then for a few years wrote for *Fortune.* "But I hated being a writer and was worried about working for the same company as my father" (who at the time was managing editor of *Life*). "So I looked around at what else was available. Working for business publications had been confining, and I had no interest in women's magazines. Since most general-interest magazines had already folded, that left *Reader's Digest.*"

The tall, gregarious Thompson rose rapidly through the ranks. He was a gifted editor, tough but fair in personal relationships, firm (and conservative) of opinion but open to the arguments of others, including the few liberals on the staff. But his early impatience remained, and by the summer of 1975 it was running thin.

"In my view," he says today, "Bun Mahony was ruining the magazine. So that fall I let it be known that if a decision about Hobe's replacement wasn't made by the following spring I would be gone. The new boss didn't have to be me. But it had to be someone other than Bun. And the change had to come soon, because Hobe wasn't doing the job. Wally knew this. But he was old and tired, and he didn't want to think about it. So he delayed and delayed, until finally Hobe's own behavior made change unavoidable."

In September 1975, a manuscript arrived on Tony Oursler's desk with a covering memo from Lewis. The manuscript was a *Time* essay about the growing popularity of Zen Buddhism and other eastern religions. Adele Dillingham had sent it over from London. "Wouldn't this make a lively change-of-pace for the Christmas issue?" her note asked. Lewis's own note —addressed to Oursler as editor of the December issue—was less equivocal: "Let's use this in your issue," it said. "And I like Adele's title—'Needed: New Myths for Modern Man.' "

Oursler, a devout Catholic, disliked the piece and believed that running it in a Christmas issue was unnecessarily provocative. But he had turned down dozens of earlier Dillingham suggestions, and this made him hesitate. Lewis *was* editor-in-chief, after all, and Oursler knew that Lewis resented the staff's stubborn resistance to his friend's ideas. So he shrugged and gave in.

Two weeks later, a proof of "New Myths" arrived on DeWitt Wallace's desk at High Winds. That evening, Wallace called Oursler at home: "This is Wally. Do you mean to say you actually *liked* 'New Myths for Modern Man'?" Oursler quickly backtracked. "Not really, Wally," he said. "But you see, this . . . *umm* . . . was an order from the editor-in-chief, who obviously has rights in such matters. And I had turned down so many other suggestions from Ms. Dillingham. This one seemed less off the mark than the others, so I decided. . . ."

"For a *Christmas* issue?" Wallace interrupted. "In a *Christian* magazine?"

"Yes, sir," said Oursler. "I sure see your point."

The next morning, Oursler got a call from editorial business manager Jim McCracken. "Who exactly *is* Adele Dillingham?" McCracken asked.

"Well," replied Oursler, "she is . . . I think . . . a good friend . . . perhaps a *very* good friend . . . of Hobe's."

"I think that's right," said McCracken. "And I think she will be gone from our midst by the end of this day." McCracken explained that he had just had a call from Wallace, who had demanded a written review of all expenses pertaining to Ms. Dillingham. "Wally is not going to like it," said McCracken. "Her expense account is astronomical and her travels on RD's behalf have an odd tendency to follow Hobe's travels. Also, there is a ten-thousand-dollar retainer, and her file contains an HL note asking me to authorize rent payments for a London town house."

Wallace made several other calls on the subject of Ms. Dillingham, and what he learned dismayed him. It wasn't so much the money; he had overlooked outrageous expense accounts before. What bothered him was the invasion of his magazine, at the invitation of the editor-in-chief, by an outsider who obviously had no idea what made *Reader's Digest* tick.

After brooding about the situation for several weeks, Wallace decided to confide in Lila. He told her about the Dillingham articles, about the expense account, about the rumors that were swirling around the editorial department. Lila had forgiven Lewis for the Hollywood fiasco, the Nixon mess and the women's lawsuit. As long as he was faithful to *her,* she would let him play his boyish games. But she could not forgive him for Adele Dillingham. "Hobe is too old for the job," she told her husband. "It's time to make a change."

Two days later—on February 3, 1976—Wallace called Lewis and asked him to come up to High Winds for a walk. As they strolled across his rolling fields, the old man suggested that perhaps the time had come for his longtime colleague to step aside. "I've been talking with Laurance Rockefeller and Harold Helm," he said, leaving Lila out of it. "They feel it's time to get my ducks in a row as far as successors go, especially in editorial. You're sixty-seven now, Hobe. It's time to let the younger editors run the show."

The next morning, Wallace called Ed Thompson out of a meeting and asked him to come to his office right away. "When I got there," recalls Thompson, "I found Wally sitting behind his desk, looking down at his hands. He began to talk about a number of subjects—the Wallace Trust, his charitable interests, a lot of other things I knew little about. Then he looked directly at me. 'As editor-in-chief,' he said, 'you're going to have to handle such matters.' I was stunned. 'Did I hear you right?' I asked. 'Oh, yes,' he said. 'You're the new editor-in-chief. Now, will you please inform Adele Dillingham that her services are no longer required?'

" 'Yes, sir,' I said. 'I'll do that right away.' "

For all the old questions it put to rest, Thompson's promotion raised a perplexing new one. The top man at Reader's Digest had always been the editor-in-chief. Was Thompson now top man? No one knew. Although still on the masthead as chairman, Lewis was scheduled to leave even that ceremonial post by the end of the year. But Kent Rhodes had been made president and chief operating officer in late 1975, and thus appeared senior to Thompson. And there were several others on the business side, including Dick Waters and Jack O'Hara, a plain-spoken Scot who had risen rapidly in the international division, who had their own sights on the top job.

Even Thompson wasn't sure of his status. "Wally didn't seem to want to talk about it," he says. "He told me only that all editorial decisions would be mine. I asked him whether this included Condensed Books and General Books and he said no, that I would have enough on my plate running the magazine. 'The magazine is what counts,' he said. 'The rest of it is unimportant.' "

What was going through Wallace's mind at this point, as he struggled with his own mortality, can only be imagined. No doubt he *wanted* to make his new editor also his chief executive. But there were concerns he couldn't shake. Thompson was clearly the right man to run the magazine—to shake up the predictability and blandness that had crept in during the Lewis years. But Thompson had little business experience, and his ability to run a major corporation was a question mark. There were also personal worries. Thompson was once-divorced, and while his second marriage appeared to be successful there were already rumors (all too familiar in view of the Lewis fiasco) about a wandering eye.

What he wanted to do was make Jack O'Hara president—on the theory that O'Hara was tough, honest and committed to Wallace values—and then let O'Hara and Thompson fight it out for the top job. But he couldn't make O'Hara president while Rhodes held that title, and he couldn't promote Rhodes to chairman while Lewis was around. And he had promised to keep

Lewis on as chairman, for appearance's sake, until the end of 1976. For a man who hated titles, who had other things to think about just then (including a recent diagnosis of colon cancer), it must have been a frustrating year. But he managed to get through it, and to keep everyone more or less happy. Lewis did leave at the end of the year, and Rhodes was made chairman. And in November—over the last-ditch protests of Rhodes and Waters—Jack O'Hara became the new Digest president. (Waters left shortly thereafter, replaced as treasurer by a younger man named William Cross.)

A painful episode was over—an episode Wallace had hoped to avoid— and he was pleased with the result. Somehow, with all his other problems, he had managed to identify and raise to controlling positions the two executives most likely to carry on Reader's Digest in the Wallace tradition. They weren't perfect, either one of them. O'Hara was hard-driving and irascible; Thompson could be heavy-handed and blunt. Lila couldn't stand either one, and had made her feelings about this very clear. But on this occasion—with the future of his company at stake—DeWitt for once didn't listen.

In December, shortly after the O'Hara announcement, the old man read an article in *Forbes* magazine about how hard it was becoming for big companies to remain private. He sent the article to Thompson with a one-sentence covering memo: "Dear Ed: I hope you and Jack will always keep RDA a private corporation. Wally."

CHAPTER TWENTY-TWO

For decades, DeWitt and Lila Wallace had seemed indestructible, almost immortal. Digesters who had arrived at Headquarters in the fifties, fresh from college, were now middle-aged and worn out. Yet in all that time the King and Queen hadn't seemed to change at all. In the mid-seventies, however, age caught up with them so fast it seemed to take them by surprise.

For Lila, the process began in 1973, when Digest executives first went after Bill Kennedy. "The knives had been out for Bill for years," recalls Fred Stanyer. "But no one was going to make a real move without solid evidence. Early that year, I began to hear rumors. So I called Bill to warn him. 'Watch your ass, my friend,' I said, 'because Barney McHenry is after it. If there is anything that needs cleaning up, you'd better clean it up now.'"

But it was too late. Kennedy had been careless, and there was no longer any easy way to "clean it up." Among the several homes he maintained at the time was a beach house on the island of St. Martin. During the winter of 1972, someone from the Digest world attended a party there, and on one of Bill's walls spotted a painting that was meant to be in Lila's collection. Then an art magazine ran a story that featured several photos of Bill's Sutton Place apartment. One of the photos clearly showed another painting that belonged to Lila. Shortly thereafter, Digest treasurer Dick Waters asked Barney McHenry to locate and inventory every piece of art Lila had ever purchased, and from that point on Bill's days were numbered.

McHenry's investigation hit pay dirt on a sunny day in October 1973. Gene Doherty had driven Lila into Manhattan that morning for her weekly appointment at the hairdresser—Kazan, on Park Avenue at Fifty-seventh Street. When she emerged from her beauty session, wig in place, makeup freshly applied, she found McHenry waiting in the limousine with Doherty. The chauffeur listened impassively while McHenry jumped from the car spouting the usual compliments—"How beautiful you look, Lila! How entrancing!"—and when his passengers were safely inside drove them over to the River Club on East Fifty-second Street.

At 2:30, when Lila and McHenry emerged from the club, Doherty knew right away that something was wrong: "After her martini, Missus was usually pretty jolly. But this time she was all business." McHenry told Doherty they had an errand to run and directed him to a warehouse on West Fifty-second Street between Eleventh and Twelfth Avenues.

As the car inched through midtown traffic, Doherty became aware of a discussion in the rear compartment about art, and in particular about a painting recently purchased in Lila's name. Crossing Eleventh Avenue, he spied the warehouse on the right. "Double-park, Gene," McHenry ordered. "And come inside with us."

The three of them rode a freight elevator to the third floor and stepped out into a long, narrow room lined on both sides with storage cubicles. A man appeared and led them to a cubicle halfway down the corridor. The man unlocked the door, and he and McHenry went inside. When they reappeared, they were carrying a large object wrapped in heavy cardboard. The man removed the cardboard and held the object under an overhead light. It was an oil painting inside an ornate frame. "Abstract. That I remember," says Doherty. "And the dominant colors were orange and blue."

Lila studied the painting for several moments, her expression changing from sour to furious. *"No, no!"* she said at last. "I have never seen this painting before. It has *nothing* to do with me."

"Okay, Lila," said McHenry. "I'll take care of it."

The painting in question (which was later sold at a considerable profit) had been purchased by Kennedy, with Lila's money, and was obviously being stored until he felt confident enough to hang it in his own home. Lila was shocked by the evidence McHenry had uncovered, and deeply hurt. Yet once again she refused to bring formal charges. Charging Bill Kennedy would have meant admitting to the world that she had been wrong, that another of her "angels" had proved to be a "devil" after all. So Bill was simply given instructions to get lost. "Barney was vicious about this," recalls Fred Stanyer. "Bill was forced to sell his homes and everything in them. He stashed the money into four shopping bags and fled to St. Martin."

When Bill Kennedy was sent away, much of the fun in Lila Wallace's life was banished as well. Now there was no one to care for her, no one who knew her well enough to connect with the lonely woman hiding behind the queenly façade. The few men she continued to see—Laurance Rockefeller, Tom Hoving at the Met, Peter Mennin at Juilliard—related to the façade only, and only on the level of money. Beyond them, there was no one.

So she began, out of desperation, to befriend her servants. When she and DeWitt had cocktails in the Game Room, she sometimes asked John and Ann Tichi to join them. "I would mix the drinks," recalls John, "and then Mrs. Wallace would raise that big gold cup and propose a toast: 'Here's to the four of us!' she always said. 'Thanks be to God there's no more of us!' "

Although DeWitt was stronger physically than Lila in those days, and more active generally, in other ways he was worse off. "Once his eyesight began to go, the process went very fast," recalls Betty St. John. "He also had trouble hearing—and zero patience with hearing aids—and his memory was rapidly disappearing. He always called me first thing every morning to check his schedule. Now he began calling over and over—'Good morning, Betty, what is my schedule for the day?' No sooner had he hung up than he would call again. This could go on all morning. I answered him each time. That's what I was paid to do. But it was very sad."

He began to appear in public less often, but when he did, he always managed somehow to seem on top of things. In the fall of 1975, in the midst of a futile campaign to wrest the Republican nomination from Gerald Ford, Ronald Reagan was invited to dinner at the Guesthouse (and afterward to spend the night in one of the guest suites upstairs). Wallace came down from High Winds to host the affair, which was attended by twenty *Digest* editors, plus the candidate and a single staff person. All through cocktails, Reagan kept patting everyone on the back, endlessly reiterating how pleased he was to be there, how relieved to be off the campaign trail, able at last to relax among friends. By the time dinner was called, it was clear that Wallace's patience was wearing thin.

The group sat down and immediately Reagan started in again. But now Wallace had heard enough. "Governor," he interrupted, "I'm delighted you feel that way, and pleased as punch we could offer you this chance for relaxation. In fact, we don't have an elaborate schedule planned. When we're done with dinner, we'd like to take you over to the VFW for a visit. Just a short talk and some questions. Then I promised my friends at the Elks that you would come by. But it will be late by then, so that shouldn't take long. And . . . *umm* . . . that's about it . . ." (Reagan's smile had faded and he was glaring at his advance man) ". . . *for tonight.* In the morning, at six-thirty, you're expected at the Knights of Columbus. That will be a full-dress breakfast, with reporters on hand, and after that. . . ."

By this point there were giggles around the table, and even Reagan's own man was beginning to grin. And finally it dawned on Reagan himself that Wallace was pulling his leg. His eyes widened, and he let out a loud guffaw. "Why, Wally, you old dog! *Haw! Haw!* You really had me going. But, you see, that's what I mean! To be among friends! To share some laughs! It's great. . . ." And there he went again.

Wallace didn't like effusiveness, or falseness of any kind. Yet he had endured both in one guise or another for more years than he cared to remember. Endless editorial luncheons. Black-tie dinners in New York, with speeches that curdled the brain. Lila's elaborate High Winds affairs. Of them all, the one party he had always enjoyed was the annual Old-Timers' Dinner held in the company cafeteria for veteran Digesters. He attended every year, and every year had a wonderful time. He chatted happily with the lowliest janitor, danced with the fattest secretary, listened to the family woes of the oldest grandmother. He always ended the evening with a funny speech, and the old-timers always applauded wildly. But the speech he gave in November 1976 remains the all-time favorite.

That the old man had something on his mind had become apparent to newly appointed Digest chairman Kent Rhodes that afternoon during the course of an unexpected phone call. "Kent," Wallace had asked, "do you happen to know the current rate of inflation?"

"Well, Wally, I think it's about six percent."

"Oh. Okay. Thank you." And he hung up.

Now, up on the dais with his top executives, Wallace was concluding his little talk in top form and the audience was howling. But not Rhodes. Wallace clearly had something up his sleeve, and it worried Rhodes because business had been slow that year and the Digest's profit margin was skimpier than usual. While Wallace waited for the old-timers to quiet down, he sucked at the side of his cheek the way he did when he was pleased. "Now," he went on, "Lila and I would like to end the evening with an announcement. We think it would be nice if everyone got a raise to match inflation . . . which Kent Rhodes here tells me is *six* percent."

The audience roared its approval, and again the old man had to wait for quiet. "On top of that, we want everyone earning less than forty thousand dollars a year to have an additional increase of *five* percent." More howls. Rhodes and Dick Waters, their bottom line crumbling beneath them, stared glumly at the floor. "And everyone earning over forty thousand dollars an additional *two* percent. We hate . . ." the crowd was on its feet now, with Wallace raising his arms for quiet ". . . we hate to make these promises unilaterally, without waiting for the board of directors to approve. But . . ." grinning broadly now, his dim eyes somehow twinkling ". . . we rather think they will."

It was a marvelously symbolic moment. With the end of his reign at hand, he had delivered an unmistakable message: What mattered to him were his people, his family of employees. The evening's little surprise had raised the cost of doing business by nearly 10 percent. But so what? The bottom line could go to hell.

After 1976, there were not many more such moments. Wallace had long been famous for his Christmas cards—hundreds of them every year, each with a personal note complimenting the recipient (friends, writers, heads of state, his barber, Digest editors) on some specific achievement. In 1976, this tradition came to a sad end. The card he and Lila sent out that Christmas was a somber gray, with a few dark birds sitting on the branches of a leafless tree. Inside, in place of the familiar Wallace handwriting, was a printed slip of paper: "My close-up vision has deteriorated so badly in recent months that I have difficulty reading my own handwriting. Hence I refrain from inflicting upon you a personal note, something I enjoyed doing in the past. DW."

His world was closing in on him, in several ways and faster than his colleagues understood. On a sunny afternoon that fall, he threw some tools into his Jeep and set off down one of his familiar roads. He drove slowly, cocking his head right and left, searching for the spot where his labors had ended the day before. By now he was working mostly on his knees, feeling the ground for obstacles, cutting brush, lifting and rolling away stones, operating more by touch than sight. It was exercise, slow going but purposeful. Exercise *without* purpose—all those editors jogging around the roads down at Headquarters, for example—left him mystified.

At some point during that long afternoon, a thick vine blocked his way. He tried to push it aside, leaning into it with his shoulder. It wouldn't budge. Several feet above his head, beyond where he could see, a tree had fallen across the vine, and the weight of the tree put the vine under extreme tension. Using a heavy-duty brush cutter, he tried to slice through the obstruction, squeezing the long handles with all his strength.

Suddenly, the vine gave way. The end under pressure snapped upward, smashing into his face. He was knocked backward, and for several seconds lay stunned on the ground. When he came to, he reached up with one hand and gently touched his lower jaw. His hand came away covered with blood and bits of broken teeth.

It was almost dark when John Tichi found him and brought him back to High Winds. A doctor came that night and sewed up his wounds, and the next morning Doherty drove him into New York for a painful session of dental surgery. When he recovered, he insisted on going back to his roadwork. But from this point on, a small group of those closest to Wallace—Gene Doherty, Betty St. John, Gordon Davies, James Stewart-Gordon—agreed among themselves that he could never be left alone again. "We let him keep to his schedule," says St. John, "but wherever he went we made sure there was someone on hand who knew the situation, who could be trusted to watch out for him, to get him over the awkward spots and pass him on to the next person. This went on for the rest of his life."

Thanks to this loyal band, and to his own iron determination not to give in, Wallace was able to fool most of his colleagues for another few years. But he did not fool his lawyer. "Oh, of course Barney knew!" says St. John. "He knew before anyone, from the first moment Mr. Wallace began to slip."

Beginning in 1976, McHenry began spending more and more time up at High Winds, often arriving uninvited and unannounced. "What's *he* doing here, Lila?" the old man would stage-whisper. "Did *you* invite him?" McHenry ignored such comments and did what he could to insinuate himself into the void so many before him had failed to fill. He never arrived at High Winds without gifts for Lila. He had his own children bake cookies for the Wallaces at Christmas. As DeWitt's eyes faded, he insisted on reading to him every Sunday from the *New York Times*. "Wally *hated* that!" says James Stewart-Gordon. "In fact, he hated McHenry, period. But he couldn't get rid of him."

Everyone down at Headquarters knew what was going on up at the Castle, and everyone worried about it. But McHenry had become the royal advocate, and there was no denying his power. He conferred with King and Queen daily, advised them, represented them, seemed at times almost to *be* them. To challenge him was to challenge the Wallaces themselves, and no one was willing to risk that.

But even as he neared his goal, McHenry paid a heavy price. "I was their *employee*," he explains, not bothering to hide his resentment. "Lila Wallace never let me forget this. We lunched often at the River Club, and I had certain jokes I was meant to perform. For example, I would point at the river. 'See that tugboat coming up there, Mrs. Wallace? Can you read its name?' And she would say, 'No! You *know* I can't!' 'Oh!' I would say. 'It's the *Lila*! It says so right there! L-I-L-A!' And she would *laugh* with pleasure. Thought that was the *height* of amusement. *But if I was ever late!* Say she lunched with someone else and I was to meet her at the club afterward to ride up to the Met. If I was one minute late . . . one *second* late . . . her car was gone! Lila Wallace would not wait one second for the likes of me!"

On a lovely Saturday afternoon in June 1977, McHenry and Fred Stanyer co-hosted a lavish garden party to celebrate the "Second Opening" of Boscobel. (Bill Kennedy's original furnishings had proved to be "historically inaccurate," so Lila had had to pay for a multi-million-dollar redecoration.) Lila arrived shortly before two, in a limousine driven by Gene Doherty, and was quickly wheeled to a table inside a huge tent set up on the Great Lawn between the mansion and the Hudson River. For several minutes, to her considerable irritation, the Queen of Reader's Digest sat alone. Then Stanyer caught sight of her and hustled over. *"Lila!"* he exclaimed. "I never saw you arrive! I *am* sorry!"

Stanyer waved to a waiter, and soon Boscobel's benefactress was sipping moodily from a plastic glass. Stanyer sat with her, and while he talked Lila gazed upon the passing throng. What she saw did nothing to improve her humor. Here and there she recognized a face, and returned a friendly wave. But for the most part this crowd of jet-set New Yorkers—the cream of Manhattan's arts establishment and clearly disdainful of everything *Reader's Digest* stood for—was far removed from the world of Lila Wallace.

After several minutes at Lila's side, Stanyer decided to risk a break. "Now, Lila," he said, "there are some very important people here—important to *Boscobel*—and I really should get around to greet them. Would you mind?"

"Of course not, Fred," said Lila. "After all"—and here she tossed a little Lila knife—"it's *your* party."

Before mixing with his guests, Stanyer located McHenry—the lawyer was holding forth for several attractive females—and pulled him aside. "For God's sake, Barney, get over to see Lila. *She's all alone!*" For the next half-hour, McHenry escorted small groups to Lila's table, presenting them to "the Founder of *Reader's Digest*" and "the lady we have to thank for this wonderful restoration." The New Yorkers nodded and smiled and were briefly polite. But there was condescension in the air and Lila sniffed it instantly. She sipped at a second glass of champagne, growing angrier by the minute, and when she was alone again she looked around for Doherty.

Before she could catch his eye (he was standing by the tent's entrance, not ten feet away), McHenry reappeared. He knelt by her chair, so his face was level with hers, and began to speak directly into her ear. From where he stood, Doherty could not hear the conversation. But as he watched his mistress's face, it was clear that the lawyer's words were not having the desired effect. Lila's eyes narrowed in anger, and suddenly she said something that caused McHenry to stand abruptly and stalk away.

Now Lila turned and waved furiously to Doherty. The chauffeur hustled to her side. "Gene," she muttered, "let's get out of here! *Now!*" She was beside herself—so mad, Doherty recalled later, that he thought she was going to order him to drive the limousine right through the tent, smashing the tables and stampeding the guests. He wheeled her quickly to the car and somehow —ignoring her wild gesticulations—got her safely inside. As he was packing up the wheelchair, he heard someone shout *"Lila!"* It was McHenry. The lawyer came running over. "Lila!" he said again, kneeling by the car window. "Where are you going? The ceremony hasn't. . . ."

"That may be," snapped Lila Wallace. "But I am leaving even so."

"But . . . this party is all for you. Please don't leave!"

"Gene!" she snapped. *"Let's go!"*

As the limousine rolled slowly away, Lila fumed in the backseat. Just after Doherty turned south onto Route 9D, her anger exploded into a tirade against McHenry. "Can you imagine the nerve of that man, Gene? He borrowed forty thousand dollars from me—*three years ago!* Now all of a sudden he says he wants to pay it back. To *Boscobel!* He must think I'm *stupid!* I told him he borrowed it from me, he can damn well pay it back to me. He should be *fired!*"

"Yes, ma'am," Doherty murmured. "Terrible. Just terrible." But a knowing smile spread across his face. Had Lila Wallace said yes to McHenry's suggestion—a pretty good bet, thought Doherty—then the borrowed money would have been returned to Boscobel. *And wouldn't that make a tidy tax deduction,* mused Doherty. *Who kept track of such things? Hell, that was Barney's job.*

But the lawyer's timing had been wrong. Lila's anger had kept her mind clear, and so the little scheme had failed. Thinking about this, the smile faded from Doherty's face. Part of McHenry's job was to protect Lila Wallace from the gathering sharks. *What if he was a shark himself?*

Something else happened that spring that boded ill for the Wallaces. In late March, John and Ann Tichi gave notice, promising to stay on only until a replacement couple could be found. A few days later, John and Mary Strasburger drove through the High Winds gate in a battered '67 Cadillac. They ran out of gas halfway up the hill, and the new butler/cook team had to coast silently back to the cottages, where Doherty pumped them a few gallons out of the estate tank. Doherty then accompanied them up to the Big House. They had only two suitcases between them, he noticed, and one of them was empty. It appeared to Doherty that they were stone broke.

Given the stature of their new employers, the Strasburgers' references seemed shockingly weak. John had worked for a time as a salesman in an upstate lumber yard, and most recently as assistant director of a funeral home in the Bronx. He was in his late forties, about five foot nine, with graying hair and pleasant Teutonic features. Except for an open, friendly manner, Mary Strasburger appeared to have no qualifications at all. She had been a housewife in Chicago—had no experience at anything else—and spoke in an accent that was part South Side street-tough and part West Virginia hillbilly.

Shortly after the Strasburgers' arrival, Jean Rossi began coming up from the Digest Guesthouse to help out part-time in the High Winds kitchen. When she first encountered John, she could not believe her eyes. "It was pitiful that people like the Wallaces should have to live in a house run by someone like John Strasburger," she says today. "I kept asking myself: *Why? Why? Why?* Mr. McHenry knows they don't belong here. *Why did he hire them?*"

Although it was immediately apparent that neither Strasburger knew how to cook, John was clever enough to fake the basics, so he prepared the meals while Mary served. Except when there were guests. Whenever company came, John told Mary to disappear ("Keep your mouth shut and stay out of sight") while he cooked and served and somehow brought it off. "John was a real smoothy," says Doherty. "He could put on a show when he had to."

Shortly after his arrival, Strasburger asked caretaker Neil Gollogoly to install new locks on all the doors in the servants' wing and in the warren of storerooms that had once been DeWitt's handball court. Gollogoly was a wise old Scot who had worked for Harry Wilcox long enough to know a crook when he saw one. He did as Strasburger ordered, but had an extra set of keys made. That summer, while the Strasburgers were on vacation, he and Doherty went exploring. They discovered that John had already moved dozens of items—antiques, rugs, clothing, even valuable artworks—from Lila Wallace's attic to the storerooms. Doherty immediately reported this discovery to McHenry. "John is takin' things, Barney!" the chauffeur insisted. "We got to do an inventory. Without an inventory, we can't prove a thing!"

McHenry listened, shook his head impatiently and promised to look into it.

CHAPTER TWENTY-THREE

"For the first time in years one feels electricity at the shop, an unleashing of new energies which bodes well for the future. Its generator is Ed Thompson . . . a brilliant choice as Editor-in-Chief, certain to grow quickly to the stature of Chairman. Unlike his predecessor, he will never avoid making a decision. Also unlike his predecessor—and very much like you yourself—he has much to heart the interests of the little guy."

So began a memo to DeWitt Wallace from Dennis McEvoy, written in the fall of 1976. McEvoy had returned to Pleasantville after several years as a roving editor in Europe at least in part to serve as Wallace's spy down at Headquarters—to check on Thompson, to analyze the changes he was making, to assess morale. His report was favorable. Ed Thompson had gotten off to a flying start as editor of the world's largest magazine, and the old man was pleased.

During the Lewis years, the *Digest* had grown stale. Many of the writers hired by Wallace decades before were still on the payroll, grinding out formula pieces on subjects that may have been relevant once but were no longer, and Lewis simply let them keep writing. As new writers were added to the ranks, the number of original articles being produced began to exceed the magazine's capacity to use them, so many of these articles ended up in "inventory." With so many articles in inventory, pressures rose to use more of them in the magazine, leaving less room for material from outside sources. By the mid-seventies, calling the *Digest* a "digest" was stretching matters, since up to 80 percent of its contents was original.

As diplomatically as possible, Thompson pensioned off a dozen of the old warhorses (the youngest in the group was sixty-eight), while quietly revising their pensions so that to a man they were better off in retirement than they had been as semiactive writers. A few new writers were hired, but mostly Thompson looked to other magazines and newspapers to fill the gap. "We are meant to be a reading service," he pointed out. "Wally's original idea was to offer subscribers a selection of the best writing from all sources. I believe that providing that service has always been our real secret."

One thing did change, however. "The *Digest* is a conservative magazine," said Thompson. "We have always believed that problems can be solved, that corruption needs to be rooted out, that tax dollars should be spent wisely. But these problems exist no matter which party is in power. The bureaucracy tends to operate as a juggernaut, and juggernauts tend to make mistakes. Our political role is to attack the mistakes. It doesn't matter whether they are made by Republicans or Democrats."

During the summer of his second year in command, Thompson invited eighty *Digest* editors from around the world to a weeklong meeting at Jackson Hole, Wyoming. "We are here to get to know one another," he said during his opening remarks, "and to discuss our common problems and opportunities." The new editor then moved bravely into a subject that had been dividing Digesters for decades. Conservatives in Pleasantville, and even more so in the Washington bureau, had always regarded the *Digest*'s international editions as propaganda vehicles charged with establishing the superiority of the American Way over the evils of communism. But others, including virtually all of the foreign editors, saw a different role. Wallace's original vision, they argued (echoing Thompson's own conviction), had not been about politics at all, but about offering subscribers a "service." That service was the key to the U.S. edition, and providing a similar service—offering a broad sampling of the best journalism produced in each individual country—ought to be the goal of the international editions.

To the delight of the foreigners, Thompson quickly made it clear that he supported their view: "I believe every edition should assume as much autonomy as it can handle. Accordingly, editions which have shown an aptitude for producing their own original material will be encouraged to produce several articles a year not subject to prior Pleasantville approval."

Thompson's words infuriated Washington staffers at the meeting, and they immediately met behind closed doors to work out a response. The vehicle they chose to deliver their verdict was a blunt one. Melvin Laird had resigned as Nixon's defense secretary at the height of Watergate and immediately thereafter accepted a position as the *Digest*'s Washington lobbyist on postal affairs. His contract also called for him to sign four *RD* articles a year (the actual writing to be done by John Barron, an editor at the bureau with close connections at the CIA), and it was in this capacity that Laird had been invited to the Jackson Hole meeting.*

Now Laird was more than willing to stand before the "liberated" foreigners and drop a bomb. "I've just returned from a tour of Europe for the White House," he began. "It strikes me that the only country in the Western alliance with a *real leader* is the United States." Smiling at his stunned colleagues, Laird went on to deliver a speech extolling America and implying that only by aping the United States could the countries represented by his audience ever achieve similar greatness. The foreign editors were thunderstruck. When Laird sat down, several rose to their feet to denounce his message. But Thompson himself appeared unruffled by the controversy. "Only by putting our problems on the table can we bring our collective wisdom to bear on solving them," he said. "This requires frankness and candor, and sometimes a bit of heat. But let's not be shy. I expect everyone to work very hard at this."

Beneath his gruff exterior, Thompson was a man who placed great faith in

---

* The Laird/Barron collaborations inevitably served the needs of the Pentagon or the CIA. In one article, Laird accused the Russians of "cheating on SALT." When a *Digest* researcher checked this with Paul Warnke, the senior SALT negotiator, Warnke was furious. "Mel knows that's not true," he fumed. "The Soviets haven't dismantled those missiles because the weather's been too cold. They told us about the problem, and we said okay." Faced with Warnke's objection, Barron shrugged. "I only wrote what Jamie told me," he said, referring to Donald Jameson, a senior officer in the CIA's Soviet Division who regularly fed information to trusted journalists.

his colleagues, and this quality tended to bring out the best in them. But among those at the Washington bureau it brought out something very different. To these men, Thompson's openness—his insistence on seeing both sides of controversial issues—marked him as a liberal. And in their minds, liberals were the enemy.

Thompson's challenge had been to return *Reader's Digest* to its former ways, a process accomplished (for the most part) with the support of his colleagues and the approval of DeWitt Wallace. The problems new president Jack O'Hara faced were very different. The business operations of Reader's Digest had never veered far from the old ways. Although Al Cole had always longed to exploit the company's vast potential for greater profit, Wallace had stood in the way. Advertising was allowed in, and Sweepstakes. But beyond those two concessions, Cole had run into a stone wall.

Now, for the first time, the keys to the gold mine had been turned over to a businessman, and Wallace himself appeared to be fading from the scene. Cole's successors—ambitious young ad salesmen who had learned their trade at his feet—were eager to prove him right. "It's time to make money," they insisted, and they could hardly believe their ears when O'Hara hesitated. "But where is the Digest *going?*" they demanded. "We are so stodgy —a stale old magazine, some musty books and records. Other companies are expanding, getting into new products, changing their ways. What about us?"

Experts in the media industry agreed with these arguments, and routinely criticized O'Hara for failing to exploit the power of the *Digest* name and its priceless mailing lists. But O'Hara held firm. "We march to a different drummer," he insisted. "We will not abandon our traditional values even if this means sacrificing growth. How big do we have to be, anyway? *Why* do we have to grow? These are philosophical questions, and I don't have the answers. If you are achieving your primary goals—providing customers with good products at a fair price, caring for your employees, offering them a good place to work—why change?"

For the most part, O'Hara's colleagues weren't interested in philosophical questions, and pressures to make more money—from young Turks like George Grune and Dick McLoughlin—were unrelenting. "But in those days I could still turn to Wally for help," recalls O'Hara. "He had a little speech he would make: 'If your only reason for being in business is to make a profit, then it doesn't matter what you produce—beans, Cadillacs, screwdrivers, socks. But I am not in this because I have a Messianic vision that the world needs better *hosiery!* The Digest has a *mission* in the world!' "

Throughout the spring of 1977, Grune and his colleagues hounded O'Hara about using merchandise premiums to attract new customers. "Everybody else is doing it," Grune insisted. "We can double our response." When O'Hara had heard enough, he turned on Grune. "Look, George," he said, "if you want to press the matter, go up and see Wally yourself." Grune did this, and when he came back down from High Winds it was obvious he had received a lecture. "The limitation on using merchandise as premiums comes from DeWitt Wallace," he wrote to his colleagues. "I've discussed the matter with Mr. Wallace. He feels the same way today. He is *not* in favor of using merchandise premiums to sell books and other RD products."

Later that summer it was Dick McLoughlin's turn. As director of magazine operations, McLoughlin was eager to raise the price subscribers paid for the *Digest*. "Our current price is ridiculously low," he insisted. "We are practically giving the thing away, and it is costing us plenty. We've got to raise the price!" When O'Hara grew tired of this, he pointed again toward High Winds. "Take your arguments up there, Dick," he said. "See what the old man says." McLoughlin did as O'Hara sugggested and got another lecture.

But Wallace couldn't be counted on to hold back the tide forever. He was old and tired, and there were times when the arguments of his younger colleagues overwhelmed him. From the beginning, he had refused to allow advertising for cigarettes or alcohol into his magazine. Over the years this policy had cost the company tens of millions in revenue—money that came from his and Lila's own pockets—but the old man never showed the slightest interest in abandoning it. Cigarettes were bad for people, period. Believing that, how could he accept advertising for cigarettes? And if he *did* accept cigarette ads, how could he crusade against smoking? For him, the issue was that simple. His feelings about alcohol were similar but not as deeply held. No one had tried to change his mind about cigarettes, but over the years a number of ad directors had sought to persuade him to accept ads for liquor.

In January 1977, Charles Hepler was *Digest* publisher, and in that year Hepler began to think the old man might finally be ready to change his mind about liquor ads. But Hepler had been turned down before, so he approached Wallace this time through Ed Thompson.

"Charlie asked me to do it, and I agreed," says Thompson. "I was more or less neutral on the subject, so I simply asked Wally what his views were. His answer was impressive":

1. People have faith in the Digest because the Company appears to put the public interest above making as much money as possible.
2. An ideal if impractical RD advertising policy would be to accept ads only on the basis of presumed interest and informative value to the reader. Liquor and beer ads have less intrinsic appeal to most people than any other class of advertising.

3. Most moderate drinkers consider the custom a pleasant social diversion. Yet all too often drinking becomes a curse and a cause of untold anguish. Drinking is responsible for frightful auto accidents and many deaths. For an alcoholic, seeing ads for liquor in a family magazine certainly accentuates the problem. Wally 1/4/77

The matter simmered for a year, during which time the ailing Wallace heard plenty about liquor ads. "McLoughlin and the others were relentless," recalls O'Hara. "They chipped away at him and chipped away at him, and eventually he got sick of it." In April 1978, after suffering a mild stroke, Wallace spent several days in Northern Westchester Hospital. While he was recovering, a memo announcing acceptance of liquor ads was prepared by the advertising department and sent up to High Winds under a cautious note from Ed Thompson. "Wally," wrote Thompson. "Would you confirm, by initialing this memo, that it is now RD policy to accept advertising for beer and wine products?" Underneath this message, Wallace scrawled, "OK. DW. 4/8/78," and that was that. "It was the only compromise I ever knew him to make," says O'Hara.

In his efforts to maintain "Wallace standards" at the Digest, Jack O'Hara found a ready ally in Ed Thompson. Yet the relationship between the two men was complicated from the beginning by their ill-defined authorities. As editor, Thompson had expected to become overall boss, as Lewis and Wallace had been before him. Wallace had withheld this. As president, O'Hara controlled the real power centers of the company. But O'Hara was unsure of his strength. His personal relationship with Wallace was not as close as Thompson's, and he was well aware of the editor's traditional dominance.

When Wallace asked him to outline an "executive structure" for the future, O'Hara respectfully suggested that he and Thompson, as president and editor, should become co-chairmen of the board when Kent Rhodes retired in 1977. Thompson was not so reticent, arguing that the chief executive of the company should always be the editor-in-chief. "For the moment, our titles are irrelevant," he suggested in a note to Wallace. "Jack and I understand our roles and where our authorities lie. It's the future that worries me. To preserve the traditional final word for the Editor-in-Chief, I suggest that the President be named Chief *Operating* Officer and that the Chief Executive Officer always be the Editor-in-Chief."

Thompson's aggressiveness may have done him in. He was a *journalist*, after all, and his outspoken conviction that the Digest had a mission in the world made his business colleagues uneasy. If Thompson became CEO, they figured, the long-awaited opportunity to push the profit button might vanish. O'Hara, despite his obvious commitment to Wallace values, was felt even so to be a tough-minded businessman with a clear appreciation for the bottom line.

But only DeWitt Wallace could make the final decision. While he pondered what to do, he turned for advice to Harold Helm and Laurance Rockefeller. In January 1977, on the basis of their recommendation, Wallace dismayed his editors by naming Jack O'Hara CEO. "O'Hara has the best-rounded background," Harold Helm told the press. "He was the obvious choice for the job."

Perhaps. But the naming of O'Hara left the direction of the Digest almost as murky as before. O'Hara was CEO, yet he reported to Wallace. Thompson was "only" editor-in-chief. Yet he did not report to O'Hara. "It wasn't clear *who* I reported to," he says. "In my own mind I, too, reported to Wallace."

So who, really, was running things? No one seemed to know. O'Hara ran the business side. Thompson ran editorial. Where the two sides overlapped —at just the point where a single strong individual was needed to lead the company into the post-Wallace era—there was a vacuum. To some, it seemed a vacuum made for mischief. And now for the first time there were murmurings in the corridors about the growing influence of Laurance Rockefeller.

For years, the Digest's directors had met once a month in what was known as the editorial conference room, a modest space located between the editorial and business ends of the Headquarters building. Wallace, who in any case rarely attended board meetings, thought the room perfectly adequate. So did Hobe Lewis. So did Jack O'Hara and Ed Thompson. But in the late seventies there came rumblings of dissatisfaction. "Laurance wasn't happy with that room," says O'Hara, "and he used Barney McHenry to hound me about it. 'The room isn't right,' Barney kept insisting. 'We need something bigger, something that reflects the stature of Laurance Rockefeller.' "

Eventually, funds were allocated to construct a new board complex. Several existing offices were vacated, and under great secrecy the work began. When it was completed, a single huge door existed where before there had been several smaller ones. The door was kept locked, and this inevitably led to wild stories about what lay behind it. In fact, the new complex was every Hollywood director's vision of how an American corporate boardroom should look. The main space was sixty feet long, with twelve-foot ceilings from which hung crystal chandeliers. The walls, hung with several of the finest paintings in the Wallace collection, were paneled in rich wood. In the center of the room was an immense mahogany table surrounded by oversized mahogany-and-leather chairs. Along the right side of the room were doors leading to several smaller spaces—committee rooms, a telephone room, a bar, an elaborate kitchen, a men's room lined with marble and glistening with brass.

As descriptions of the plush facility spread around Headquarters, old-timers shook their heads in bemusement. The new boardroom seemed to them to symbolize everything DeWitt Wallace despised in the world—ego, pretense, hypocrisy—and also in some vague way to be a harbinger of things to come.

After the Affair of the Boardroom, the whispering about Rockefeller rose several decibels. *What was he up to?* people wondered. *Why would a Rockefeller sit on the board of Reader's Digest?* No one could answer these questions. Rockefeller himself was seldom seen at Headquarters. He attended board meetings once a month, arriving in a helicopter that landed in the field behind the Guesthouse. But he paid little attention to the proceedings and afterward was quickly off again. No one seemed to know him very well, and his opinions about the *Digest,* to the extent that he had any, were never quoted by anyone.

In 1975, Rockefeller had prevailed on Hobe Lewis to publish an article he had written called "The Case for a Simpler Life-Style." Digesters read his article eagerly, searching for clues to the great man's presence among them. "What is meant by such a life-style?" Rockefeller asked. "In my own experience I know that cutting and splitting firewood can bring spiritual reward. . . . More and more people are walking to work or riding bicycles. . . . Others have discovered that leaving lights on unnecessarily is a habit that cannot be justified by convenience. . . . Some may find it ironic that one who has been blessed with material resources should be advocating such measures, but . . ."

Digesters found his advocacy more hilarious than ironic. In fact, Laurance had made himself an easy target, recommending that others walk to work while he himself traveled by personal helicopter, private jet, silver Bentley, and converted PT boat. Yet there was something ominous in the very fact of the article. Laurance was playing Wallace's song (all those references to "chopping wood" and "turning off lights") so blatantly as to give rise to further questions: *What was he after? Who is running this company?* In the absence of hard answers, a consensus began to grow among the employees that in some mysterious way Laurance Rockefeller was "closing in."

CHAPTER TWENTY-FOUR

Even as a child, Laurance was the Rockefeller most often compared to John D., Sr. The two men shared a strong physical resemblance—deadpan face, straight nose, mocking eyes that seemed to absorb and dismiss most of what passed before them. There was also in each man a marked sense of irony

Janet Davis Wallace, mother of DeWitt, shown here at age forty with her three eldest children: Benjamin Bruce, Helen and young Robert. (Macalester College Archives)

James Wallace, DeWitt's father, in a portrait painted when James was seventy-eight. (Macalester College Archives)

DeWitt at age fourteen, with his bicycle behind the old frame house at 1596 Summit Avenue, across from the Macalester campus. This was Janet Wallace's favorite photo. (Macalester College Archives)

The Macalester College hockey team, winter of 1908–1909. DeWitt is third from left in the bottom row; to his left is Barclay Acheson, whose sister Lila would become DeWitt's wife and co-founder of *Reader's Digest*. (Macalester College Archives)

From left to right: Jane,
Evangeline, Lila Bell and Marta
Mae Acheson. (Macalester
College Archives)

Lila at her graduation from the
University of Oregon in 1911.
(Macalester College Archives)

The basement storeroom at 1 Minetta Lane, in New York's Greenwich Village, where *Reader's Digest* was born. (Wallace Estate)

Pendleton Dudley's fieldstone garage in Pleasantville, New York. The Wallaces moved here from Greenwich Village in July 1922, establishing living quarters above the garage and "business headquarters" in the tiny pony shed at far left. (Wallace Estate)

Lila at her "editor's" desk in 1936. Although she contributed little to the magazine, she was in every sense Co-Owner and Co-Boss, and no one was allowed to forget it. (Wallace Estate/Wendell MacRae)

Lila's brother Barclay was a Presbyterian minister and executive director of the Near East Foundation. In 1935, he abandoned the preacher's role to become Lila's lieutenant in Pleasantville. (Wallace Estate)

Opposite page

DeWitt and Lila circa 1930. They had much to smile about: Circulation of their magazine was now 400,000, with annual revenues nearing $1 million. "They were a formidable combination," a family member later recalled. "Part Presbyterian fundamentalist; part nineteenth-century Dakota street fighter."(Macalester College Archives)

Downtown Pleasantville in 1936. *Reader's Digest* editorial offices were now housed on the top floor of the Mt. Pleasant Bank & Trust Co.(building on the left); the business offices were in the First National Bank Building (from which this photo was taken); additional departments of the growing company were located in fourteen other places around town. (Fortune)

The Wallace estate outside Mt. Kisco, New York—the "perfect home" Lila had dreamed of since she was a child. "This is my fairy castle," she wrote to her mother in 1939. "I call it . . . HIGH WINDS." DeWitt called it "Lila's place," and worried that it was "too extravagant." (Wallace Estate)

The living room at High Winds, with Lila's favorite Renoir on the wall above the fireplace. (Wallace Estate)

The Teahouse at High Winds. In her later years, Lila "meditated" here in a canopied four-poster draped with gauzy curtains. (Wallace Estate)

Looking west from the pool at High Winds. This was DeWitt's favorite view—across the rolling hills of Westchester County all the way to the Hudson River and the Catskill Mountains. (Wallace Estate)

Reader's Digest headquarters in Chappaqua, New York, in 1939. (Wallace Estate)

A statue of Pegasus, Reader's Digest corporate symbol, presides over an intimate garden on the Digest grounds. (Wallace Estate)

Fred and Judy tie the knot before a cast of hundreds. Several Wallace servants can be seen observing the ceremony from Lila's bedroom terrace and Wally's Tower window. (Courtesy of the Thompson family)

With the reception in full swing, DeWitt and friend Wendell MacRae flew overhead in DeWitt's silver airplane, snapping photos of the "fairy tale come true." (Courtesy of the Thompson family)

At the High Winds Lookout, with Byram Lake far below, DeWitt charms the bridesmaids. (Courtesy of the Thompson family)

Judy and Fred Thompson— the "new" Lila and the "new" Wally—strolling at High Winds before their wedding in May 1939. (Courtesy of the Thompson family)

Lila and Fred "march down the aisle" following the wedding rehearsal. "This is the quintessential Lila," Fred's son Geoffrey Thompson has observed. "The belle of the ball forever." (Courtesy of the Thompson family)

In 1951, Lila and DeWitt made the cover of *Time*. This portrait by Boris Chaliapin perfectly captures her indomitable conviction and his shy determination. (Copyright 1951 Time, Inc. Reprinted by permission.)

Opposite page

General Manager Al Cole, surrounded by his key executives. Seated (from left): Harry Wilcox, Kent Rhodes, Cole, secretary Suzanne Quarenghi; standing: N. R. Norton, Les Dawson, Frank Herbert, Fred Thompson, Jack Maloney, George Sprague. (Wallace Estate/Wendell MacRae)

In 1964, the Wallaces stunned Al Cole by choosing handsome editor-in-chief Hobart Lewis to be the new president of *Reader's Digest*. (Time)

W. Barnabas McHenry became RD's corporate counsel in 1959. By the early seventies he was handling the Wallaces' personal affairs as well, and by 1976—despite the distrust he aroused at Headquarters—he was firmly established as the Founding Couple's "royal advocate." (Marilyn K. Yee/NYT Pictures)

COMPANY NEWS

Reader's Digest: Scene of A Struggle

Continued From Page A1

old, did not assume control of the voting stock.

"It was coincidental that Lila died shortly after Jack's resignation," said William J. Cross, referring to Mr. O'Hara.

Mr. Cross, who has become president and chief operating officer, is now one of two trustees of the trust controlling the company's voting stock. The other is Laurance S. Rockefeller, who is 74 and a former chairman of the Rockefeller Brothers Fund. Together they will name four other trustees during the months to come, Mr. Cross said.

Mr. Cross, who is also 56, said he could not speculate on who the new trustees might be, but he indicated that he and Mr. Rockefeller would probably choose two officers of the company and two outsiders.

A Look at the Candidates

Lila Wallace
Co-founder of Reader's Digest

Changes at Reader's Digest

Shortly before the death of Lila Wallace, crucial changes were made in the Wallace Trust's board of directors — which would control Reader's Digest after her death. The company's two top executives, who also served as directors of the Trust, resigned, leaving the voting stock controlled by two men.

Remaining

Laurance S. Rockefeller

William J. Cross

Resigned

Edward T. Thompson
Former editor in chief of Reader's Digest

John A. O'Hara
Former president of Reader's Digest

The New York Times / June 1, 1984

When *Outward Bound* (a recipient of Wallace millions) suggested a rafting trip on Utah's Green River in 1977, DeWitt eagerly accepted. He was eighty-eight at the time and almost totally blind and deaf. (Wallace Estate)

In June 1984, a front-page story in the *New York Times* revealed to the world the bizarre details behind the "Great Pleasantville Coup." (New York Times)

For twenty-five years, Gene Doherty served Lila and DeWitt Wallace as trusted chauffeur, caretaker and friend. When the Digest fired him after Lila's death, he could hardly believe it. (Courtesy of the Doherty family)

After a brief stint as head of the Voice of America, Ken Tomlinson returned to Pleasantville in 1984 to help new editor-in-chief Ken Gilmore lead the world's most widely read magazine away from the "independent journalism" of the Wallace-Thompson era into the paths of political righteousness as defined by Ronald Reagan. (USIA)

Following the coup that shook Pleasantville in 1984, former ad salesman George
Grune became the Digest's new Chairman and CEO. (Duke University)

and a personal coldness only partly ameliorated by a self-deprecating laugh. "Mr. Senior" had become the richest (and most vilified) man in America not by creating things so much as by orchestrating power. So it was with Laurance. "Orchestrate" is a word he likes to use, and he has made it a lifetime practice to observe and analyze situations—people, opportunities, circumstances—and then, from behind the scenes, to orchestrate the whole in a way that produces the result he desires.

After graduating from Princeton in 1932, Laurance spent two years at Harvard Law School discovering that his real interest, like that of his grandfather, lay in business. In the late thirties, sensing that the coming war might offer numerous opportunities for profit, he began to pour venture capital into a number of small companies in the fields of aviation, electronics, rocket engines and nuclear energy—companies that offered great promise at great risk. Then he set about eliminating the risk by exerting Family connections and the kind of money others could only dream about.

By the mid-fifties, through the shrewd orchestration of capital, power and influence, Laurance had converted $9 million into $40 million. But that was as far as he could go. Taking the logical next step—openly assembling the pieces necessary to obtain a controlling position in some industry, for example, or seeking in any direct way to make *really* big money—was off limits. His father, John D., Junior, had spent a lifetime and a vast fortune rescuing the Family name from the moral opprobrium brought on by Rockefeller Senior's "industrial terrorism." This achievement—the creation of a Family Myth that portrayed the Patriarch as a moral paragon and his heirs as superior beings devoted only to the well-being of their fellow citizens—could not be put at risk.

So Laurance began to look for some other way to make a name for himself. In 1947, when he and his brothers divvied up the Family's philanthropic arms, Laurance had been put in charge of Jackson Hole Preserve, Inc., the foundation set up by Junior to further the Family's conservation aims. Although he enjoyed this responsibility, considering himself an "outdoorsman," it was not something he took seriously. This attitude changed in 1952 with the publication of a far-reaching presidential report called *Resources for Freedom*. Put together in large part by Nelson Rockefeller and other Family associates, the report equated "conservation" with the opening of federal lands to private interests. Suddenly, Laurance began to take a different view of conservation. "We can take this development [the environmental movement] in stride," Laurance reassured the Congress of American Industry in 1963. "It will turn out in the end to be just good business."

In 1964, after Lady Bird Johnson indicated that "beautifying America" would be her primary concern as First Lady, Laurance got himself named to her husband's Presidential Task Force on Natural Beauty. Soon he and Lady

Bird were fast friends. In a courtship that foreshadowed in eerie detail his later pursuit of Lila Wallace, he invited Mrs. Johnson and her daughters to lengthy stays at the JY Ranch in the Grand Tetons, to his wife's mansion in Woodstock, Vermont, even to the great Rockefeller demesne at Pocantico. Soon a starry-eyed Lady Bird was publicly calling him "America's leading citizen-conservationist," and LBJ himself was paying attention. In 1965, after establishing a Citizen's Advisory Committee on Recreation and Natural Beauty, President Johnson asked Laurance to serve as chairman, making him in effect "adviser to the White House on environmental matters." But as the great conservation battles of the sixties began to unfold, it soon became apparent that Laurance Rockefeller's goals had little to do with preserving the environment.

Storm King Mountain rises like a great gray sentinel guarding the entrance to the beautiful Hudson River Highlands. In 1962, the Consolidated Edison Power Company announced a plan to hollow out the entire top of the mountain so that a hydroelectric pumping station and reservoir could be installed. Local residents quickly formed an organization called the Scenic Hudson Preservation Conference to fight the plan, arguing that it would disfigure one of the country's most scenic sites, and that releases from the reservoir would lead to massive fish kills and destruction of the river's marine environment. But when these citizens looked to their state's leading conservationist for support, they were sorely disappointed.

Why would Laurance Rockefeller favor the Con Ed plan? There were several reasons. Brother Nelson backed the plan because it would provide thousands of jobs for the Building and Trades Union, his political base in organized labor. Rockefeller Family members had been among the earliest investors in Con Ed stock, and estimates were that in 1965 the Family's Con Ed holdings were in the range of $10 million. Beyond that, there was the matter of "philosophy"—Laurance's belief in the "efficient use" of natural resources.

As the two sides in the angry Storm King debate firmed up their positions, a local congressman named Richard Ottinger introduced a bill that asked the Interior Department to make the entire Hudson Valley a federal preserve to protect it from local interests, and in particular from the interests of Nelson and Laurance Rockefeller. The Rockefellers responded like defenders of a country threatened by invasion. With reason, they regarded this part of the world as their own feudal domain, pointing to the 3,600 acres of the Family's great Pocantico estate, the entire Palisades Interstate Park given by Junior, the renovated manor estates of Historic Hudson Valley (Phillipsburg, Van Cortland, Sunnyside and Annandale, all of them owned by the family) and the several great tracts of farmland maintained by family members farther up the river.

With a gift from Laurance's American Conservation Association, Nelson created the Hudson River Valley Commission in 1965 "to protect the river and its surrounding area," and named Laurance as its chairman. "It is a matter of who can best save the Hudson," Laurance insisted at the time. "The burden should not be shifted to the Federal government so long as the state can do the job."

By "state," Laurance clearly had in mind himself and his brother the governor, and the real nature of their concern for the Hudson became clear later in 1965 when "their" state suddenly announced plans to build a six-lane superhighway connecting Manhattan in the south with Croton-on-Hudson to the north—right up the eastern bank of the river they were so intent on "protecting." Outraged environmentalists quickly assembled a one-two argument against the highway: one, no conceivable need for such a road had ever been demonstrated; two, the expensive dredge-and-fill operations required to build it would devastate whole populations of shad, striped bass, sturgeon and other local game fish. Secretary of the Interior Stewart Udall agreed: "Such an expressway in this highly scenic and historically significant corridor . . . would seriously impair the very values we are all trying to preserve."

What were the Rockefellers up to? Conservationists suspected that plans for the road had been drawn with the Family's land holdings in mind. So did the Interior Department. "The greatest financial benefit to the Rockefeller Family," said a confidential department memorandum written at the height of the controversy, "would accrue from the fact that the Expressway . . . will open up the Rockefeller land holdings to people as far away as New York City."

"Their father had been interested only in keeping people *away* from Pocantico," point out biographers Collier and Horowitz. "Yet Nelson and Laurance were looking ahead to a time when taxes would make the Family's 3,600 acres there a financial burden. Land for residential development in the area was selling for $100,000 an acre, and the brothers were intrigued with the idea of Pocantico's potential for tasteful condominium and single-family dwellings."

Under the guise of "protecting the river," the brothers were proposing to spend billions of taxpayer dollars on a road that would in fact "seriously impair" the river—while at the same time adding potential millions of dollars to the value of the Rockefeller land holdings at Pocantico and farther north. Originally opposed to the road, Secretary Udall began to crumble under the kind of heat only Rockefellers can bring to bear. "Laurance leaned on me very hard not to interrupt his plans for the Hudson," Udall said.

In 1968, when Udall announced his decision in favor of the road, the Sierra Club and other leading environmental groups obtained an injunction in federal district court prohibiting construction. Two years later, the Supreme Court flatly declined to hear New York's appeal of the matter—the issues really were that clear—and the expressway became a dead issue. At the same time, the National Environmental Policy Act—a direct outgrowth of the long battle over Storm King—became the law of the land. The act asserted that the public's interest in the environment was as weighty as the interests of special groups like Consolidated Edison or the Rockefeller brothers, and required all federal agencies henceforth to consider the environmental consequences of their actions.

As 1970 approached, it was clear that Laurance had reached the same sort of dead end as his brother Nelson. He had always prided himself on his ability to see through people and events, and to use this knowledge to stay ahead of the curve in whatever game he played. But the conservation movement had passed him by. While he was advocating "efficient use," the movement had fallen into the hands of "environmentalists"—serious people who meant what they said about saving the planet—and he had been left behind. "I feel sorry for Daddy," his daughter Lucy told Collier and Horowitz in 1970. "He missed the boat. He could have been creative."

But Laurance Rockefeller was not a man to be counted out prematurely. As his sixtieth birthday approached, a new game finally did appear—of all things, in the person of Lila Wallace—and Laurance was smart enough to see right off that this game offered possibilities for "creativity" that were irresistible. In his grandfather's day, at the height of the vilification, the humorist Mr. Dooley had said of the old pirate: "He is a kind 'iv society for the prevention of croolty to money. If he finds a man misusing his money, why, he takes it from him an' adopts it." Looking at Lila Wallace and her husband, sizing up the unexploited potential of their company, its global reach, its matchless mailing lists, its quaint notions about "serving readers," Laurance apparently began to chafe at the thought of all that money being "misused." There was an enormous opportunity for profit waiting in Pleasantville—it was like a giant Sitting Duck—and Laurance seemed to understand this from the beginning. And he was able to convince himself (as he had so often in the past) that taking advantage of the Duck was not only wise but *the right thing to do.*

In this, it must be admitted, he was not all wrong. With the Wallaces aging fast, their Duck would soon become an orphan in any case. If *he* didn't step forward to claim it, someone else (some greedy corporate raider, perhaps, with motives less charitable than his own) surely would. So a plan began to form—the most elaborate orchestration of his career—that in its essence amounted to a proceeding of adoption.*

---

* Mr. Rockefeller, who retired from the Digest board in 1993, declined to be interviewed for this book.

CHAPTER TWENTY-FIVE

Despite the murky conditions under which they operated, Ed Thompson and Jack O'Hara managed to get along remarkably well. "Jack and I thought the same way about most things," says Thompson. "At the outset, we made a decision that RD would not be run to maximize profits. It would be important to *be* profitable, but the magnitude of the profit would be irrelevant. That isn't necessarily how I might have run another company, or Jack either. But this was Wally's company, and we had promised him to run it his way."

"Ed and I were in lockstep on this," echoes O'Hara. "Wally wanted things done a certain way. Ed and I agreed to go along."

About the only thing the two didn't agree on was what to do about Barney McHenry. "Barney was a *lousy* counsel for a company the size of the Digest," says Thompson. "Once, when he drew up contracts transferring blocks of RD stock to certain charities, he neglected to put in language giving the company a right of first refusal should the charities want to sell. This could have been disastrous. We were a private company, after all, and wanted to stay that way." ("RD retained control over that stock in any case," insists McHenry today. "The missing language was irrelevant.")

Within a year of becoming editor-in-chief, Thompson wanted to fire McHenry, but he couldn't persuade O'Hara to go along. "Jack was unsure of himself vis-à-vis the Wallaces, and was therefore afraid to move against Barney," says Thompson. There was also concern that a move against McHenry might be seen as a move against Laurance Rockefeller. During the early seventies, as McHenry's position next to the throne solidified, Laurance had begun to take a friendly interest in the young attorney, and this interest had paid immediate dividends. Millions of Wallace dollars had already found their way to such Rockefeller institutions as the Metropolitan Museum, the Bronx Zoo and Lincoln Center, and a record of Wallace interest in other areas of concern to Laurance was steadily being established. "In effect," says James Stewart-Gordon, "Barney had become Laurance's inside man at High Winds. During the seventies, the Wallaces were frequently furious at Barney, and on several occasions Lila wanted to fire him. But Laurance had great influence over Lila. He praised Barney continually, and Lila listened."

As 1978 began, concern about who was running the Digest—and what would happen to the company when the Wallaces were "no longer with us" —became widespread among employees. To allay this concern, Thompson and O'Hara invited the Wallaces to lunch at the Guesthouse. "Without invading your privacy," they explained, "we would like to discuss the future of the company."

The King and Queen came down from the Castle for this occasion, but they weren't inclined to answer probing queries about their private affairs. "You may ask whatever you like," Lila declared at the outset of the lunch. "We may or may not deign to answer." DeWitt was less regal, but equally noncommittal. "These are complex issues," he said as the lunch was ending. "Why don't you submit something in writing."

With McHenry's help, Thompson wrote a memo that described what he believed to be the Wallaces' wishes for the future. The Wallaces studied this document carefully, then signed it without making a single change. It was subsequently distributed to all Digesters:

> We would like to put to rest speculation about the future of Reader's Digest after we are no longer with you:
>
> First, and most important, the Company will continue to be managed, as at present, by a group of executives dedicated to maintaining the kind of Company we founded—one that is privately owned (we will *never* go public) and that will always have the interests of its employees *as its highest priority.*
>
> Second, taxes on our personal estates will be paid by the estates. There will be no need to sell the Digest to pay taxes.
>
> Third, there are no outside stockholders. All stock in the Corporation is now owned by ourselves, by the Corporation, and by certain employees and directors.
>
> Finally, we individually own all of the voting stock of the Company. After our deaths, this stock will go into a Trust which will be administered by voting trustees already selected by us. The Digest is in good hands, and will remain in good hands.

At the time, that memo was generally accurate (except for the fact that 10 percent of RD's nonvoting stock, pledged to a variety of individual charities, was already on deposit at an umbrella group called Community Funds, Inc.). Within a few months, however, a series of events got under way—what insiders came to call "the War"—that would make it hard to tell *whose* hands the Digest was in, or indeed what kind of future lay ahead for the Kingdom.

The seeds of the War were sown in 1977, when it dawned on Al Cole that his old colleague Wallace was no longer making consistent sense. (The same insight Barney McHenry had reached two years earlier.) But if Wally wasn't "with it"—was forgetting things, agreeing to things he shouldn't agree to, signing papers he couldn't read, and so forth—then someone had to protect him and, even more, protect the Kingdom. Since neither Thompson nor O'Hara seemed positioned to accomplish this, Cole decided he would have to handle the job himself.

"Al was up at High Winds frequently throughout 1977," recalls Betty St. John. "He was the only one who could do that—go up there and pound on the door and get inside to see Mr. Wallace. He kept trying to explain what was going on, what Barney was up to, and so on. By the time he would finish, Mr. Wallace would be ready to *fire* Barney. They met once down at the office during this period, and I remember that Mr. Wallace became very upset. 'Oh, why do you let him *do* this, Al?' he kept asking. '*Why? Why?*' And Al said, 'That's why I'm *here*, Wally. That's why I'm asking you to make these changes.' So Mr. Wallace would agree to the changes. But then he would forget. The next day, Barney would go up to High Winds and explain that Al was a meddling old man who didn't understand anything. And Mr. Wallace would listen to this and reverse himself."

In January 1978, frustrated because his efforts to protect the Kingdom had gotten nowhere, Cole began lobbying for reappointment to the Wallace Trust. When McHenry learned of this, he decided the time had come for a confrontation. "Barney told Al to give up on the trust business, or else," says Peggy Cole. " 'If you don't cease trying to get on the trust,' he said, 'I will have the Wallaces declared incompetent. Then the courts will take over and we'll have a real mess.' *Just like that!* Al thought that threat was the worst thing he had ever heard. On the one hand, Barney swears Wallace is competent when he signs codicils prepared by Barney. But when Al tries to get on the trust, Barney insists Wallace is *incompetent!* What a nasty business! It caused Al to back off." (In fact, McHenry's threat of a court struggle caused *everyone* to back off. Under a court-appointed guardian, the rules governing the candy store were sure to change in unpredictable ways. No one seemed to favor that.)

Whatever his misgivings, Cole didn't back off for long. On February 17, 1978, an eighth codicil to the Wallace wills was quietly signed. Under its terms, Cole joined Rockefeller and Helm as an outside trustee, and (to keep things even, a crucial consideration) RD treasurer Bill Cross joined Thompson and O'Hara as an inside trustee. McHenry was furious, but did nothing to carry out his threat. ("Barney's threat was idle," says Ed Thompson. "He had more to lose from a declaration of incompetence than anyone.")

Later that spring the Wallaces' need for protection suddenly became much greater. On a Sunday evening early in April, DeWitt, now eighty-nine, was taken to Northern Westchester Hospital in a state of confusion following what was diagnosed as a mild stroke. On Monday, Lila insisted on being driven down to see him three times. When she emerged from the hospital after her second visit, she was clearly upset. Before the limousine had left the hospital grounds, her secret came bursting forth. "Wally has signed a document giving power of attorney to McHenry!" she confided to Doherty. "*I can't believe it!*

In his right mind, he would never have done that. *Never!* When he comes home, we will get that power back. I will see to it myself!"

It was a trying week for Lila Wallace. She had always been terrified of senility—"going mad," she called it—and the prospect of a senile husband wore on her nerves. "I can take the pain in my hips," she told Doherty. "But going mad . . . *that* I couldn't take."

When DeWitt returned to High Winds on Friday, the two of them had a quiet supper together in the breakfast room, then went to bed. The next morning, when Doherty went upstairs to help Lila with her wheelchair, it was immediately apparent that something had gone wrong. "She was like a child," Doherty says today. "Didn't know who she was or what was going on." A doctor was summoned and later that day Lila was taken to Northern Westchester. She had suffered her own stroke, less than a week after her husband, and clearly hers had been more severe. Four days later, she returned to High Winds. But her mind would never be the same again.

Lila's stroke posed a new problem. In her altered state, she didn't always recognize John or Mary Strasburger, and she frequently became agitated or angry when they appeared. She also tended to get up at night, and this was obviously dangerous. There was no choice but to hire a nurse.

For a few weeks, McHenry tried to get by with a day nurse only, using Mary Strasburger to tend Lila at night. But John complained so loudly that nurses had to be hired to work three shifts around the clock. John hired these nurses himself, and they reported directly to him. His rules were simple: "You are here to watch Mrs. Wallace, period. You do nothing without clearing it with me first. No schedule changes. No phone calls. And stay away from Mr. Wallace." Nurses who complied with these rules kept their jobs. Those who did not were quickly dismissed.

From this point forward—roughly from mid-1978 until their dying days —DeWitt and Lila Wallace were more or less totally isolated. Since DeWitt was blind, partially deaf and forgetful, and Lila lost in confusion, they were also completely helpless. John Strasburger controlled their world, and Strasburger in turn reported to McHenry. And McHenry had decreed that High Winds was now off-limits to all visitors not cleared with him in advance.

The lawyer's position in the Kingdom had suddenly become eerily powerful. He was a member of the Digest board and executor of the Wallace wills. His word at High Winds was law. And if the Wallaces (or anyone else) tried to fire him, he could cry "incompetence." And he would be right.

Yet seemingly he wanted more—wanted, in fact, to gain control over the Wallace Trust itself—and as 1978 came to an end he appeared to be almost there. But then he made a foolish error. Sometime that fall, in front of several friends, he boasted about his growing power in the Digest world. One of those who heard his boast was a friend of Harold Helm, and this man later told

Helm what he had heard. Helm then discussed the matter with Al Cole, and just after Christmas the two men had lunch with Wallace at High Winds.

During their meal, Cole asked Wallace whom he had named to be executors of his will. "Wally couldn't remember," Cole recalled later. "So we suggested to him that perhaps it was time to have outside counsel look over his and Lila's wills to see that they still made sense. He agreed to this."

Immediately after the lunch, Cole wrote a memo to Wallace to confirm their agreement. He showed the memo to Gordon Davies, Wallace's nephew and closest living relative. (Davies had been hired as Wallace's "administrative assistant" after World War II and for thirty years had labored in a small Headquarters office shared with Betty St. John.) At Cole's request, Davies sent a copy of the memo to Lord, Day senior partner Herb Brownell, and at the same time forwarded a backup copy to Cole. "I hope you will work closely with DW on this, Al," warned Wallace's next of kin in a covering memo. "Otherwise, the matter may simply be deferred from day to day."

Two weeks later, well aware of the potential for delay hinted at by Davies, Cole wrote to Wallace again. Both letters, and all the letters that followed, were typed on Betty St. John's special large-type machine. Yet, even so, Wallace was unable to read them. Cole had to deliver the letters to High Winds in person and read them aloud. The new letter, dated January 12, 1979, raised a different issue:

> You asked me to tell Barney McHenry that you *approved* of the idea of having Herb Brownell review the major factors that have to do with your estate and with the future of Reader's Digest. I did that. Barney . . . was quite upset with me for believing that such a review was desirable. Barney also told me he was the *sole executor* of your estate. For any one person to be in that position I believe is a mistake. You said on the phone that you agreed. If your sole executor should die, a *court* would have the right to appoint a new executor. Courts usually appoint a *politician. I can't think of anything worse for Reader's Digest. . . .* I hope you will tell Barney that you want him to meet with Brownell and to proceed with a proper study of the details that pertain to your estate and the future of Reader's Digest. You might telephone Brownell and tell him you have told Barney that his phone number is 212-344-4401. Al Cole.

Under the heat generated by Cole's efforts, McHenry suddenly took a reckless step. On the twenty-sixth of January, he appeared at High Winds bearing in his briefcase a tenth codicil to the Wallace wills. By means of this codicil, McHenry made official his status as sole executor of the two wills (Dewitt had been co-executor of Lila's will, and she of his). More importantly, he made himself the *seventh* trustee of the Wallace Trust, thus upsetting the carefully worked-out fifty-fifty balance between inside trustees and outside trustees—and, in effect, awarding to himself the swing vote on all matters relating to the Wallace estate and the future affairs of Reader's Digest. The codicil was signed by each Wallace—their barely legible signatures scrawled untidily in the general area above and (in Lila's case) slanting down across the dotted line—and the signings were witnessed by McHenry and two female employees from McHenry's own office. And that was that.

The copy of the codicil signed by DeWitt ended with a claim that he had "read aloud to us the final clause of the codicil"—a feat clearly impossible for a man who could not read, even with a magnifying glass, the large-type memos prepared on Betty St. John's special typewriter, who had reluctantly confessed *three years* previously that he was no longer able to read even his own handwriting. Moreover, the changes made by the codicil were in direct conflict with the understandings reached by DeWitt, Cole and Helm just days before. So DeWitt either didn't understand what was in the codicil— making it worthless—or, understanding, forgot what he had just agreed to.

As for Lila, there are dozens of individuals—from Ed Thompson to Gene Doherty, including secretaries, nurses, maids and kitchen help—who have described her thorough and worsening senility from April 1978 forward. A woman who frequently failed to recognize longtime members of her own staff —who had taken to calling her own husband by the name of her long-dead brother—can hardly be described as being "of sound mind, memory and understanding, not . . . in any respect incompetent."

The tenth codicil made one other change: Individuals named as Wallace trustees would be disqualified from service upon reaching the age of seventy —except for Cole, Helm and Rockefeller. Cole would be disqualified at age eighty-seven, Helm at eighty-two and Rockefeller at seventy-nine. At first glance, these ages appear arbitrary and irrelevant, and if anything more restrictive of Rockefeller than of Cole and Helm. In fact, they meant that Cole would be forced off the trust in 1982, and Helm in 1983, while Rockefeller would remain qualified until the end of 1989. "Barney desperately wanted Al out of the picture," recalls Peggy Cole. "He put a lot of thought into those age restrictions, and in the end they worked out just as he had planned." *

But not right away. In fact, McHenry's battles with Al Cole over the tenth codicil were just beginning. On February 5, in compliance with DeWitt's request, Lord, Day senior partner Palmer Baker produced a twelve-page memo on the wills, and this memo served as the basis for a luncheon discussion at High Winds on February 9. Attending the lunch were Baker, Thompson, O'Hara and the Wallaces. Among several points made by the Baker memo, the following were of greatest importance:

1. There were roughly seven million shares of Class A nonvoting stock outstanding, and nine thousand shares of Class B voting stock. The Wallaces, individually and through their four charitable foundations, owned 86 percent of the Class A stock and 100 percent of the voting stock.
2. Upon the death of the surviving Wallace, all of the voting stock (and therefore control of the corporation) would go to the Wallace Trust. The trustees were: Rockefeller, Cole, Helm; Thompson, O'Hara, Cross. And also—thanks to that tenth codicil—Barney McHenry.
3. The trustees were required to manage the RD stock for the benefit of the DeWitt Wallace Fund and the LAW Fund, and hence for the benefit of charity, subject to a continuing right of review and supervision by the New York attorney general "on behalf of the ultimate charitable beneficiaries of these two organizations."
4. The memo concluded by pointing out that Lila Wallace had executed a proxy, "effective at the death of Mr. Wallace," authorizing the trustees to vote her shares. This proxy, Baker carefully noted, could be revoked "if Mrs. Wallace wishes to do so."

During the course of the luncheon, Thompson and O'Hara were persuaded that the Wallaces did *not* want McHenry as a trustee (although they had signed documents naming him one just fourteen days previously), and that they wanted to make their two top executives co-executors of their wills.* After the lunch, Thompson phoned McHenry to review these decisions. During the call, he jotted down several revealing bits of information provided by the lawyer:

Basic problems:
1. There is no paper saying he [Dewitt] wanted ALC [Cole] or Helm to look into his affairs
2. Barney has read Cole's letter to him 2 or 3 times. He doesn't understand.
3. He hasn't made any real decisions in several months.
4. *Probably doesn't know where he is.*
5. He will sign anything I [Barney] send him.

Over the next two weeks, to deal with the lack of a "paper" showing that Wallace had *invited* the Cole/Helm investigation (needed to protect them-

---

* McHenry argues it was the other way around: that O'Hara and Thompson insisted that they be named co-executors.

selves from charges of meddling), Thompson, O'Hara and Cole produced a lengthy "Memo from Harold Helm and Al Cole" which began: "Wally: You asked us to look at plans for your estate as they now exist. Also to report our observations and to give you suggestions. . . ." The memo went on to reiterate the two key points: that McHenry should come off the trust; that "two top RD people" should be added as co-executors of the wills.

To keep the pressure on, Cole followed this memo with several others. Finally, on March 27, Wallace sent his own letter to McHenry, via messenger: "After further thought, I believe we should have two additional executors. One to be Jack O'Hara and one to be Ed Thompson. I also feel sure it would be better to have you as counsel to the trustees rather than to be one of the trustees. . . . Please prepare a proper codicil. . . ."

But nothing happened. On May 10, prodded by Cole, DeWitt sent yet another letter to McHenry: "We hope the codicil necessary to bring our wills in line with our proposals . . . can be presented to us for signature not later than June 1, 1979. Wally."

Still nothing happened. To find out why, Thompson spoke directly to McHenry. "I'm not going to make those changes," McHenry told him. "Al is a meddling old fool and Wally has no idea what he is doing. I have this tenth codicil, signed and sealed, and I'm not going to change it. It involves the Wallaces' personal business, and I'm their personal lawyer. Period."

"It was just that blatant," says Thompson today. "I told Barney he was in no position to take such a stand. But, in fact, he *was* acting as their personal lawyer. So it was a tricky situation."

As the pressure from Cole and Thompson mounted—and as it became clear that outside attorneys were beginning to focus on the "tricky situation" at High Winds—McHenry's resistance crumbled. On June 13, he agreed to meet at High Winds with the Wallaces and Ed Thompson to discuss "possible revision of the Wallaces' wills and changes in the directorships of their various philanthropic funds." During this meeting—as described in a detailed "memo for the files" prepared by Thompson—the parties agreed that Thompson and O'Hara would be added as co-executors and that McHenry would be dropped from the Wallace Trust. In addition, new directors would be named for each of the four Wallace Funds: directors of the DeWitt Wallace Fund would be McHenry, Thompson, O'Hara and Cole; directors of the Lakeview Fund would be McHenry, Thompson and O'Hara. Directors of the LAW Fund would be McHenry, John Walker (former head of the National Gallery and a friend of Lila's through her art benefactions), Laurance Rockefeller and Thompson; directors of the High Winds Fund would be McHenry, Dr. Frank Stinchfield (the surgeon who had replaced Lila's hips), Rockefeller and O'Hara.

Thompson's memo indicated that McHenry would have the paperwork on the executorships and the trust completed by June 30, and that the various directorships (according to McHenry) "could be handled with the verbal authorization I received at the meeting." Yet *still* McHenry stalled. The June 30 deadline came and went with no new codicil available for signing. On July 5, Cole appeared at High Winds one more time, bearing one more letter to Wallace urging action. "Al was a *very* tough salesman," recalls Thompson. "But at this stage it took every ounce of his ability to get through to Wally."

After the July 5 meeting, Wallace demanded immediate action from McHenry. And now, finally, there was no more room for delay. On July 11, at High Winds, an eleventh codicil to the Wallace wills was signed, removing McHenry from the trust and adding O'Hara and Thompson as co-executors. A second document was also signed on this occasion, in its way as important as the codicil itself.

On an earlier date, Lila Wallace had executed a proxy, effective at De-Witt's death, authorizing the trustees to vote her shares of Digest stock (and thus to run the company), "said proxy to remain in effect until Mrs. Wallace dies or revokes it by a written instrument." Now, all too aware of McHenry's ability to get signatures from either Wallace "on anything I send them," Thompson and O'Hara insisted that Lila sign a new proxy "of infinite duration to be terminated only at my death." Once again, McHenry resisted. But then, says Thompson, "we let him know he had to get us the new proxy or he would have worse troubles than he ever dreamed of."

The proxy was prepared, and on July 11 Lila Wallace—smiling like a child, thrilled as always to be the focus of so much undivided male attention —obediently scrawled what now passed for her signature in the space indicated by her attorney. "We *had* to force this issue," says Thompson. "Had Wally died in the absence of such a proxy, Lila might have been 'persuaded' to revoke the earlier proxy. Then there would have been hell to pay."

With the signing of the eleventh codicil and the irrevocable proxy, the War begun by Al Cole two years before appeared to be over. McHenry had lost, and it was clear now to both sides—given the impaired mental states of the Founders—that further alteration of the wills was out of the question. Yet still DeWitt rained memos on his attorney, sometimes two on the same day, demanding fresh changes, new executors, additional directors. The War he had been pressed into joining had set something off in him, some ancient instinct to do battle. He had labored to build a certain kind of company, and he seemed to understand that this company was in danger now of evolving into something very different.

As things turned out, Wallace's suspicions were right on target. When the dust of the War had settled, it became apparent that control of the crucial Wallace Funds—into which the RD voting shares would be deposited upon the eventual dissolution of the trust—had *not* gone to the slates of directors agreed upon during the June 13 meeting. Instead, using the "verbal author-ity" granted during that meeting, McHenry had eliminated O'Hara, Thompson and Rockefeller.* McHenry and Cole were named to direct the DeWitt Wallace Fund, and McHenry alone to direct the Lakeview Fund; McHenry and John Walker would direct the LAW Fund, and McHenry and Frank Stinchfield would direct the High Winds Fund. Since Walker and Stinchfield were elderly outsiders named mostly out of friendship, and Cole at eighty-five was finally becoming as forgetful as Wallace himself, the net effect of these moves was to put McHenry in control of all four funds. Thompson and O'Hara —either out of deference to Laurance Rockefeller or because they were otherwise occupied running an international corporation—made no objection. Additionally, the age limitations written by McHenry into the tenth codicil had attracted no one's attention during the War and therefore were unchanged by the terms of the eleventh codicil. So Laurance's future window as sole outside trustee remained open.

On a Sunday morning shortly after the eleventh codicil was signed, DeWitt's longtime friend and neighbor, Dr. Robert Patterson, showed up at High Winds for the weekend walk that had been part of their routine for years. As the two old gentlemen were leaving the house, a car bearing Barney McHenry pulled up at the main entrance. "Doc" Patterson nodded to McHenry, and McHenry smiled and said "Good morning." Wallace ignored his lawyer completely.

The two friends then strolled off together in silence, making their way slowly across a rolling field in the general direction of the Patterson estate. "Then, as he often did, Wally asked about the hospital," recalls Patterson (who was surgeon-in-chief of New York's Hospital for Special Surgery for many years), "and as always I began to fill him in. The subject of some money he was giving for a new operating room came up. I wondered how I should go about making the arrangements. 'Should I see this fellow McHenry?' I asked. Well . . . Wally blew his top. *'Hell, no!'* he shouted. *'Not him! Don't go* near *him!'* He was so agitated that I dropped the subject. In all the years I knew him, that was the only time I ever saw him lose control."

* A wholesale transfer of RD shares from the funds to various Rockefeller-connected charities was about to take place—a process that would have involved considerable conflict of interest had Rockefeller himself remained a director of the funds.

CHAPTER TWENTY-SIX

By the beginning of 1979, John Strasburger had figured out that his position at High Winds was secure no matter how he performed his duties. DeWitt and Lila Wallace were sole owners of a worldwide publishing empire whose managers, incredible as it seemed, still looked to them for the final word on every major decision. Senility had overtaken them more or less simultaneously, and now it was doubtful whether any truly *legal* transfer of power could be carried out without the assistance of a court. Strasburger was aware of this, just as he was aware of the "signings" that took place at High Winds on a regular basis. On occasion, he was asked to witness these events himself. Not actually to be present—the signings generally took place upstairs, in Lila's and DeWitt's private rooms—but later, when McHenry spread the papers across his kitchen table, to sign on the dotted line as if he *had* been present and so could attest to the signers' "sound mind and understanding."

Strasburger was also aware—more so than anyone—that the Wallaces did not seem competent to sign anything, least of all legal documents. Knowing this gave him a not-surprising sense of power. Nobody was going to fire *him*.

As spring turned into summer, High Winds began to seem less and less the Wallaces' home and more and more the Strasburgers' playground. John's mother moved in for a prolonged stay, and later Mary's mother as well. Other Strasburgers showed up on a regular basis, including small armies of nephews, nieces and grandchildren. "We're going to the Castle in the Sky!" they would sing as they headed up the highway. "We're off to see the King and Queen!"

Food for the Strasburgers and their guests—steaks and hams, smoked salmon and shrimp, fancy wine and the finest cheeses—filled the two large refrigerators in the kitchen, while a smaller fridge in the pantry was meant to serve the Wallaces and the nurses. "But that fridge was nearly always empty," recalls Jean Rossi. "So there was nothing, really, to feed the Wallaces. You just had to make do with what you could find." But woe to the maid or nurse who opened even the unstocked fridge without first asking John Strasburger. "All the jars and bottles in our fridge were marked with lines so John could tell when anything was taken," says nurse Janine Ardohain, who served at High Winds from March of 1979 until Lila's death in May of 1984. "If John saw that the apple juice was an inch below his line, he would have a fit and accuse us of stealing."

"The Wallaces didn't get enough to eat or drink," adds Julie Waldrun, an

RN from Northern Westchester who came to work at High Winds in August 1979. "We all knew this and we all worried about it." Later that summer Dorothy Little, Lila's longtime secretary, also began to worry. A meeting was held, presided over by McHenry and including Little, Doherty, Strasburger and Lisa Collins, an accountant from McHenry's office. As a result of this meeting, a diet plan was worked up, with menus for every day of the week, and a special account was opened at the Chappaqua Market to supply the necessary items. "But that was all for show," recalls Collins. "Within days it was business as usual."

As John Strasburger's confidence grew, the pace of his stealing at High Winds increased dramatically. Rare books and first editions disappeared. The Meissen dinner service. Lila's silver was stored in a floor-to-ceiling wall safe in a closet behind the pantry door—all her flatware, trays, punch bowls, creamers, and so forth. All of it disappeared. Mary Strasburger's son-in-law remembers visiting High Winds during this period and being shown "all the valuable stuff" by John (or "Jack," as the family called him): "Once, Jack showed me this stack of gold plates. 'Try to pick'em up,' he says. So I did, and I go, 'Holy Mackerel!' They weighed a ton. Solid gold!" But not too heavy to steal. Those plates, too, soon were missing.

Somehow, amid all the rancor and plotting, the aged King and Queen eked out what passed for a daily life. Lila asked for little more than an occasional male visitor, a change of flower arrangements, and the opportunity once or twice a day to sit in her chair before the fire in the living room and commune with her alter ego. Not much for a Queen to expect. Yet even these simple desires were frequently frustrated.

Few of the men who had courted her so ardently in the past came near High Winds now that she was old and helpless. John Allen, promoted to public-affairs director, showed up every few weeks. But Allen's visits were clearly official, his real mission being to check on things and report back to Jack O'Hara. Laurance Rockefeller appeared once or twice a year, and so did Al and Peggy Cole.

"But no one else," says Julie Waldrun. "Only people who were paid to be there. We thought it was very sad. She loved having male visitors—just sparkled all over whenever a man came into the room. But McHenry controlled the situation, and his orders were to let no one in without his permission." (Many of those who might have come, including friends, former staff members and an army of nephews and nieces from both sides of the family, stayed away for fear of offending McHenry. Over the years, the Wallaces had set up dozens of "irrevocable trusts" for such people, conferring modest annual incomes, and they continued to do this until their last years. From 1974 on, McHenry was in charge of this process, and from 1978 on he was free to establish such trusts entirely on his own. Or *not* establish them. So once again the Wallaces' own money and generosity was the chief cause of their isolation.)

In many ways, DeWitt's dream had collapsed even further than Lila's. His editors had given him a television with a giant screen, and when he sat close enough, with the volume going full blast, he could vaguely follow what was going on. But he had a terrible time operating the remote control and so had to rely on others to find the right channel and turn the volume up. Then he would settle in happily, usually to watch a Yankee game.

But the noise of this activity irritated Strasburger—"I can hear that god-damn game all the way in the kitchen," he would growl—and so he generally found a way to cut it short. "John would wait until the Boss left the room," says Doherty. "Then he would sneak in and turn the sound down. When the Boss got back, he could never figure out what had happened. He would fiddle with the remote, then become frustrated and go up to bed. I found out about this one evening when I was watering plants in the flower room. I saw DW go to the bathroom, and then I heard the sound go down. 'What'd you do, John?' I called. *'Fuck you!'* he called back. Later I asked Connie the maid about this. 'Oh, yeah,' she said. 'John always turns the sound down on Mr. Wallace. The bastard!' "

Although DeWitt had finally given up his roadwork, his need to manage some life-affirming task had not diminished. Coming in from his afternoon walk one day that fall, he passed an area where head gardener Joe Guignardi was working with a chain saw. That evening, he called Guignardi at home. "Joe," he said, "I've always wanted to operate one of those saws. Would you show me how?"

They met the next afternoon, and Guignardi led the old man into the nearby woods until he located a downed sapling lying at a convenient angle across a stone wall. "Here's a tree that will be easy to cut, Mr. Wallace," he said. The old man reached out and felt the sapling. "No," he said. "I want a bigger tree, Joe. And it has to be standing. I want to *fell* a tree. "

With great misgivings, Guignardi selected a small maple that was clear of underbrush. "Okay, Mr. Wallace. Here's a good tree. Let me get the saw started." "No," said Wallace again. "If you don't mind, Joe, I'd like to start the saw myself. Will you show me how?"

Guignardi went through the motions, and then the old man himself pulled the cord. When the machine crackled to life, he smiled with pleasure. Guignardi reached around him with both arms to guide the saw blade against the little maple. Then the gardener stepped back and watched as Wallace set about his task. Within seconds, the tree began to lean, and then with a satisfying *thump* it fell to earth.

Wallace laid the saw down. "Thanks, Joe," he said. "Be seeing you." And the old man headed off in the general direction of High Winds. Guignardi had to grab the saw and hustle to catch up.

By this time, the Wallaces took supper most nights in Lila's sitting room, with its splendid view over Byram Lake. But what should have been a pleasant time together was often anything but. "There was a lot of tension," recalls Janine Ardohain. "Mrs. Wallace would get frustrated because Mr. Wallace couldn't remember anything. And Mr. Wallace got tired of being called 'Barclay.' Whenever the conversation faltered, he always returned to the same theme: *'Cheer up, Lila! Think how lucky we are!* We have all those buildings down the road, where all those people work. *Perhaps we should give them away.'* And she would glare at him. 'Be careful who you give your money to,' she would say."

At bedtime, the same scene repeated itself every night. When Lila was settled in her quarters, DeWitt would come in to kiss her good-night. Then he would forget he had done this and come back for another kiss. Sometimes this would happen several times, and eventually Lila would become impatient. "All *right!"* she would say. "Enough of kissing! Go to bed!"

After nine, the house would settle down, except that sometimes—if Lila had trouble falling asleep, or woke from a bad dream—she would cry out *"Barclay! Barclay!"* Then, more silence. The nurse on duty in Lila's room would nod off in her chair. For a time, the only sound would be the wind keening around the High Winds towers. Then, *bedlam.* "Mrs. Wallace always woke up during the night," recalls Janine. "Sometimes those moments were funny, like slapstick comedy. Sometimes they were very sad.

" *'We're having a meeting!'* How many times have those words startled me from a sound sleep! Mrs. Wallace would rap on her bed rails with that big diamond ring. *Rap! Rap!* 'Everybody quiet!' *Rap! Rap!* She was conducting a board meeting, and she clearly could see the other directors in a circle around her bed. She shook her finger at them. 'We have bad problems here and we've all got to start *thinking* better!' Then she would mumble on about this problem or that problem, and after a while she would doze off again.

"Other nights she would have bigger plans. *'I'm going to Headquarters!'* she would announce. *'Everybody up!'* I would have to get her out of bed and help her dress. That meant everything—pearls, perfume, makeup, the works. You did not say no to Lila Wallace! *'Call Gene!'* she would command. I would pretend to dial Gene's number. Then we would take the elevator downstairs and wait in the rotunda for Gene. And wait and wait. 'Where *is* he?' she would demand. 'Call him again!' He doesn't answer, Mrs. Wallace. 'Then he is *fired!'* How many times has she fired Gene at three in the morning!

"In the middle of all this hubbub, Mr. Wallace often appeared, in his pajamas, coming down the stairs in search of food. When he sensed that someone was there, waiting below him in the rotunda, he would stop and squint his eyes in our direction. '*Whooo* is it?' he would ask. '*Lila?* Is that you, Lila? Whaat are you *dooing?* Go to bed, Lila!'

" '*No!*' she would say. 'We are leaving for Headquarters. It's time to go to *work.*' " There was no talking her out of it. When he tried, she let him have it. *Zap!* Like a knife. 'You're not my *husband!* Who are you?' And Mr. Wallace, he would just . . . he would be *crushed.* So he would turn and go back upstairs and disappear into his room.

"Eventually, if you were lucky, Mrs. Wallace would get tired of waiting for Gene and then you could convince her to go back to bed. Other times, she would ask to go into the living room. The light that illuminated the *Jeune Fille* would be on, and she would sit there in the dark and look up at her painting. Since it was always cold in that house, I would light a fire. And there we would sit, just the two of us, waiting for the sun to come up."

CHAPTER TWENTY-SEVEN

At this point it should have been clear to anyone who spent two minutes with DeWitt or Lila Wallace that neither one of them was competent to do much of anything. Not competent in a legal sense, for sure, but also not competent to care for themselves, or even to be left alone for very long. Yet there they were in that huge old house, still in nominal control of a worldwide publishing empire, still in possession of a fortune growing vaster every year. By the middle of 1979, they had given away only 14 percent of their stock. Eighty-six percent of Reader's Digest—hugely profitable even when run as a kind of philanthropic candy store—remained in their possession. So it is not surprising, as word of their declining health spread, that DeWitt and Lila began to attract increased interest from every side and from all who understood what the candy store might be worth if operated as a real business.

In July 1979, a delegation representing Macalester College arrived at High Winds to bestow upon DeWitt an honorary doctor of humane letters degree. It was an odd occasion. DeWitt's anger at Macalester—his conviction that the school had been "spoiled" and would benefit from a "period of austerity" —had cooled by 1975 to the point where he had been persuaded to finance five professorships. But there is no evidence that he had forgotten what had gone wrong in the sixties, nor any reason to suspect a desire on his part to resume his former pattern of unstinting generosity. As for the honorary degree

—over the years he had turned down dozens of similar offers out of hand (including the one made by his own father in 1936). "He hated the very idea of honorary degrees," says James Stewart-Gordon. "He thought they were a scam, a high-powered way to con rich people into giving money."

On this occasion, the Macalester delegation was high-powered, indeed. Chief Justice of the Supreme Court Warren Burger, a Macalester graduate and trustee, was on hand, as were John W. Davis, president of the college, and Carl Drake, chairman of the St. Paul Companies and also a Macalester trustee. Despite all the brass and hoopla, and the academic robes someone pulled over his head, it is doubtful Wallace understood what was going on. "Your pioneering spirit enabled the dream of your youth to become a unique and successful phenomenon of the publishing world," intoned the chief justice. "Your generosity will continue to help generations of those who love Macalester to shape and reach out for their own dreams."

"The Boss stood there listening to this with an irritated frown on his face," recalls Gene Doherty. "When the ceremony was over, the chief justice and several others crowded around him, all of them babbling about what an honor it was to meet him. The Boss kept mumbling 'Yes, yes,' all the while looking to escape."

Suddenly, Wallace suggested that the group might like to go for a walk. Without waiting for an answer, he headed for the front door, and the others —with raised eyebrows and inquiring looks—followed after him. Joe Guignardi was working in the rhododendron beds that day, and he will never forget the sight of all those pinstriped men heading out across the High Winds fields. "Except for Burger, the others were in their forties or fifties," Joe recalls. "DW was ninety. But you could pick him out from the rest because he stood straighter and walked faster. He seemed to be trying to get away."

The record would now show that Macalester and its wealthy benefactor had been reconciled after all (there was wide coverage of the event in the press). And exactly seventeen months later—as Wallace lay dying in his darkened bedroom at High Winds—a legal entity called "The DeWitt Wallace Fund for Macalester College" was suddenly established. Barney McHenry handled the details, transferring into the fund some 250,000 shares of Reader's Digest stock. One year later (nine months *after* DeWitt's death), an additional 188,500 shares were turned over to the Macalester "Support Organization," as the fund was called, followed in 1984 by a final allotment of 75,000 shares. The purpose of the S/O (technically, a "conduit trust") was to hold the Digest stock "for the benefit of" Macalester.

Under the bylaws of the fund, a board of directors was appointed that included two representatives from Macalester, two from RD and two who were (at least in theory) independent. The Digest's representatives were meant to be its two top executives—the editor-in-chief and the CEO. But when the dust settled it turned out that Barney McHenry was serving and Ed Thompson was not. "The tax considerations involved in the deal were arcane and complex," says Jack O'Hara. "Barney was the only one who understood them, so it seemed to me he had to be included on the board."

Thompson shakes his head at this argument. "In hindsight," he says today, "that was a dumb play. Barney should have been *adviser* to the board, not a member. *I* should have been the other member. But I was Barney's enemy— I had tried to fire him, after all—and Jack was afraid. So I was kept off." The slight seemed a small matter at the time. But it would turn out to be a very large matter, indeed. As with the Wallace Funds themselves, Thompson had been shoved aside. O'Hara was on the S/O board, but willing to leave the details to McHenry. So McHenry was in charge, and McHenry, more than ever, was Laurance Rockefeller's man.

At the time of the Macalester transfer, it was hard to put a meaningful value on the 515,000 shares involved. The price of the stock during those years floated from a low of around $5 to a high of around $30, based on a formula (devised by Morgan Guaranty) that was frequently changed by RD management. At $30 a share, the gift totaled an impressive $15,450,000. But everyone involved understood that even at $30 the stock was ludicrously undervalued.

The formula in use during the early eighties arrived at a price by multiplying the Digest's earnings-per-share by the Dow-Jones price-earnings multiple, and then (because there was no public market for the shares) discounting by 15 percent. In 1982, under this highly volatile arrangement and in the face of some bad economic news, the price of Digest stock collapsed to around $5.25 per share. But later that year (for complicated reasons), the Dow P/E ratio soared over 80, which would have sent the Digest stock up to around $100. Because this was deemed to be an "unreasonable" price, Digest treasurer Bill Cross (with approval of the Morgan bank) quietly changed the formula, dropping the Dow figure in favor of the less-volatile multiple of the S&P 400 Industrials. Under this new formula, the stock actually *dropped* from $5.25 to around $4.75.

Why all the subterfuge? In addition to tax considerations, there was the problem (soon to grow) of large blocks of stock being dedicated to charities like Macalester. Under the "conduit-trust" setup, the RD-controlled S/Os were meant to hold the stock while distributing modest dividends (2 percent was the norm) to the selected charities. But if the stock rose toward anything like its *real* value, the selected charities—eyeing all that unrealized wealth —would naturally want to sell "their" stock to the highest bidder for cash that could be reinvested for a higher return. This would have caused a crisis. Although controlled by the Digest, the S/O boards would have come under tremendous pressure to accept such a bid (or face serious legal repercussions), and this would have forced the company either to borrow heavily to buy the stock back itself, or to seek a public market long before such a move made sense.

What *was* the stock worth? A rule of thumb used during this period to evaluate successful media companies like the Digest involved multiplying aftertax earnings times 25. In 1978, a good year, Digest earnings were almost $80 million, which works out to an overall value of $2 billion, which, divided by the seven million shares then outstanding, produces a price per share of $285—a far cry from $30 (and *light-years* away from $4.75).

But the $80 million in earnings had been achieved with Jack O'Hara and Ed Thompson at the helm, operating under DeWitt Wallace's rules for doing business. *What if you got serious?* What would happen if you dropped Wallace's "service" concept and ran the place as a bottom-line mail-order juggernaut, cutting here and slashing there? Profits might double or triple, sending the stock price soaring and converting gifts like Macalester's modest $15 million into vast fortunes. (Even at a relatively low $285, the Macalester bequest would have totaled $150 million.) The possibilities were mind-boggling. But the first challenge was to move the stock from the Wallaces' funds into a series of newly created S/Os, and while this was going on the less said about golden future possibilities the better. In fact, the huge undervaluation of the stock was crucial to the whole operation. With the real value of these dubious transferrals hidden from view, publicity would be limited and few questions—especially questions from the IRS—would be asked.

Whether, in his right mind, DeWitt Wallace would have committed even a small fraction of those 515,000 shares to a school he believed already "too affluent" is unknowable. What *is* known is this: He had promised himself that his father's travails would not be in vain, and that was a promise he had kept. And whatever questions one may raise about the size of the Macalester bequest, the real question marks—and the truly *questionable* behavior—lay ahead. "The Fund for Macalester was only the first of seven separate S/Os funded by the Wallaces," points out Robert Gavin, the school's current president. "Our fund was meant to serve as a model for the ones that followed, and they all got their stock after we got ours."

Funded by the Wallaces? It is a phrase that gives one pause. Neither Wallace at this point was legally competent to make decisions that funded *anything.* So who *did* make these decisions? The Wallace trustees? Not possible. The trustees would not exist in a legal sense until both Wallaces were dead. But the trustees-to-be held Lila's proxy for the voting shares. Did *that* give them the power to make these decisions? No, on two counts: The proxy would become effective "only at my husband's death"; and while the proxy would at that point empower the trustees to vote Lila's shares at board meetings, it granted them no right to give away her money or her stock. That was *her* business.

So who, then? Consider the next delegation that came to High Winds in that busy year of 1979.

Sometime that October, Carlisle Humelsine, chairman of the board of Colonial Williamsburg, and Donald Gonzales, Williamsburg's vice president for public relations, arrived at High Winds to present a proposal for the creation of a "Decorative Arts Museum" at the restoration. In a pamphlet entitled *The DeWitt and Lila Wallace Legacy* (which amounts to an "authorized version" of the Williamsburg/Wallace connection), Humelsine describes this visit:

> After pleasant conversation, Mr. Wallace asked us about the proposal and its cost. I outlined the program and said it would require $12 million. Mr. Wallace didn't gasp, but turned to Mrs. Wallace and said, "Lila, this is a fairly heavy sum for me to handle at this time; would you be prepared to help me?"
>
> She answered, "No, DeWitt. While I'm very fond of Williamsburg, you know we never share projects." But she added, "We'll talk about it, the two of us."

At this point it may be useful to consider some Williamsburg history. From its beginnings, Williamsburg had been a Rockefeller project. John D., Jr. had provided the initial funding back in the late twenties, and for many years thereafter underwrote the costs of keeping his "favorite philanthropy" in operation. When "Mr. Junior" died in 1960, his son Winthrop picked up the Williamsburg torch for the Family, and much of the financial burden as well, and bore both until in his own death in 1973. But then the situation began to change. When none of the other Rockefeller brothers—JDR III, Nelson, Laurance or David—stepped forward to accept the challenge, or to provide funds, it became apparent that a source of support outside the Rockefeller Family would have to be found. "A remarkable series of events then occurred," writes Don Gonzales in *The Rockefellers at Williamsburg,* "the results of which have to be listed in the miracle category of fund-raising."

In 1976, a major fund-raising program was launched under the leadership of newly hired Roger Thaler. When Thaler was informed that Lila and DeWitt Wallace had been visiting Williamsburg for years but had never been asked for money, he wasted little time. In July he wrote to the Wallaces to determine whether they would be interested in covering some portion of the development program's $13 million price tag. "The deaths of John D. Rockefeller, Jr., and Winthrop Rockefeller have created an urgent need . . . for someone else to bridge the gap," wrote Thaler. "Our 'want list' includes a new visitor's entrance to Colonial Williamsburg, with a new theater in which to show the orientation film *Story of a Patriot*. Also of high priority is our need for a Decorative Arts Museum and Gallery." (The Rockefeller Family had amassed an impressive collection of "decorative" Americana that for want of display space was stored in Williamsburg warehouses.)

DeWitt wrote back expressing thanks for the "compliment implicit in your willingness to let us participate." Mrs. Wallace was not in a position to consider the proposals, he said, but he himself "might consider a modest donation for a building used exclusively" to show *Story of a Patriot*. Over the years, Wallace had viewed this film dozens of times, and his child-like fondness for it was well known. "The Boss *loved* that movie," says Gene Doherty. "He felt every American ought to see it. Even when his eyes were gone, he still went to the *Patriot*. And when he came out of the show, there were always tears streamin' down his cheeks."

But it bothered Wallace that the theater was so far from the restoration itself. "All the tourists had to line up for buses to get to the movie," says Doherty. "The Boss thought that was terrible." To alleviate this problem—to make it easier for millions of ordinary Americans to see a movie that so stirred his own patriotism—Wallace agreed in late 1976 to provide $4 million for a new theater. "This is the *only* building proposal that has ever interested me," he wrote to Thaler. "I have never had my name on anything before, but in this very special case I might like it."

Now things begin to take a curious twist. In early 1979 (three years *after* Wallace's hesitant offer of $4 million), blueprints for the new *Patriot* theater were finally coming off the drawing boards. But then Williamsburg announced a sudden change in plans: "We are shifting our emphasis—in view of grim economic forecasts—in favor of the Decorative Arts Museum and Gallery." Work on the theater was postponed, and Wallace was "persuaded" to shift his $4 million to the new plan. (These negotiations, it should be noted, were taking place in the middle of the McHenry/Cole War, at a time when Wallace was having trouble keeping track of simple things from day to day, or even hour to hour—when, as McHenry told Thompson, "he will sign anything I send him.") Then it turned out that the new plan, which was being "emphasized" because "economic problems" made the old plan too expensive, was, in fact, far *more* expensive than the plan it replaced. "As important as Mr. Wallace's gift was," confided Humelsine in the authorized history, "it fell far short of the resources needed to create the Decorative Arts Museum. So I asked to see the Wallaces again."

Which brings us back to the visit paid by Humelsine and Gonzales to High Winds in October 1979—a visit that even the official history admits ended inconclusively. "We'll talk about it," Lila had promised, "just the two of us."

Perhaps they did talk about it. Who is to say? What *is* known is that DeWitt—when he understood that his beloved *Patriot* theater had been shelved in favor of a "decorative arts" museum—managed to rouse himself sufficiently to ask several friends what a decorative arts museum *was*. "I got a call from Wally that October," recalls Noel Oursler (Tony's wife). "He wanted to know about decorative arts, and whether I thought a museum devoted to that purpose was worth supporting. He was hesitant and confused. He seemed to feel that a museum full of 'decorative' things was in some way a contradiction of everything he had supported in the past."

"In any event," Humelsine continues (deftly spanning the chasm between Lila's willingness to "talk about it" and the wonderful gifts soon to flow), "Mr. Wallace made the gift of $12 million. In addition, he set up the DeWitt Wallace Fund for Williamsburg, to which he made an additional gift of 250,000 shares of Reader's Digest stock that was expected to produce an annual income of at least $600,000. Colonial Williamsburg had the big non-Rockefeller gift it needed!"

Following the Macalester model, a board of directors for this second S/O was established that included two insiders (Humelsine and Williamsburg president Charles Longsworth), two outsiders (the ubiquitous Chief Justice Burger and his Supreme Court colleague Associate Justice Lewis Powell) and, again representing the Digest, Barney McHenry and Jack O'Hara.

But go back briefly to the words following Humelsine's chasm-spanner: *"In any event,"* he writes, "Mr. Wallace made the gift . . . and set-up . . . the Fund." If that is true, he must have done so at some point between December 1980, when the Macalester model was established, and March 30, 1981, when he died. Yet, during that period, he was lying in his darkened bedroom in the High Winds tower, blind, deaf, disoriented and ill. For three weeks in February and March, he was at Columbia-Presbyterian Hospital. Then he was returned to High Winds to sleep away his final days. So it doesn't seem likely that he spent this particular period negotiating the financial salvation of Colonial Williamsburg.

"The S/Os were Laurance Rockefeller's call," says Ed Thompson. "Sure, Barney McHenry was out on the streets of New York at the time, telling everyone in sight he could get them Wallace money. On minor gifts—a million here, five million there—Barney did control the situation and could in fact make such gifts. But Barney didn't have the stature to pull off the S/Os. With the S/Os, it was a matter of Laurance saying to Barney, *'Let's do this,'* and then Barney doing the paperwork. The Wallaces had no idea what was going on. Neither did I. Neither did the other proxy holders. It wasn't proxy business and it wasn't trust business. It was *Wallace* business."

"Wally knew he was being sold out by Laurance," adds Jack O'Hara. "He had worried for years about who was telling him the truth and who was not, and in those last difficult days I think he understood that Laurance was not. But he was tired and sick, and he didn't want to think about it. And they were very clever. Barney was careful during the seventies to guide Wallace giving in the 'right' directions. The result was a record that could be used later on to justify the huge gifts made to the S/Os. When the appropriate time came, Laurance simply nodded his head and Barney set up the whole operation.

"After the Williamsburg Fund was established, I had a talk with Warren Burger and Justice Powell. I wanted them to understand, now that Williamsburg would be relying on income from RD stock, that the Digest's fortunes were subject to extreme ups and downs and that it would be prudent for them to husband their income in some way—to create a reserve that would enable them to meet their needs during down periods. *They looked at me as if I were daft!* I mean, I had been holding back the dam at RD. But eventually, no matter what I did, it was going to go *Booom.* Through the roof! And Burger and Powell clearly understood this. So all my talk about creating reserves made no sense to them. When I saw the expression on their faces —the utter incredulity—I knew the game was lost."

But what of the other Wallace trustees? Thompson was "kept out of it" and O'Hara played it safe. But what about Al Cole and Harold Helm on the outside, and Bill Cross on the inside? Why did they voice no objections to the grandiose sting taking place before their eyes? "Al was eighty-five at this point, and Harold seventy-eight," says Thompson. "We used to compare them to the old Muppet gentlemen at the opera, who always fall asleep when the singing begins. At board meetings, Al would doze off almost immediately. Then Harold would follow suit. If there was a need to vote on something, we shook them awake and they voted with the rest of us. That's how they were with Laurance. They went along with whatever he wanted."

Which leaves Bill Cross, the least powerful of the inside trustees (but a man with fierce ambitions to become Digest chairman), as the only one left in a position to protect the ailing Founders. "Bill Cross was a hothead," recalls Dick Waters (Cross's former boss). "Because of this, Wallace never liked him, and Bill resented this. I left the Digest just when Wally began to fade, and after I was gone Bill began to have dreams of power—and he saw Barney McHenry as the way to make those dreams come true. Bill and Barney were quiet about it, but they were allies, no question." ("Like *that,*" says Gene Doherty today, crossing two fingers. "Every time I dropped something at Cross's office, Barney was in there conferring. And every time Barney got a call up at High Winds, it was Cross on the line.")

In view of his alliance with McHenry, it seems likely that Cross figured out early on which way the wind was blowing, and chose thereafter to place his money on Rockefeller. This was clearly a shrewd move, and as things turned out it almost brought him the jackpot. But win or lose, Bill Cross was no more likely to stand in the path of Laurance Rockefeller's plans than Jack O'Hara had been. So the answer to the question about who was protecting the Wallaces is: absolutely no one.

A third hunting party came to High Winds that year, and this time the target was Lila. Millionaire investment banker C. Douglas Dillon was chairman of the Metropolitan Museum's board of trustees (and a valued member of Laurance Rockefeller's inner circle) and Kevin Roche was architect of the museum's master plan. In view of Lila's past interest and generosity, the two men were eager to discuss a new wing at the museum to be devoted to twentieth-century art.

But by now the situation had changed. Tom Hoving had resigned in 1977, and with his departure (and her own increasing confusion) Lila's interest in the museum had faded. There is no record of the conversations Dillon and Roche had with her during 1979, but whatever was said the two men were apparently as persuasive with Lila as the Macalester and Williamsburg delegations had been with DeWitt. "Mrs. Wallace had never shown much interest in modern art," wrote Calvin Tompkins in *Merchants and Masterpieces,* his history of the Met. "Yet now she appeared quite ready, through her charitable foundation, to give more. The negotiations actually took place with Barnabas McHenry, who was then administering the Wallace funds. According to McHenry, 'Dillon and Roche so captured Mrs. Wallace's enthusiasm and trust that if they had said they wanted to re-create the Eiffel Tower at twice its original height, she would have said, "Do it!" ' "

This was no doubt true: Lila Wallace was ready for anything. But her willingness to give to the Met had little to do with "enthusiasm and trust" and everything to do with loneliness and confusion. By this time in her life, she was offering diamond rings to nurses who were "nice" and valuable paintings to the butler's wife who brought her food. She had become a helpless old woman who would give anything to anyone in return for a little kindness.

What she "gave" to the Met was more money: $11 million for a new wing to be devoted entirely to twentieth-century art. It is also worth noting that shortly after the successful Dillon/Roche negotiations, Barney McHenry was appointed to the museum's board of trustees. To the average American, that might not seem an excessive reward for the services he had rendered. But Met trustees are not average Americans, nor is the Met by any means an average museum. It is, in fact, the richest, most powerful institution of its kind in the world. "To serve on the board of the Met," writes Tom Hoving, "is to gain the apex of the social, intellectual and artistic position in the nation. . . . The public impression of the Met trustee is a person of privileged rank moving in a serene and elegant world of impeccable manners, a world devoted to the encouragement of beauty and taste."

Precisely the world Barney McHenry longed to enter. And now, by the grace of Lila's money and his own clever machinations (and the clear willingness of the museum's trustees to overlook the obvious), he had attained his goal. He was a member of the most exclusive club in town, sitting at the same table where Vanderbilts, Morgans, Astors and Rockefellers had sat before him.

As with DeWitt's earlier gifts to Macalester and Williamsburg, Lila's gifts to the Met in the seventies became the justification for yet another grand final gift. In 1982, Barney McHenry initiated a process whereby 588,424 shares of Reader's Digest stock were quietly transferred from Lila's personal fund to the "Fund for the Metropolitan Museum of Art." In time, those shares would come to be worth a vast fortune—the greatest gift ever given to the Met, or for that matter to any cultural institution in the world, ever in history.

Lila's earlier gifts, arranged by McHenry, had gained the attorney a coveted seat on the museum's board of trustees. This new gift, credited to Laurance Rockefeller, was far greater, and in its way (in the circles where Rockefellers dwell) no doubt earned Laurance a commensurately greater reward. And all it had cost him was an Egyptian cup, two brooches from Van Cleef's, and a modest application of Rockefeller charm.

CHAPTER TWENTY-EIGHT

Although DeWitt's physical condition deteriorated steadily throughout 1980, the nurses remained under orders to stay away from his bedroom. "But by now it was obvious that he needed help," recalls Dorothy Evans, a private nurse who was Lila's favorite. "So whenever John wasn't around I would sneak in there to see what I could do." One day in November, she found him lying in bed with the blankets under his chin and his feet uncovered. His toenails, she saw at once, were a mess—black and twisted, with the fleshy area around the nails swollen and pink with infection. "His feet were so painful that even the weight of a blanket was too much," says Evans. "So I decided to take a chance. 'Mr. Wallace,' I said, 'would it be a good idea, do you think, if I got a bowl of hot water and some soap, and helped you with your feet?' He gave me an embarrassed look, and at first I thought he was going to refuse. But then he smiled like a child. 'Would you do that?' he whispered. 'Would you really do such a thing?'

"So I got the water and gave his toes a long soak. Then I sat on the bed with his feet in my lap and trimmed those terrible nails. He kept murmuring the whole time, partly from embarrassment, but also, I think, partly from pleasure. I doubt whether anyone had ever done such a thing for him in his entire life. When I was done, I shook on some talcum, then wrapped his feet in warm towels. 'My, my,' he said. 'That's much better.' "

Later in November, the cancer in his abdomen began to produce digestive problems and considerable pain. He mentioned this to no one, preferring as always to keep a stiff upper lip and hope the problem would go away. But the problem persisted, and got worse. He was a ninety-one-year-old billionaire wasting away from a terrible disease, unable to eliminate the food he was eating, his insides racked with discomfort. And no one seemed to understand that he was ill.

"Jack and I were kept in the dark about the cancer," says Ed Thompson. "We heard nothing from any doctor, and nothing from Barney. In fact, Barney didn't *want* us to know. Wally was still capable of changing his will and this I think scared the hell out of Barney. Frankly, it scared all of us. Because we knew that the last voice in his ear might upset everything."

So nothing was done. The old man's situation grew worse every day, and no one in authority did a thing to help him out. "We weren't even told he *had* cancer," says Janine Ardohain. "We knew he wasn't eating much, and we began to worry about how terrible he looked. But we were under orders to stay away. The only person who entered his room in those days was John, to bring him food he couldn't eat. When Dr. Fisher came from the Medical Group, it was only to see Mrs. Wallace. When we asked John why Fisher couldn't check Mister as well, he told us Mister preferred to see his doctors in New York."

Betty St. John was also worried. "In December," she recalls, "I got a call from Dotty Evans. She was hysterical. She told me Mr. Wallace had become violently ill at dinner. His insides had just . . . *erupted!* John helped him to his bed, *and left him there!* No one called a doctor! No one did a *thing!* So Dotty called me to see if I could get someone at Headquarters to do something. I spoke with Jack O'Hara, and Jack spoke to James Stewart-Gordon."

"After clearing it with McHenry, I made an appointment with Irving Wright," recalls Stewart-Gordon. (Wright is a well-known cardiologist who operated his own geriatric center in Manhattan. Wallace had known him for years and supported his center financially.) "When I picked Wally up at High Winds on the morning of the appointment, I was shocked at how awful he looked. Skin and bones, and obviously suffering. McHenry was there, and before we left he slipped me an envelope to deliver to Wright. 'DW wants to make another gift,' he told me. 'There's a check inside.'

"When we got to Wright's office, the three of us chatted for a few minutes. Then I gave Wright the envelope and suggested he examine Wally. 'He's feeling rotten,' I said, 'although he won't admit it.' Wright then gave him a brief examination. Palpated his stomach, said it felt okay, and that was that. We went home."

Back at the Castle, Wallace retreated to his darkened bedroom to grapple with his pain in solitude. No one came to see him. No one called to inquire about his health. Complex arrangements had been made for the future of his Kingdom—for the dispersal of his power, his titles, his money—and now it seemed that those most blessed by these arrangements were waiting with the greatest impatience for him to die. O'Hara worried that McHenry might persuade him to sign another codicil. Cole worried that Thompson and O'Hara had turned their backs on him, and dreamed still of putting Fred Thompson on the Throne. McHenry worried that Cole might succeed in this. Or even that Ed Thompson, always unpredictable, might do something rash. There was still much work to be done—new S/Os to create, more stock to move—and as long as the old man was alive there was a chance something could go wrong. So everyone worried and waited and plotted. And nothing was done to help him.

At 2:15 P.M. on February 22, Dotty Evans sat reading in an armchair in Lila Wallace's bedroom, trying unsuccessfully to ignore the sounds coming from down the hall. Her shift had begun at 11:00 P.M. the night before—a double shift so the other nurses could be with their families over the weekend—and Evans was exhausted. Tending to Lila's needs was far from easy. The Queen of High Winds didn't always know who she was, but she knew perfectly well what she wanted and how she expected her days to unfold. "I like all my nurses," she was fond of saying. "But some of them"—her voice rising slightly—"some of them I like *better* then others."

Since DeWitt's illness had worsened, the after-lunch drives had been canceled, so on this day Lila had gone upstairs for her nap at two and was now fast asleep. In the stillness that filled the house, the sounds coming from DeWitt's room were impossible to shut out. His breathing was raspy and labored, and every few minutes he would have a spasm of violent coughing. Then the raspy breathing would begin again, punctuated by a series of low, rising moans.

When Evans could stand it no longer, she rose and went to his room. She opened the door a crack and peered inside. The room was dark, and the old man lay on his side with his back to the door, his emaciated body curled in a fetal position. A deep moan escaped him, and Evans's hand tightened on the doorknob. Every instinct urged to her to enter the room, to call a doctor, to summon an ambulance. Instead, she closed the door and returned to Lila's bedroom. As she waited out the final fifteen minutes of her shift, tears of frustration and anger welled in her eyes.

Later, driving down the High Winds hill, the tears fell freely down her cheeks. As she passed Gene Doherty's cottage, she suddenly pulled over and stopped her car. *Gene is as frustrated as I am,* she thought. *Maybe he will know what to do.*

Seated in Doherty's kitchen, Evans poured out her tale. "He's dying, Gene! I am sure of it! The sounds are *horrible!* But John won't let me in there. 'Mister is not your business,' he says. 'Stay away from Mister.' So I stay away. *Everyone* stays away!"

After Evans departed, Doherty brooded about the situation. His Boss was suffering, alone and uncared for. To ignore this was impossible. *But where were all the others?* What about the Wallace trustees? What about Barney McHenry? Where was Gordon Davies? These people should be doing something. *Why weren't they?*

"Perhaps they've given up," said Ilse. "Perhaps they've decided to let nature take its course." Doherty shook his head. He thought Evans was right: the old man was struggling to stay afloat, and the sharks were circling closer.

After a sleepless night, Doherty rose on Monday morning determined to do something. At 8:30, he dialed the Mt. Kisco Medical Group and asked for Dr. Fisher. He was told that Fisher would not be in until 1:00. At 10:30, he drove to the Leonard Park Building in Mt. Kisco, where the Wallaces kept offices for the managers of their charitable funds, and spoke with Gordon Davies. "DW's very sick, Gordon," said Doherty. "I'm thinkin' of takin' him to the hospital."

Davies was aware of his uncle's illness. But he also knew where the power lay just then at Reader's Digest, and who controlled the various trust funds established by the Wallaces for family members and friends. "Do what you think is right, Gene," he said.

Back at High Winds, Doherty killed time over a second cup of coffee. At 12:30, he climbed into his limousine and drove up the long hill to the mansion. As he crossed the foyer, John Strasburger emerged from his kitchen. "Where are *you* going?" he demanded.

"To get Mr. Wallace. He has an appointment at the Medical Group."

"Who authorized that?"

"Don't mess with me, John. He has an appointment. That's it."

Doherty glared at the little Austrian, and for a moment the two men seemed on the verge of a physical clash. Then Strasburger turned and slipped into his kitchen. Doherty proceeded up the curving main staircase, turned right down the upstairs hallway, walked past Lila Wallace's bedroom and down another short hallway to Dewitt's bedroom. Although it was almost one o'clock, venetian blinds were still drawn over the long leaded windows. The old man lay on his side, his back to Doherty. He seemed to be asleep. Doherty stepped into the room. "Mr. Wallace," he said. "It's Gene. We have an appointment at the Medical Group."

Wallace struggled to sit up. "What?" he said. "An appointment?"

"Yes, sir. At the Medical Group."

Doherty helped the old man dress, then led him down the hallway. As they descended the staircase, they became aware of John Strasburger glaring up at them. "You have no authority!" he hissed. "McHenry doesn't know of this!" Doherty glared right back. "Out of my way, John," he said. "Or you'll be goin' to the hospital yourself."

Ten minutes later, the limousine pulled up to the Medical Group's rear entrance. Doherty got Wallace inside, parked him in a chair by the receptionist's desk and asked for Fisher. "I have DeWitt Wallace with me," he said. "He needs to see the doc right away." While the receptionist hustled off to find Fisher, Doherty went outside to park the limo. When he returned, his charge was gone.

Doherty sat for a few minutes, then pushed his way into the nearest examination room. Fisher and a colleague were peering at an X ray. Wallace dozed in a nearby chair, moaning softly. "If you'll wait outside," said Fisher, "we'll be with you in a few minutes."

Doherty ignored him. "Is that DW's X ray?" he asked, stepping forward. Dorothy Evans had told him she suspected Wallace had an intestinal blockage. "Does it show a blockage?" The doctors looked at each other. "As a matter of fact, there is a blockage," said Fisher. "But there's not much to be done about it."

"I'm takin' him to the hospital," said Doherty. "Better have somebody call over."

By 4:00 P.M., Wallace was resting in a suite at Northern Westchester. Satisfied that he had done all he could, Doherty left the hospital and drove again to Leonard Park. He told Davies what had happened, and suggested that Davies inform McHenry. Then he drove to his cottage to await developments. Around seven, the phone rang. "I will be up to the hospital tomorrow morning," McHenry announced. "I want to talk with you."

When Doherty arrived at Wallace's suite the next morning, he found the old man's bed empty. The duty nurse told him the patient had been taken off for "prepping." "His intestinal obstruction is life-threatening," she said. "The doctors plan to operate right away."

"*Oh, no, they won't,*" said Doherty. "If they operate on him now, the way he is, he'll die!" The nurse shrugged. "You tell them no operation," Doherty said. "Tell them I'm calling his nephew."

Doherty went to a pay phone and called Gordon Davies. "We can't let these guys operate," he told Davies. "If they do, the Boss will die. We need to get him down to Columbia-Presbyterian. Let Doctor Latimer and the others down there take a look." Davies agreed to come straight to the hospital. "Make it fast, Gordon," begged Doherty. "I need you here."

Davies got to the hospital around eight, and after a brief conversation the nephew concluded that Doherty was right. The two men spoke with the nurse, and she made some calls. The operation was put on hold. Then Doherty called McHenry to tell him what they had done. The lawyer exploded. "Who the hell do you think you are?" he raved. "Don't do another thing! I will be there in an hour."

When McHenry arrived, around ten, there was "smoke pourin' from his ears." But Doherty stuck to his guns. "Mr. Wallace deserves the best medical care, Barney," he insisted. "He should see Doctor Latimer in New York. These doctors don't know him. If they operate today, with the Boss so weak, he'll die. If you authorize the operation, you must *want* him to die!"

McHenry's eyes bulged. *"That's not fair!"* he shouted. "I've been doing everything possible!" The lawyer glanced toward the nurses' station, then lowered his voice. "I know what's good for Mr. Wallace, Gene," he said. "You aren't the only one."

"Then it's simple, Barney. Let's get him down to Harkness Pavilion at Columbia. They'll know what to do."

McHenry considered these words. "All right," he said, glaring into Doherty's determined Irish face. "You want him there, *you* get him there." And the lawyer stalked away. Doherty asked the duty nurse to order an ambulance. "And you better call Harkness Pavilion and let them know we're on our way."

At Harkness, Wallace was wheeled to a private room on the tenth floor, where three physicians waited. One of them came forward. "Hello, Mr. Wallace," he said, sticking out his hand. "How are you?" Doherty recognized Latimer's assistant, Dr. Phillip Weidel.

After a brief exam, Weidel concluded that intravenous nutrition and hydration should begin immediately. While these arrangements were being made, McHenry strode into the room. "I'm Mr. Wallace's attorney," he announced. "Thank you all for getting here on such short notice." Before he could continue, a team of technicians arrived to connect Wallace to an array of IVs. Then Weidel again approached the bed. "You're in good hands now, Mr. Wallace," he said. "We're going to build you up a bit. When you've regained your strength, we'll run some tests. Nothing to worry about, but you'll be with us for a few weeks."

The doctors departed, and for a long moment the room was quiet. Doherty was standing on the far side of Wallace's bed; McHenry on the near side. The old man looked better than he had the day before, and when he spoke his voice was surprisingly firm. "Barney," he said, "I'd like to see my will. Would you bring it to me?"

McHenry's eyebrows lifted. "Sure, Wally," he said. "I'll take care of it. Don't worry about a thing."

McHenry signaled to Doherty that they should leave. In the hallway, the attorney put a hand on Doherty's shoulder. "Gene," he said, "I apologize for what happened at Northern Westchester. You were right about bringing Mr. Wallace to New York." The two men began to walk toward the elevator. "I rely on you greatly at High Winds, Gene," McHenry continued. "It's a difficult situation, and you and I have to work together. If we do, you can be sure of one thing: You will always have a job with Reader's Digest."

"That's great, Barney. I appreciate it." Doherty looked closely at the lawyer. "But what about the will?"

"He was kidding about that. You know DW. Always on my case."

"It didn't sound like kidding to me."

McHenry's smile faded. "Let me worry about that," he said. "You've got other things to worry about."

It was well after dark when Doherty finally got home. "What happened?" asked Ilse. "Well," he said, sitting heavily in a chair by the kitchen table, "Barney and I went to war. I won the opening round, I think. Now we have to wait for the bomb to drop."

When Doherty got Wallace to Columbia-Presbyterian that Tuesday, the old man was almost dead. Four days later, having been fed, hydrated and purged of sedatives, he was as close to normal as a cancer-ridden ninety-one-year-old man can be. By Saturday, he was deemed strong enough to withstand an exploratory operation. What the doctors found inside wasn't good: the cancer had spread from his colon, and was clearly untreatable. But they were able to clear away the intestinal blockage and otherwise to rearrange his insides so that eating would again be possible. A colostomy was performed and a tube installed to drain his urine (since his prostate was also involved). He had been in terrible agony; now he would be comfortable. The cancer was widespread but so slow-moving the doctors thought he might live for several months.

While Wallace recovered in the hospital, a debate raged back at Headquarters over how the old man had been allowed to reach such a shocking state. Not surprisingly, McHenry came under a lot of heat. In defense of McHenry, it should be noted that Wallace was a reluctant patient. "Wally simply wouldn't go for a physical," McHenry recalls, "And I couldn't persuade him." During a meeting with Betty St. John, Dorothy Little and Gene Doherty, Wallace was pressured to hire a new doctor, and he asked Dr. Robert Salerno, the Digest's in-house physician, to take over the case. Salerno agreed to do so, but within a week arranged to shift responsibility for the Wallaces to a younger associate.

When DeWitt came home on March 3, Dr. James McAvey was in charge, and now finally there were nurses on hand for the old man twenty-four hours a day. "There had been a lot of questions about what went on before his hospitalization," says Dorothy Schmidt, an RN from Northern Westchester who was hired later that spring. "With a blockage like that, records should be kept so you know what is happening and when things become serious. Had proper records been kept, something might have been done for Mr. Wallace much earlier."

From this point on, records were kept on everything that happened in the Pink Room. But records alone didn't help. The old man was hooked up to an IV and to something called a Foley catheter, and these devices made it difficult to get him out of bed. "He needed to get up and walk around," says Dotty Evans. "But he couldn't do this without help, and he hated to have anyone help him. So the nurses assigned to him watched TV all day and never went near him. He lay there in one position and naturally his lungs became congested."

When Gene Doherty entered High Winds on the afternoon of March 28, he felt as if he had entered a tomb. The kitchen to his left was empty, as was the butler's office to his right. There was no sign of John or Mary Strasburger, and only the wind rattling loose windows in the living room broke the silence. Doherty turned to his right and began to climb the staircase.

Because the hospital bed DeWitt now required was too large to fit into his own bedroom, he was occupying the south guest suite near the top of the stairway—known to staff as the Pink Room. Doherty pushed his way inside. Thin light streamed through the south windows. The old man was lying on his back, staring at the ceiling. "Hiya, Mr. Wallace!" Doherty said in a cheery voice. "How're we doin'?" Wallace struggled to sit up. A smile creased his face—the slow, sweet smile of a child—but when he spoke, his voice was gravelly and weak. "Hello, Gene," he said. "What time is it?"

"Four o'clock, Mr. Wallace. Just droppin' by to see how things are goin'." Wallace smiled again, leaning back now against his pillows. Despite all his troubles, his mood had brightened in recent weeks. He seemed gentler, more aware of the people around him. "Well," he said, repeating a joke between them, "given the alternative, Gene, things are goin' all right. But Gene"— his voice grew serious—"I was thinking this might be a good time to go in and see Mrs. Wallace. Could we manage that?"

"Sure, Mr. Wallace. No problem." Doherty helped his Boss into a bathrobe, a difficult process, and then more or less carried him through the sitting room and down the hall toward the distant suite occupied by Lila Wallace. He knocked once and quietly opened the door. The Queen of High Winds was sitting in bed, surrounded by pillows. Dorothy Evans occupied a nearby armchair, a book open in her lap.

As the two women looked on in surprise, Doherty gently deposited the old man onto Lila's bed, bracing him carefully against its padded footboard, then retreated several steps toward the door. Wallace raised his head to stare into the eyes of the woman who had shared his dreams for sixty years. "Hi, sweetie," he said. "It's me."

Lila glared back in angry incomprehension. The old man sighed, then looked away toward the French doors that led to Lila's balcony. The view beyond the windows was still wintry, but here and there—in the buds on Lila's magnolia, in the relative brightness of the late-afternoon sky—signs of spring could be detected. "Your flowers will be coming up soon, Lila," he said. "Daffodils. Hyacinths. . . . Won't that be nice? Aren't *hyacinths* your favorite?"

The old woman frowned. Her thoughts were clearly far away, focused on some sunny long-ago from which he was forever excluded. She closed her eyes. "When I'm feeling better, Lila," DeWitt continued, "we'll go for a drive. To West Point, perhaps? Or Ridgefield? Would you like that?"

When she made no reply, the old man pursed his lips. He appeared to be reaching for something, some happy image or memory that would please his wife and earn him the nod of approval that was all he had ever wanted from the world. But nothing came to him, and as the minutes ticked away his own confused thoughts seemed to wander off as well.

Watching them, Doherty thought how strange it was that two people who had traveled together for so long should have arrived at such separate destinations. He glanced at Evans. In response to his nod, the nurse rose from her chair and the two of them silently left the room. When Doherty returned several minutes later, Lila was asleep, and DeWitt was slumped against the bed's footboard, his head resting on his arm, his withered cheeks glistening with tears.

Near tears himself, Doherty laid a gentle hand on his Boss's shoulder. The old man looked up at this, and from somewhere again produced a childlike smile. "Gene," he said, "I'm a little tired. Maybe we'd better go back."

As Doherty was helping him toward the door, Wallace stopped in mid-shuffle and turned to look one more time in the direction of his wife. For a long moment, he strained to take in that familiar face, a face he had first glimpsed seventy Christmases before, coming toward him across Reverend Acheson's crowded living room, smiling and eager, taking his breath away. Another sigh escaped him. His little plan, hyacinths and all, had failed. There had been no nod, no smile of approval. With a visible effort—aware that this might be his last chance—he turned away.

The two men slowly renavigated the passage to the Pink Room. When

Doherty was satisfied that the old man was comfortable, he prepared to leave. "Okay, Mr. Wallace," he said. "You take care, now."

"Wait a minute, Gene." The old man clutched at Doherty's sleeve. There was something he wanted to say, some . . . *connection* . . . he wanted to make, but it wasn't coming easy. He had given away millions of dollars at the drop of a hat, sometimes to individuals he barely knew. Now, face-to-face with his honest servant, he was nearly overcome with shyness. He began again. "You've been a good friend, Gene. A very good friend. If there is anything you need . . . anything at all . . . you better ask me. And you better ask me *now.*"

"No, no. I don't need anything, Mr. Wallace," said Doherty. "I'm fine. As long as I have my job, I'm fine. Don't you worry about it. And don't you worry about Mrs. Wallace. I'll always be here to care for her."

"Good!" The old man released Doherty and lay back on his pillow. He appeared to be exhausted but also strangely pleased. Gene Doherty had served him loyally for many years—had been his friend, his *real* friend, not like the others. Yet, in all that time, he had never been able to acknowledge this fact, to put it into words, face-to-face. Now he had done so. It was a small step; he was aware of that. Still, he had taken it. And he was glad.

March 30 was a busy day in the Pink Room. Around three that afternoon, Judy Thompson arrived at High Winds for her first visit since the Christmas Massacre sixteen years before. "I had heard that Wally was dying," she says today, "and I decided—whatever the situation at High Winds—that I was going to see him one last time. To my amazement, he insisted on getting out of bed, and when I admired his tartan bathrobe he put one hand on his nurse's shoulder and one on mine and performed a Highland fling. I was astonished. Then he sat down and for thirty minutes we had a wonderful chat. He asked about my children and grandchildren, what they were doing for pleasure, what their school plans were. He was very gentle, very *connected.* For the first time in years, I felt I was talking directly to DeWitt Wallace, the real man behind the screwy façade."

At five o'clock that afternoon, Julie Waldrun wheeled Lila into the Pink Room to say hello. "I had begun doing this every evening, knowing he might die at any time. But Mrs. Wallace didn't like these visits. She wanted to go to her own room and she kept talking about 'Barclay.' During his first weeks at home, Mr. Wallace tried every way he could to cheer her up—'We've had a wonderful life, Lila! We've been so lucky!'—things like that. But on this occasion he looked at her sadly, and said nothing. And she kept looking at the door."

Shortly after seven, DeWitt's night nurse—a pretty young woman named Joan, barely out of her teens—helped him into the bathroom. On their way back to the bed, DeWitt suddenly fell forward, clasping his arms around Joan's waist. *"Oh!"* he cried. "You stepped on my toe!" Then he straightened and smiled at the startled nurse. "Only kidding," he murmured, releasing her waist. The nurse regarded him with astonishment—a ninety-one-year-old dying man behaving like a teenager. "Why, Mr. Wallace," she said, smiling back at him. "You are something else!"

He had pulled off his Final Stunt. And Joan the Nurse had rewarded him with a smile that was all he could expect just then by way of approval. It would have to do.

Around nine o'clock, Joan came down to Lila's room to ask Julie to watch the old man while she went downstairs for a pitcher of ice water. "I had a feeling, standing there by his bedside, that it was almost over," recalls Julie. "And one hour later—at 10:02—his breathing stopped and he was gone."

In the week that followed DeWitt's death, all those who had stayed away during the last years suddenly rediscovered High Winds. Lila was inundated with flowers and phone calls, and a parade of cars bearing well-wishers began to pour through the gates. She was ninety-three years old, weighed barely one hundred pounds, and no longer understood who or even exactly where she was. She was also sole owner of one of the largest private corporations in the world, and therefore (although such things are hard to judge) possibly the Richest Woman on Earth. So it is not surprising that so many sought to register their concern. "Everybody wanted to be the *first* to console Lila," recalls James Stewart-Gordon, "because no one knew yet what was in the will. Once it became clear that everything was going to charity, her phone went dead again overnight."

The week between Wallace's death and his memorial service on April 6 was a nervous time for Barney McHenry. He asked Ilse Doherty to write down the names of everyone who came through the High Winds gate. But there was no way to keep these people out, or to screen all the phone calls, and thus no way to control what was said to the Queen. He was concerned as well about the memorial service. The interior of the Castle was a disgrace— empty shelves, missing furniture, peeling paint—and this would surely be noticed. Lila herself, after a few calm days, was off the wall again, and there were people coming who would not understand this.

Mary Strasburger also had a nervous week. "Today has been a hell day," she wrote in her diary on April 2. "People are mad because McHenry don't invite them. . . . What will happen to us when Mrs. dies? We will get pushed out, and I know why. We know too much."

Back in 1978, Wallace had scratched out instructions "in case of death": "LAW and DW desire cremation; ashes to be spread in Lila's Rose Garden; simple, private service (no eulogy) at High Winds, conducted, if available, by NV Peale (to be paid $500)." On the reverse side of the note, he listed the guests he wanted to be invited. For such a famous man, the list was very short: just twelve names, including his brother Robert (the sole surviving sibling), his nephew, his and Lila's secretaries, and the eight men who had been his closest associates. Barney McHenry was not on the list, nor was Laurance Rockefeller, an oversight corrected by McHenry when he put together an "official" list that included forty names. (But not the name of Dotty Evans. When Gordon Davies protested about this—"It was only Dotty and Gene Doherty, after all, who kept screaming about DW's illness. Everyone else ignored their repeated cries for help"—McHenry relented.)

At 10:00 A.M. on the morning of the service, the lawyer arrived at High Winds carrying a square box in his arms. Gene Doherty was in the rotunda at the time, giving instructions to drivers hired to bring guests up from "down below." After checking on the seating and the flowers, McHenry headed back out the door, still carrying the strange box. "I'll be right back," he told Doherty.

Curious, Doherty followed the lawyer around the garages and out to the small terrace that sits above Lila's Rose Garden. For a moment, the two men stood there—McHenry at the top of stone stairs leading down to the garden, Doherty several steps behind him. Then McHenry turned and glared at Doherty. "What do *you* want?" he growled. "You stay here!"

So Doherty watched from the terrace while the lawyer descended the stairs and walked to the center of the garden. "I won't ever forget what happened next," says Doherty. "Barney opened the box, tipped it upside down and dumped its contents on the ground. Just like that. When he passed me coming back up the steps, he gave me a nasty look. 'Don't be so nosy,' he said."

The service began at eleven o'clock, and was short and to the point, as Wallace had requested. Lila was there in her wheelchair, looking confused, with Dotty Evans on one side and Dot Little on the other. McHenry took up a position in the rear of the High Winds living room, and remained there as various guests rose to speak their words of affection and respect. Despite instructions, Norman Peale did deliver a eulogy, and his words were so excessive that had Wallace himself somehow been present he would surely have fled the room in embarrassment: "I don't suppose we'd say that he was perfect. Who among us is? But he was as near to perfect as anybody could be because he loved people. He believed in America, in freedom, in free enterprise, in goodness, in decency, in morality. The man who lived in this house, who looked out over these hills, of him it may be said that he saved America. It's not too much to assert . . ."

As the Positive Thinker's final "Amen" floated over the heads of the mourners, Barney McHenry edged away from his position in the rear of the room, quickly crossed the rotunda and exited to his waiting car. Questions were sure to be asked during the luncheon that followed the service: How had it happened? What about the *future?* McHenry clearly wanted no part of them. In particular, he wanted no part of Gordon Davies, Betty St. John or Al Cole, each of whom had been active in the War and each of whom knew in some detail the role McHenry had played. He resented them for this, and would later find ways to pay them back.

(As executor of DeWitt's will, one of McHenry's responsibilities was to distribute to friends and family members various of the dead man's personal belongings. Gordon Davies had had the effrontery to complain about his treatment of Dotty Evans. To loyal Gordon, McHenry awarded the old man's false teeth. Betty St. John had typed up every memo created during the War with Al Cole, and her knowledge of the details they contained burned in her eyes every time she looked at him. To angry Betty, he gave the little jade box DeWitt had kept on his bureau for holding cuff links. The box had a broken hinge, and when it arrived at Betty's house it contained—as if in compensation for forty years of devoted service—three broken sand dollars and a note from McHenry: "Thought you might like these. Barney." Al Cole had fought him tooth and nail, and almost won. Al had always wanted to be a rich man, and to have a rich man's fine estate. To stubborn Al, he sent a faded aerial photograph of High Winds, cracked where it had been folded in half. Across the bottom, as on a souvenir, was the legend: "High Winds, Byram Lake, N.Y.")

It turned out that McHenry's early departure from the memorial service was a wise move. Halfway through a second drink, Cole began to mutter darkly about the lawyer, and about the War, and about "all the things I should have done." Standing in the rotunda, talking with Fred Thompson and Gene Doherty (but loud enough so several others heard him), the old salesman worked himself into a teary-eyed fury. "I should have done something," he said. "He threatened to declare Wally incompetent, even to have him committed. *And I let him get away with it!*"

Later, as the party gathered steam, a Digest public-affairs executive named Bob Devine began escorting various guests, including Peggy Cole and Judy Thompson, out to the Rose Garden. "Look," he exclaimed to Peggy Cole, pointing to a small pile of ash and bits of white bone. "That's all that's left of DeWitt Wallace!"

The next morning, as Gene Doherty was wheeling Lila Wallace along the upstairs hallway past the Pink Room, the old woman suddenly raised her hand for him to stop. "Where did the man go?" she asked, clearly upset.

"What man, Mrs. Wallace?" asked Doherty. For several seconds, she struggled for his name—for *his* name, not Barclay's—and when it failed to come her blue eyes flashed with irritation.

"The . . . *man,*" she said again, nodding toward the Pink Room. "From in there. The one they took away."

THE YEARS AFTER

1981–1994

PART VI

Strange Coincidence

1981–1984

CHAPTER TWENTY-NINE

In the weeks following DeWitt's funeral, Lila Wallace slipped ever deeper into a world of her own. Her chief diversion remained the daily drive with Gene Doherty, and her favorite destination that spring was the corporate paradise she had created down at Headquarters. Doherty would cruise around the grounds, pausing here and there so she could look out at certain settings—the Daffodil Field, the Pegasus Fountain, the Dogwood Walk. "Oh, beautiful," she would murmur. "*Soo* beautiful."

At noon, Doherty would park in a quiet corner of the farthest lot. A window would roll down and a tiny old woman could be seen sitting quietly in the rear seat, head canted to one side, listening as the carillon atop the Pegasus Tower played a medley of popular tunes. When the music ended, after fifteen minutes, the window went back up and the limo rolled away. If the weather was nice, Doherty sometimes stopped by the Guesthouse to pick up a picnic basket prepared by Jean Rossi—lemonade and little ham sandwiches with the crusts cut off—before driving across the rolling field behind the Guesthouse to a knoll that was the highest point of land on the Headquarters property. He would park the car facing west, so Lila could survey the working portion of her Kingdom while she ate.

That she was no longer Queen of what she surveyed did not occur to her.

Nor did she comprehend that there were men at work in the Headquarters building—her former dukes and barons, now her keepers—to whom she had ceded all rights and powers, her voice itself. She was the Richest Woman in the World, and very likely one of its most wretched, bereft of husband, friends, family, shorn of privilege and position, left to the mercies of a loyal chauffeur and the assorted caretakers her keepers saw fit to provide.

But at least Lila's life was simple now. For her keepers, life was increasingly complex. Outwardly, her six proxy-holders appeared to be divided into two well-defined groups: the young insiders—O'Hara, Thompson and Cross; and the aging outsiders—Rockefeller, Cole and Helm. But the appearance of symmetry was misleading. O'Hara and Thompson were committed to running the Kingdom the way Wallace had run it (as they had *promised* him they would run it), and therefore could be counted on to vote in favor of a management philosophy emphasizing *service*. Rockefeller controlled his elderly colleagues, and thus by himself represented three votes in favor of a different way of running things, emphasizing *profit*. Unlike Thompson and O'Hara, Cross had made no promises to the Wallaces, and, in fact, looked upon the Wallace traditions as foolish. So Cross saw himself as isolated between the two groups.

His was a position with many possibilities. If he voted with his inside colleagues against the three old men, the result would be a stalemate and, in effect, a victory for the Wallace faction. If he went the other way, his vote would tip the balance in Rockefeller's favor, turning on a green light and setting off a stampede for profits. Then there was the matter of Lila. When she died, her proxies would terminate and the six former proxy-holders would become trustees. If she died in 1981, the situation would remain unchanged. If she died in 1982, Cole would be disqualified by age from serving as a trustee, and therefore the numbers would switch to 3 to 2 or 2 to 3, making Cross's vote more potent still. If she died in 1983 or later, Helm would also be disqualifed, producing the worst possible situation for the Rockefeller faction: a possible 3 to 1 vote against or—again depending on Cross—a 2 to 2 stalemate that was just as bad. In either case, O'Hara and Thompson would control at least 50 percent of the votes and be unbudgeable.

Before that happened—at some point while Rockefeller still enjoyed the upper hand—there was the distinct possibility that O'Hara or Thompson, or both, might *themselves* be disqualified (through termination), and this would produce at least two additional sets of numbers to contemplate (including a set in which Cross and Rockefeller would be the *only* trustees). The possibilities were mind-boggling, and it was not lost on Cross that the mathematics varied according to whether Lila was alive or dead.

Yet, whatever happened, Cross himself was likely to remain in the middle of the fray, sought after by both sides and thus in a position, when the time came, to expect a proper reward in return for his vote. Meanwhile, it would be important to keep his options open, but also to bear in mind that Laurance Rockefeller was the master player in the game and likely to win in the end. Which, in Cross's view, would be the proper outcome. To him, Reader's Digest was a business, pure and simple. As a business, its sole function was to maximize profits.

McHenry felt the same way, and as 1981 progressed the two men became closer than ever. McHenry knew the numbers and their ramifications even better than Cross, having created them himself, and it must have seemed to him just then that they were working out as planned. Laurance looked like a sure winner, and since his victory would depend in part on Cross's vote, Cross was likely to win as well. As the ally of both men, McHenry could count on a large reward: control over the Wallace Funds, and the great wealth and power they would comprise in the years that lay ahead.

But it all depended on Laurance, and therefore McHenry lost no opportunity to cement their relationship. In 1978, he had pleased Laurance by making a million-dollar gift of Lila's money to the Juilliard School at Lincoln Center (where Laurance's brother John served as chairman). In 1979, when a fund drive for Asia House (another of John Rockefeller's interests) seemed likely to come up short, McHenry had supplied a second million. In 1981, he arranged for a million dollars' worth of Digest stock to be transferred from the DeWitt Wallace Fund to the Fund for Spelman College. Spelman had been the Atlanta Female Baptist Seminary until receiving a large gift from John D. Rockefeller, Sr., in 1884, after which it was renamed in honor of Senior's wife, Laura Spelman Rockefeller (from whom Laurance's own name —*Laurance Spelman* Rockefeller—is derived). Thus blessed with Digest stock, the Spelman Fund stood ready—like the S/Os themselves—to benefit spectacularly when the green light went on in the Kingdom. (In fact, the Spelman gift would come to be worth nearly $42 million.)

But all these miscellaneous services were dwarfed by the help McHenry provided in the creation of additional S/Os funded by huge transfers of Digest stock and devoted to charities with deep and abiding connections to the Rockefeller family, and to Laurance Rockefeller in particular. The process that had begun in 1980 with Macalester, followed by Williamsburg and the Metropolitan Museum, continued during the early eighties with gifts to the following organizations: 550,000 shares to Lincoln Center; 250,000 shares to the Bronx Zoo; 200,000 shares to Sloan-Kettering Cancer Center; and 475,000 shares to a mysterious entity called the Fund for Hudson Highlands. When this final gift was in place, nearly two-thirds of the ownership of Reader's Digest had been transferred from Wallace Funds to Rockefeller charities.

As 1981 came to a close, Laurance could take great satisfaction in the progress of the plan to "adopt" the only child DeWitt and Lila Wallace ever had. Phase I ("Courting the Founders") was over and Phase II ("Moving the Stock") was right on schedule. Yet the course ahead was not without shoals and foggy areas. Jack O'Hara had proved a disappointment as chief executive, and had begun to show signs of cracking under pressure. Would he ever shape up as a proper leader for the post-Wallace era? If he did not, was Ed Thompson the answer? Laurance clearly worried that the blunt-spoken editor might be too independent and (like O'Hara) too committed to the Wallace way of doing business. But if not Thompson, who?

Then there was the problem of Lila. For the time being, her longevity was a blessing, offering a breathing space in which to complete the transfer of the stock, and for making whatever executive changes proved necessary. But these matters would have to be expedited because it was clear that Lila would not be around much longer.

They would give it a year. If O'Hara wasn't able to turn things around during 1982, changes would be made. Someone had to be in place when Lila died who understood "good business." Al Cole had begun to lobby for George Grune, the aggressive director of RD's books-and-recorded-music division, and Laurance was inclined to agree. Grune was the kind of man who wouldn't shrink from the steps necessary to launch Phase III of the overall plan (which came to be known as "Pumping the Stock").

In late April of 1981, Lila Wallace was invited down to the Bronx Zoo to attend the "christening" of three California condors—the first condors ever born in captivity. Doherty drove her down, with Dotty Evans along to provide nursing assistance. The baby condors had been named "Lila," "Bell" and "Wallace," in the great lady's honor—a modest gesture, in view of her generosity to the zoo—but when they were formally presented to her, Lila grimaced in disgust. "Ooh, *ooh!*" she said. "They're soo *ugly!*" Doherty had to walk away to hide his laughter, and Dotty Evans giggled behind her hand.

Although Evans was resented by the other nurses (because of a tendency to "take over"), she was by this time very close to Lila. But Evans's days at High Winds were numbered. In early May, after straining her back, she asked for time off. McHenry agreed. But when she phoned about coming back, the lawyer told her she had been replaced. So Lila had lost another friend. (In her diary entry for May 5, Mary Strasburger makes note of Evans's departure: "Dottie Evans not coming back! Now everything going good for us!")

Later that year, when the weather turned cold, the worst problem the nurses had with Lila was keeping her warm. "High Winds was incredibly drafty," recalls Dorothy Schmidt. "When the wind blew, it didn't matter how high the thermostat was set. The place was freezing. We had to pile several blankets on Mrs. Wallace's bed, and wrap blankets around her in the wheelchair."

In October, Janine Ardohain became upset over the state of Lila's nightgowns. She spoke to John about the problem, and John nearly took her head off. "He went berserk," recalls Jean Rossi. "Screamed at Janine. Told her to mind her own business." For a time, Janine did this. But in December, with the wind whistling through every room at High Winds, she wrote a note to Dorothy Little:

Dear Mrs. Little: Could you please send Mrs. Wallace three long nightgowns, preferably of heavy cotton flannel? Her two remaining gowns are in rags. When I mentioned this to John he became enraged, so I don't dare ask him again. Please don't let him know about this note. It would create another scene, which we certainly don't need.

Little purchased some decent flannel nightgowns, and arranged for Gene Doherty to get them up to Lila's room. So by Christmas of that year the Queen of High Winds had something warm to wear at night. But it wasn't much of a holiday, even so. "No one came to visit her," recalls Janine. "She was all alone—no husband, no friends, no family. In the evenings, I would park her wheelchair so she could see the Christmas tree in the rotunda from her spot by the fireplace. Then I would play a tape of Christmas carols—a Digest tape, all the old favorites—and the two of us would sit there and sing along. She always reached out and grabbed my hand at such times, and when we sang certain carols—'O, Come, All Ye Faithful,' 'Joy to the World,' others like that—huge tears came pouring down her cheeks. Her mind was far away, back in her childhood, and the memories that came to her were overwhelming."

CHAPTER THIRTY

Although much has been written about Jack O'Hara's "disastrous" reign as RD's chief executive, in fact, as 1982 began, he could look back on a record that was at worst mixed. There were problems ahead, no doubt. But the company had earned before-tax profits of $78 million in 1981, on revenues of $1.1 billion—both all-time records—and had done so with no lowering of Wallace standards. It was also true that the problems looming most seriously were industry-wide and could not be blamed on O'Hara alone.

Every magazine was faced with falling newsstand sales during this period. Back in the late sixties, *Digest* single-copy sales had peaked at just over two million a month. This number had fallen steadily during the seventies, and by 1982 was under a million. To make up for these lost sales (and to maintain the eighteen million in overall circulation guaranteed to advertisers), the magazine had been forced to spend heavily on promotion activities. By 1982, these expenditures were nibbling seriously at profits from circulation.

Advertising revenues were also down, but, again, this was not O'Hara's fault. There was a recession going on in 1982, and ad revenues were falling throughout the industry. At RD, the losses were substantial but not ruinous: pages were down 14 percent for the year, and revenues down 7 percent (from $112 million to $105 million).

These losses were compounded by a frustrating situation overseas. Although the company's foreign editions were doing fine, a strong U.S. dollar was resulting in losses through currency translations of several million dollars a year. "Overall, the company's earnings are solid," Bill Cross told the *New York Times.* "But they are not at the level we've enjoyed in recent years."

As the profit picture soured, O'Hara was criticized by Wall Street and Madison Avenue for his conservative policy toward growth. "They sit there with this enormous storehouse of mailing lists," said one self-appointed expert. "If they were truly aggressive, they would do far more." Responding to such criticism, and to ever-mounting pressures to "do more" from aggressive colleagues like George Grune and Dick McLoughlin, O'Hara began to plunge into other businesses. And then he was criticized again when these ventures performed indifferently in the face of the 1981–82 recession.

The one bright spot in the company's fortunes in the early eighties was the books-and-recorded-music division presided over by George Grune. "We're in the research business," Grune boasted at the time. "We research every book we publish so thoroughly as to leave nothing to chance." The process began with an idea—say, for a history of the American Indians. The idea was converted into a brochure that was mailed to a sampling of "scientifically selected" names from the Digest's huge list. If enough of these names expressed interest in buying such a book, the brochure was translated into an outline that was sent out to another sample to test the relative appeal of various subject areas. Whatever sections of the outline survived this step were then further refined during a series of focus-group interviews. The result—in effect, a "book blueprint"—was fed into the

Digest's computers. If the numbers churned out by the computers indicated a sale large enough to cover predicted costs *plus* a hefty profit, the editors were given a green light. "Every book we publish," crowed Grune, "is a guaranteed best-seller!"

Although grateful for the revenues produced by Grune's division, O'Hara worried that Wallace standards were being ignored. "In the early days of that division, you could not publish a book that did not pass muster with Wally," he says. "Whatever its potential for profit, every book had to meet three tests —for value, quality and service—or it wasn't published. Under George, that began to change."

Wallace himself had worried from the beginning that the book business might get away from him, and had made his concern clear to the entire staff in a 1964 memo:

> In considering books for publication, the first questions asked should not be: "Can we promote this product? Can we sell it? Can we make a large profit from it?" Instead, we should ask ourselves: "Will this book be read? Will the buyer be happy with it? Will he feel he got his money's worth?"

During this same period, O'Hara was faced with the problem of *Families* magazine, the first new publication launched by the company in fifty-eight years. Three test issues distributed via newsstand in 1980 and 1981 had been successful, and the magazine was officially launched as a monthly in October 1981. Readers were enthusiastic, as were Wall Street and Madison Avenue, and for a time *Families* looked like the big success O'Hara needed. But then the fledgling magazine ran into the recession, and its numbers began to fade. To save money, the company had introduced *Families* on newsstands only, hoping to establish it there before risking the $30 million required for a full-scale subscription campaign. But when early newsstand sales failed to reach the level guaranteed to advertisers, O'Hara began to get cold feet.

In the spring of 1982, just when everything else was going sour for him, O'Hara was faced with a go/no-go decision on *Families*. Ed Thompson was eager to forge ahead. "Our figures showed us going into the black during the third year out from 1982," says Thompson. "But only if we discounted losses incurred up to that point—roughly thirteen million dollars. If we had to include those losses—money that was already spent—then the black was several years farther out."

O'Hara wasn't sure he believed the figures. If his colleagues were right, fine. If they were wrong, the company's exposure could run over $100 million. So O'Hara made a rule: If there was a way to demonstrate profitability for *Families* within five years, including every penny spent to date, it would live.

If not, it would die. *"Families* would have been a winner," says Thompson. "But there was no way to meet Jack's rule, so that was it. We folded our tent."

There are many possible explanations for O'Hara's cold feet: the recession, the grim advertising climate, his colleagues' tendency to be over-optimistic. But it is likely that something else was involved. Long term—eight to ten years down the line—*Families* appeared a sure winner. Every study supported such a view. But for Digest executives, long term had become a dangerous way to look at things. Ownership of the company was being turned over to charities eager to maximize financial returns. Keeping those charities in line (and keeping their powerful benefactor happy) would be difficult enough without complicating the situation by dedication to a new endeavor that promised to lose money for several years.

The failure of *Families* dug a crater in the Digest's 1982 bottom line, and the company's stock plunged to below $6. O'Hara's own stock headed for the cellar as well, and as it did the once-feisty Scot began to show signs of strain. "There was always this tremendous pressure," he says today. *"Give way! Relax the standards!* But you couldn't do it. If you gave an inch, those guys took a mile. It simply wasn't possible to run the Digest to Wally's standards and please Laurance and his charities at the same time. They wanted one thing: *Money!* Same for Grune and McLoughlin and the rest of them. 'Wally's gone and good riddance,' was their attitude. 'If we can get rich quicker by doing this and this and that, *let's do it!'* So that was it. The tide was rising. You couldn't hold it back."

During this same period, Ed Thompson was engaged in an endgame of his own, although he was too honest and unsuspecting to realize it. In fact, whatever problems existed on O'Hara's side of the equation, Thompson himself had every reason to feel secure as editor-in-chief. By the beginning of 1982, his tenure was widely regarded as extremely successful—as good, many in the company felt, as the best years under Wallace himself. Even outside observers were impressed. "Readers are well satisfied with the magazine," reported the *Columbia Journalism Review* in 1983. "The 'enthusiasm quotients' measured in monthly readership surveys have risen steadily during Thompson's years, and the magazine's subscription renewal rate stands at an impressive 70 percent."

Yet beneath the praise there were problems. In fact, there were clouds gathering over Thompson's future as dark as any surrounding Jack O'Hara. One of them was cast by the unlikely figure of James Stewart-Gordon. Back in 1976, when Thompson had been struggling with the aging-writer problem, he had tried to persuade Stewart-Gordon to surrender his freelance status and come on board as a salaried employee. "That way," he explained, "you'll be able to retire in a few years with a decent pension." But Stewart-Gordon had turned him down. He had a note from Wallace promising a lifetime retainer, and he regarded the note as a solemn contract. "I want to keep doing what I have been doing," he insisted.

"But you haven't been doing *anything*," Thompson pointed out. "We can put you on pension at *twice* what Wally's letter offers. If you want to keep writing occasional pieces, fine. We'll pay you."

But Stewart-Gordon was adamant. "If you feel I'm not contributing," he said, "perhaps I shouldn't get a retainer at all."

"Perhaps that's right," said Thompson. "Let's cut off your retainer and raise your article rate."

The meeting ended on that note, and Stewart-Gordon chose to interpret Thompson's final offer as tantamount to dismissal. He wrote less for the *Digest* after that, and became openly bitter. Soon he was telling everyone that Thompson was "ruining the magazine." He assembled a file of articles sponsored by Thompson—articles he considered "liberal and negative"— and in August 1981 showed the file to Al Cole. Cole had his own complaints about Thompson, feeling that the younger man didn't listen very well, and his resentment had festered into a conviction that Thompson was wandering from the magic formula his friend Wally had perfected.

After his meeting with Stewart-Gordon, Cole pulled several old *Digest*s from his bookshelf and compared the number of "art-of-living" articles they contained with those in current issues.* He sent the result of his study to Thompson. "Perhaps I'm wrong about this, Ed," his memo concluded. "But I am sure that for many years it was art-of-living articles that helped RD's sale to grow and grow."

Thompson replied with a lengthy analysis of his own, the gist of which he summarized in a short note: "The percentage of art-of-living is as high as it ever was, Al. The actual number of articles may be down slightly, but that is because the *total* number of articles is down. I thank you for your concern."

Thompson had his analysis hand-delivered to Cole in Greenwich. But the old salesman ignored it, and his campaign against Thompson gathered steam. He and Stewart-Gordon met with Rockefeller to discuss Thompson's short-comings, and Laurance appeared to be intrigued by what they told him. Flimsy as their complaints were, it was possible to see a use for them down the line should the "trustee situation" ever make a case for Thompson's elimination.

But Thompson's problems went far beyond the rantings of Cole and Stew-art-Gordon. Under Hobe Lewis, the *Digest*'s Washington bureau had grown

---

* A perennially popular category comprised of human dramas at the core of which readers are meant to discover certain "life-enhancing" principles.

accustomed to being the magazine's dominant political voice. Although himself a staunch Republican, Thompson infuriated the bureau by regularly allowing other voices into the mix, including some that seemed "damn liberal" to the conservatives in Washington.

And then there was the "intelligence" problem. For decades, ever since the OSS had been so helpful with those first international editions, *Reader's Digest* had been a willing conduit for CIA and FBI propaganda.* This relationship became especially intense during the early sixties as the CIA, in an effort to build support for its coming invasion of Cuba, sponsored a series of violent anti-Castro articles in *RD*'s pages ("The Facts about Castro's Propaganda," "The Sinister Man Behind Castro," "Castro Betrayed Our Country!"). When the landing at the Bay of Pigs failed (largely because of CIA mismanagement), the Agency vented its frustration in a fresh series of *Digest* articles defending its plans and bitterly attacking the Kennedy administration for "cowardice" ("Lessons of the Cuban Disaster!," "The Truth About the Bay of Pigs," "Cuba, Castro and John F. Kennedy," etc., etc.).

Later in the sixties, with Richard Nixon in the White House and Hobe Lewis running things in Pleasantville, *Reader's Digest* became a virtual house organ for the administration and its right-wing allies. But when Ed Thompson became editor in 1976, all this began to change. The magazine remained as patriotic and anti-Communist as ever, perfectly willing to cooperate with the intelligence agencies when their information appeared valid and could be independently confirmed. In 1977, for example—with substantial assistance from the CIA—the *Digest* became the first popular medium to reveal the wholesale slaughter of Cambodian civilians at the hands of the Khmer Rouge under the murderous Pol Pot. Written by John Barron and roving editor Anthony Paul, under the guidance of Ken Gilmore, "Murder of a Gentle Land" (published by Reader's Digest Press and simultaneously condensed in *Reader's Digest*) appeared to confirm the direst predictions of Vietnam hard-liners and thus to justify the Vietnam trauma itself (and in that way to cleanse a "resurgent America" of the dreaded Vietnam Syndrome). Although scholars would later prove that "Murder" was in part propaganda (based on faked interviews and studies fabricated by the CIA), the book was widely praised at the time and became a best-seller.

Yet Thompson remained wary of the CIA/FBI connection. He listened to

* That dozens of America's most powerful news media were cooperating with the CIA became public knowledge in 1977, when reporter Carl Bernstein published his groundbreaking "The CIA and the Media" in *Rolling Stone*. Curiously, Bernstein failed to mention *Reader's Digest*—an oversight corrected in 1983 when the *Atlanta Journal* published a series on CIA infiltration of the press. During the sixties, claimed the *Journal*, Time/Life had been favored by the Agency. "But in recent years CIA watchers have seen *Reader's Digest* achieving 'most favored status' by the CIA."

their propositions, as conveyed by his Washington colleagues, and sometimes went along. But he wasn't willing to accept as gospel whatever the two agencies "made available." Instead, he encouraged his editors in Pleasantville to follow the facts wherever they led. On several occasions in the late seventies *Digest* writers actually *sued* the CIA, under the Freedom of Information Act, for documents the Agency preferred to withhold. None of this sat well with the Washington bureau, whose editors often seemed closer to the intelligence agencies than to *RD* itself. Thus the rift between Washington and Pleasantville yawned ever wider. When a former KGB major named Yuri Nosenko showed up, the rift became a chasm no one could bridge.

The origins of the Nosenko affair go back to 1962, when a senior KGB officer named Anatoli Golitsyn defected to the United States. Information provided by Golitsyn quickly established him—particularly in the eyes of James Angleton, legendary director of U.S. counterintelligence—as the most valuable defector in years. But Golitsyn brought with him several disturbing messages.

The Cuban missile crisis had recently ended in what was being hailed as a triumph for the Kennedy administration and the CIA. "Not so," said Golitsyn. Secret missile documents obtained by the CIA via double agent Oleg Penkovsky, which had been considered vital during the crisis, were in fact KGB "plants" designed to "provoke and control" the U.S. response. The missiles themselves, said Golitsyn, "had been placed in Cuba as bargaining chips."

For two years prior to the crisis, the CIA had been trying (with John Kennedy's approval and via such exotica as exploding seashells, toxic diving suits and poisoned fountain pens) to assassinate Fidel Castro. The young president, "outblustered" by Nikita Khrushchev during their initial meeting in 1961, appeared determined to reassert his authority by eliminating Khrushchev's surrogate in the Caribbean. The "Missiles of October" were Khrushchev's response. And the missiles were removed only after Kennedy agreed "to recognize the legitimacy" of the Castro regime. (Despite this agreement, the attacks on Castro—carried out by an army of rogue CIA agents, Mafia gangsters and embittered Cuban exiles—continued.)

Golitsyn's news—that a U.S. "triumph" might, in fact, be a Soviet deception—was not something the Kennedy brothers or the CIA wanted to hear. Indeed, the CIA was already preparing a book, based on what it claimed were Oleg Penkovsky's personal diaries, hailing the triumph. Published by Doubleday in 1965, *The Penkovsky Papers* became a huge best-seller and was subsequently excerpted in *Reader's Digest.* "But all of it is nonsense," insisted Golitsyn. And James Angleton believed Golitsyn.

Golitsyn also warned that a Soviet operative had penetrated U.S. intelligence at a high level, and that in the near future the KGB would start sending false defectors to divert attention from this valuable "mole." Sure enough, a stream of high-ranking Soviet intelligence officers began to show up at various U.S. installations around the globe, including a UN diplomat, codenamed "Fedora," who despite Golitsyn's warnings quickly established himself as a valued source for the FBI in New York.

On November 22, 1963, John Kennedy was assassinated in Dallas, under circumstances that strongly suggested KGB/Cuban retribution for the attacks on Castro, and for a time the world teetered on the edge of chaos. Then Yuri Nosenko defected to the CIA in Geneva—just as Golitsyn had predicted—and on the basis of the messages he brought with him the world was able to step back.

Golitsyn was wrong, Nosenko said. There was no Soviet penetration of the CIA. And he had more important news: He had been Lee Harvey Oswald's control officer during Oswald's three years in Moscow, and had reviewed Oswald's entire KGB file just prior to defecting. Suspicions about KGB involvement in the assassination were totally unfounded, said Nosenko. The KGB "had not had the slightest operational interest in Oswald," and had played no role in the killing of the president.

Here was a riddle fit to tie any intelligence service in knots: If Nosenko was telling the truth, the world could breathe easier. But if he was lying—if he was in fact a disinformation agent—only two conclusions were possible: That the KGB had killed Kennedy. Or that Oswald, despite clear ties to the KGB, had nevertheless acted on his own in Dallas, causing the panicky Soviets to dispatch Nosenko with his reassuring lies.

Although initially regarded with disbelief (because the KGB had *obviously* been interested in Oswald; in fact, Oswald had been seen meeting a KGB officer in Mexico City just two months prior to the assassination), Nosenko's claims were strongly supported by Fedora and other Soviet defectors now working for the FBI. To deny Nosenko was thus also to deny Fedora, and this was something J. Edgar Hoover (who was passing Fedora's secrets directly to Lyndon Johnson) was reluctant to do. Among other things, Nosenko and Fedora were telling Hoover precisely what Hoover wanted to hear—that Oswald was a "lone nut" and that therefore the FBI could not be held accountable for his fatal presence in Dallas.

But whatever Hoover thought (and however convenient it would have been to agree with him), James Angleton's counterintelligence staff soon caught Nosenko in a web of lies and contradictions that eventually led to his incarceration as a hostile agent. For four years, under brutal interrogation by the CIA, Nosenko refused to crack. Finally, in 1968, his interrogators gave up.

Nosenko was set free, given $137,052 in "back pay," and hired as a consultant to perform "nonsensitive" duties for the Agency.*

In this role (and under the guidance of Donald Jameson, RD's media contact at the CIA), Nosenko was sent to the *Digest*'s Washington office in May 1970 bearing an offer to tell his story to the editors. The initial result of this collaboration was a best-selling book entitled *KGB: The Secret Work of Soviet Secret Agents*, published by Reader's Digest Press and excerpted in several issues of *Reader's Digest*. Written by bureau staffer John Barron, under the guidance of Ken Gilmore, the book presented eye-opening tales of Soviet evil-doing and CIA/FBI counterheroics (in the pattern of *The Penkovsky Papers* and similar accounts). Nosenko and Barron (himself a former naval intelligence officer) became close friends, and in subsequent years the *Digest* continued to publish articles based on information fed to Barron by the "former" KGB man turned CIA consultant.

In 1975, when Tony Oursler began discussing a book on the Kennedy assassination with Edward Epstein, the highly acclaimed author of *Inquest: The Warren Commission and the Establishment of Truth*, Nosenko's name immediately came up. "You ought to spend some time with Yuri Nosenko," Oursler told Epstein. "He can tell you a great deal about Oswald and the KGB." Epstein did this, but after several talks with Nosenko concluded (as Angleton and Helms had concluded before him) that the Soviet defector was a phony. So instead of a book about the assassination, Epstein began writing a book about Oswald and the KGB, to be called *Legend*, that supported Angleton's belief that Nosenko's tale was nothing more than an elaborate "legend" concocted by the KGB—which also meant, of course, that Nosenko himself had been a KGB plant all along. Which raised the likelihood that Soviet defectors who had supported Nosenko's claims—including Fedora— also remained under KGB control. In fact, if *Nosenko* was a mole, then it was hard to avoid the conclusion that the entire U.S. intelligence apparatus was KGB-penetrated. (The case for KGB complicity in JFK's murder was also strengthened, but no one wanted to think about that.)

Given these stakes, the CIA went to great lengths to suppress *Legend*. On February 2, 1978, Tony Oursler received a call from Melvin Laird in Wash-

---

* Despite this seeming vindication, Nosenko was still regarded as a KGB agent by James Angleton and CIA director Richard Helms. "No one familiar with the facts," insisted Helms, "can find Nosenko's statements about Oswald and the KGB to be credible." But disbelieving Nosenko and openly declaring him to be a KGB agent were different matters. As Helms explained it to the Senate Intelligence Committee in 1975: "If Nosenko were to be believed, then one could conclude that the Soviets had nothing to do with the assassination. If, on the other hand, Nosenko was shown to be giving us false information about Oswald's contacts with the KGB, then it was fair to surmise that Oswald was acting as a Soviet agent when he shot President Kennedy. And if that were true, the consequences for the United States—indeed, for the entire world—would have been staggering."

ington. "The Agency is very upset about your project," Laird said. "They want to talk with you." The next day, two agents from the CIA's Soviet Division appeared in Oursler's office. Publication of *Legend*, they insisted, would place key intelligence operatives (including Fedora) in danger, and thus cause great harm to the national security. Oursler suggested that U.S. intelligence might be in danger *precisely because* of blind loyalty to dubious agents like Fedora. An impasse was reached and the CIA men departed.

But it didn't end there. Oursler was called to Washington the next day to meet with George Kalaris, Angleton's replacement as chief of counterintelligence. Kalaris demanded that key portions of the book be killed. When Oursler asked for proof that these portions were in fact inaccurate and/or damaging to U.S. interests, Kalaris refused even to discuss the matter. Ed Thompson was also called down to Washington to receive a Kalaris lecture. And a delegation from the *Digest*'s Washington office, led by John Barron, traveled to Pleasantville to present an impassioned plea for killing *Legend*. "If you publish this book," Barron told Thompson, "it will be the greatest tragedy ever to befall the *Digest.*"

But nothing anybody said altered the fact that Nosenko had lied, and was still lying, on several key points. Unlike the men who now controlled the CIA, Thompson refused to brush this inconvenient fact aside. "I was prepared to be persuaded," he says today. "If they had been able to prove that *Legend* did present a real danger to U.S interests, and not just to certain reputations within the intelligence community, I would have killed it on the spot. But to kill it merely to satisfy political considerations seemed wrong, seemed like the first step down a very slippery slope. So we went ahead."

This was a brave move on Thompson's part (and would lead to severe personal consequences). But the stakes, as he saw them, were high. The murder of John Kennedy had never been convincingly explained to the American people. The conclusion of the Warren Commission—that Oswald had acted alone in Dallas—remained the official position of the U.S. government. Yet fewer than 5 percent of Americans believed it. Thompson thought this was a disgrace. And he was determined to use his magazine to put pressure on the government to produce a more convincing answer.

First published as a two-part book section in the March and April 1978 *Digest*s, *Legend* caused a sensation. The *Washington Post* ran a front-page story. AP, UPI and Reuters all wrote dispatches that appeared in dozens of papers around the globe. *Time* and *Newsweek* each covered *Legend*—not in reviews, but as breaking news—and a separate condensation of the book ran in the *Sunday Times* in London. The *Digest* had achieved a scoop of great significance, and much credit was paid in the journalistic community. But not by the CIA or the FBI, and not by Thompson's enemies in the Washington bureau. In their minds, the editor-in-chief was now beyond the pale.

CHAPTER THIRTY-ONE

As 1983 began, it was clear to Laurance Rockefeller and his colleagues that change was in order. The "safe" year of 1982 was over. From 1983 forward, unless O'Hara was fired, or Thompson (or both), the approaching death of Lila Wallace would instantly place 50 percent of the voting power into their hands. To avoid that situation, one or the other had to go. Since the company's business situation was clearly more pressing than its "editorial problem," O'Hara was the obvious candidate.

Under normal circumstances, that would have been that—a 4 to 2 vote of the proxy-holders against O'Hara. But under the circumstances then prevailing in the Kingdom, 4 to 2 wasn't good enough. Four to two would have involved an alliance of the three aging outsiders with the juniormost insider against the CEO and the editor-in-chief—the two men Wallace himself had handpicked to lead the Digest into the post-Wallace era. It would have looked terrible; it might even have led to a board revolt. To make the move against O'Hara stick, Thompson's vote was also needed.

Early in February, George Grune and Dick McLoughlin (director of magazine operations) invited Thompson to join them for lunch at the Kittle House, just up the road from Headquarters. After pleasantries in a private room off the main dining area, the two men got down to business, pouring out their unhappiness with O'Hara. He was wasting the company's money, they claimed, buying businesses that quickly failed and that, in any case, weren't worthy of the Digest's time and attention. As a result, the company's financial performance had not recovered from the recession. "We have problems in this company," concluded Grune. "Instead of paying attention, Jack is focusing on peripheral things. *He has to go!* We think you should become chairman—the titular head of the company—while Dick and I run the business end of things as CEO and chief operating officer. We want you to join us in taking this message to the board." *

As Thompson listened, the thought occurred to him that his colleagues were not acting entirely on their own. *What is going on here?* he wondered. *Who is pulling whose strings?* When they were done, he found himself shaking his head. "I'm sorry," he said. "It's a flattering offer, but I just don't think the time has come for a cabal against Jack. I don't disagree with what you're saying. Much of it is clearly true. But Jack is the man Wally picked to run

---

* Kent Rhodes had retired, so the RD chairmanship was empty.

the company. And whatever his problems, Jack is running the company more or less the way the Wally wanted it run."

Grune and McLoughlin were astonished. They had offered Thompson the chairmanship on a platter. Yet he had turned them down, putting loyalty to O'Hara and the Wallaces ahead of his own self-interest. They pressed him on his decision, reviewing the facts, emphasizing O'Hara's emotional problems. But Thompson was adamant. "I just don't think the situation is as bad as you think it is," he said. "This may change. But for now, I'm not willing to turn against Jack."

"I'm sorry you feel that way," said Grune, making no attempt to hide his displeasure. "Let us know if you change your mind. And I hope you will keep this conversation between the three of us."

"Of course," said Thompson. "I understand your position, and as far as I'm concerned this meeting never happened." It was a promise he kept, although in hindsight he may have wished he hadn't. Thompson wasn't conspiratorial. He didn't understand the numbers involving Lila's proxies, and so had no idea that by saying no to the plot against O'Hara he was, in effect, saying yes to a plot against himself.

Since Thompson wouldn't cooperate in the elimination of O'Hara, the only way to solve the numbers problem was to enlist O'Hara in the elimination of Thompson. Plan A would have to become Plan B. But Plan B was more complicated. The case against O'Hara was clear. The case against Thompson, to the extent that a case existed, was circumstantial, pitting rumor and political bias against a record of solid achievement. To build support for Plan B—and to convince O'Hara to go along—a stronger case would have to be developed.

As a first step, Al Cole and James Stewart-Gordon were dispatched to Headquarters in early March (while Thompson was in Europe) to confer with O'Hara and Bill Cross about "the editorial problem." For over an hour, the two executives listened patiently as the old man and the angry writer laid out their case against Thompson. "He is abandoning Wally's traditions," insisted Cole. "All these damn exposés. They're *boring!*" Stewart-Gordon was even harsher. "He's *ruining* the magazine. He doesn't understand what makes the *Digest* tick!"

O'Hara and Cross heard them out, and when the presentation was over thanked their visitors and said good-bye. But now O'Hara made an unfortunate decision. Although no promises had been made about confidentiality, he chose to keep his friend Thompson in the dark about the meeting. It wasn't that he had turned against Thompson. But he saw that there were several options still available—several courses the plot might follow—and he wanted to keep as many of his own open as possible. He was invited to a luncheon at the Links Club in Manhattan that spring. Hobe Lewis was present, along with Cole, Stewart-Gordon and Mel Laird, and the subject of discussion was Thompson. "He's got to go!" insisted Stewart-Gordon. "How about it, Mel? Can't you get him an embassy?" Lewis thought this was a fine idea: "Ambassador to Abyssinia! Called to a higher duty!" O'Hara listened to their laughter, and kept his peace.

In late April, Thompson flew to the Middle East for a series of meetings with leaders in Israel, Jordan and Lebanon. On May 20, he arrived in Monaco to host what he hoped would be the most memorable meeting of his tenure as editor-in-chief. Over a hundred *Digest* editors had gathered at the posh Loew's Monte Carlo Hotel for the Third Worldwide Editorial Conference. On the conference's last evening, Thompson chartered a 120-foot yacht that had once belonged to the king of Sweden. The entire *Digest* party steamed grandly west along the Mediterranean coast to the seaside village of Ville Franche, where a lavish catered dinner was served al fresco and everyone danced under the stars. The next morning, several of those in attendance were ferried from hotel to airport by helicopter, a frill laid on by meeting coordinator Connie McGowan because of the views thus afforded of the spectacular Mediterranean coast. It was a nice touch, but one that came back to haunt Thompson. For several weeks, the usual gossip in the business end of Headquarters was spiced with references to "yachts" and "helicopters" and "Who the hell does Thompson think he is?"

Two pieces scheduled for the July *Digest,* waiting to be put to bed back in Pleasantville, also raised questions in some minds about who the hell Thompson thought he was. One was a piece by roving editor James Nathan Miller that slammed the Reagan administration for crippling the Environmental Protection Agency. Entitled "What *Really* Happened at EPA," the piece led off with a blurb that seemed designed to infuriate the Reaganites in the magazine's Washington bureau: "When industry's foxes were hired to guard the national chicken coop, no one—least of all the President—should have been surprised at what followed." The second piece was even more controversial. Written by roving editor Irwin Ross, it sharply criticized the growing influence of political action committees and was a particularly courageous move on Thompson's part in view of the fact that the Digest's business side had only recently established its own RD PAC (primarily to exert influence on postal matters). Resistance to "Why PACs Spell Trouble" from Jack O'Hara and other key Digest executives was so great that the piece was scheduled and pulled from three consecutive issues. When it finally did appear in July, it was accompanied by a sidebar strongly defending PACs written by Senator Steven Symms, a Republican from Idaho who was himself a recipient of Digest PAC money.

To those struggling to build a case against the strong-willed editor-in-chief, these two articles, coming on the heels of the Monaco bash, were seen as vital ammunition. "He's hanging *himself,*" they murmured to each other. "All he needs is a little more rope. . . ."

Meanwhile, up at High Winds, Lila Wallace was having trouble with her jewelry. Although the most expensive items were now in storage at a Manufacturer's Hanover branch in New York, Lila insisted on keeping her personal favorites at High Winds. One of these was a necklace of freshwater pearls. Whenever a nurse tried to remove this necklace in the evening, Lila would become agitated. *"No, no, no,"* she would mutter, so the nurse would leave it on. Then, during the night, Lila inevitably rolled on the pearls in a way that broke the string. In the morning, the nurse would have to crawl around on the floor to gather the missing gems, and later in the day Doherty would take the necklace down to Tiffany's to be repaired.

Lila's diamond, appraised by Harry Winston at $250,000, was another problem. "Her fingers were so shriveled that the ring often fell off," recalls Doherty. "She might be sleeping in her wheelchair by the fireplace, and drop her arm. The ring would roll across the floor. This happened once when John was there—the ring rolled almost to his feet. He looked down at it, and I swear his eyes *dilated.* 'Don't even *think* about it, John,' I said."

Eventually, all the jewelry remaining at High Winds was removed from Lila's control and placed in the walk-in safe off the pantry. One day that summer, Doherty got a call from McHenry. "We need to inventory Mrs. Wallace's jewelry," the lawyer said. "Get whatever is in the safe and bring it to my office in the Pan Am Building. Wear your pistol. Those jewels are worth a fortune."

Doherty did as he was told, but stopped at Headquarters on the way to the city to pick up security officer Ed Cermak, whose gun permit, unlike Doherty's, was good in Manhattan. When the two men reached McHenry's office on the thirty-fourth floor, they found Lisa Collins and Josephine Brucelleri, McHenry's secretary, seated at a large table. There was no sign of McHenry himself.

After spreading the jewels on the table, Collins produced a list and began to identify everything. "Hold it!" said Doherty. "There are things on the list that aren't here on the table. Where are they?"

"Who knows?" said Collins. "Our job is to produce a new list of what is actually here, so we can get it appraised. That's all."

For another few minutes, while the two women worked on the list, Doherty remained quiet. Then he shook his head. "Wait a minute," he said. "That list you have, Lisa . . . that was done in the early seventies, after the robbery, right?" Collins nodded. "Well, Missus has bought several pieces since then. Some of them are missing, too!"

"What pieces, Gene?" asked Collins.

"Her necklace—the one from Olga Tritt? That's not here. She also had a Chinese ring, very old. That's not here. And a diamond-and-sapphire bracelet. And a diamond choker. And . . . let's see . . . a fancy compact, gold and sapphires. Hell, there's lots of things missing!"

The women regarded him with irritation. "That's not our problem, Gene," said Collins. "McHenry wants a list of the jewels that exist today. That's what we have here on the table. Then the jewels go to Sotheby's to be appraised, and on the basis of the appraisal we get a new insurance policy. And all the jewels go back in the safe. When Mrs. Wallace dies, they will be sold and the proceeds will go to the Metropolitan Museum. That's it. That's all we have to do."

Doherty subsided into angry muttering while the women completed the list. Then he, Cermak and Brucelleri packed up the jewels and delivered them to Sotheby's, on Seventy-third Street and York Avenue, and that was that. Mission accomplished.

As fall came on, the pressures on O'Hara to act against his friend, exerted mainly by Cole, McHenry and Cross, with ever-increasing support from Washington, were becoming hard to resist. "You know, Jack," Cross said to him one day, "you *could* just fire Ed. After all, you are the chief executive."

"That's fantasy land," snapped O'Hara. "I'm CEO, sure. But Ed is the one Wally named to be editor. Anyway, I don't think things have reached that point. There's got to be a better way."

But that November Thompson gave the plotters, including finally O'Hara himself, all the rope they needed. For two years, under tight security, he and Tony Oursler had been working with roving editor Henry Hurt on a second book about the Kennedy assassination. Called *Reasonable Doubt*, the Hurt book was based on startling new information about a massive conspiracy to murder the president, and once again was highly critical both of the CIA and the FBI. By pursuing this new book, Thompson and Oursler hoped to persuade the Justice Department and the FBI to reopen the investigation and, at long last, to produce an explanation the American people could believe. But their hopes for such a result were quickly disappointed.

"When we spoke to the Bureau about our evidence," recalls Oursler, "they refused even to discuss it, and advised us—in *very* angry terms—to drop the project." During the early months of his research, Henry Hurt visited the Assassination Archives and Research Center in Washington, D.C., a facility founded by prominent Washington lawyer Bernard Fensterwald. When Hurt described his plans for *Reasonable Doubt*, Fensterwald shook his head. "Good luck," he said. "But I doubt a single word of your book will ever appear in *Reader's Digest*. There are those in our government who do not want such matters discussed in so large a forum."

Thompson's intention was to run *Reasonable Doubt* in three installments. The first—in which a self-confessed member of the alleged conspiracy would make inflammatory charges about an FBI cover-up—was scheduled to run in the November *Digest*. Then Thompson got cold feet. "That section was the natural way to begin the series," he says. "But there was still too much speculation in it, too many points we hadn't nailed down. I decided if it ran at all, it would be the third installment, not the first. And since the other two parts weren't finished, I chose to put the whole thing off until the spring of 1984."

But the damage had been done. Although distribution of the manuscript was meant to be limited to a few trusted people in Pleasantville, the Washington office had somehow obtained a copy.* *Reasonable Doubt* accused the FBI of deliberately misleading the Warren Commission, and was an even more damning indictment of the intelligence community than the controversial *Legend*. To people like John Barron and Ken Gilmore, it was little short of treason.

"It's true the book was going to make the intelligence community look bad," says Thompson today. "In fact, both agencies *had* performed miserably both before and after the assassination. But to say that in the *Digest* was clearly a no-no. There were several people—in the Washington office and also at the CIA and the FBI—who felt this shouldn't be allowed. I had shown a copy of the first installment to O'Hara, and it clearly made him nervous. But when the others—Cole, Stewart-Gordon, Laurance Rockefeller—began to lean on him about it, he became terrified."

As 1983 drew to a close, the rift between Pleasantville and Washington had become a chasm. In Pleasantville, Thompson's editors were working on a book that *attacked* the CIA. At the same time, in Washington, Gilmore's editors were working *with* the CIA on an article about the alleged shooting-down of a Korean airliner by a Soviet fighter plane. (Cited by the Reagan administration as evidence of "Soviet brutality," "What *Really* Happened to KAL 007" was, in fact, part of a massive propaganda campaign to conceal a deliberate U.S. penetration of Soviet airspace.)

Clearly, something had to give. For several years, the Washington bureau had lobbied behind the scenes for the replacement of Thompson by someone more "reliable," someone who would stop parading articles critical of the CIA before 100 million readers. That fall, at the height of the campaign against Thompson, William Casey suddenly recruited veteran covert agent George Lauder to be his new "director of public affairs." "Why me?" asked

* During this period, an odd machine materialized in an unused office on the third floor at Headquarters. "I assumed at the time," recalls Tony Oursler, "that copies of *Reasonable Doubt* were going from that machine—some kind of early fax—straight to Washington. There were reports of strange men prowling our corridors after-hours. And I was told that a *Digest* writer visiting the Washington bureau overheard Bill Gunn [a bureau editor and former FBI "researcher"] reading the manuscript over the phone."

Lauder (as reported by Bob Woodward in *Veil: The Secret Wars of the CIA*). Casey told Lauder he needed someone "to control the news media—to stop all these damaging stories."

With *Reasonable Doubt* about to be published—a "damaging story" if ever there was one—the plotters in Washington believed they had a convincing case against Thompson. Yet they lacked the authority to force him out. But now the cabal in Pleasantville also wanted Thompson out. And this group—Rockefeller, McHenry, Cross, Cole and Stewart-Gordon—had all the authority they needed. What they had lacked was a case. As they absorbed the Bureau's charges against *Reasonable Doubt*, they realized they had their case at last.

But before they moved, one last attempt was made to resurrect Plan A, an attempt that indicates just how cynical their case against Thompson really was. That December, during a Christmas party at the home of Digest research director Sue Wanner, Thompson was pulled away from a group singing carols around the piano by Martha Farquhar, Barney McHenry's deputy in the legal department. "There's something I need to tell you, Ed," she whispered. "Let's go sit by the fire."

At the far end of the Wanner living room, sitting alone on a couch by the fireplace, Thompson and Farquhar had a brief chat. "You made a terrible mistake last February," the lawyer said. "I know all about your meeting with George and Dick. What they proposed then is the right thing to do. *O'Hara has got to go!* George and Dick know I am speaking to you. They *approve.* In fact, their offer is still open. They want you to be chairman and you should think about it."

For a long moment, Thompson studied the dying embers in the fireplace. "I *have* thought about it, Martha," he said finally. "I realize Jack has problems, and it may be that he will have to go. But not yet. The financial picture is improving. Things can still be turned around. So tell them I'm thinking about it, but . . . I'm not ready. . . ."

As the New Year began, any lingering thoughts about Plan A were dropped. Thompson had been given his chance—*twice*—and had turned them down both times. Now it was time to concentrate on Plan B, and that meant first of all deciding on Thompson's replacement. The Washington office insisted that Ken Gilmore was the right man. Although staffers there privately scorned their former boss, the prospect of having one of their own in the editor's chair —a man who had participated in dozens of CIA-connected RD projects, whose own *sister* was an Agency employee—was irresistible. Cross and O'Hara were inclined to go along. To them, Gilmore was a nonentity, and for that very reason—because it made him unlikely to cause trouble—they found him acceptable.

Only Al Cole expressed misgivings. He felt that Gilmore was wishy-washy —"not tough enough to do the job." But the others leaned on him, and he began to come around. He spent a lot of time in January and February talking with Gilmore on the phone, and whatever he heard from the eager editor-in-waiting clearly did the trick. When the time came—during a meeting of the plotters at Cole's estate in Florida—the old salesman agreed to go along. "Ken's all right," he told everyone. "He'll get things back in the Wallace swing."

In late January, O'Hara attempted to set up a meeting with Thompson and Cross to "discuss some important matters." Because of Thompson's busy travel schedule, however, the meeting was put off until Monday, March 19. In mid-February, while Thompson was in Hawaii, proofs of an article scheduled for the April issue kicked up yet another storm. "Mr. President, This Isn't Russia" was the title, and the article strongly condemned the Reagan administration's Directive 84, which proposed to censor government employees privy to sensitive information. "The use of lie-detector tests, secrecy oaths and censorship for life is a threat to the very freedoms the Directive seeks to keep secure," wrote veteran roving editor Carl Rowan. "It should be withdrawn completely, and for good."

The same issue contained a "coming attractions" box that described several articles scheduled for the May issue. One of them was the long-delayed first installment of the controversial *Reasonable Doubt*. It was time to act.

CHAPTER THIRTY-TWO

As March began, Cross and McHenry kept the pressure on O'Hara, using all the ammunition Thompson had given them during the previous twelve months. Slowly, grudgingly, O'Hara came to believe that they were right, that his friend had indeed wandered from the traditional Wallace path. "In any case," he says today, "there was nothing I could do to stop the process. *Nothing!* Ed was going. That was clear. You can stall, delay, postpone. But it doesn't work. In the end, things fall apart, and that's it. The tide rises. . . ."

March 8. Still unsuspecting, Thompson and his family departed for Mexico aboard the Reader's Digest jet. Also on board were Jerry Dole (who recently had been named executive editor for the international editions) and his family. The group planned to be in Mexico for ten days, and hoped to divide their time between business and pleasure.

After dinner on their second day in Mexico City, the conversation turned to the turmoil back in Pleasantville. "What about O'Hara?" Dole wondered. "His behavior has been pretty erratic in the last year." Thompson nodded wearily. "There are those who feel Jack should go," he confessed. "I'm beginning to agree with them."

March 10. Hardly able to believe his good fortune, Ken Gilmore, the secret editor-designate, departed on a sudden trip to China—a fitting place to be, all in all, in view of the upcoming event. With Gilmore and Thompson out of sight, McHenry prepared the legal documents required for Thompson's termination, while Cross arranged for Cole, Helm and Rockefeller to be in the right place at the designated hour on March 19.

March 19. On Monday morning at 8:30, Jerry Dole's international staff gathered in the editorial conference room to hear his post mortem on the Mexican trip. He was just getting into his act when there was a knock on the door and Thompson walked in. Despite a case of *turista* that was growing worse by the hour, the editor-in-chief launched into a monologue on how Mexico's problems with corruption could best be solved.

He was interrupted by a second knock on the door. An unfamiliar face looked in—a secretary from O'Hara's office. "Mr. Thompson?" she said. "I'm sorry to interrupt, but Mr. O'Hara and Mr. Cross are waiting to see you. You were scheduled to meet at nine."

"Good Lord, you're right," said Thompson, glancing at his watch. "Tell Jack I'll be finished here in twenty minutes. I'll stop by then."

"Well, sir," she said, clearly embarrassed, "Mr. O'Hara insisted I bring you right away. He said to track you down wherever you were. He and Mr. Cross are waiting in the boardroom."

"Okay, okay," said Thompson, frowning in irritation. He apologized to Dole's staff and promised to return as soon as he could. In the boardroom, he found Cross sitting quietly in a leather chair, while O'Hara paced back and forth, smoking a cigar.

"Sorry I'm late, gentlemen," he said. "What's up?"

O'Hara stopped pacing and stared at his editor-in-chief. "What's up isn't good," he said. "The other proxy-holders aren't happy with your performance. They want you out." Thompson was stunned. "What are you talking about?" he said. "What the hell have I done?"

O'Hara launched into a tirade: "They feel you aren't running the magazine the way Wally wanted it run. Al in particular was furious about that anti-PAC piece. And what was that other one . . . oh, yes, 'Mr. President, This Isn't Russia!' *Good God,* your editors are accusing Ronald Reagan of censorship! The proxies don't like these articles, Ed. And the Hurt book is the final straw. The entire intelligence community is furious. . . ."

"Bullshit!" said Thompson. "Jack, that's all bullshit, and you know it." He turned to Cross. "What's your version of this?"

Cross pursed his lips. "The same as Jack's," he said. "The others are fed up, Ed. The situation looks hopeless. . . ."

O'Hara interrupted. "Look, Ed, there may be a way out of this. The others might be satisfied with the establishment of an editorial board. You'd be on the board, of course, no question of that. But you'd have no veto power over its decisions."

Thompson snorted. "That's *ridiculous,*" he said. "I can't run a magazine with a committee looking over my shoulder."

"I know, I know," said O'Hara, lighting a second cigar. "But . . . it's the only thing I can think of. And beyond that . . ." He shrugged.

Thompson was furious. "Look, Jack," he said, "we both know Laurance is upset about our financial results. I don't blame him. But those results aren't *my* fault. So why are they going after me?"

Cross and O'Hara looked at each other. Then O'Hara stubbed out his second cigar. "We'll soon find out," he said. "Al, Laurance and Harold are expecting us in New York at eleven. My car is waiting out front."

The ride to New York in O'Hara's limousine was silent and uncomfortable. At the Pan Am Building, Cross led the three of them to a conference room on the thirty-second floor. Laurance Rockefeller sat at one end of a long table. Cole sat in the middle, and Harold Helm, already nodding off, at the far end. As counsel to the proxy-holders, Barney McHenry sat on Rockefeller's right, a large stack of documents on the table before him. Palmer Baker, the senior partner from Lord, Day & Lord, was also present.

When everyone was seated, Laurance began. "Our feeling, as I'm sure Jack and Bill have explained, is that you are not running the kind of magazine DeWitt Wallace would have liked. Since the rest of us are committed to such a magazine, we feel we must act."

Thompson glared at him, but resisted the temptation to say what was really on his mind *(What makes you rich old bastards think you understand Reader's Digest?).* "I believe I've honored Wally's values and traditions in every respect, Laurance," he said. "Maybe I'm wrong. Maybe I've made mistakes. But you have to give me specifics."

Rockefeller frowned. "I believe you know what we're talking about," he said. "Too much negative stuff. All these exposés . . . all this *sensationalism.* That's not the *Digest* way."

"We've been running such material for fifty years," replied Thompson. "If you have a problem with it, give me specifics."

"*Art-of-living* is the problem!" Silent up to this point, Al Cole now burst into his favorite speech. But Thompson interrupted. "For God's sake, Al!" he said. "We've been through all that! If you had read the study I prepared, you would know—whatever your personal feelings—that the charge is not true."

Cole subsided into red-faced sulking. O'Hara was staring at his hands. No one had raised the possibility of an editorial board and clearly O'Hara wasn't going to do so on his own. Thompson turned back to Rockefeller. As he studied the older man's hooded eyes, he felt his last vestige of hope leak away. The gulf between them was unbridgeable. Rockefeller couldn't comprehend how someone "in business" could be as innocent and trusting—as *unaware*—as Thompson appeared to be. Even now, with his betrayers openly arrayed against him, the younger man didn't seem to get it. He was talking about "values and traditions"—about *DeWitt Wallace*, for God's sake—while Rockefeller, behind his fabricated arguments and phony commitment, was talking about something very different. About money. And most of all about power.

At 11:45, Thompson was excused from the meeting so the others could "debate" his arguments (to the extent he had been allowed to make any). When he returned twenty minutes later, he found the room deathly still. McHenry was standing at the table, shuffling documents. O'Hara was still gazing at his hands. Cross stared out the window. Helm and Cole appeared to be asleep. "The vote was unanimous," sniffed Rockefeller. "I'm sorry. We intend to ask Ken Gilmore to be your successor."

McHenry studied Thompson's expression. "I have some papers here for you to sign, Ed," the lawyer suggested. "Might as well get it over with. Then things will go smoother later on."

"Barney," said Thompson, glaring at the man he should have fired years before, "take those papers and shove 'em! I'm not going to sign a damn thing. Not now, maybe not later." He stood up. "Thanks a lot, everyone," he said. "It's been a pleasure." As he headed for the door, a thought occurred to him, and he stopped and turned around. "Does Gilmore know about this?" he asked. Everyone looked at Rockefeller, who shook his head. "Then may I have permission to inform him myself?" Rockefeller nodded and Thompson left the room.

March 20. At 10:00 A.M. on Tuesday morning, an ambulance arrived outside the main entrance at High Winds. A stretcher bearing the emaciated form of Lila Wallace was placed aboard, and the ambulance sped off toward nearby Northern Westchester Hospital. Although the admittance forms would describe her condition as "congestive heart failure complicated by apparent pneumonia," Lila's real problem on that first morning of spring stemmed from something very different: alone in her Castle, frightened and confused, she had lost all interest in food and drink, and had thereby brought herself to the edge of starvation. Despair had done to her precisely what a cancerous colon had done to DeWitt.

In the hospital's intensive care unit, Lila was quickly hooked up to three separate IVs that began flooding her depleted body with glucose, potassium and multivitamins (the same regimen used to resuscitate her husband three years before). For a while, she hovered at death's door. Then, slowly, she began to show signs of returning strength. On her third day in the ICU, doctors agreed to permit family visits. When no one showed up (because she *had* no family now), they ruled that Gene Doherty was close enough and allowed him to approach her bedside.

What he saw came as a terrible shock. "Missus had been confined to her bedroom for the previous three weeks," he recalls. "I hadn't seen her during that time, so I was unprepared for how she looked. Her arms were *emaciated* —nothin' but skin and bones. Her eyes were frozen shut. She was wired up to everything, and she looked . . . *awful*. Like she was already dead. . . ."

March 21. On Wednesday morning, still not getting the picture, Thompson confronted O'Hara in his office. "If those old men really *believe* the magazine has changed, make them prove it!" he said. "They should get three experts —any three, I don't care—and have them compare issues from the sixties with issues from today. Here's a memo that describes how that might work. If those *experts* can prove the magazine has been trending away from what it was, then I'm wrong and *should* be fired. But that's a damn big if!"

O'Hara took the memo. "Okay, Ed," he said. "I'll show this to the others. But I don't think it will help."

"Well, do what you can, will you? And another thing. Gilmore won't get back until Friday and meantime the May issue needs to be closed. I assume I'm still the one to handle that?"

"No!" said O'Hara sharply. "Ken can handle it over the weekend."

Thompson's eyes narrowed. "Listen, Jack," he said. "If *Reasonable Doubt* is the real problem here . . . with you and others I won't bother to mention . . . why not just tell me? I'm willing to hold it from the issue." O'Hara said nothing. Thompson strolled over to the window.

"When I reached Ken in China on Monday night," he said, "he didn't seem all that surprised by my news. Do you suppose he may have had an inkling? Just a *hint* of what was coming?" O'Hara shrugged. Thompson glared at him. "You know, Jack," he said, "I'm only the first course here. Your turn is coming."

O'Hara nodded. "I know," he said. "I don't give myself much time."

"Then why on earth have you gone along with them?"

O'Hara had no answer.

Later that day, Bill Cross appeared in Thompson's office. "The board will meet on Friday to make all this official," he said. "These resignation papers have to be signed and it might be less embarrassing if you do it now. I'll hold on to them until Friday. That way, if the vote goes as expected, you won't have to be called down."

Thompson regarded the little financial man with distaste. "Okay, Bill," he said. "Whatever you say." And he signed the documents.

March 23. The special board meeting on Friday morning didn't last long. Rockefeller presented the case against Thompson in stark terms, and the other directors—who in any case were powerless against the proxy-holders —offered little resistance. Except for Chemical Bank chairman Don Platten, a friend of Thompson's. "Aren't we acting a bit precipitously here?" Platten asked. "Have we really explored these issues with Ed?"

"You *can't* explore these issues with Ed!" snapped Rockefeller. "He hasn't the faintest notion what we are talking about. And, in any case, we have his signed resignation. The fact that he has signed these documents is proof enough he understands the issues."

And that was that. Cross had not held on to the documents until after the vote, as promised. Each director had been given a copy before the meeting began, and so each was under the impression that Thompson's termination was a *fait accompli.* The vote to fire the editor-in-chief was therefore unanimous. "Ed Thompson has accepted early retirement," read the announcement that went out to all employees later that day. "This decision arises out of fundamental differences of editorial philosophy with the other representatives of Lila Acheson Wallace, owner of all voting shares in the company. Ken Gilmore becomes the new editor-in-chief."

When word of the vote reached his office, Thompson called his wife, Susie, and the two met for a dreary lunch. Later that afternoon, he called a meeting of his staff and broke the news. Amid cries of outrage, several key questions were raised. "I have no answers," Thompson said. "Their announcement is bullshit, but beyond that. . . ." He shrugged. "The truth is, I don't know why I was fired. Just that it's done. Now . . . why don't we all go over to my house."

A boozy wake followed that lasted several hours. As the liquor flowed, talk of rebellion gathered steam. The phone began to ring as *Digest* editors from around the world checked in. Several of the foreigners, out of loyalty to Thompson and to defend their hard-won freedom to publish truth instead of propaganda, wanted to fly immediately to Pleasantville to man the barricades.

For each of them, Thompson had the same message: *"Don't do it.* The votes are against us, and these old men will not be swayed. My hope is that the magazine can go on as before, and you will be needed."

Later that evening, when his plane from China arrived at JFK Airport, new editor-in-chief Ken Gilmore ordered his driver to detour into Manhattan on the way north to Westchester. He stopped at the office of Digest lawyer David Fuller, where he was handed a thick Manila envelope. When he finally reached home, after ten o'clock, the exhausted Gilmore pulled from the envelope a proof of the first installment of *Reasonable Doubt,* still scheduled for the May issue. Along with the proof were the customary reports supplied by the *Digest*'s research and legal departments, plus a third report that was anything *but* customary. Gilmore read this third report very carefully. Then, over the weekend, he typed up a lengthy memo.

March 26. On Monday morning, in his first act as editor, Gilmore walked abruptly into Tony Oursler's office and dropped a ten-page document on his desk. "I'm pulling *Reasonable Doubt* from the May issue," he said. "I haven't time to talk about it now. This memo will explain my reasons."

Oursler, having invested three years of his life and a great deal of Digest money in the effort to make *Reasonable Doubt* succeed, was stunned. Gilmore's memo turned out to be a detailed attack on every claim made in the book. "But that memo wasn't Ken's doing," Oursler says today. "Henry Hurt was a very close friend. Yet whenever the memo referred to Henry, it said things like '*Hurt* says this' or '*author* claims that.' It was *bullshit!* The Bureau was behind every page."

Unwilling to concede defeat, Oursler took the memo to Nancy Tafoya, the veteran researcher assigned to *Reasonable Doubt.* "I want you to double-check every claim this memo makes against the book," he told her. "Call every major source. Don't leave a stone unturned." The report Tafoya handed Oursler later in the day bore the same notation at the bottom of every page: *"No changes necessary."* Oursler took her report to Gilmore. "Ken glanced at it and shook his head," he recalls. "He wouldn't even read it."

With nowhere else to turn, Oursler called Hurt to report that their book was dead. After absorbing the blow, Hurt became philosophic. "Well," he said, "I guess that's that. What's my next assignment?"

"Unforgettable Shirley Temple," said Oursler, and both men laughed. (To replace *Reasonable Doubt* in the May *Reader's Digest,* Gilmore selected "Uncommon Courage," a patriotic tribute to an Air Force pilot downed in Vietnam.)

Several months later, *Reasonable Doubt* was quietly released by Holt, Rinehart & Winston, to glowing reviews: "A compelling analysis," reported the *New York Times.* "Convincing and meticulous," wrote the *Washington*

Post. "It is hard to imagine a better introduction to the subject," concluded the *Village Voice,* "or a more devastating indictment of official obfuscation." Although the book was dedicated to Tony Oursler and Ed Thompson (for their "courage and integrity"), *Reader's Digest* itself got no credit. Nor were the *Digest's* 100 million readers ever exposed to what the intelligence community (and, in his own way, Laurance Rockefeller) surely considered a "damaging story." Sales were modest, and as the months passed *Reasonable Doubt* faded from sight.

Shortly after Thompson's dismissal, a group of powerful industrialists gathered for lunch at the Links Club in Manhattan (where much of the plotting against Thompson had taken place). CIA director William Casey was guest speaker, and his message was a simple one: "Intelligence is too important to be left to professionals. I look to all of you for help. In fact, I rely on you." As described by Joseph Persico in *Casey:* "The Director's audience gave him a standing ovation. To people for whom the power of money had lost its novelty, here was a taste of another form of power, and they savored it." Among those applauding most enthusiastically on this occasion was . . . Laurance Rockefeller.

CHAPTER THIRTY-THREE

March 30. During her first week in the hospital, Lila amazed everyone by recovering sufficiently to be moved from the ICU into the Wallace Suite. But when Doherty visited her bedside on the tenth day of her stay, he was shocked to find her suddenly worse than ever. The organisms that had caused her "apparent pneumonia" had escaped from her lungs into her bloodstream, and with her resistance near zero they were thriving. "Every vital organ is under attack," Dr. McAvey told Doherty. "She is not going to get better."

April 5–8. As the furor over Thompson's dismissal subsided in Pleasantville, Jack O'Hara and a dozen subordinates, including George Grune and Dick McLoughlin, traveled to Lisbon to attend a meeting of the Digest's international advertising directors. O'Hara was in a terrible state—"absolutely wired," recalls a colleague. On the second day of the meeting, a closed-door strategy session was scheduled for a limited group of key people. O'Hara ordered a security man to guard the door and under no circumstances to allow Grune or McLoughlin to enter—a calculated insult that infuriated his two rivals. Later that day, O'Hara waved several documents in the air during a speech to the ad directors. "These memos list everything George and Dick think is wrong with the company," he ranted. "The two of them are full of ideas because they don't seem to believe I can think for myself!"

After dinner on the meeting's final evening, Jerry Dole was introduced to speak about "international editorial problems." As the lone editor in a sea of businessmen—at a moment in Digest history when the gulf between business and editorial could not have been deeper—it was not a task he relished. To make matters worse, he had decided at the last minute to set aside his prepared remarks and instead to raise the subject that had been ignored by his business colleagues throughout the week:

> Two weeks ago today Ed Thompson strode into my office and asked me if I would give this speech in his place tonight. I said I would, and asked the obvious question: "Why?"
>
> "Something has come up," Ed said. "I can't make it."
>
> That "something," of course, was the fact that he was being fired—an event that has caused a degree of trauma in our editorial offices around the world. That "something" has also caused me to do some hard thinking these past few days: About the real meaning of *Reader's Digest,* and about the common future that ought to be ours.

Normally a low-keyed man, Dole spoke with an edgy determination that did not sit well with the ad directors. He mentioned several memories of Wallace, concluding that their late employer had been "unpredictable and occasionally eccentric, but also a civilized and generous-spirited man, and in his way a kind of genius. . . ."

> He had a simple idea about *serving readers.* About exerting a real influence on readers' lives, and leaving readers better off than they were before they encountered the *Digest.* As editors, that's our job—our *mission*—and we do it proudly. Skeptics maintain that editors and their business colleagues are doomed to a clumsy twilight combat. I don't feel that way myself. But I do believe that if we are to achieve our common goal—the success of this company—we must agree on two points: First, that the health of the magazine is essential to the health of the company. And second, that our magazine is *not* a product—not tubes of toothpaste or bottles of Coca-Cola, or something we peddle just to make money. It is an *Idea.* And while it is a good idea, having survived for sixty-two years, it is not imperishable. Given abuse, it *can* be killed. . . .

Glancing up from his notes, Dole stared into a sea of stony faces. *Almost through,* he told himself, and plunged ahead. . . .

If the *Digest* is not Coke or toothpaste, neither are its editors. I'd like you to think of us as keepers of the flame—as the people entrusted with the preservation of DeWitt Wallace's magnificent obsession. . . . I don't think you can survive without us, gentlemen. And we are not so ignorant as to think we can survive without you. In the future, I hope we can deal with one another with greater honesty and respect. Thank you.

There were a few scattered handclaps, then silence. Dole stepped from the speaker's platform and walked slowly through the silence, past the tables of glowering ad men, headed for the men's room. He was standing at a sink when the door opened and Jack O'Hara entered. The embattled CEO looked terrible—pale and exhausted—and when he saw Dole his face stiffened with anger. "So," he said, looming alongside his younger colleague, "you editors are the only keepers of Wally's flame, is that it?" O'Hara shook his head in frustration. "Has it ever occurred to you that there are some on the business side—one or two, anyway—who have also tried to keep the faith? Huh? *Huh?* Has that thought ever occurred to you?"

April 10. On their return to Pleasantville, Grune and McLoughlin were still steaming over O'Hara's insults. "He's out of control," insisted Grune. "If we don't get him soon, he is going to get us." The two men were puzzled over the failure of Plan B to move forward. Needing support from at least one proxy-holder, they went to Cross to find out what was holding things up. "You've got to be patient," Cross told them. "Laurance is in Europe. When he returns, there will be time to handle the O'Hara problem."

Cross, of course, understood the Lila numbers, whereas Grune and McLoughlin, not being proxy-holders, did not. To avoid the 2 to 2 stalemate, Cross and McHenry had pushed hard for Thompson's ouster. Now, with Thompson gone, the interests of both men were best served by putting the brakes on as far as O'Hara was concerned.

It was a matter of sequence. If Lila died first, while O'Hara was in command, the voting power would reside with three *trustees:* O'Hara, Cross and Rockefeller. To gain Cross's support for the ouster of O'Hara—the last obstacle to Phase III—Rockefeller would have to agree to make Cross CEO. With Cross as CEO, McHenry's control over the Wallace Funds and High Winds would be assured. But if O'Hara was fired *before* Lila died, the voting power would reside with the four surviving *proxy-holders*—Cross, Rockefeller, Cole and Helm—and Cross's vote would count for nothing. Moreover, Cole and Rockefeller had made it clear in recent months that they preferred George Grune for the top spot once O'Hara was gone, and Dick McLoughlin for number two, leaving Cross as third man on the totem pole and McHenry (whom Grune despised) in all probability looking for work.

For the lawyer and the financial man, success or failure depended on Lila. If she died before O'Hara's ouster, they were winners. If she died after his ouster, they were losers.

April 15. Worried about Lila's condition, Janine Ardohain decided to visit the Wallace Suite when her shift on the pediatric floor at Northern Westchester ended in midafternoon. Coming off the elevator on the seventh floor, she ran into Barney McHenry, who told her that he and Dr. McAvey had just decided to send Lila home. "Keeping her here is pointless," the lawyer said. "She told me on several occasions that she wanted to spend her last days at High Winds. It's the right thing to do."

Janine nodded. "I agree," she said. "It's what she would want."

"We'll keep her on the IVs for as long as possible," McHenry added. "But no heroic measures. When she goes, she goes. That's it."

April 23. With time running out, Grune and McLoughlin met with Cross a second time. "We can't wait for Laurance's return," they told him. "We're going down to see Don Platten. We'd like you to come with us." This put Cross in a dilemma. If he helped them, the strategy he and McHenry were relying on would be at risk. If he refused and they succeeded without him, he could be fired. "Okay," he said. "Let's go."

In Platten's office, Grune outlined their reasons for wanting to move against O'Hara. "Where have you been?" Platten asked. "I've been expecting you guys for weeks. Laurance won't be back until early May, but meantime you can count on me to get the ball rolling."

Meanwhile, up at High Winds, Lila Wallace was having a terrible time with her IVs. For some reason—perhaps because her veins were old and tired—the tubes kept plugging. Whenever this happened, a special team had to be summoned from Northern Westchester to get things started again. The process involved probing for a new vein, and was very painful. "Finding a fresh vein in a woman Lila's age is not easy," recalls Janine Ardohain. "It was very difficult for her, very unpleasant."

Later that day, McHenry showed up. Informed about the IV problem, he summoned Dr. McAvey and the two men conferred. "This is not what she would want," McAvey concluded. "If the IVs infiltrate again, that should be the end of it. It makes no sense to return her to the hospital just to keep her breathing." McHenry nodded. "I agree completely," he said. "Prolonging her struggle would be cruel." The nurses were told to monitor Lila's vital signs hourly, and to phone any changes to McAvey's office.

April 26. Janine Ardohain called Dr. McAvey around nine that morning to report that all three IVs had plugged again. After conferring with McHenry by phone, McAvey ordered their removal. This was clearly the humane thing to do, and the nurses were relieved that Lila would be spared further needles. They fully expected her struggle to end within a day or so. To their amazement, she showed no change at all. "Her heart just kept pumping away," recalls Janine. "It was very strong . . . like a locomotive."

Early May. By the time Rockefeller returned from Europe, Don Platten had already spoken by phone with Al Cole and Harold Helm. Rockefeller scheduled an emergency meeting of proxy-holders (minus O'Hara) to be held at 3:00 P.M. on May 5, a Saturday, in the boardroom at Headquarters. McHenry was told to prepare termination papers. Cross was put in charge of getting Cole up from Florida.

May 5. McHenry arrived at High Winds very early that morning. After conferring with Strasburger and checking on Lila's status, he was called to the telephone in the kitchen. Gene Doherty, moving from room to room watering flowers, tiptoed into the rotunda to eavesdrop. McHenry was conversing with Bill Cross. In urgent tones, he mentioned the need to send the Digest plane immediately south to pick up Cole. (Clearly, the two had delayed until the last minute. Had Lila died overnight—a real possibility— sending the plane for Cole would have been pointless because her proxy would have died with her. In fact, her death would have made the meeting itself pointless. With Cole and Helm proxyless, Rockefeller would have had to make his deal with Cross and McHenry. But Lila *hadn't* died, and thus her stubborn heart had dashed their last hopes.)

McHenry emerged from the kitchen wearing a sour expression. Catching sight of Doherty, the lawyer glowered. "Whatever you heard, Gene," he snapped, "you'd better forget."

The Headquarters meeting that afternoon was brief. The four proxy-holders—Rockefeller, Cole, Helm and Cross—agreed to oust O'Hara. George Grune would become the new Digest chairman and chief executive officer. Richard McLoughlin would be vice chairman. William Cross would be president and chief operating officer. The board would meet on Monday to make the changes official.

May 7. At midmorning, the directors convened in the boardroom and in short order ratified what the proxy-holders had decided on Saturday. Beaming with excitement, Al Cole shook George Grune's hand and pounded his sturdy back. For fifty years, round after round, Cole and Lila Wallace had fought for the soul of Reader's Digest. Now, in what amounted to the last second of the fifteenth round, Cole had scored a clean knockout. George Grune was *his* man—a salesman, a *go-getter*—and Cole was confident that George would do all the things he himself had longed to do for many years. Although his pleasure was unbounded, Cole was no longer sharp enough to appreciate the irony of his final triumph: that Lila had made it possible by her stubborn refusal to die on schedule. Nor did he comprehend how brief his moment in the sun would be. Within days, Grune would banish him from the Kingdom forever.

As the meeting broke up, Barney McHenry and Bill Cross appeared to be in shock. Victory had been within their grasp, so close that defeat now seemed impossible to accept. Laurance Rockefeller, on the other hand, looked relaxed and satisfied. The right man—a man who understood "good business"—was in place at the company helm, and every other obstacle to the prosecution of Phase III had been swept away.

Later that afternoon, at a business meeting in Connecticut, Bill Cross confronted his old friend O'Hara with the news of his ouster. O'Hara seemed more relieved than angry. His long endgame was finally over, and he could feel the tide falling away at last. He had been brought down less by his business failings than by an emotional collapse brought on by constant pressure—to ease standards, to abandon Wallace ways, to betray his friend and, ultimately, to betray himself. He had sworn allegiance to the goals of a Founder whose company was now controlled by people whose goals were very different. Thus he had felt himself lost whichever way he went: damned by the new owners if he kept the faith; damned by his own conscience if he did not.

Chapter Thirty-four

At 9:00 A.M. on May 8, Janine Ardohain sat in the sitting room outside Lila Wallace's bedroom and waited for her mistress to rouse herself from sleep. A thought occurred that made Janine smile. Before Lila's hospitalization, Strasburger would have insisted on serving breakfast by eight o'clock. Now he lets her sleep. *John is becoming a softy,* Janine mused. *A real pussycat.*

Around nine-thirty Lila rang her bell. Janine entered the bedroom and carefully helped the old lady from bed to bathroom. Minutes later, as she was lowering Lila back into bed, the Queen of High Winds suddenly leaned forward and kissed her on the cheek. "I love you," she whispered hoarsely. "You're my favorite nurse!"

"That's nice, Mrs. Wallace," said Janine. Then, while she was plumping Lila's pillows, she noticed that her patient had begun to hyperventilate. The rapid breathing got steadily worse, and suddenly all color drained from Lila's face. Her chest rose one last time, and fell, and she was dead.

Janine sat on the bed. For several minutes, too upset even to record the time of death, she held Lila's lifeless hands and said good-bye. Then she buzzed Strasburger. "Mrs. Wallace is gone," she said. "Better call McHenry."

Precisely at 10:00 A.M. copies of a press release entitled "New Management Team at Reader's Digest" began to flood the offices at Headquarters. Stunned employees left their desks to gather in small groups in corridors throughout the building. *What can this latest upheaval mean?* they asked each other. *What is going on?*

In the office of the editor-in-chief, a very different conversation was taking place. Ken Gilmore had informed Tony Oursler of Lila's death, and the two were discussing what to do next. "There will be an announcement over the PA system," Gilmore said. "Any minute."

"But, Ken," Oursler said, *"you're* the editor-in-chief. That announcement should be made by *you."* Gilmore thought about this, then nodded his head. "I guess you're right," he said. "I'd better go."

Ten minutes later, the hallway debates were silenced when the building's rarely used public-address system squawked into life: "It is with deep regret," Gilmore's voice intoned, "that I must inform you that Lila Acheson Wallace passed away at nine-forty-eight this morning."

Now, especially among older employees, the debates dissolved into a general sense of shock and sadness. The King had been dead for three years, but as long as the Queen survived—however old and frail she was—the magic remained alive. Now the Queen was dead, and everything in the Kingdom had been turned upside down.

Later that morning, Gene Doherty, Joe Guignardi, and Ross Cutri gathered in the High Winds kitchen. Doherty produced a bottle of scotch whisky from somewhere, and the three men commenced to drink a tearful farewell to their dead mistress. In the midst of this ceremony, Barney McHenry appeared. "Gene," he said, frowning at the scotch, "open the safe, please. I need to remove the jewels for safekeeping." The three men stared at McHenry in disbelief. There were no words of greeting from the lawyer, nor any acknowledgment of their tearful faces. ("We was all *crying,"* Ross Cutri recalls. "But McHenry, he wasn't like that.") Doherty went into the pantry and opened the wall safe. McHenry removed the few pieces of jewelry entrusted to the Queen during her final months of life, and left without another word. The safe, Doherty noticed, was now completely bare. Even Nefertiti's cup had disappeared.

—

In the immediate aftermath of Lila Wallace's death, many questions were raised about the timing of the power plays that preceded it, and about how those power plays might relate to various aspects of her last will and testament. But it was difficult even for seasoned reporters to pierce the wall of mystery and denial that rose like a medieval battlement around her beleaguered Kingdom. To veteran Digesters, these disavowals sounded like a chorus out of Orwell, Big Brother speaking in several voices simultaneously. And it was not lost on anyone that the year in which all this happened was 1984:

"It was purely coincidental that Lila died when she did," Bill Cross told reporters. "The resignations of O'Hara and Thompson had nothing to do with a power struggle."

"All this speculation is silly," said Barney McHenry. "There was no plotting at the deathbed here. Nor was control of the voting stock a factor in anything that happened."

"I have no comment," said Ken Gilmore. "All I want to do is to get on with my job."

But of all the statements issued on this occasion, the most Orwellian came from George Grune. At a gathering of Digest executives, the new chairman was asked about the "strange coincidence" of his ascendance to the throne only hours before Lila's death. "You could call it that," the burly executive said, smiling at his troops. "But you could also look at it another way. Suddenly she saw the sun shining on the Digest, and she felt . . . relieved."

Lila's memorial service was held at High Winds on May 25, a glorious spring day with every flower and shrub on her hillside in radiant bloom. Barney McHenry arrived early, as he had before DeWitt's service. He parked by the garages and walked directly to the Rose Garden, carrying the familar urn from the crematorium. Mary Strasburger, out of sight at the far end of the garden, was snipping roses for a table decoration. "I was down there," she recalls today, "and McHenry came and he took that thing . . . the urn, ya know . . . and he was just throwin' and throwin' it all around. Not nice, ya know. Just dumped the stuff. You could see it lyin' there. White ashes. Pieces of bone. Every time I went down there I could see it. . . ."

The service, in the High Winds living room, opened with a singing of "America, the Beautiful." Then, as he had for DeWitt, Norman Peale delivered a brief eulogy. "On this day," he began, his resonant voice quickly warming to its task, "when Lila has taken her way to the higher country, all nature is aflame with beauty because she walked in beauty. She could have become the greatest women's rights leader of her time. Instead . . . she lost herself in Wally . . . and Wally lost himself in her. . . ."

The service ended with a singing of "Abide with Me," and then the guests were invited into the dining room where two cocktail bars had been set up and a lavish spread of food laid out. The solemn mood dissipated quickly enough, and soon laughter and animated chatter filled the air. Observing this change from a position by the front entrance, Fred Stanyer shook his head sadly. "I found it all distasteful," he says today. "One minute everyone was misty-eyed and solemn. The next minute . . . *party-time!* It seemed wrong to me. The King and Queen were dead, and now their subjects were running about the Castle like parentless children on a field trip. *Yuck!* I lasted five minutes, and then I went home."

As the party gathered steam, three minor incidents took place that bear reporting:

George Grune, as close to a King as could be found now in the Kingdom, made no effort to hide his simmering resentment. "I have never been to High Winds before," he told several people. "You all have partied here for years, but not me. I was just an ad man."

Sometime later, Fred and Judy Thompson, drinks in hand, were seen wandering across the South Lawn. When they reached the Lookout, they turned and faced each other, standing in the very spot where their marriage vows had been exchanged forty-five years before. Fred was waving his glass from side to side, pointing to this or that aspect of the gorgeous view spread beneath them. Judy, leaning against him, was shaking her head. "Look at that," someone muttered from a vantage point on the Main Terrace. "Isn't that the saddest sight you ever saw?" (Had they played their cards differently, of course, Fred and Judy would have owned everything they now surveyed— indeed, the Kingdom itself. Instead, they would settle for a single modest bequest: by the terms of Lila's will, Judy was given what remained of the Queen's clothing. The tax man valued the lot at $100.)

Later still, a group formed to make a tour of the second floor. As they started up Lila's magnificent staircase, they met another group coming down. This group was led by Norman Peale and his wife, Ruth, and included Tony and Noel Oursler. Halfway down the stairs, the elderly Dr. Peale paused to rest, forcing those behind and in front of him to pause as well. At the foot of the staircase, hidden from Peale's view but no more than ten feet away, Ken Gilmore's wife, Janet, sat on a bench side by side with Al Cole.

"You know, Ruth," Norman said, his gravelly voice echoing throughout Lila's two-story rotunda, "the one thing I can't understand is why they gave the editor's job to *Gilmore!* I thought for sure young *Oursler* would get the nod!"

An audible and collective gasp followed this observation, and everyone on the staircase and crowded about the rotunda turned to see how poor Janet Gilmore would react. Her face turned bright red, and she cast a furious glance in Peale's direction. Cole, briefly at a loss, put a protective arm around her shoulder. "You know, Janet," he said, searching for a way to change the subject, "the thing . . . the whole damn thing . . . is going through the roof!"

"What is, Al?" asked a grateful Janet.

"Why, my dear, the *stock!* Now that George and Ken are in, the stock is going to go *through the roof!*"

The old salesman was right about that, of course. He had known all along how to make it happen, and now, by God, the process was finally going to start. Phase III was on the launch pad. The green light was on. And for good or ill the roof at Reader's Digest was about to blow sky-high.

PART VII

Hello, Wall Street!

1984–1996

CHAPTER THIRTY-FIVE

At the heart of Reader's Digest Headquarters, in a kind of No-Man's-Land between the editorial and business offices, there is a large octagonal room lined with glass display cases. Dominating the south end of the room in the summer of 1984 were oil paintings of DeWitt and Lila Wallace, and the display cases that spread out to their right and left were filled with items attesting to the fullness of their long lives: letters and photographs, early editions of *Reader's Digest*, awards, honors and other personal memorabilia. The room served as a kind of corporate shrine, and was known officially as "The Wallace Memorabilia Room." Unofficially (and particularly among the editors), it was called "Wally World."

During his first weeks in office—the first weeks of the post-Wallace era —new Digest chairman George Grune attracted considerable media attention, not least because of the implausible timing of his sudden rise to the throne. Although DeWitt Wallace had granted no more than two or three interviews in his entire career, Grune began welcoming reporters into his office on a regular basis. And he made it a habit to begin these sessions with what he called "a walk down memory lane."

"I want to show you something," he would say, leading the reporter down the hall to Wally World. There, surrounded by Wallace artifacts, he would talk proudly of the Digest's history. "I am drawn to this room," he assured his visitors, "to contemplate the past while I plan for the future. It's such a wonderful heritage . . . a link with everything that makes this company great."

Walking back to his office, Grune made a point of emphasizing that he and his associates were determined to do whatever was necessary to preserve the Wallace heritage. "We will maintain the family atmosphere they created," he insisted, "and their sense of loyalty and community, high ideals and service to others. We also expect to retain the generous salaries, lengthy vacations and all the other employee benefits the Wallaces pioneered. To do this we must remain a private company, and to remain private we must increase our profitability. But . . . *we will do it.* That is what the Wallaces wanted. And that is what I want."

These words, or variations thereof, became Grune's personal mantra, and he repeated them over and over, whenever the subject of the Wallaces came up. Yet, in fact, he understood from his first day in office that anything beyond symbolic deference to the old ways was out of the question. What had been the ultimate long-term company (because the owners had insisted on it) was about to become the ultimate short-term company. And whereas profit had never been a priority in the past, now profit would be the *only* priority. The days of "family" were over, and for all Grune's talk about staying private the company was in some ways *already* public, its stock held by charities every bit as demanding as Wall Street itself. It was also true (and Grune was well aware of it) that under the terms of the wills and the tax laws of the land some form of outright public ownership would have to be in place within fifteen years of Lila's death.

So Grune's mantra was really only public relations. From his first day as chairman, he began to change every aspect of the Kingdom, replacing the benevolent capitalism of the Wallace era with the bottom-line rapacity of the Greed Decade. And merely by *saying* it wasn't happening—by insisting, over and over, that black was white and up was down—he was able to convince Digesters that all was well. Laurance Rockefeller saw that he had picked the right man to lead Phase III, a man willing (as Ed Thompson and Jack O'Hara had not been willing) to do what the times and the situation demanded.

Yet there was always a spark of tension between the two men. Each understood that the central issue was to travel from Point A to Point B— from $20 Digest stock to stock selling somewhere in the stratosphere—and then to take the company public and send the stock higher still. They agreed, more or less, on the steps necessary to make this happen, and they had a common understanding of the perils they would face along the way. Where they differed was in their perceptions of who should benefit, and by how much, from all the wealth they were about the create.

At the time of Lila's death, 60 percent of the company's stock had already been transferred out of the four Wallace Funds into the seven Support Organizations established by Laurance and Barney McHenry. Thirty percent remained in the funds, its income to be disbursed according to guidelines established by the Wallaces; 8 percent was committed to a variety of charities (principally the New York Public Library, Spelman College and New York University) and held at the Community Trust; and 2 percent was owned by company executives. Laurance's goal for the stock was to raise it from A to B as fast as possible, in the process enriching his charities beyond their fondest dreams and elevating his own reputation as a philanthropic rainmaker to heights unreachable by lesser mortals. Grune's goal was to get the stock from A to B as well, but when it came to enrichment his thoughts were understandably focused less on Laurance's charities and more on himself and the few cronies whose help he would need along the way.*

But one thing was clear: neither man could reach his goal without the other. Laurance needed Grune to execute his plans, to be his captain in the trenches, wielding the ax. Grune needed Laurance because in the aftermath of Lila's death Laurance was the supreme power at Reader's Digest. All the voting stock was held now in the Wallace Trust, and with O'Hara and Thompson eliminated from the trust, and Cole and Helm disqualified by age, the only remaining trustees were Laurance and Bill Cross. But Cross reported to Grune and so could be eliminated (if need be) at a nod of Laurance's head.

So the canny philanthropist had brought the company to the start of Phase III with barely a hitch. The adoption proceeding he had launched a dozen years before was over, and the Sitting Duck of Pleasantville was now firmly in his control. Yet problems remained. It was time to fatten the Duck for market, and this was bound to be a perilous process. During the years of Phase II (1980–1984), the undervaluation of RD's stock had been a plus, providing a useful cover for the unprecedented "gifts" arranged by Rockefeller and McHenry. The undervalued shares had accumulated quietly in the S/Os, paying out modest dividends to the selected charities, who were grateful for what they got and not inclined to ask questions. ("We didn't even give them annual reports," recalls Ed Thompson. "So they had no way of knowing whether the dividend was reasonable.")

But with Lila's death Phase II was over. The seven selected charities now understood that they had been blessed with more than modest incomes— that, in fact, they owned huge blocks of stock in one of the world's most

---

* Mr. Grune declined to be interviewed for this book.

profitable publishing operations. And they wanted more from this ownership than 2 percent dividends. Under ordinary circumstances, that would have been that. By demanding an opportunity to sell their shares, the charities would have forced Digest management to go public long before such a move made sense.

But Laurance Rockefeller had not orchestrated ordinary circumstances. Because he controlled the boards of each S/O—and because he was a Rockefeller—he was able to exert enormous influence. "Laurance understood what the stock was *really* worth," says Ed Thompson. "He told the charities to be patient, that they would do better if they waited. And the charities listened."

Yet the situation remained volatile. In the months after Lila's death, the price of Digest stock, as determined by the formula, hovered between $20 and $30. But Digest insiders understood that its real value—if only they were given time to push the necessary buttons—might be ten times higher. Might be *twenty* times higher. There was a huge fortune lurking within those mailing lists, and the only real question was who would get to exploit it.

What would happen, for example, if the inside information they possessed somehow leaked to outsiders? Suppose an offer was made that was four or five times the listed value of the stock? Would the charities be able to resist? Could Rockefeller and the S/O board members counsel *against* such an offer? Wouldn't that be *risky?*

In fact, several raiding parties did come sniffing around Pleasantville (including one led by Rupert Murdoch), and several offers were under consideration. But the Digest had always been obsessively secretive, and hard figures about its prospects were impossible to obtain. While the various interested parties thought about the problem, George Grune and his colleagues began to take the steps necessary to lift Reader's Digest—and their own future financial prospects—out of its perilous position.*

The plan they came up with, after several weeks of closed-door deliberations, was simplicity itself: Reader's Digest was a direct-mail company with four core products and a list of 100 million customers. Henceforth, they would focus on selling as many of the core products—magazine, condensed books, general books and recorded music—to as many of their customers as

---

* The situation at RD in 1984 was remarkably similar to the situation at RJR/Nabisco in 1988, before the takeover battle celebrated in the best-seller *Barbarians at the Gate.* The stock at both companies was deceptively undervalued: at RJR because of public distaste for tobacco investments; at RD because of DeWitt Wallace's distaste for profits. RJR was a cash cow, with money pouring in no matter how management performed; merely by plugging holes, insiders knew, profits could be made to soar. Same at RD. And at both companies the gap that existed between listed value and *real* value—known only to insiders—represented an extraordinary opportunity for personal gain.

possible, by whatever means would yield the most profitable result. At the same time, everything else—everything not directly connected to the profitable peddling of the core products—would be eliminated. "We asked ourselves a simple question," Dick McLoughlin told reporters at the time. "Is it nice or is it necessary? What is necessary we will keep. What is nice is history."

The Digest's Spanish company was an early candidate for the dustbin. Begun in the heady days following World War II, *Selecciones* had been a money-loser for decades. Yet it had a large circulation and always seemed on the verge of becoming profitable. "Spain will make it eventually," Wallace had insisted. "Until it does, the French can carry it, or the British or the Germans." His was a long-term view predicated more on keeping the *Digest* message alive in Spain and Digest families employed in Madrid than on short-term profits. Since such concerns were now clearly in the "nice" category, Spain was shut down shortly after Grune took over.

The same fate quickly overtook the Digest's Educational Division. Although it, too, had never been a moneymaker, Wallace kept the division going because he felt it encouraged young people to read and hoped that over the long term these young readers would become *Digest* subscribers. In recent years, partly in response to pressure from eager beavers like Grune and McLoughlin, the division had taken a gamble on selling educational software, and this had proved a major failure. Now, apparently feeling that the future would care for itself, these same eager beavers sold it off.

Of all the changes initiated that first summer, none was more shocking to Digesters than what became known as "The Purge." In 1984, the company employed eleven thousand people worldwide. Within two years, that figure would be reduced to seventy-five hundred. Nothing so unpleasant had ever happened in Pleasantville. DeWitt Wallace occasionally dismissed overreaching top executives (with Lila doing the heavy pushing), but beneath the highest levels job security had been virtually guaranteed and people counted on being "Digesters" for life. No longer. Employees began to disappear, many of them highly paid veterans committed to the Wallace way of doing business. And it was noted that in many cases there appeared to be an age or medical problem involved (or even something as relatively innocent as a tendency to smoke or drink too much). No doubt some of the firings could be justified. But the abruptness of this change—the sudden transformation of what had been a "family" into what now seemed a "jungle"—left people breathless.

Other changes compounded the problem. Employee benefits, legendary at the Digest since the days of Ralph Henderson, were an easy target: subsidized meals were suddenly priced at the market rate; the workweek was lengthened, vacations shortened, free bus service ended, health coverage reduced; bonuses shrank and salary levels were capped. In the end, and somehow symbolic of everything else, even the free Thanksgiving turkeys disappeared.

The war to eliminate what was merely "nice" focused with special heat on the editorial department. From the early days of the Digest, Wallace had treated his editors as a breed apart. He saw them as his frontline troops, doing the real work of the organization, while everyone else was ancillary. Editors worked in the best offices, with flexible work hours and longer vacations than other employees. They got up to High Winds more often, communicated with Wallace more frequently, and in various other ways acted like the special Knights of the Kingdom. And this made executives in the business departments furious.

So when the ax began to flash in the summer of 1984, those wielding it headed first for editorial. Aware that his own job was on the line—that even the editor-in-chief now served at George Grune's pleasure—Ken Gilmore offered zero resistance. So it fell to deputy editor Tony Oursler to defend the department, and Oursler did what he could in a cause he knew from the start was lost.

"I was named editorial representative to a new group called the Management Committee," he recalls. "As far as I could tell, the committee's sole function was to fire people, and in particular to fire editors." To make sure Oursler got the message, Chairman Grune hammered it home during a meeting of the Management Committee later that summer. "I have a question," the big man announced. He picked up a crayon and began to draw on an easel. Working very deliberately, he sketched a picture of a funnel. Beneath the funnel he drew a picture of a magazine, which he labeled "RD." Above the funnel, he drew what looked like sheets of paper, which he labeled "magazines, newspapers, books," and with arrows indicated that these papers were meant to filter through the funnel into the magazine. Above the papers, he drew several human hands.

"Now," he said. "What would be wrong with having the hands that feed these papers into the funnel be attached not to the arms of high-priced editors but, let's say, to high-school English teachers? What would be wrong with letting those *teachers* select the articles that go into our magazine?"

Oursler was in the front row for this demonstration, and when Grune posed his question the deputy editor laughed out loud. A dead silence followed. "You think that's funny?" Grune asked.

"Well," said Oursler, "if you lived my life, George, you would know why I laugh. I go home every night and help my children with the writing exercises their English teachers have assigned. The next day, they bring these exercises home with comments scribbled in the margins. And you know, George, those teacher comments need more correcting than my children's own work! So that's why I laughed."

Grune allowed the flicker of a smile to cross his face. But there was nothing funny about the point he had made, and its underlying message was soon circulating throughout the editorial department: In the opinion of Chairman Grune, the magazine's editors were replaceable by high-school English teachers who would work for a fraction of what editors were paid, and do the job as well.

At the end of 1984, Oursler was asked to submit to management a report on editorial cost projections for the next three years. His covering memo neatly summarized the conflict heating up between the "Church" of editorial and the "State" of business:

> In recent years there has been a steady diminution in the number of editorial pages we offer our readers. This erosion continues this year with the decision to cut back an additional 32 pages even as the price of the magazine rises once again. . . . We believe the limits of this policy (charging readers more for less) have been reached. . . . In pondering the figures on the following pages, two additional thoughts should prevail:
> 1. In 1984, edit costs represented 4.5% of the cost of producing the magazine;
> 2. Reader's Digest magazine is the soul of RDA. *No one* can X-ray a soul. . . .

CHAPTER THIRTY-SIX

Although Oursler's warnings clearly had the ring of truth, just as clearly the new management team and the new editor-in-chief were not impressed. In fact, Ken Gilmore's first action as editor—the swift killing of *Reasonable Doubt*—was symbolic of all that would follow. The bold, independent journalism that had flourished under Ed Thompson was abandoned, replaced by right-wing propaganda and the sort of fluff favored by advertisers— adventure, art-of-living, sex, diet and self-help. Nothing controversial was allowed, and stories addressing the *real* problems of the country (all those "exposés" Laurance Rockefeller had complained about) were once again discouraged.

One of Thompson's last moves as editor had been to ask roving editor

James Nathan Miller to conduct an investigation into the Reagan administration's record in the area of civil rights. A first draft of Miller's article, highly critical of the administration, arrived in Pleasantville shortly after Gilmore took over. It was immediately killed without explanation—as if, by definition, criticism of Reagan was wrong. (Reagan was overseeing the largest transfer of wealth in U.S. history, from the middle class to the very rich. And the very rich—people like Rockefeller—did not like to see him criticized.) An alarming report on the overuse of toxic chemicals by U.S. agribusiness was also killed, as was an article praising the election of a liberal-democratic president in Argentina.

With the Washington bureau now ascendant, Gilmore consolidated his power base by bringing Washington insider Ken Tomlinson back to Pleasantville to be his new managing editor. A former reporter for the *Richmond Times-Dispatch*, Tomlinson had spent fifteen years writing ultraconservative articles for the bureau before coming to Pleasantville as a senior editor in 1981. Bearded and heavyset, the thirty-eight-year-old West Virginian had displayed few editorial skills, found it hard to make friends with others on the staff, and seemed to take pleasure in affecting a hillbilly persona that grated on the nerves of the Pleasantville Ivy Leaguers. He liked to listen to country music and could be counted on at social occasions to say things like "Lordy, aren't we havin' fun!" or "Hot *dawg!* Red meat 'n' *browwwn* whisky!"

But there was more to Tomlinson than met the eye—a mixture of ambition, shrewdness and political savvy that made it risky to dismiss him as the Appalachian buffoon he sometimes appeared to be. In 1982, just as clouds began to gather over Ed Thompson's future, the Reagan administration summoned Tomlinson back to Washington to serve as director of the Voice of America. Many on the Digest staff were astonished by this move. Beyond his "political reliability," Tomlinson appeared singularly unqualified to manage an important government agency employing several thousand people.

But others on the staff, older hands who understood the *Digest*'s role within the intelligence community, weren't surprised at all. To these veterans, it was perfectly logical that Reagan should regard Tomlinson's political reliability as more important than his lack of managerial experience. In fact, Tomlinson had been summoned to Washington to accomplish at VOA precisely what Ken Gilmore would soon be asked to accomplish at *Reader's Digest*.

During the fifties and sixties, VOA had been a highly politicized weapon in a war of words against the evil Soviet Union. So had *Reader's Digest*. But with the arrival of détente in the mid-seventies, a new philosophy emerged at VOA. "Warts and all" was the operative phrase, the idea being that revealing the truth, even when the truth presented unflattering aspects of

America, was the best way to gain lasting respect around the world. A similar change occurred at *Reader's Digest* when Ed Thompson became editor in 1976. Both institutions had been involved in international propaganda. In the late seventies, both began again to practice real journalism.

But in 1980 Ronald Reagan became president, and at that point—to combat what Reagan kept calling the "Evil Empire"—the clock was turned back. Reagan appointed his California friend Charles Wick, a former bandleader, to run the U.S. Information Agency (the umbrella under which VOA operates), and Wick subsequently appointed Ken Tomlinson to run VOA. The "Brown Whisky Kid" served in this capacity from 1982 until mid-1984. His tenure was unremarkable, except that beneath the seeming calm it is clear that VOA quickly resumed its predétente role as a political weapon. According to a 1993 Ted Koppel report on ABC's *World News Tonight*, during the years when Tomlinson was director, VOA was used to broadcast secret messages to U.S. agents working undercover in the Soviet Union and elsewhere (by, among other devices, playing certain songs at agreed-on times, accompanied by coy signals indicating who had requested which tunes, and why). "At issue is the credibility of VOA itself," summed up ABC's James Walker, "whether it is acceptable to violate the trust between broadcaster and listener in the name of 'national security.' "

In the summer of 1984, shortly after Ed Thompson was fired, Ken Tomlinson was released from VOA to facilitate his return to Pleasantville as managing editor. Now even old RD hands became upset, and soon the corridors buzzed with rumors. One held that Tomlinson was a kind of "Manchurian Candidate" (after the title character in the famous political thriller), programmed by his Washington colleagues to help a shaky Ken Gilmore lead the world's most widely read magazine away from the "independent journalism" favored by Thompson loyalists into the paths of political righteousness as defined by Ronald Reagan and William Casey.

There was no proof of this, of course; nothing beyond Tomlinson's background, his obsessive secretiveness, and the suspicious timing of his otherwise inexplicable emergence as *Digest* heir apparent. But the rumors persisted even so, and it didn't help that the magazine's attitude toward the nation's intelligence agencies—sharply critical during the Thompson years—changed abruptly following the coronations of Gilmore and Tomlinson. Articles lauding the triumphs of U.S. intelligence (or pushing themes that CIA director Casey considered "politically useful") became regular events. And the watchful skepticism that had marked the Thompson years—the insistence on speaking truth even when truth was inconvenient—was banished from *Reader's Digest* as thoroughly as it had been banished from the Voice of America itself. Two episodes in particular—each involving CIA/FBI/*RD* collaboration in the "spinning" of a major news event, and each peaking in 1985, following the Gilmore/Tomlinson ascendancy—lent weight to the rumors.

The origins of the first episode go back to 1981, on the day after Reagan's inauguration, when secretary of state Alexander Haig made a widely reported speech blaming world terrorism on the Russians (a theme that soon became the centerpiece of the administration's propaganda). Pressed for evidence to support his charge, Haig cited *The Terror Network*, a just-published book written by *RD* roving editor Claire Sterling under the watchful eyes of Ken Gilmore.

As expected, Haig's speech made headlines around the world. Sensing an opportunity to score points against the Evil Empire, William Casey called for a special national intelligence estimate—an in-depth report from his senior Soviet analysts—on the subject of Soviet terrorism. When the experts were done, however, their report cleared the Russians of involvement (Sterling's methods were called "preposterous") and concluded that Sterling had been misled by the CIA's own "black propaganda"—anti-Soviet tales planted around Europe by Agency operatives. This was *not* the conclusion Reagan and Casey wanted to hear. "I paid $13.95 for Sterling's book," Casey sneered at his analysts, "and it tells me more than you bastards who cost me $50,000 a year!"

Four months later, on May 13, 1981, a right-wing Turkish radical named Mehmet Ali Agca shot and nearly killed Pope John Paul II in Rome, and in this shocking event director Casey clearly saw a fresh opportunity to cast aspersions on the Evil Empire. An intelligence consultant named Paul Henze, the CIA's former station chief in Turkey, was "made available" to *RD*'s Washington bureau (just as Yuri Nosenko had been "made available" nine years before). The bureau hired Henze, a specialist in propaganda, to write a report on the attempted assassination, and on the basis of Henze's report Gilmore and "Dimi" Panitza, *RD*'s European editor, assigned Claire Sterling to write a book about the attempt on the pope's life. "Take as long as you like," they told Sterling. "Go wherever you please, spend as much as you must to get as close to the truth as you can."

"The Plot to Kill the Pope" appeared in *Reader's Digest* in September 1982, and to no one's surprise presented "strong evidence" that the assassin's trail led through the Bulgarian secret service straight back to the KGB in Moscow. Other media soon took up the cry. NBC News broadcast an hour-long special. William Safire of the *New York Times* gave the theory his official approval, as did *Time, Newsweek,* CBS News, and the *Wall Street Journal.*

The *Digest* thesis—that Soviet leaders had actually ordered the murder of the pope—reflected grotesque evil. *Could it be true? And if it* was *true, how should the world react?* From the Kremlin came furious denials, including a lengthy article in *Literaturnaya Gazeta* that "proved" the Sterling charges false. In Washington, an alarmed Congress demanded more information. Analysts at the CIA were asked once again to conduct an in-depth study, and in early 1983 they produced a secret report that once again exonerated the Soviets. Although Casey's deputy Robert Gates quietly briefed the Senate Intelligence Committee to that effect, the report itself was not made public. Reagan and Casey continued to insist that the Evil Empire had done it, and that's what they told the world.

In the summer of 1983, with the press uproar at its peak, a Soviet journalist named Oleg Bitov (who "just happened" to have written the *Gazeta* article) suddenly defected to the British. Hoping that Bitov might have additional information about the murder plot, Dimi Panitza arranged to meet with him in London. After a lengthy interview, Panitza sent Bitov to see John Barron in Washington. And soon Barron was at work on a new article.

What did Bitov tell Barron? No one will ever know. In September 1984, just as Barron was completing his article (supervised now by newly appointed editor-in-chief Gilmore), the alleged defector suddenly fled back to the Soviet Union. At a press conference, he railed that he had been kidnapped by Western intelligence, drugged, tortured and forced to make "anti-Soviet" statements. The notion of Soviet complicity in the plot to kill the pope, he wrote in a subsequent *Gazeta* piece, was a lie conceived by the CIA—"and John Dimitri Panitza, European editor of *Reader's Digest,* was instrumental in bringing it to the world." Bitov had been brought to John Barron's home in Washington, he claimed, to meet a CIA contact who had tried to force him to testify against the accused Bulgarians. "Many leading staffers of *Reader's Digest,*" Bitov concluded, "do not deem it necessary to conceal their CIA attachments."

Who was telling the truth? For political reasons, Ronald Reagan and William Casey wanted the world to believe that the Evil Empire was guilty. And *Reader's Digest* had cooperated by assuring its 100 million readers that this was so. On the other hand, the Soviet Union angrily denied every charge in the *Digest*'s report. And William Casey's own senior analysts *agreed with the Russians*.

But not, as it turned out, for long. In 1985, alarmed at the warming relationship between Reagan and Soviet leader Gorbachev, Casey ordered deputy Gates to produce a new report "stating the case for Soviet involvement." As described by Anthony Lewis in the *New York Times,* this new report "read like a novelist's fantasy of Red conspiracy." Yet Gates sent it to Reagan, as ordered, under a memo that described it as "a comprehensive examination of who was behind the attempted assassination." So much for truth in government. As for the *Digest*'s conspiracy theory: In 1986, the three Bulgarians charged with arranging the assassination at the behest of the

KGB were acquitted on all counts by an Italian court (after a trial during which the would-be assassin, though claiming to be a reincarnation of Jesus Christ, failed to produce a single piece of evidence to support his claims of Bulgarian involvement).

The second episode began in May 1985 with the FBI arrest of John Walker, a former naval officer whose espionage ring had been selling top-secret communications documents to the Russians for two decades. Seeking to put the best face on what was, in fact, an intelligence calamity, the Bureau asked John Barron to write a book about the case focusing not so much on the lost secrets as on the brilliance of the FBI's investigation (". . . the U.S. now has a chance to restore the sanctity of its communications," Barron would conclude, "thanks to those who broke the ring").

In the midst of Barron's research, a KGB colonel named Vitaly Yurchenko —the highest-ranking KGB defector on record—suddenly turned up at the American embassy in Rome. "The advantages provided by the Walker gang no longer exist," Yurchenko insisted. And there was something else. "As it happens," Yurchenko said, he had recently served as deputy chief of the KGB unit responsible for espionage against the United States. So his knowledge in this area (like Nosenko's knowledge about Oswald) uniquely qualified him to identify KGB moles within the CIA.

This was, in fact, the first question put to Yurchenko by his debriefers. So many U.S. intelligence assets had already been "burned" in 1985 that both the CIA and the FBI were convinced there had to be an active mole in their midst. Yurchenko confirmed these suspicions by identifying two U.S. agents who had worked for the KGB: Edward Lee Howard, a CIA officer fired in 1984; and Ron Pelton, who had sold communications secrets to the Russians during a just-ended career at the National Security Agency.

Beyond Howard and Pelton, said Yurchenko, there was no one—not a single active penetration by the KGB of any U.S. intelligence service. Period. And the CIA, hearing once again what it desperately needed to hear, believed him. Director Casey actually bragged about Yurchenko to the media—he even authorized a Yurchenko book, along the lines of *The Penkovsky Papers*, to demonstrate to the world this "great triumph" over the KGB.

In truth, the Agency had little choice. Because if Yurchenko was lying, then his sudden presence among them led inexorably to an alarming conclusion: That there *was* a mole—a mole of such extraordinary importance that Yurchenko (like Nosenko) had been dispatched to divert attention from the penetration by fingering Howard and Pelton. And if *that* were true, then every U.S. espionage operation going back to the acceptance of Nosenko in 1968 and the purge of Angleton in 1974 would have to be reassessed, with political and security implications excruciating to contemplate.

So the CIA chose against all the evidence to believe Yurchenko, and stubbornly kept believing him even when, in November of that year, he redefected to the Soviet Union. Like Bitov, he held a press conference, and like Bitov he claimed he had been abducted, drugged and tortured by U.S. intelligence. And *still* they believed him.

"Yurchenko's redefection," sniffed William Casey, "was due to CIA mishandling." During hearings that March to confirm his appointment as the Agency's new deputy director, Robert Gates stated flatly that "Yurchenko was genuine." And when *Reader's Digest* published John Barron's analysis of the Walker case in April 1987, it too exonerated Yurchenko. There were some, Barron admitted in *Breaking the Ring,* who doubted Yurchenko. But "officials aware of the totality of what Yurchenko provided remain convinced that he was authentic."

It is always easy to be wise in hindsight. Yet it must be said that those who insisted on Yurchenko's credibility in 1985—despite all the evidence of KGB deceit—were guilty of more than ignorance. The blindness they displayed was stunning and the damage it has caused is only now, in the wake of the Aldrich Ames fiasco, finally coming clear.

Recruited by the KGB in April 1985, Rick Ames soon established himself as a spy of extraordinary value. As chief of the CIA's Soviet counterintelligence branch, he had access to every operation against the Russians, and he didn't hesitate to make this information available. One by one, Western "assets" began to disappear. At CIA headquarters, concerns about a Soviet mole—a hideous prospect—rose to feverish proportions. And then Yurchenko turned up in Rome. "There *is* no mole," he said. And the CIA believed him.

As it happened, *Rick Ames himself* led the interrogation of Yurchenko. So here we have an interesting situation: Ames the Mole (terrified at first, as he later admitted, but able somehow to ignore the interior voice that kept repeating, *If only they knew, If only they knew*) interrogating his own KGB Spymaster on the subject of whether Ames the Mole existed. And Yurchenko the Spymaster replying (with what must have been a *very* straight face) that Ames the Mole did not. *And the CIA believed him.*

The full costs of that belief are higher than anyone has been able to calculate. Rick Ames identified to the KGB every CIA spy working against the Soviet Union during the 1980s—more than one hundred U.S. and Allied operations were exposed and as many as thirty-four individual agents arrested. Following the usual practice, these agents were not immediately executed. Instead, they were left in place to channel KGB disinformation (whatever the Kremlin wanted U.S. policymakers to believe) back to Washington. When they *were* executed (or, in a few cases, imprisoned), replacements were quickly established, with help from Ames, and the flow of disinformation continued. And even when the CIA *realized* there was a problem, it did nothing. For seven years, the Agency routinely passed "tainted" reports to the president and the Pentagon—*knowing they were false*. When this extraordinary behavior was finally revealed to members of the House and Senate intelligence committees, in October 1995, they professed astonishment. "Mind-boggling!" concluded Senate chairman Arlen Spector. "Inconceivable!" echoed House chairman Larry Combest.

In fact—as a review of recent Agency history makes abundantly clear—this behavior was not mind-boggling at all, but the inevitable result of the slippery slope Ed Thompson had worried about during the Agency's attacks on *Legend* in the late seventies. The leadership of the CIA had opted to "believe" Yuri Nosenko not because his message was true (they understood it was not) but because it was convenient, and because Nosenko himself could be used (in *Reader's Digest*) for propaganda. They chose to "believe" Claire Sterling in the early eighties not because her tales made sense (they were based on the Agency's own "black" propaganda) but because (when published in *Reader's Digest*) they created support for the Reagan weapons program. And they "believed" Vitaly Yurchenko in 1985 because believing Yurchenko made the Agency look good and because his message (that there *was* no mole) was convenient (and, true or false, could be published in *Reader's Digest*).

A CIA that would believe all this was *destined* to produce an Aldrich Ames. And when Ames appeared, right on schedule, it was precisely in character for this credulous CIA to pass along the information he made possible—*even knowing it was bogus*. In fact, the Ames disinformation (vastly overstating Soviet military and economic strength) was passed along precisely because, true or not, it provided support for the administration's weapons program. "First, I will build," Reagan had boasted to Pope John Paul II in 1981. "Then they will build. Then I will build again, and they will build again. But the next time . . . they will have to quit." And he kept his word.*

Yet it is clear now that Mikhail Gorbachev was ready to quit long before the Soviet Apocalypse of 1991. Gorbachev understood that war between the superpowers would be a catastrophe for the Soviet Union. He was eager, therefore, to negotiate agreements to end what he called "these unnecessary arms expenditures." But his powerful generals, pointing to the Reagan

---

* Is it possible that Ames was a "created" traitor? Repugnant as this theory is, it is the only explanation that covers all of the events that comprise the otherwise "inconceivable" Ames "fiasco." Consider:

1. In the early eighties, reports from U.S. agents behind the Iron Curtain were clearly indicating vast weaknesses in the Soviet economy and military establishment—precisely what Ronald Reagan, William Casey and their hawkish friends at the Pentagon *didn't* want to hear.

2. In 1983, with Congress (in view of these reports) increasingly reluctant to bankroll Reagan's weapons splurge, Aldrich Ames—an Agency hack whose record featured alcoholism, insubordination,

spending spree, would not let it happen. The Americans kept building, so the Russians kept building. And then, just as Reagan had predicted, their world collapsed. This has not been altogether a good thing. Indeed, the consequences of those unnecessary arms expenditures—for a bankrupt Russia that cannot feed itself; for a "triumphant" America staggering under a $4 trillion debt—will haunt the world for decades to come.

CHAPTER THIRTY-SEVEN

By the spring of 1985, the initial cost-cutting moves made by George Grune, Dick McLoughlin and Bill Cross had produced results beyond their wildest dreams. Although revenues remained level, profits for the fiscal year ending in June promised to be *twice* what they had been the year before. It almost seemed too easy. Merely by firing people and shutting down operations, Grune and his pals had caused profits to rise from $30 million to $60 million, and the value of the company's stock to soar from less than $20 in early 1984 to $60 in mid-1985. *What will happen when we get serious?* they asked themselves. *We can send this stock through the roof!*

But there was a catch. As the stock's value rose, so, too, did pressures from the charities to get at what was after all (in large part) *their* fortune. And as this happened it became evident to Grune and his colleagues that they had been left with a serious problem—an internal weakness they began to call "our Achilles' heel":

1. Ninety-eight percent of the company's stock had been given to various charities.

aberrant behavior and failed polygraph exams; who had talked openly of "leveling the playing field" between East and West—was suddenly and inexplicably appointed to one of the most sensitive posts in the entire CIA, with access to the files on every Agency operation against the Soviet Union, the very operations that were producing the intelligence that Reagan and Casey found so "inconvenient."

3. Faced with this unexpected opportunity to "level the playing field," Ames quickly succumbed. And soon the reports coming from Russia were very different. "The net effect [of the new reports] was that we overestimated the U.S.S.R. as a credible military and technological opponent," says current CIA director John Deutch. "The new reports were used to justify multi-billion-dollar investments in weapons systems."

So the question remains: *Was* the Ames case a fiasco? Or was it, in truth, one of the most cynical and sophisticated political manipulations in history—in the course of which the Soviets were deceived into writing the script that justified the weapons program that brought the Evil Empire crashing to the earth?

2. To retain control, most of this gifted stock remained within "conduit trusts" dominated by RD (the S/Os) and under contracts that strictly limited the right of the charities to sell.
3. After the deaths of the Wallaces, these limitations came under fire. Were they legal? Or were they a clever but illegal subterfuge—an attempt to have it both ways, to give *and* to retain—that would eventually put the tax treatment of the gifts in jeopardy?
4. If the charities ever became dissatisfied—if, for example, they sought to sell to an outsider in search of a higher return, and were blocked from doing so by the Digest—they would have a right to seek relief in the courts. Indeed, there was a worrisome precedent: In 1984, when the charitable foundation that owned all of the B. Altman's department-store chain turned down the offer of a raiding investor, the New York attorney general forced the foundation to sell and invest in assets that provided a better immediate return for the beneficiaries. Nevertheless, Digest lawyers were confident—*except for that damned Achilles' heel.*
5. Two percent of Digest stock had been sold to a small group of employees under contracts that gave them the right to dispose of it whenever and to whomever they pleased (with the sole restriction that they offer it first to the Digest). The fact that these employees could freely sell their stock further weakened the limitations placed on the charities, and raised the possibility of ultimate loss of control to an outsider.
6. To deal with the problem, management let it be known—via the grapevine and through brutal example (though they put nothing in writing) —that employees who sought to exercise this right would be fired. As long as the stock price remained low, this outrageous threat proved effective.
7. But now, with the stock soaring upward, management feared that some employees might sell despite the threat. If they did, even the counsel of Laurance Rockefeller might not suffice to hold back the impatient charities. And if the charities insisted on selling, the whole elaborate house of cards might come crashing down.

It was indeed a terrible problem. The S/Os alone were sitting on stock with an "official" value of $250 million and a "real" value somewhere above $2 *billion*. Perhaps *far* above $2 billion. Lurking on one side of this hidden fortune were raiders hunting for ways to get at it. Lurking on the other side were employee-shareholders whose right to sell might open a door.

Grune's initial approach to the problem—a stock buyback that would eliminate the employee-shareholders even as it offered Grune and his closest colleagues a chance to get rich—was as brutally direct as the man himself. Employees at the time owned roughly 120,000 shares. With the price already double what it had ever been before, some were eager to cash in. Those who weren't eager, Grune must have reasoned, could be "induced" to go along by use of the threat to terminate jobs. That this scheme might be grossly unfair did not seem to bother him. Longtime employees—who had bought their *unrestricted* shares over decades of bank payments—would be forced out just when the stock was finally heading up. At the same time, the Rockefeller charities—whose *restricted* shares had been a *gift*—would be advised to wait for the far-higher prices that were coming.

At the conclusion of the stockholders' meeting that October, Grune stood before his assembled executives brimming with confidence. "So that's it, ladies and gentlemen," he said. "It has been an excellent year, and you can all be proud. Are there any questions?"

For several seconds, no one responded. Then an executive in the third row stood up. It was Lynn Mapes, associate publisher and a thirty-five-year RD veteran. "George," he said, "there is a rumor flying around about a company buyback of employee stock. Anything to it?"

The room abruptly quieted. "Thanks for your question, Lynn," said Grune. "The answer is yes. We are working on a plan to buy back all the stock at sixty dollars. Any other questions?"

The room was buzzing. Was this good news? Bad news? What, really, was management up to? They had questions, all right. Every executive in the room had a question. But, again, only Mapes was brave enough to rise. "One other question, George," he said. "This buyback you've described . . . will it be . . . *voluntary?*" Grune forced a smile at the obvious relevance of Mapes's query. But he chose to duck it. "I don't know, Lynn," he said. "We're studying it." He looked slowly around the room. "Anyone else?" he asked. You could almost hear the arm muscles contracting. But not a single hand was raised.

As it turned out, Lynn Mapes had put his finger on the sticking point. If the buyback was voluntary, there were sure to be wiseguys who held out, who sensed that profits were not only going to keep rising, as Grune had indicated, but were about to rise dramatically. And all it would take to ruin the scheme was a few. But there were problems, too, with forcing the buyback. If, under threat of dismissal, stockholders were coerced into selling, and thereafter the stock doubled or tripled, how many lawsuits would they face? It was tempting, but too dangerous. The corporate grapevine was already buzzing, and company lawyers were shaking their heads. In the end, amid assurances that some other path to riches would be found (tied no doubt to Grune's success in raising the value of the stock), the $60 buyback died a quiet death.

Stymied in his efforts to eliminate the Achilles' heel, Grune turned to the problem of the Wallace Funds. Under the wills, 100 percent of the corporation's voting stock (nine thousand shares in all) would eventually be transferred from the Wallace Trust (controlled by Laurance Rockefeller) to the

Wallace Funds. At that point, whoever controlled the funds in theory would also control the corporation. It was not lost on Grune that the man in charge of all four funds after Lila Wallace's death was none other than Barnabas McHenry. Nor could Grune have been unaware of the fact that McHenry, despite his earlier disappointment, remained very much Laurance Rockefeller's man.

From his first days as chairman, therefore, Grune seemed determined to eliminate the wily attorney. Among other things, he argued that it was wrong —an obvious conflict of interest—for the Digest's counsel to serve also as director of the independent Wallace Funds. In July 1985, combining this argument with a bountiful golden parachute, Grune induced McHenry to resign his corporate position. One year later, under relentless pressure, McHenry resigned from the funds as well. "I had eaten all the Grune crow I could stomach," he says today. "George was just . . . *unbelievable*. A real sleazy guy."

In fact, there was more to McHenry's second resignation than met the eye. McHenry had been Rockefeller's man at the funds, and he was removed only after Grune agreed to take on Stephen Stamas, former director of the Exxon Foundation and a member of the Rockefeller inner circle, as McHenry's replacement. But Grune had a few cards of his own to play. At his insistence, the four Wallace Funds were merged into two and renamed the Lila Wallace/Reader's Digest Fund and the DeWitt Wallace/Reader's Digest Fund. In October 1986, Stamas became president of both funds. But Grune became chairman of the funds at the same time, so it was clear to everyone who was in charge.

The two men clashed from the outset. Among other things, Stamas was opposed to renaming the funds, arguing that the new names were in conflict with the Wallaces' wishes and made it appear that the funds were being used (unethically and perhaps illegally) to promote the business interests of Reader's Digest. Grune disagreed. "Everything that has been done since the Wallaces haven't been with us has been in support of their wishes," he insisted. A second area of contention grew out of rising pressures on the funds to meet their philanthropic obligations. To the forthright Stamas, the only sensible option was to bite the bullet and take the company public. But again Grune resisted, and Stamas found it impossible to find out why. What he failed to understand was that Grune had no intention of going public until he had figured out how to retain control—and had positioned himself to become a prime beneficiary of the higher price sure to develop in a public market.

The struggle between the two men worsened later in 1986 when Bill Cross suddenly resigned. Although "poor health" was cited, Cross quit in part because he agreed with Stamas about selling the Digest and in part because he had gone as far down a slippery path with Grune as he was willing to go. ("I didn't want to be part of all that," he says today. "I . . . resisted.") Convinced that the financial affairs of the company were hopelessly tangled, Stamas demanded that a high-powered outsider be brought in to straighten out the mess. Instead, Grune promoted Vernon Thomas, an unassuming Digest veteran, to fill the Cross vacancy. For Stamas, this was the last straw. In January 1987, the frustrated foundation executive followed Cross out the door.

There were other problems at the funds that also required tough action. For example, the original Wallace wills had been hastily drawn up just before passage of a 1969 law that limited the amount of stock private foundations can hold in a single company (because Congress believed that wealthy people were using such foundations to gain unfair tax benefits and commercial advantage). But while it was legal under the pre-'69 law for the Wallace Funds to be comprised mostly of Digest stock, the funds themselves (to avoid problems with the IRS) had been set up not as company-sponsored institutions but as separate private foundations meant to distribute money according to clear guidelines established by the Wallaces.

But the required arm's-length relationship between Reader's Digest and the two funds was ignored from the outset, and the funds have been used as vehicles for retaining control within the corporation. George Grune was chairman of the Digest and of the two funds, and virtually all of the funds' trustees were directors or executives of the company. "In effect," concluded Daniel Kurtz, former head of the Charities Bureau in the New York State attorney general's office, "the Wallace Funds have been precluded from receiving disinterested advice, because almost everyone who is in a position of responsibility—that is, the directors of the funds—wears another hat, as a director or officer of the company. But what is good for Reader's Digest is not necessarily good for the funds."

Grune adamantly denied any conflict. "It so happens that the Wallace/Reader's Digest Funds own shares in Reader's Digest," he explained to a reporter. "But they operate as separate entities. There is no influence of Reader's Digest over the Wallace Funds. Period."

Despite Grune's denials, legal experts raised serious questions about this relationship. What would happen, to cite just one possibility, in the event of a downturn in the company's fortunes—a downturn that caused the funds' holdings to decline in value by tens (or even hundreds) of millions? Under such circumstances, the funds' directors might be expected to consider changing Digest management—might even feel a *responsibility* to do so. But the funds' directors *were* Digest management, and these managers were clearly not eager to fire themselves. "The current setup at Reader's Digest is a blatant charade," concluded the comptroller of one of the country's largest foundations. "It makes you wonder if the funds are there for charitable purposes or for some ulterior motive."

To preclude just such a "blatant charade," the tax laws stipulated that within fifteen years of Lila's death 50 percent of the RD voting stock would have to be sold off. When that happened, control of the Wallace Funds would no longer be an issue, and Reader's Digest—at least in theory—would be a public company answerable only to shareholders. This was the problem that had convinced Bill Cross the company should be sold at the height of the market and before it came under the gun of the law. "It is unlikely that current managers can retain control," Cross told a reporter for *Forbes* in 1987. "If they have found a loophole, it would be something that has eluded a lot of good minds for a number of years."

By "good minds," Cross was referring to lawyers at Lord, Day & Lord, who had advised Grune that retaining control after the inevitable public offering would be impossible. Not satisfied with this answer, Grune and Cross had sought a second opinion from lawyers at Cleary, Gottlieb, Steen and Hamilton, by reputation the sharpest trust attorneys in New York. But the "good minds" at Cleary, Gottlieb also said no, and at that point a discouraged Bill Cross announced his retirement.

But George Grune understood that if you search long enough you can usually find a lawyer who will produce the answer you want. Shortly after Cross's departure, trust attorneys at Proskauer, Rose, Goetz and Mendelson considered the Digest's predicament and after due deliberation arrived at the long-sought solution. Under the Proskauer plan, 50 percent of the RD voting stock would be retained in the two funds, 20 percent would be sold over time to the Digest's profit-sharing plan (also controlled by Grune and his colleagues), and only 30 percent would be offered to the public. Thus 70 percent of the voting power would remain within entities controlled by Digest management. The company would be "public" in a way that satisfied the requirements of the excise laws, but "private" where it counted.

Lawyers, of course, thrive in gray areas, and this elusive loophole seemed to some very gray, indeed. And also very clever. Because although the arrangement seems to offend the law's spirit (by allowing the company to retain tax benefits without having to surrender control), there are no identifiable injured parties and thus no plaintiffs to bring the lawsuit that finally arouses the IRS. "There are no vigilant shareholders watching over these funds," points out Barney McHenry. "In fact, *nobody* watches this stuff! New York State has exactly *two* people manning its philanthropic-frauds office."

In private letters to Digest lawyers, the IRS and the New York Attorney General's office have found no fault with the arrangement, and even critics have not claimed that the clear appearance of conflict necessarily indicates a conflict in fact. But there will be plenty of time for real conflicts to arise, and meanwhile any serious downturn in the company's fortunes would by itself constitute a conflict of interest. This has been a terrible burden on management. If profits should ever falter, they could lose control.

So there were many things to worry about as 1987 began, but nothing truly to fear. Profits *were* rolling in, and the stock was soaring ever higher. And by the time these other issues came to a head, it was likely that Chairman Grune would be enjoying a very golden retirement, while the charities of Philanthropist Rockefeller would have cashed in their billions and reinvested elsewhere for the long haul. As the Founder himself used to say when things began to fall apart at High Winds: "Well, it's too bad. But . . . *umm* . . . I guess the next tenants can worry about it."

CHAPTER THIRTY-EIGHT

In the months following Lila's death, Gene Doherty began to understand that the wishes of the King and Queen might not carry much weight now that they were dead. Among other things, the Wallaces had made clear to everyone that they wanted High Winds to remain in the Digest world as a corporate meeting place and social center (with Doherty as caretaker and all other staff employees provided for). They had discussed the necessary arrangements with McHenry, and a favorable ruling on the tax issues had been obtained from Lord, Day. Only when Lila believed it would happen—that her Castle would remain within the Kingdom forever—did she confide to DeWitt her desire to have their ashes spread in the Rose Garden. She seemed to feel that the presence of their remains at High Winds would in some way protect the Kingdom after they were gone.

But the Wallaces' pleasant vision for High Winds was not based on anybody's bottom line. High Winds did go to the funds, as stipulated by the wills, and from the funds to the Digest. But the Digest was under no compulsion to *keep* what it had bought, and it didn't take Grune, Cross and McLoughlin long to decide that the Founders' Castle was very much in the "nice-but-not-necessary" category. Within weeks of Lila's death, word leaked out that High Winds was for sale.

Overnight, feelers from the rich and famous (everyone from Ralph Lauren to Steven Spielberg to Carl Icahn) began to fill the air. Never one to miss a trick, John Strasburger contacted a local realtor and secretly offered—for a sizable concession—to show the place to interested parties in advance of the public market. On an afternoon in September of that year, Gene Doherty looked out his cottage window to see a long black limousine sweep through the High Winds gate. Still fiercely protective, Doherty climbed into his own vehicle and chased the limo up the Wallaces' hill. But when he reached the main entrance, Strasburger barred his way. "This is a private matter," the butler told him. "It's none of your business."

In the rotunda behind Strasburger, Doherty spied two very large gentlemen with decidedly unfriendly faces. *What the hell,* he thought. *It really* isn't *my business. Not any more.*

The mystery visitor turned out to be Bob Guccione, publisher of *Penthouse* magazine, and Guccione subsequently offered the Digest $5.5 million for High Winds "should it come on the market." When news of this offer inevitably leaked, the local papers had a field day: "Pets in the Swimming Pool??" ran one headline; "Porn King of Pleasantville??" another. Neighbors on Byram Lake Road were titillated by visions of bare-breasted girls romping across the Wallace hillsides. But the reaction down at Headquarters was very different. "High Winds can't be for sale," employees murmured to one another. "High Winds belongs to RD. Hell, High Winds *is* RD!" Alarmed by all the commotion, Grune and Cross quickly made it clear that High Winds was *not* for sale (not yet, anyway), and that Mr. Guccione would have to look elsewhere for summer quarters.

But this was only a delaying action. Six months later, with Guccione out of the picture, High Winds was quietly put on the market for $8 million— the highest price ever asked for a private residence in Westchester County. In November 1985, it was sold to mystery man Nelson Peltz, chairman of a conglomerate known as Triangle Industries, for $6 million. And now Doherty began to worry for real. Shortly after the sale was announced, he cornered McHenry. "What about my job, Barney?" he asked. "What about my Digest pension?" McHenry shrugged. "Can't help you, Gene," he said. "Better make a deal with Peltz." Furious, Doherty drove down to Headquarters to confront Bill Cross. "This isn't right, Bill," he pleaded. "What about my twenty-five years? What about all the promises?"

"You got paid, didn't you?" Cross replied. "That's all we owe you."

At the time, the Digest had a policy under which severance could be spread over several years or, in special cases, conveyed in a lump sum at the time of termination. Needing cash to set himself up in a private limousine business, Doherty arranged for a lump-sum payment. But Cross vetoed this as well. "No special deals, Gene," he said. "You'll get paid over time like everyone else."

Today Doherty shakes his head when he thinks about this. "Cross and

McHenry had a problem with me because I knew so much," he says. "By spreading the payments out, they were sending me a message: *Start blabbing and your checks may stop.* With Strasburger, they went the opposite route. John knew even more than I did, so with him they used kid gloves. Barney wrote him out a fat check to keep him quiet, then put him on the Rockefeller payroll over at Laurance's place in Pocantico Hills." (According to a document filed at Surrogate's Court in nearby White Plains, in January 1985 McHenry did in fact settle a "claim for services" by paying John Strasburger $75,000 out of Lila's estate. It is also worth noting that Strasburger's demands did not stop at $75,000, and that shortly after undertaking his new responsibilities as a sub-butler for Laurance Rockefeller he suffered a brain hemorrhage and died.)

Christmas 1985 was not a happy time for Gene and Ilse Doherty. Although the High Winds sale would not be approved by the IRS until the following March, Peltz rented the estate in the meantime and quickly decided he wanted former Wallace retainers off the premises. The Dohertys moved from their cottage at the foot of Lila's hill into a condominium in nearby Bedford Hills, and Gene struggled to get a livery business started. "I had lost everything," he says today. "My home, my job, my future. The world I had lived in for twenty-five years, where people were good to one another, had disappeared."

The sale of High Winds put a quick $6 million into Digest coffers, and caused an upward blip in the company's stock. But $6 million wasn't the answer to the problems facing George Grune. Profits were still rising, but the charities—like so many greedy grandchildren—wanted more from their inheritance, and fast. ("I was after the Digest continually in those days," admits Robert Gavin, Macalester's president.) As the second summer of the post-Wallace era got under way, therefore, the cost-cutting ax began to flash again.

First to fall, after forty years of publication, was the Digest's Japanese company. Wallace had always been fascinated by the Japanese. He admired their hard work, their thrifty nature, their ingenuity and openness to new ways of doing things. He thought America could learn a lot from Japan, and it pleased him that the Japanese seemed to feel they could learn from America —and especially from what they read in the pages of *Reader's Digest.*

From the end of World War II, *RD*'s circulation in Japan had remained above one million. But in recent years, as Japan became an economic power in its own right, its obsession with America had moderated. As this happened, circulation of *Reader's Digest* tapered off, eventually bottoming out at 500,000, and the once-profitable company began to struggle. It was partly in response to this situation that Ed Thompson had launched his program of increased local autonomy for foreign editions. But turning Japan around was going to take time—several years, at least—and the new managers in Pleasantville did not have several years.

When the Digest announced it would cease operations in Japan in 1986, the Japanese labor movement took it as a mortal insult. The union eventually sued RD, and a dozen workers traveled to the United States to set up a picket line outside the main gate at Headquarters. It didn't do them any good, of course, yet there was something deeply moving in their protest. It caused old-time Digesters to shake their heads in frustration. And it would have made DeWitt Wallace very angry. (Asked by a reporter about this, Grune bristled. "I wasn't put here to be a caretaker," he snapped. "Caretakers mow the lawn.")

The Scandinavian editions were next on the hit list. For years, these little companies—in Norway, Denmark and Sweden—had had their ups and downs, making money in some years, losing money in others. It hadn't bothered Wallace. In fact, it pleased him greatly just to have a presence for his magazine in countries whose pioneers had settled Minnesota. But all three companies were in a down cycle in the mid-eighties, and therefore something had to be done. The three editions were consolidated into one, published out of Copenhagen, and hundreds of additional Digesters were thrown out of work.

The biggest change of all came at home. From the early days in Greenwich Village, the *Digest*'s U.S. circulation had risen every year, peaking in the late seventies at 18.25 million. Keeping it at that level had become difficult because of a drop-off in newsstand sales. To bring in the last one or two million subscribers, several mailings were required, and this was expensive —more expensive, in terms of the bottom line, than the subscriptions were worth. This, too, had never bothered Wallace. His goal was to put the *Digest*'s message before as many readers as possible, and it didn't matter to him what this cost as long as the company remained profitable overall.

Beginning in January 1986, the Digest announced that the magazine's rate base would drop by more than 10 percent, from 18.25 million to 16.25 million. It was the first such cutback in RD's history, and it meant that the *Digest* could no longer claim the largest circulation of any magazine in the world. (That honor now went to *TV Guide*, with a rate base pushing 17 million.) But Madison Avenue didn't mind. "This cut gives the advertiser a better buy for the buck," said Leo Scullin of Young & Rubicam. "It's a sign that the Digest is finally paying attention to profitability." While accepting the plaudits of the advertising world, Grune and McLoughlin managed to trample on the memory of the Founder. The previous circulation policy had been a mistake, they told reporters. Wallace had insisted on it "because it pleased his personal vanity to be Number One."

Although sharply criticized by the Digest's old guard (for straying from the Wallaces' concept of a "public trust"), and even by members of the financial press (for failing to promote real growth), Grune, Cross and McLoughlin could not be faulted on the central issue: When it came to profits, they were getting the job done. When Grune took over in May 1984, after-tax profits for the fiscal year ending that June were $30 million. One year later, profits had doubled, to $60 million, and one year after that they were up another 50 percent, reaching $90 million. In two years, profits had tripled. It began to seem as if the upward momentum would never stop. And since the stock was tied to earnings (by the formula), its value rose along with profits —from less than $20 in 1984 to $60 in 1985 to an astonishing $153 in the summer of 1986.

All of this was very satisfying to Grune and his colleagues, and to Laurance Rockefeller and his charities as well. But there was a nagging problem. The surging profits had been achieved with no growth in revenues: total sales had edged upward from $1.3 billion in 1984 to $1.4 billion in 1986. So all the extra cash was coming from cost-cutting alone—"squeezing the orange," as Digesters put it. And by the middle of 1986 the squeeze was beginning to pinch.

CHAPTER THIRTY-NINE

In the fall of that year, with employee-stockholders still buzzing over the surge in value of their once nearly worthless shares, Grune made a second attempt at dealing with the problem of employee ownership. A few days before the annual meeting, he startled everyone by distributing a tender offer that became known as the "One Third Plan." The tender proposed to buy back the holdings of employee-stockholders over a three-year period—one-third in 1986 at $153 per share, and the second and third thirds in 1987 and 1988 at then-current prices. To participate in the offer—which was being made, shareholders were informed, for "the good of the company" and because the current situation "perpetuates a serious morale problem"—you had to sell on schedule. No waiting for the second or third years to see where the price might go. Take it all, now, was the idea. Or leave it all. And the clear implication was that anyone who "left it all" faced a bleak future at Reader's Digest.

The offer made two additional points: (1) that selling now was "appropriate" in view of upcoming revisions in the tax laws that were expected to cause a drop-off in the stock market (which would cause a drop-off in the RD stock); (2) that the corporation had no "specific" plans under consideration for a public offering (a legally mandated notice buried at the bottom of page 6).

In fact, Grune knew perfectly well that a public offering was coming. The only questions were when and how it would happen. If the offering came too soon, before the stock attained its full potential, outsiders who bought in low would reap gains that by right ought to come to management and the charities. If the offering came too late, the impatient charities—goaded by the cash-ins of employees eager to get rich—might jump the gun by throwing themselves at an outside suitor.

Grune desperately needed to control the situation. Taking the Digest public was going to be immensely complicated. There were so many strings involved—the employees, the charities, the Wallace Funds, the SEC, the IRS, the New York Attorney General—and each seemed to be pulling in a different direction. Grune needed to have as many of the strings in his own hands as possible, and a major step in that direction would be to gain control over the employee stock. With that goal in mind, he stood before his fellow Digesters on the evening of October 9, looked them sternly in the eye, and delivered a lecture based on thinly veiled threats and an outright falsehood.

"Just to be sure we're together on this," he began, "let's recall Wally's original purpose in letting certain employees buy stock. It was intended as a nest egg for retirement. [*False:* Wallace had told the selected executives that he wanted them to have a "proprietary interest" in the company, and the stock contracts spoke only about providing "additional incentives" and "rewarding outstanding service."] His rule was simple: If you leave or retire, you turn in your stock. [*True.*] And conversely, if you turn in your stock, you leave or retire." [*False:* The "leave-on-tender" rule was a management fabrication used to bully employees into selling at times and prices advantageous to management; the contracts gave employee stockholders a clear right to sell freely and without penalty.]

The chairman surveyed the room with a challenging frown that turned by slow degrees into a cold smile. "Now," he continued, "as some of you know, we have just relaxed Wally's Rule a little. Our new one-third/one-third/one-third buyback policy gives us all—you and the company—a little more flexibility. If you elect to follow this program, you do not have to leave. [*Threat #1.*] But I don't want anyone to be misled. If you elect to dispose of your stock in any other way, you *must* leave—at a time determined by the executive committee to be right for the company. That won't necessarily be when *you* want to go. [*Threat #2.*] Please don't interpret this as a threat. It's a simple truth. You need to recognize that you are severing your ties when you sell outside the plan. That fact should be part of your decision-making process." [*Threat #3.*]

At this point, after a long pause, Grune's smile broadened into a friendly grin: "We all know there have been major inequities in this stock situation. But let's not worry about the past. Let's look to the future. For ours is a company with a very bright future indeed!"

As with the aborted 1985 buyback, the One Third Plan set off a buzzing debate among employee-stockholders. Was it a good deal? Was it a bad deal? Only eight months earlier Grune had contemplated a plan to take back their stock at $60—which, had it gone forward, would already have cost each of them $93 a share. Now he was offering this new plan. *Why was he so eager to get his hands on their stock?* Was it going to keep rising? Was there perhaps a giant rise on the horizon? What would happen to employees who *didn't* sell? Grune's little lecture—and the language of the tender offer itself —had been very threatening. Could it be . . . was it remotely conceivable . . . that nonparticipants would be *fired?*

Given these understandable fears, the employee-stockholders went for the new plan en masse, obediently turning over the first third of their Digest shares at $153. Some were resigned about this; others were furious. But no one thought to ask why the majority stockholders—the charities holding 98 percent of the shares—weren't selling, or why they were so quiet about it. The employees were being pressured to sell "for the good of the company" while the *charities* were allowed to wait for a higher price.

For a few months, as Ronald Reagan's tax reforms pushed the market down, $153 seemed like a good deal. By January, the Digest stock had dropped to $130. But it didn't stay down for long. Profits poured in that spring as Grune's brutal cost-cutting continued, and the stock responded, surging past $200, then past $250. By summer, with the price approaching $280, excited stockholders waited with bated breath for their chance to sell the second third.

It never came. On June 6, Grune sent a curt note to each stockholder. The One Third Plan was canceled, the note said, "pending decisions as to certain legal matters now under review."

Furious executives met behind closed doors. They had been coerced, more or less, into selling a third of their shares at a low price. Now they were being denied the promised chance to sell a second third at what seemed a high price. *What was going on?* No one knew for sure, although there were plenty of theories. According to one, the price had got too high, too fast. If "key executives" (who presumably knew the score) were selling out at $280, the charities would also want to sell, forcing management to put the company itself on the block. At $280, they weren't ready for that—not yet. Another theory held that a public offering was *already* in the works; that the rapid run-up in price had caused the company's "general" plans for such an offering (which legally could be kept from stockholders) to become "specific" —so specific that it was no longer legally feasible to press employees to sell under the One Third Plan without also telling them of the coming public market and the much higher prices likely to develop.

On August 11, Chairman Grune was interviewed on CNN, and the interviewer asked him point-blank whether the Digest planned to go public. "No," said Grune. "We have no such plans." The next morning, by coincidence, Grune was scheduled to discuss this very issue with Tony Oursler over breakfast at the Digest Guesthouse. Oursler got quickly to the point. "I saw you on TV last night, George," he said. "You told the interviewer that we're not going public. If that is true, why are we spending all this money telling the world how profitable we are?"

GRUNE: Silence.
OURSLER: *"Are* you going to sell?"
GRUNE: Blinks and smiles. Says nothing.
OURSLER: *"When* are you going to sell?"
GRUNE: "Good question." More silence.
OURSLER: "What about the second third, George? Will we ever get a chance to sell those shares?"
GRUNE: "There are legal matters under review."
OURSLER: "You do realize you may lose some of your best editors? Because they are worried about all this—about the stock, about the future. Some may feel they have to cash in to protect their families."
GRUNE: "I'm fatalistic about that. They will get a fair price. And they can easily be replaced."

Thinking about this later, it occurred to Oursler that Grune was *daring* them to sell. The editorial budget had just been drastically slashed (during a period of record-breaking profits) and Gilmore was having a terrible time making ends meet. The departures of several top editors would go a long way toward solving the problem. *Yes,* mused Oursler. *And when these overpaid editors are gone, George will bring in his band of English teachers to sit at their desks and drop manuscripts into a funnel.*

In the weeks following cancellation of the stock buyback, rumors spread around Headquarters that Wall Street was headed for a crash. Digest treasurer Ross Jones volunteered this information to a senior editor, and this editor nervously spread the word. "The S&P multiple is going to fall by 40 percent," Jones insisted. "That will cause a 40 percent drop in RD's stock." Worried about this, several of the company's best and brightest tendered their stock despite Grune's threat, and were immediately terminated. Others, unwilling to risk careers, swallowed bravely and hung on. Calculators were working furiously in many offices as the full costs of termination—in lost salary, pension benefits, medical coverage, reputations—were finally becoming clear.

When the annual stockholders meeting opened on Thursday afternoon, October 15, the room was buzzing with the news that the stock market had lost a hundred points. With the market imploding, there was fear that management would change the formula once again, causing Digest stock to plummet. Grune eased these fears by confirming that the price would hold through the end of the year. But he said nothing about letting employees sell. In fact, chief financial officer Vernon Thomas went out of his way to warn once again that the penalties for "unauthorized" selling were "extremely severe."

On October 19—forever after known as "Black Monday"—the stock market plunged 500 points. Because the Digest share price was tied to the market, it, too, would inevitably fall—but not until the next quarterly valuation on January 1. So an odd situation was set up: Digest shareholders could hold on to their stock and celebrate the New Year by watching a third of its value go down the drain. Or they could sell now to avoid that certain loss— and suffer the "severe penalties" alluded to by Thomas: loss of jobs, pensions, futures.

The irony wasn't wasted on many: DeWitt Wallace had made stock available to valued employees precisely with the wish that one day it would make them rich. He had helped them make their stock purchases by arranging loans—with the stock as collateral—at Chemical Bank. In 1971, when the stock fell below $5 and the bank threatened to foreclose, Wallace *personally* guaranteed payment. For seventeen years, these employees had worked to pay off loans on stock that was frequently worth less than they bought it for. Now, with the loans paid off and the predicted rise in value finally taking place, the man who had usurped the throne of Wallace's chosen successors was warning these same "valued employees" that if they tried to make Wallace's wish come true—even tried to avoid becoming *poorer*—they would face immediate termination from jobs they had performed well for years.

For many, Black Monday was the last straw. The trickle of cash-ins became a flood and the Guesthouse was booked solid through Christmas with what were mockingly called "retirement parties." Senior editor Dan O'Keefe, a thirty-six-year Digest veteran, was so outraged he refused to attend his party—refused even to participate in the traditional "Boscobel ceremony" (the awarding of a crystal bowl from the Boscobel restoration, with words offered by the editor-in-chief). "Tell Gilmore to back off," O'Keefe told Connie McGowan, Gilmore's assistant. "I have been fired, without severance, after thirty-six years, and it is an outrage! If he tries to put me through this ritual of degradation, *I will throw the Boscobel Bowl out the window!*"

"Oh, please don't do that, Dan!" said McGowan. "Gilmore might have a breakdown!"

"Then get him off my back! That wretched bowl symbolizes all that has gone wrong at the Digest! Wealth *we* labored to create has gone to these fascist Rockefeller charities, and now, when longtime employees try to cash stock they bought on years of loans, they are thrown out the door without severance. *It is an outrage!*"

When the dust kicked up by Black Monday finally settled, several top business executives had sold their stock and been fired, along with the deputy editor-in-chief (Tony Oursler), the executive editor, one of two managing editors, the art editor and two senior staff editors. With the departure of these veterans—all of them Thompson loyalists—the entire upper tier of editorial management had been purged. Of the ten editors whose names had immediately followed Thompson's on the masthead, only one—the ever-obsequious Ken Gilmore—remained. Outsiders of a predictably right-wing political bent were brought in to fill the vacated positions, and Ken Tomlinson, the mystery man from VOA, was named to succeed Oursler as Gilmore's deputy.

George Grune was a happy man that Christmas. By canceling the One Third Plan—without explanation, actually *taunting* his executives to do something about it—he had induced many of them to cash in their stock despite his threat to invoke "Wally's Rule." This had resulted in a threefold payoff: the Achilles' heel of employee stock had been virtually eliminated; he had rid himself of another dozen top-level executives, men and women with the highest salaries and bonus packages, who had known DeWitt Wallace and believed in the old ways; and since it could be argued that by selling their stock these people had in some way "invoked their own terminations," Grune decided that he did not have to pay them severance. (A federal judge later ruled the employees had been terminated.)

CHAPTER FORTY

In January 1988, RD's stock took its predicted plunge, falling to $170. But with profits pouring in (and the broader market snapping back), the beast soon recovered. It rose again with the spring, and kept rising, past the old record, past $300, soaring upward as if it would never stop. The veteran Digesters who might have resisted Grune's increasingly aggressive methods were all gone now, so the coast was clear and the sky the limit. DeWitt Wallace's modest "reader service" had become a direct-mail juggernaut, and Grune and his colleagues were clearly determined to squeeze every possible penny from their list of 100 million customers.

That list was now the real jewel in the Digest's corporate crown. *Reader's Digest* remained important, accounting for a quarter of gross revenues (a share that is steadily shrinking). But the primary role of the magazine was no longer to make money, and certainly not to inform or inspire. The magazine's real value now lay in its ability to produce names for the list. To maintain a worldwide circulation of twenty-eight million, the magazine must acquire (via Sweepstakes and other promotions) eight million new subscribers every year. Once acquired, these subscribers become potential customers for the company's other products, all of which have higher profit margins and greater growth potential than the magazine.

So getting new names (by whatever methods pass muster with the Federal Trade Commission) is obviously a high priority. Say you've just received a mailing for the Digest's $12 million Sweepstakes. Aware that the odds against winning are virtually infinite (they are one in 215,000,000), you're tempted to toss the package away. But the envelope is emblazoned with assurances that your name has already passed several levels of "strict computer selection"—"ONLY TEN OF EVERY 100 RESIDENTS IN YOUR STATE HAVE PASSED THESE TESTS!" These promises make you hesitate. You begin to muse about your chances, and to wonder what you would do with the $5 million Grand Prize.

This concept—advising potential entrants that they have ALREADY BEEN SELECTED from a larger group—has been used by direct-mailers for years. But as long as DeWitt Wallace was alive, it was not used at Reader's Digest. "We tried often enough," recalls retired sales promotion director Tom Bundrick. "Once, in the early seventies, we wrote some copy that said, 'You and your neighbors *have been selected* to receive . . . ,' etc. Wally called me down to his office. 'This is not true,' he said. 'Yes, it is, Wally,' I said. 'Because, you see, we go through our overall lists and we select only those people who are already *RD* subscribers.' 'But,' he said, 'there are *sixteen million RD* subscribers!' 'Yeah,' I said. 'That's true, Wally. But there are *two hundred million* people in the country. And we are selecting only these sixteen million for our offer.' He glared at me. 'Are you telling me,' he said—really angry, red in the face—'*are you telling me* . . .' 'Wait, wait, wait!' I said. 'I see your point, Wally. We'll change the copy.' So that's the way it went with him. Anything that smelled of trickery was not allowed. You just couldn't do it."

But that was then. Beginning in 1984, the smell of trickery pervaded

Pleasantville: the slickest, most sophisticated Sweepstakes in the business; "special promotions" offering "guaranteed" prizes (but only to customers who order the product); "free" gift tokens valid when returned with a "free" thank-you certificate (the return of which automatically triggers an order), etc., etc. Since these methods tend to work best on older Americans (who are often confused and lonely), in the late eighties the Digest purchased four new magazines clearly aimed at a senior audience: *Travel Holiday, New Choices for Living Better After 50, Family Handyman* and *American Health.* Although these magazines have lost money every year, they did bring in three million new customers for RD's more profitable products. "The company has determined," said a press release mailed to stock analysts, "that the response rate to product solicitations from *Digest* readers is low relative to the response rate generated by our special-interest magazines." In other words, the over-fifty crowd is easier to seduce than the younger and presumably more skeptical *Digest* audience.

In 1984, RD achieved after-tax profits of $30 million on gross sales of $1.3 billion. In 1989, on sales that had risen to $1.8 billion, after-tax profits surged to *$152* million. In 1984, Digest stock was valued at $18. In mid-1989, the formula placed its value in the neighborhood of $400. At that price, the corporation was worth close to $3 *billion*—a very Fat Duck, indeed. And now it was clear that the long-awaited public offering could be postponed no longer. The charities were demanding liquidity, and at $400 Grune and his powerful mentor were finally ready to let it happen.

On December 20, 1989, after receiving a green light from the Rockefeller-led board, Grune initiated the fourth and final phase of Laurance's master plan—"Payday," as it came to be known. READER'S DIGEST BREAKS 67-YEAR SILENCE, ran the headline in the *Wall Street Journal.* "The closely-held magazine and publishing company, widely-known but obsessively private, allowed the public a glimpse of its finances in a filing with the SEC yesterday. Seeking to tap public markets for the first time, the company plans to raise up to $550 million for a global expansion."

The part about raising funds, of course, was nonsense—a smoke screen to hide what was really happening. After a 20 for 1 split, 28,750,000 shares of nonvoting common stock—roughly 25 percent of the total—were put on the market on behalf of the charity owners at an offering price set by the underwriters at $22 ($440 presplit). The $630 million raised by this sale was not used for "global expansion." Instead, 60 percent of it—$370 million—found its way into the coffers of the seven Support Organizations and the Community Trust, and 40 percent—$260 million—into the two Wallace/Reader's Digest Funds. In return, a grateful Laurance Rockefeller and his compliant (and well-rewarded) fellow directors opened the Digest treasury to Grune and his colleagues.

The SEC filing included details of a dozen separate compensation plans for Reader's Digest's top five executives. Here, for example, is a list of the splendid benefactions that fell upon George Grune during 1989 alone:

1. Salary and bonuses	$1,460,707
2. Cash-out of equivalent stock units	$4,528,590
3. Cash awarded under earlier ESU plan	$991,995
4. 56,000 "performance shares"	$1,232,000
5. Cash accrued from performance shares	$860,910
6. 72,000 "restricted shares"	$1,584,000
7. Interest accrued on various other shares	$90,160
Total	$10,748,362

The filing also indicated that Grune still owned his original 240,000 shares of common stock, worth more than $5 million at the time of the offering (and more than $12 million in 1995), and made it clear that still-larger sums would flow into his pockets and into the pockets of his colleagues for years to come. Even if they were fired. Even if they quit. Even if some outside raider bought the company and sent them packing. Among the various plans established for the sole benefit of these five executives were the following:

The *Management Incentive Compensation Plan,* the *Long-Term Incentive Plan for Senior Officers* (under which the fortunate five became eligible to receive huge annual awards of stock options, stock appreciation rights, restricted stock, performance shares, performance units and various other stock-based benefits doled out by the "Compensation Committee"), the *Deferred Compensation Plan,* the *Excess Benefit Retirement Plan* (enabling the top five to exceed federal limits on retirement amounts), the *Supplemental Retirement Agreements* and the *Income Continuation Plan.*

A dozen years earlier, George Grune had been selling advertising space in *Reader's Digest.* In 1990, according to *Business Week,* he was the ninth-highest-paid executive in America. Already chairman and CEO, in July 1990 he appointed himself president and chief operating officer as well (Dick McLoughlin having departed under a $15 million golden parachute). DeWitt Wallace, who never held any title other than editor, would have considered this string of honorifics ridiculous. But Grune was thinking less and less of Wallace now, and on the rare occasions when he spoke of the Founder his attitude was strictly matter-of-fact. "Wally was a humble man," he told reporters in defense of his own high-profile approach. "It was a nice personality trait. But I'm not DeWitt Wallace."

In fact, by this point Dewitt and Lila Wallace were seldom mentioned by anybody down at Headquarters, and their once-pervasive presence was evaporating faster than their employees were being terminated. Lila's ornate office on the main editorial corridor had been maintained for decades as a kind of corporate sanctuary, its splendid antiques and glorious watercolors a drawing card for Digesters and visitors alike. In 1989, as part of the drive to cut costs, Lila's paintings and antiques were carted away and her office was divided into two smaller spaces for junior editors. Shortly thereafter, an even sadder transformation began to unfold at Wally World. The Wallace memorabilia disappeared, replaced by lavish displays of products from the Grune era. Then the Founders' portraits themselves were taken down, and a framed photo of Albert Leslie Cole was installed in their place. The Great Salesman, who died in September 1989, had known all along what the Grune era would bring ("Through the *roof,* my dear!"). Now he had returned from the grave to smile over this demonstration of his astuteness.

CHAPTER FORTY-ONE

In the weeks following the public offering, it became apparent that the underwriters (Goldman Sachs and Lazard Frères) had set the offering price too low. The public *loved* RD's stock—it was like buying a slice of Mom and Apple Pie, wrapped in the American flag—and the price rose steadily. By May of 1991, the stock had reached $32 ($640 in presplit terms), and at that price the charities were allowed to sell an additional twenty million shares. And still the stock climbed. Early in 1993, it reached $57, and there finally it paused. Some thought $57 ridiculously high. At that price, the company was selling for twenty-five times earnings. The average in the industry at the time was around fifteen, and RD—as a mature company with a low dividend and a serious growth problem—ought to have rated somewhat below average. But the public would not be denied.

At $57 per share (*$1,140* in presplit dollars, up nearly *6,000* percent since 1984), George Grune had become a very rich man. But the biggest beneficiaries of "Payday" were Laurance Rockefeller's charities, and to a lesser extent the Wallace/Reader's Digest Funds. Although the gifts received by these charities were largely ignored by the press, they have turned out to be the largest charitable gifts in history. From their uneasy graves, Lila and DeWitt were "raining porridge" on the world, and as usual Laurance Rockefeller's bowl was right side up (see table, below).

What would the Wallaces have thought of this? That their company had gone public despite all the promises they had extracted would have made them very angry. That former ad salesmen now were running the show (and paying themselves millions for the privilege), would have turned their anger into fury. But what of the seven Support Organizations? Certainly Laurance Rockefeller considers them worthwhile. With the exception of Macalester, they are his Family's institutions, ideally suited to add power and prestige to the Rockefeller name. But what of the Wallaces? Would they be pleased? Consider:

Chief Beneficiaries of Lila and DeWitt Wallace			
	Proceeds of 1/90 Sale	Proceeds of 5/91 Sale	Value of Remaining RD Holdings, 2/93	Total
MACALESTER COLLEGE	$57,842,148	$52,032,000	$363,375,000	$470,000,000
COLONIAL WILLIAMSBURG	$27,206,912	$25,344,000	$169,290,000	$220,000,000
METROPOLITAN MUSEUM	$64,037,006	$59,648,000	$398,658,000	$522,000,000
BRONX ZOO	$27,206,912	$25,344,000	$169,290,000	$220,000,000
LINCOLN CENTER	$59,855,400	$55,744,000	$372,261,000	$488,000,000
SLOAN-KETTERING CANCER CENTER	$21,765,590	$20,288,000	$135,489,000	$178,000,000
HUDSON HIGHLANDS	$51,693,290	$48,128,000	$321,822,000	$422,000,000
Total to the Seven "Support Organizations":			$2,520,000,000
COMMUNITY FUNDS	$55,012,540	$51,200,000	$342,000,000	$448,000,000
DW/RD FUND	$151,190,000	$76,224,000	$538,490,000	$765,904,000
LAW/RD FUND	$116,691,000	$44,096,000	$311,584,000	$472,371,000

1. *Macalester College.* In the early seventies, after giving Macalester more than $60 million, DeWitt decided the college was "too affluent" and shut off further gifts. Although there is no evidence that he ever changed his mind (beyond financing a few professorships), he did relent to the point of accepting that honorary degree in 1979. But no number of degrees would have induced him to end his "period of austerity" with a gift that has increased Macalester's endowment from $60 million to more than *$500* million. In fact, Wallace had given up on college kids. In his last decade, he determined to focus his support on younger students, as indicated in the guidelines he established for his own funds:

> Support primarily for independent schools and activities fostering qualities of leadership and character in young people, including scholarships, summer camps, experiences abroad, speaking contests and explorations, and projects promoting an understanding of the history and economy of the United States.

It is hard to see how raining almost $500 million on Macalester *College* has been an effective way to support these goals. In fact, the Macalester S/O had little to do with the wishes of DeWitt Wallace. It was meant to serve as a model for the S/Os that followed. If the "conduit trust" concept (conferring income while retaining control) passed legal muster at Macalester (a safe bet, in view of the Wallace background), then it was likely to pass muster elsewhere. As it surely has.

2. *Colonial Williamsburg.* As noted earlier, neither Wallace was inclined to shower money on Williamsburg. Lila refused altogether ("Wally and I *never* share projects"), and DeWitt reluctantly agreed to provide $4 million for the new theater only because he hoped thereby to make it easier for ordinary Americans to see *The Patriot.* In the context of that "reluctant" $4 million, the final total of DeWitt's generosity to Williamsburg is breathtaking. At $57 per share, the five million Digest shares awarded to the restoration came to be worth more than $280 million—a sum greater than the donations of the Rockefeller Family over more than four decades.

3. *The Metropolitan Museum.* In defense of Lila's gift to the Met of $522 million, mention is always made of her "long-standing" commitment. Between 1969 and 1984, after all, she provided $47 million to renovate the Great Hall and the Egyptian Galleries, and to build the Twentieth-Century Wing. Why would she have done this if she hadn't been committed?

In fact, beyond her sad musings about Nefertiti, Lila Wallace had no particular interest in Egyptology, and she *detested* modern art. She gave to the Met—and by extension to Tom Hoving, Barney McHenry, Laurance Rockefeller and all the other men who courted her in those sad last years—out of the same desperate need that allowed Harry Wilcox and Bill Kennedy to rob her blind, and Hobe Lewis to rise in the Digest Empire while Al Cole and Fred Thompson sank. She would give *anything* to attract the attention of such men.

But the *real* Lila was different. The real Lila prided herself on bringing art and culture into the lives of ordinary Americans. The real Lila provided hot meals for factory workers, then served art-appreciation courses for dessert. The real Lila hung million-dollar paintings in the corridors and cafeterias at Pleasantville, so that mail clerks and secretaries could enjoy what is ordinarily reserved for CEOs and top executives. As she explained herself to Rudolf Bing: "I happen to *come* from the provinces, Mr. Bing. And I believe there are people out there who appreciate art as passionately as anyone here in New York."

Lila's own fund is based firmly on this belief. Now the largest private provider of cultural grants in the country, it spends millions each year to bring art exhibits and other cultural events and happenings to small towns from coast to coast—from the Atlantic Center for the Arts in New Smyrna Beach, Florida; to the Community School of Music and Arts in Mountain View, California; to the Anchorage Concert Association in Anchorage, Alaska. This is what the *real* Lila wanted. What she *didn't* want—what she religiously avoided while she was still thinking straight—was for *her* money to disappear into the general funds of other institutions, to be used by others as *they* saw fit. "She always supported *specific* projects," recalls Lisa Collins, accountant at the Wallace Funds. "To hand over a lump sum, with no strings —that she would *never* do."

4. *Bronx Zoo.* In the mid-sixties, Laurance Rockefeller and his friend Fairfield Osborn persuaded Lila to contribute $4 million toward construction of the zoo's "World of Birds." Lila thought birds were beautiful. She also liked horses, and in her earlier years was partial to dogs. Other animals she could do without. And the concept of "conserving species" was not something that had ever captured her imagination. Her sole philanthropic concern was to bring the experience of culture into the lives of ordinary people—"to make the arts a vital part of everyday American life," as her own fund's statement-of-purpose expresses it.

Laurance Rockefeller, on the other hand, has spent the better part of his adult life seeking to establish himself as a leading conservationist. He became chairman of the Bronx Zoo's executive committee in 1940, vice president in 1948, and served as president from 1950 until 1970. Against this background, his success in delivering to the zoo (now known as the "New York Wildlife Conservation Park") 220 million of Lila Wallace's dollars must be seen as a substantial triumph.

5. *Lincoln Center.* From its origins in the fifties, Lincoln Center was the pet project of Laurance's older brother, John D. III. John was its first chairman and chief fund-raiser, and John alone pushed it forward through swirling clouds of controversy. As with other Rockefeller real-estate projects (the World Trade Center, Morningside Heights, Caneel Bay Plantation), there was much talk about the enhancement of surrounding Rockefeller landholdings, and it didn't help that brothers David (the Banker), Laurance (the Developer) and Nelson (the Governor) were also deeply involved.

The late Lincoln Kirstein, creator of the New York City Ballet and a member of the Lincoln Center board, resigned over this issue. "Having worked so long with artists," he wrote to John Rockefeller, "I had imagined Lincoln Center might answer *their* possibilities—fantasy, imagination, selfless capacity. Four years have taught me different: The criterion is manipulation of real-estate."

When Lincoln Center was finally completed in 1969, costs had risen to $185 million—at the time the largest sum ever devoted to the arts from the private sector. In all, various Rockefellers gave over $40 million. But, eventually, Family members faced the same problem at Lincoln Center that had troubled them at Williamsburg: How to maintain the place without constant infusions of Rockefeller cash. As at Williamsburg, Laurance found a way to use Wallace dollars to solve a Rockefeller problem.

Digest stock transferred by Barney McHenry from the Wallace Funds to the Fund for Lincoln Center came to have a value of $488 million—more than twice the original cost of the entire project. Although few appreciate the fact, Lincoln Center today is essentially a Wallace institution, its future as a playground for sophisticated New Yorkers assured by the unwitting generosity of two unsophisticated Middle Westerners.

Would the Wallaces be pleased by this? In DeWitt's case, the answer surely is no. He had no interest in music or dance, and would be mystified at the thought of so much money being lavished on something so seemingly ephemeral. Lila's interest would no doubt be greater, but her earlier support for various Lincoln Center constituencies was owing more to the flatteries of John and Laurance Rockefeller, Barney McHenry and Peter Mennin of the Juilliard School than to any deep personal commitment. To the extent that she *was* committed, the attraction would have been (as with the treasures of the Metropolitan) to make Lincoln Center's performances available to average Americans. But that is not what is happening at Lincoln Center today.

Like many of America's great urban arts complexes, Lincoln Center is in danger of becoming a cultural dinosaur. Part of the problem is cost. Ticket prices have risen to the point where only the well-off can afford to attend. But a bigger problem is *education*. Audiences of knowledgeable, discriminating people—people from every level of society who have been exposed to music, drama and dance—are disappearing. "The days when twenty-five hundred people crowded into Avery Fisher Hall are over," says Jane Moss, director of programming at Lincoln Center. "The failure of our school systems to teach these subjects to young people is having major consequences for the arts."

As a result, Lincoln Center these days attracts ever-smaller audiences of ever-richer people, and the money lavished on it by Lila and DeWitt Wallace may only make matters worse. DeWitt believed that the key to society's problems was education. Had his $488 million been devoted to *educating* young people about the performing arts, it would have had a greater impact —on their lives, surely, and on the future of less-grand cultural institutions around the country, if not on the reputation of Laurance Rockefeller.

6. *Sloan-Kettering Cancer Center.* Over many decades of philanthropy, DeWitt Wallace was always reluctant to support hospitals. He gave occasionally to specific hospital *projects*, particularly when a friend was involved. And he was generous to Northern Westchester Hospital, as he was to other local institutions. But general giving to big-city hospitals was out. "He just wasn't interested," says Ed Thompson. "He felt that most large hospitals already had their own substantial sources of private support."

But Laurance Rockefeller was chairman of Sloan-Kettering, and Laurance was determined that his hospital would become the world's foremost cancer center. "Laurance has always hoped that the final breakthrough against cancer would come at Sloan-Kettering," says Barney McHenry. "Thus it would be *his* breakthrough—the capstone to his career and the achievement for which he would be remembered down the ages." So Laurance worked on DeWitt. And over time, by dint of skill and persistence, he wore down the old man's resistance. The modest donations that resulted were later cited as evidence of "long-standing interest," and long-standing interest eventually became justification (years after Wallace was dead) for the establishment of the Fund for Sloan-Kettering. So, in the end, the man who wasn't interested in hospitals became a supporter of Laurance Rockefeller's hospital to the tune of nearly $200 million.

7. *The Fund for Hudson Highlands.* Of all the Support Organizations established in the Wallace name, none seems so clearly designed to further Rockefeller interests as the one Laurance saved for last. Given the extent of the Family's landholdings in the vicinity of this spectacularly beautiful fifteen-mile gorge—from the thirty-six hundred manicured acres at Pocan-

tico in the south to the three thousand farming acres owned by David and Peggy Rockefeller in the north—it is not surprising that Laurance's interest in conservation should have focused on the Highlands. Yet there is ample historical evidence, most strikingly seen in the bitter battles he and his brother Nelson waged over Storm King and the Hudson Expressway, that his deepest interest in the area has always had more to do with "efficient use" and "profitable development" than with saving a unique and priceless environment.

The stated purpose of the Fund for Hudson Highlands is to preserve the area in its natural state by buying conservation easements on riverfront land. To the extent that preservation is in fact the purpose of the fund, the Wallaces' joint gift of more than $400 million will surely help. But even if the money *is* spent to further the stated goal, a deeper question remains: Is it a goal that DeWitt and Lila Wallace would have supported to the extent of $400 million?

Those who knew them best—including the two men they chose to lead their company into the future—seriously doubt it. "They would *never* have supported that kind of gift to the Hudson Highlands," says Jack O'Hara. "The Wallaces had nothing to do with that gift," echoes Ed Thompson. "That gift was all Laurance's doing."

Lila Wallace's real interest in the area of the Hudson Highlands was the Boscobel restoration (which happens to look directly across the Hudson at Storm King Mountain, where Laurance and his brother had been so eager to build a power plant). Yet, in stark contrast to the various Rockefeller interests listed above, Boscobel today is strapped for money. "Lila provided us with a modest endowment of Digest stock within the Community Trust," says Fred Stanyer. "It pays the expenses, with a little hedge for inflation. But that's it." There is no Support Organization for Boscobel, and no money has ever been forthcoming from either of the Grune-controlled Wallace Funds. "The funds claim we're 'elitist,' " adds Stanyer with a wry smile. "We can't get a nickel from them, even though Lila was far more attached to Boscobel than, say, to the Metropolitan Museum."

By the time Lila Wallace died in May of 1984, two-thirds of the fortune she and her husband had accumulated had been transferred to these seven charities (plus the Community Trust). From the evidence listed above, it is clear that these transferrals would have pleased neither Wallace. In their early years, each of them had lived and worked among the people of small-town America—Lila as a teacher and social worker; DeWitt as a peddler of maps and farm brochures. These everyday Americans would later become the readers of their magazine and the source of their wealth. And when they prospered and could think of charity, it was these Americans they thought of first. To *give back* to their fellow citizens ("to benefit all the people of the United States," as they put it in their wills) became their overriding goal.

But Laurance Rockefeller had a different goal, and a plan for implementing it that in the end proved unstoppable. And so it was that the bulk of the Wallaces' Digest stock was removed from their own funds and awarded to a handful of elite New York institutions beloved of Manhattan's upper classes (the "fancy New Yorkers" Lila Wallace so resented). This has not been without consequence. For the Digest shares that escaped this process—worth today roughly $2 billion—remained in the Wallace Funds. And the story at the Wallace Funds is very different.

The mission of the DeWitt Wallace/Reader's Digest Fund is to foster improvement in the quality of educational and career-development opportunities for school-age youth, and in particular to increase access to such opportunities for young people in low-income communities across America. With total assets of $1 billion, the fund paid out grants totaling $60 million in 1994. A sampling:

1. Under the fund's *Pathways to Teaching Careers Program*, $450,000 was awarded to Clark Atlanta University to provide scholarships for 125 noncertified minority teachers working in the Atlanta area. Since 1989, Pathways has provided scholarships for three thousand prospective teachers enrolled in forty-five institutions in thirty-two cities around the country, at a total cost of $38 million.

2. Under its *Library Power Program*, the fund has invested $40 million since 1988 in a national effort to revitalize library services in public elementary and middle schools, and to turn school libraries into true centers of learning for entire student bodies. In 1994, for example, $1.2 million was awarded to the "Wake Education Partnership" in Raleigh, North Carolina, to implement Library Power programs in twenty-four schools serving more than twenty-four thousand students.

3. To improve services to children and young people in various community-based organizations, the fund in 1994 approved new grants totaling $4.6 million. The Congress of National Black Churches in Washington, D.C., received $741,108 to expand Project SPIRIT, an afterschool program for six- to twelve-year-olds that offers academic instruction, social activities and life-skills development.

Grants from the Lila Acheson Wallace/Reader's Digest Fund focus on the arts, and in particular on programs that enhance the cultural life of communities. In 1994, out of assets worth $760 million, Lila's fund paid out grants totaling $44 million. Three examples:

1. To the New England Foundation for the Arts, $5.1 million to support a consortium of performing-arts presenters and regional arts organizations formed to increase touring opportunities and community outreach programs in the jazz field. Since 1991, the fund has invested almost $19 million in jazz projects.

2. To the Mid-America Arts Alliance in Kansas City, Missouri, $1.1 million to continue Exhibits/USA, a national traveling exhibition program that serves small and midsized organizations around the country, including regional museums, community-college exhibiting spaces, community centers and public libraries. Fund support for the visual arts has totaled more than $38 million since 1989.

3. To the Fund for Folk Culture in Santa Fe, New Mexico, $2.45 million to support locally based projects that identify, document, preserve and present folk-art traditions to the public. Since 1991, fund investment in the folk arts has totaled $9.3 million.

So that's the good news: that a third of the Wallace fortune is at work doing what they wanted it to do. The bad news, of course, is that two-thirds of it— three *billion* dollars—is not. It is frustrating to contemplate what those vanished dollars might be accomplishing had they remained in the Wallace Funds, reaching out to young people, providing the kinds of opportunities for education and exposure to the arts that are rapidly disappearing in this country. In an era increasingly dominated by "brain-power" industries, investments in education of the kind being made by the DeWitt Wallace Fund are crucial. "Yet our government is doing precisely the opposite," points out economist Lester Thurow in *The Future of Capitalism.* "We are lowering investment in the future in order to raise consumption in the present."

AGING AUDIENCES POINT TO A GRIM FUTURE FOR THE ARTS, ran a recent headline in the *New York Times.* The article that followed deplored "the declining engagement of younger Americans in all aspects of civic culture," and singled out the Lila Acheson Wallace Fund as "one of the few remaining efforts to broaden audiences of young theater-goers." That the Wallace Funds are addressing crucial national needs is obvious. That they could be doing twice as much is therefore that much sadder.

But philanthropy was only part of the Wallace dream. The original idea had been to earn their living by offering a "reading service" to their fellow citizens ("the best possible magazine at the lowest possible price"). And to provide rewarding lives for their employees. When these goals were accomplished, they had set their sights (through their wills) on the most ambitious goal of all: to keep both elements of this original dream alive and thriving "for five hundred years." And here again, on both counts, their wishes were defeated.

The Magazine. One of the first ads in the million-dollar public-relations campaign launched by George Grune in 1985 referred to *Reader's Digest* as "the tip of our iceberg"—a phrase that aptly described the situation that soon evolved under the new managers. For years, of course, *Reader's Digest* had *been* the iceberg, and everything else (in Wallace's words) was "only a way to make money." In those earlier days, the man who ran the magazine also ran the overall enterprise. By 1990, when poor health forced Ken Gilmore to surrender the editorial reins to Ken Tomlinson, the primacy of the magazine had vanished. "Gilmore was number four on the corporate totem pole," noted an editor at the time. "But it became apparent very quickly that Tomlinson's ranking was far lower—about twentieth. He wasn't on the executive committee or the board of directors, and he had no voice whatever in corporate policy."

Nevertheless, Tomlinson *was* in charge of editing *Reader's Digest.* To help him carry the load—and in particular to assist him in shaping the political information fed to *RD*'s 100 million readers around the globe—he came to rely on four key associates: managing editors William Schulz and Dimi Panitza remained as bureau chiefs in Washington and Paris; newly appointed executive editor Christopher Willcox was placed in charge of the forty-five international editions; and senior editor William Beaman was named to manage *RD*'s bureau in Hong Kong, with responsibility for Asian affairs. As it happens, each of these men was well versed in the art of political indoctrination—Willcox and Beaman having prepped for their *RD* careers at Radio Free Europe and the Voice of America, respectively, and Bill Schulz and Dimi Panitza having overseen, jointly or separately, virtually every *Digest* collaboration with the CIA and the FBI for more than twenty years.

So no one was surprised when the process begun after Ed Thompson's termination—the shift from independent journalism to right-wing politics—proceeded apace. Indeed, wherever the CIA was embattled in those years—from its struggles in Washington ("Congress Is Crippling the CIA!") to its operations in Nicaragua ("The brave *contras* look to Washington for assistance. Will we turn our backs?") to its preference for dictators over elected governments in Haiti ("American intervention will only expose us to failure") —Tomlinson and his colleagues provided a supportive chorus. And when the *Digest* launched a Russian-language edition in Moscow in 1995, they and their business counterparts were perfectly content to accept $2 million in "insurance funds" from the U.S. government (precisely the kind of "official participation" DeWitt Wallace had refused after World War II).

In recent years, however, the focus of *RD*'s political coverage has changed. As the Cold War has receded, government disinformation about the enemy outside the gates (the now-defeated Evil Empire) has been replaced by what can only be called corporate disinformation about the enemy within. Over the last two decades, as executive salaries and corporate stock prices have soared to record levels, the wages of average Americans have stagnated or fallen, and millions of well-paying jobs have disappeared. By the end of 1995, the richest fifth of the U.S. population—led by the owners and managers of our largest corporations—owned 80 percent of the national wealth, and the gap between "winners" and "losers" in America was wider (and growing wider at a faster rate) than in any other developed country on earth.

During the last years of the Cold War, the dimensions of this historic shift were hidden (for the most part) beneath patriotic rhetoric about the Evil Empire. Few Americans complained because few understood what was going on. And the institutions designed to defend their interests were generally silent. The political parties, in hock to the corporations, looked the other way. The unions had been rendered more or less irrelevant by foreign competition. And the media, either owned outright or in other ways controlled by the corporations, found it more politic to applaud the process than to criticize.*

But then the Cold War ended, and suddenly people were asking awkward questions. The Evil Empire had lost. America had won. *So why did so many Americans feel like losers?* The U.S. economy had doubled in a decade. Inflation was down, productivity up, profits soaring. So where was all the money going now? *Who was the New Enemy?*

Sensing trouble—sensing, in fact, that the middle class might eventually look in *their* direction—the corporations used their media assets to control this new threat much as they had used their military assets to contain the old one. It isn't *Us* was the message they put forth. It's *Them*. The poor, the sick, the homeless. Immigrants. Black people. "Femi-Nazis" and "Welfare Queens." Anyone who was different. Anyone without power. *They* were the New Enemy.

Although the charge was led by television and talk radio, *Reader's Digest* wasn't far behind. In 1992 (the last year of a *Republican* administration), every issue of the magazine berated the government for some excess of compassion: "We're Spending Too Much on Schools!"; "Don't *Buy* These Environmental Myths!"; "Workers' Compensation: License to Steal!" In 1993, the tone grew even harsher: "Get *Tough* with Killer Kids!"; *"Why*

---

* Corporate domination of the media has been documented in several recent books, most notably in *The Media Monopoly* by Pulitzer Prize-winner Ben Bagdikian. "The United States," writes Bagdikian, "is moving swiftly toward media control by a handful of giant corporations." In 1980, fifty corporations controlled the entire national flow of information. By 1989, according to the latest edition of Bagdikian's book, the number of dominant corporations had shrunk below twenty. And, recently, the situation has become much worse. General Electric now owns NBC. Westinghouse owns CBS. And Capital Cities, which owns ABC, has itself been swallowed by Disney.

Welfare for Illegal Aliens?"; *"Must* Our Prisons Be Resorts?" In 1994, contemplating health-care reform, the *Digest* became apoplectic: "How *Not* to Improve Health Care"; "Is *This* the Kind of Health Care We Want?"; *"What* Health Care Crisis!?" In 1995, the favorite target was helping others: "When 'Peacekeeping' Costs Too Much"; "Welfare Gone Haywire"; "The United Nations: Out of Control."

Americans *are* angry these days, with reason. Instead of addressing this anger—by identifying the economic insecurity that is its true source and suggesting thoughtful, *workable* solutions, as Wallace would have done, as Thompson did—the *Digest* exploits the anger by returning over and over to the very subjects likeliest to infuriate (and distract) its readers: race, flag, gays, God, AIDS, immigrants. In a single recent issue, *RD* repudiated the homeless ("until they summon the will to help themselves, all the help in the world is so much wasted effort"); starving Africans ("the overwhelming responsibility . . . lies with the people of Africa. No amount of money can do the job they must do for themselves"); AIDS victims ("HIV remains overwhelmingly confined to gays and drug users . . . unless you are a member of these groups, there is no reason to fear."); and union members ("from coast to coast, taxpayers are being asked to fund bloated, wasteful labor contracts"). *All in a single issue.*

How did this happen? How did a magazine designed to serve average Americans become so clearly a tool of the corporate elite? Part of the answer can be traced to the palatial boardroom built in the early eighties to salute the arrival of Laurance Rockefeller. In Wallace's day, RD's directors were insiders whose chief function was to carry out the wishes of the Founders. No longer. RD's current board is comprised in large part of outsiders who represent (through their own companies and various interlocking directorships) every center of corporate power in America: from oil (Mobil, Phillips Petroleum, Halliburton), to timber (Potlatch, Champion International), to finance (American Express, Chemical/Chase Manhattan), to consumer products (Avon, Woolworth), to communications (NYNEX, COMSAT) and chemicals (Merck) and defense contracting (Lockheed/Martin) and utilities (Con Edison) and insurance companies (Metropolitan Life).

These directors are answerable only to their counterparts at the Wallace Funds—which means, since the two groups continue to be comprised in large part of the same individuals, only to themselves. And they serve as *Digest* directors because doing so is clearly in the interest of the corporations they represent. The success of these corporations is widely dependent on government policy and public opinion, and it is clearly useful to be able to count on *Reader's Digest,* with its 100 million readers, for support in both areas. (The director from Lockheed/Martin, for example, was surely not displeased by a recent *Digest* article calling for vast increases in defense spending. Nor have the directors from timber giants Potlatch or Champion International had to lose sleep over *Digest* articles attacking the paper-and-lumber industry. And so on.)

When not being political, today's Digest seems content to give its readers whatever they say they want—as long as costs are kept low and controversy avoided. Prior to 1984, every issue of the magazine contained a dozen or more articles from America's leading publications: *Time, Newsweek, Fortune, Esquire, Harper's,* the *Atlantic Monthly,* the *New York Times Magazine,* etc. Wallace wanted *RD* to be a true compilation of the best articles from the country's most-respected publications, and he was willing to pay whatever it cost to accomplish this. Today these prominent sources have clearly become *too* expensive, and *Digest* readers are therefore likelier to encounter material from obscure magazines, local newspapers or Sunday supplements. During 1994 and 1995, each of the following sources contributed one or more articles to *RD*'s pages: *Allure, Booklist, Country Living, Daily Press, Home Life, Maine Sportsman, Middlesex News, Northeast Woods and Waters, Pursuit, Spirit, Trapper, Virtue, Working Mother, Valley News.*

This "dumbing down" of editorial matter (a process favored by advertisers who appreciate a bland background for their messages) has been amplified in recent years by the magazine's reliance on reader polls. After the close of each issue, the editor-in-charge and his executive editor meet with their business colleagues to discuss poll results and the performance of the issue on newsstands, all with an eye to "improving the numbers" and raising profits. What works well in one issue according to the polls becomes a model for the next issue, which is then also rated by poll, and so on. This process (proudly referred to as "performance editing") leads inevitably to a narrowing of subject matter (because subjects that score poorly are abandoned) and to a simplification of contents (because challenging articles are deemed too risky). "The *Digest* has been lobotomized," sums up a current senior editor. "Every issue reads like a Xerox of a former issue that has been faxed somewhere and Xeroxed again."

DeWitt Wallace published stories *he* liked, and when it turned out that millions of readers agreed with him, his magazine became a success. It had a personality—*his* personality—and that was its secret. William Shawn, legendary editor of the *New Yorker,* spoke of this shortly after Wallace's death. "Both *Reader's Digest* and *Time* succeeded because they were started by men who expressed their own values regardless of the market and thereby established an identity that made for long-range success. But editors today are growing up in a different atmosphere. *'We want to edit the magazine to give readers what they want. What do we give them??'* There is such a fallacy in that calculation! If you edit that way, to give readers only what they think they want, you never give them anything new. You *stagnate!* It is very worrisome as far as journalism is concerned."

Does it really matter to the world what happens to *Reader's Digest?* Given the fact that Wallace's magazine still speaks to 100 million readers every month—in forty-eight editions and nineteen languages, in every country on the planet, to every age and demographic group—the answer surely must be yes. These people elect governments. They raise families. They pay taxes and teach children and invest in the future. It *matters* what they think. And what they think still depends to a remarkable degree on what they read in *Reader's Digest.*

And that is the real tragedy. That Lila and DeWitt Wallace were mistreated is bad enough. That their dreams were defeated, their employees dispersed, their Kingdom dismantled—all this is sad but not lasting. What *is* lasting is the erosion of their magazine, the silencing of an editorial voice that spoke to average people everywhere about things that mattered, in terms they understood and trusted, and that generally left them feeling better about the world. In 1984, speaking to the advertising directors in Portugal, Jerry Dole had worried about this. *"RD* is *not* a product," he had warned the ad men. "It is not tubes of toothpaste or bottles of Coca-Cola. It is an *Idea.* And ideas can be killed." Ten years later, the Idea is dead.

The Employees. After a decade of repeated downsizings—even as corporate profits were hitting record levels—it is not surprising that "family feelings" among remaining Digesters have largely vanished, or that morale has dropped dramatically. As each new round of layoffs takes place, management holds pep talks with the anxious survivors. "Times are tough" is the message they deliver. "Only by cutting back can we stay competitive, and only by staying competitive can we raise salaries and increase bonuses."

What has happened belatedly at Reader's Digest (belatedly because De-Witt Wallace held the line so long) only reflects what has been happening in the country as a whole for the last twenty years. The conviction of earlier Americans that the good life flows from family, church and community was replaced after World War II by a belief in material progress, a conviction that the economic might of Corporate America contained the real answer to our problems, the "rising tide" that would lift all ships. During the fifties and sixties, with communism on the march and labor unions thriving, this was true. Feeling vulnerable, America's corporations became humane and generous. Annual raises, lavish benefits, lifetime job security—all the fabled elements of the American Dream—became the order of the day.

But as communism self-destructed, and as the labor movement collapsed in the face of global competition, the corporations reverted to form. "Lean and mean" became the new wisdom, and the social contract written in the postwar years was torn to shreds. Since the early seventies, it is only the rich who have risen in America, while the poor have sunk deeper into poverty and even the middle class has fallen back. At Reader's Digest, this process was delayed because the King and Queen, with their quaint insistence on fairness and loyalty, remained alive. But when the Wallaces died in the early eighties, fairness and loyalty died with them. Since 1984, only RD's top managers have prospered, while the average Digester has become poorer.

Along with monetary inequality has come a heightened sense of management *versus* workers. In the old days, when the company was still a family, there was a feeling that the building and its lovely grounds—indeed, the company itself—in some way "belonged" to the employees, and the employees acted accordingly. Joggers were everywhere during lunch hour. Golfers honed their games on Digest lawns. Even after-hours, people came and went as they pleased, ignoring the elderly Burns guard who was generally asleep at the front desk. On weekends, Dad might put in a few hours at his desk while Mom gave the kids bike lessons in the parking lot. People showed up with dogs in tow, or brought friends in to admire Lila's artworks.

You would not get away with that today. Big Brother arrived at Headquarters in 1984, right on schedule, and from then on any notion that the employees owned the building went out the window. As anger and frustration replaced the communal feeling, management "took measures" to see that security was maintained. Gates were installed at all entrances. Except for a brief period during rush hour, employees are required to enter the grounds through the Main Gate. A Guard House has been installed there (dubbed "Checkpoint Wally" by older Digesters) and no one is allowed through without proper identification.

Even more ominous is the twenty-four-hour surveillance. Security cameras are hidden inside shiny spheroids that dangle like bird feeders from poles installed throughout the building and around the grounds. Enter the Guesthouse and there is a spheroid with a camera inside. Park in the south lot, and there is a spheroid. Slip into the men's room on the main editorial floor; there is a spheroid. Big Brother is everywhere, always watching. "I try to stay away from the place these days," says a veteran roving editor. "The Thought Police are on the prowl and it's just not pleasant. My editor won't discuss serious matters with me in her own office. We have to go outside because she's afraid of bugs. Same with the telephones. RD has the ability to listen in on calls, so you have to be careful. It's creepy. You might as well be working for the CIA."

When the dust of the transition in Pleasantville finally settles, what will remain? The Rockefeller charities will still be rich. George Grune and his cronies will still be rich. But the *process* of their enrichment (clearly a one-time event, a rising line that sooner or later must burn itself out) will be over. Then what? How to motivate demoralized employees? What to do with a failing magazine? How to peddle stale products to aging customers whose real interest is the Grand Prize they will never win? *What about the future?*

In fact, there have been signs in recent years that the rising line in Pleasantville may already be nearing the sun. In 1993, under relentless pressure to maintain his string of record-breaking quarters, Grune suddenly upped the ante. Books, CDs and videos had been selling briskly in the domestic market, so a decision was made to pump still more product into the customer pipeline at an even faster rate. Digest customers had grown used to receiving four individual offerings a year. During fiscal 1993, the number of offerings was increased to six, and at the same time prices were raised yet again. "We had research showing that each of the new offerings would be popular individually," says a current manager. "But we didn't take time to test them as a group—breaking a cardinal rule—and we ignored earlier tests that showed negative results from six offerings a year. In other words, we pushed the system to its limits, flying blind. And the system kicked back."

The pipeline filled with unwanted products as customers whose tolerance had seemed bottomless suddenly rebelled. Sales of the books-and-home-entertainment division (which accounts for 68 percent of RD's total revenues) fell for the first time. Then management compounded the problem by sending murky signals to the financial press. "The division has been performing below expectations," a spokesman admitted in February 1993. When analysts asked what "below expectations" meant, the spokesman refused to elaborate. Nervous investors wondered what was going on, and began to sell. The price of Digest stock skidded from $57 in late January to $46 in early May. On May 4, the company finally admitted that sales for the third quarter had not only failed to rise as predicted, but had actually fallen by 6 percent. On that day alone, the stock lost 13 percent of its value, bottoming out at $37. "We have a problem," Grune admitted. "It may take us 12 to 24 months to get back on track."

But for Grune the real problem was more immediate. In less than four months, the price of RD stock had fallen by 35 percent. For the two Wallace Funds, the paper loss amounted to $500 million. Under ordinary circumstances—given the magnitude of that loss—the funds' directors should have felt an obligation to consider changes in Digest management. But in this case the funds' directors *were* Digest management. This was more than the "appearance" of conflict. This was conflict itself: the interests of management were clashing with the interests of future fund beneficiaries.

The only way to eliminate the conflict was to get the stock back up, and the only way to do that was to increase profits. But increasing profits was no longer as simple as it had been in the eighties. Everything that was "nice" was gone. Every subsidiary that wasn't producing immediate profits had been shut down, and every seemingly superfluous employee had been fired. The Sweepstakes had been hyped to the extent of the law, and the pipeline to customers was backed up with products priced as high as the market would bear.

With nowhere else to turn, Grune elected to solve his problem by attacking once again the two elements of the Kingdom that had been considered untouchable by DeWitt Wallace (that had been, in his eyes, the only reasons for being in business in the first place). The initial blow came when the corporation announced a second cutback in *Digest* circulation, from 16.25 million to 15 million. "The savings associated with a lower *Digest* circulation," Grune maintained, "can be invested more profitably elsewhere in the business." By "elsewhere in the business," Grune clearly had in mind the special-interest magazines, with their older readerships and higher response rates. It was a gamble, a short-term ploy to raise profits, and for a time it seemed to work. But insiders thought they saw an ominous pattern developing, the beginnings of a long-term slide into magazine oblivion. Under Wallace, *RD*'s circulation had always risen. Under Grune, it had fallen twice.

The second blow came in two parts: In June 1993, the company announced that 250 people—14 percent of the meager workforce remaining in Pleasantville—would lose their jobs. In November, the ax flashed for 200 more. "It is with a deep sense of regret that we've had to tell these employees they will be leaving Reader's Digest," Grune told the press. "These are our dear friends and colleagues and we will miss them. However, *times are tough*. To be competitive and productive—and to meet our growth targets for Fiscal '94—we have to operate efficiently. We intend to do this."

Management had made the costly error. But it wasn't management that suffered. Chairman Grune did not point out, for example, that his own annual compensation would have covered the salaries of the "dear friends" just departed, with a tidy sum left over to provide for himself and his family. Nor did he explain that the "regretted" terminations would produce an automatic upward blip in RD's stock, and thus an automatic increase in his own substantial net worth. His silence extended even to the fact that Reader's Digest, "tough times" notwithstanding, was enjoying record-breaking profits. That message was saved for a different audience. On June 6, two days after announcing the latest employee purge, Grune began his "Third Quarter Report to Stockholders" with these encouraging words:

> We are pleased to announce record worldwide revenues and profits for the third quarter and nine-month period ended March 31, 1993. Our overall

performance in the third quarter should lead us to a ninth consecutive year of record profits. . . .

One year later—after additional downsizings, a $62 million plunge in revenues and a worrisome drop in operating profits—Grune quietly surrendered the corporate reins to new CEO James P. Schadt and slipped into golden retirement. Before joining the Digest in 1991, Schadt had served in senior marketing positions for Procter & Gamble, Sara Lee, Pepsico, and Cadbury Schweppes. "Selling magazines and selling soda pop are pretty much the same thing," the new man observed to a reporter for the *New York Times*. The reporter wondered whether Schadt devoted much time to reading *Reader's Digest*. "No," replied Schadt. "Not since I was a kid. But *Reader's Digest* is a consumer product. So is Pepsi-Cola. They are both consumer products, and I've been selling consumer products all my life."

For all his experience with soda pop, the new CEO seemed powerless to stop the bad news bubbling out of Pleasantville. In September 1994, the Digest announced a loss for the fiscal fourth quarter of $34 million. Eight months later, when the company revealed that earnings for the third quarter of fiscal 1995 were "below expectations," its stock plunged 16 percent in a single day. "This announcement calls into question the fundamentals of the company," warned James Dougherty, media analyst for Dean Witter Discover. Even Grune's gamble on the special-interest magazines was turning sour. *Travel Holiday*, its ad pages hemorrhaging, was put on the block, and there were signs that *American Health* and *New Choices* would soon follow.

As the gloomy news mounted, RD's stock slipped ever lower, until by the end of 1995 Schadt faced the same dilemma that had troubled his predecessor: his duty to monitor RD's performance on behalf of the Wallace Funds—and, if necessary, to change management—was in conflict with his natural desire to remain in charge in Pleasantville. With his back to the wall (and a multi-million-dollar compensation package at risk), Schadt reacted firmly. In February 1996, after confessing a further 10 percent decline in operating profits for the quarter just ended, he announced that 1300 additional Digesters would be losing their jobs. And that was not all. The strategy so effectively employed by Grune to squeeze short-term billions from the Pleasantville Duck (a strategy Schadt himself had eagerly embraced) would now be abandoned. "We have been a print publisher selling sweepstakes via the single channel of direct mail," RD's new leader explained to the press (in terms DeWitt Wallace would have found incomprehensible). "Now we will become a multi-channel marketing operation by investing in such new ventures as video, CD-ROM, television and on-line services like the World Wide Web. That's where real long-term growth will be found."

RD insiders immediately identified serious problems with this approach.

Among other things, it would take time—Schadt himself spoke of "several years"—and the conflict at the Wallace Funds might not wait several years. It would also require vast editorial and marketing resources, and the company's strength in both areas had been decimated by repeated downsizings. That an undermanned and bloodied Reader's Digest could survive in the shark-infested waters of "multi-media," against such juggernauts as Blockbuster Entertainment and Wal-Mart, seemed unlikely. Then there was the problem of age. The new "marketing channels" Schadt was describing were clearly aimed at younger Americans. Yet *Reader's Digest* remains the prime source of customers for the company's other products—CDs like *Those Were the Days: 30 Years of Great Folk Hits* and videos like *The 15-Minute Acupressure Face Lift*—and the average age of *Digest* readers is forty-eight and rising. What to do about that?

At least for this question Schadt appeared to have an answer. Later in February, he announced that Ken Tomlinson would be leaving *Reader's Digest,* and that the post of editor-in-chief would henceforth be occupied by executive editor Chris Willcox. This move was greeted with enthusiasm by *RD*'s editors (Willcox being perceived as fairer and "more open" than the secretive Tomlinson). Yet the switch in editors seemed unlikely to produce a dramatic change in the magazine's political thrust. Willcox had been hired by Tomlinson, after all, and came to Pleasantville in 1988 directly from a lengthy stint as "senior program adviser" to Radio Free Europe and Radio Liberty in Munich. Created by the CIA in the early days of the Cold War, these powerful broadcast operations have been pumping propaganda into Eastern Europe for decades; ostensibly supported by "private donations," they are, in fact, wards of the CIA and the U.S. government.

But whatever the doubts of Digest insiders, Wall Street itself appeared to welcome Schadt's announcements, and for a few days RD's shares edged upward. The rally soon ended, however, and the stock resumed its downward slide. And as this happened the Pleasantville rumor mill began to stir. One theory held that the company would be auctioned off, its mailing lists, creative backlog and "good name" sold to the highest bidder. (Critics scoffed at this, wondering, *Who would bid on the* Titanic?") Another rumor insisted that only the building would be sold and that the business itself was headed to "a warehouse in South Carolina." (Several major maintenance contracts had suddenly been terminated in Pleasantville and this was cited as "proof" of the South Carolina theory.) Management itself, as a form of "persuasion" during the termination lectures it presented to "eligible employees," spoke ominously of future downsizings (to eight hundred employees, to *five hundred!*), and this, too, was cited as evidence that the company was heading south (the theory being that a skeletal workforce would be cheaper to move, and that new employees could be hired in South Carolina at bargain rates).

Amid all the rumors, a few incontestable facts stood out: The circulation of *Reader's Digest*—the rock on which the Pleasantville edifice has always rested—was down by 20 percent, and likely to fall further during the coming transition to "multi-media." Subscribers to the Condensed Book Club, RD's most profitable division, were falling away in droves; from a peak of 1.2 million, circulation of CB had dropped to 500,000. The gamble on special-interest magazines (and on the senior citizens who declined to buy them) had failed. The company's worldwide workforce, reduced to less than half of pre-1984 levels, was at rock bottom. There were no more departments to eliminate; no more people to fire. The enterprise begun by DeWitt and Lila Wallace in 1920, and nurtured for sixty-four years as an ever-growing but always-sustainable circle—where employees and customers were treated fairly, and profits were incidental to service and decency—had become in a single profit-taking decade a burned-out line pointing toward a dim, uncertain future.

Yet chairman Schadt insisted that all was well. "Reader's Digest remains in a position to reach an ever broader customer base," he assured stockholders in his latest annual report. "The Wallace Funds continue to be our principal shareholders . . . and we are pleased that they remain confident in our company as a long-term investment." This was comforting news—that the Wallace Funds retained their confidence in Reader's Digest—but hardly surprising. Since, in fact, the boards of these institutions continue to be comprised in largest part of the same directors.

The breathtaking hypocrisy of Schadt's statement conjures up a familiar image. The face of DeWitt Wallace, lips pursed, eyes blazing, emerges from the gloom. "Are you telling me," he is muttering. *"Are you telling me . . . !"* But the image quickly fades. For even in Pleasantville, death is forever. And nothing can be accomplished from the grave.

Lila Wallace's Rose Garden at High Winds, where the ashes of both Founders were buried. In 1985, after RD's new managers sold High Winds to entrepreneur Nelson Peltz, the Rose Garden was plowed up and converted into a playground and dog run. *(Wallace Estate)*

Epilogue: The Rose Garden
1986

Joe Guignardi woke early that morning—May 15, 1986—and immediately looked outside to see what kind of day it was. The sky was clear and blue, and Guignardi was eager to get to work. For two decades, he had served as Lila Wallace's head gardener at High Winds. Although he had volunteered to stay on in the employ of the new owner, it hadn't happened. Most of the staff had been summarily fired, either by Barney McHenry following Lila's death in 1984 or by Nelson Peltz when he bought the estate in 1985. These days, Guignardi worked wherever he could find a job.

While he was fixing breakfast, the phone rang. It was Ross Cutri, one of the lucky few kept on by Peltz, calling from the greenhouse at High Winds. "Listen, Joe," Cutri said. "You wanna free rosebush? Get up here! *They gonna plow it under!*"

Guignardi's favorite chore at High Winds had been tending Lila's Rose Garden. Lila had planted the first bushes herself in the early forties, and had nursed them faithfully until hip problems made such work impossible. Then Guignardi took over, proudly expanding the garden into an acre-sized paradise. During the season, it had been his pleasure every morning to snip off the freshest blossom for the Queen's breakfast tray. *But those days are long gone,* he thought sadly, gulping a glass of juice before heading for his pickup.

Twenty minutes later, driving up the familiar High Winds hill, Guignardi frowned in displeasure. Fields that Lila had sown with wildflowers had been turned over and resodded with acres of lush lawn. The cobbled pathways carved from the forest by DeWitt lay buried under layers of asphalt, with garish lights strung overhead. A helicopter pad occupied a level spot on the lawn below the swimming pool, and in a niche blasted out of Lila's cliffside Nelson Peltz had installed a giant hot tub. Guignardi frowned again. Peltz had made his fortune as one of Mike Milken's junk-bond cronies during the height of the Greed Decade. Now, from his new Jacuzzi, the former frozen-food salesman was enjoying the same splendid view that had caused DeWitt Wallace so many pangs of guilt.

As Guignardi parked his pickup outside the main garage, a smartly uniformed butler stepped from the front entrance to inquire about his business. Ignoring the butler, Guignardi grabbed a shovel and trotted around the east wing of the mansion toward the stone terrace that sits above the Rose Garden. He and Cutri had built the terrace themselves in the late seventies, so Lila would have a place to park her wheelchair during early-evening meditations above the roses. *(Oh, beautiful,* she would murmur. *Soo . . . beautiful . . .)*

But he saw at once that he was too late. Several huge machines—two bulldozers, a frontloader, two dump trucks—were already at work, rumbling up and down what was left of Lila's paradise. Cutri appeared at his side, wearing a mournful expression, and for a time the two gardeners watched in silence.

Then Cutri spoke. "I could cry, Joe," he said. "Those roses . . . they was so *beautiful.*"

"Why are they doing this?" asked Guignardi. "Don't they know . . . ?"

"Yeah, they know," said Cutri. "Gene told 'em."

"But the Wallaces are *buried* here. How can they plow it up?"

"Joe, you don't understand," said Cutri. "Peltz has a little boy, Matthew. This place gonna be Matthew's playground."

"Oh," said Guignardi. "Matthew's playground."

For several more minutes, the two men watched in silence while the machines toiled back and forth. Then Guignardi sighed. "Gotta go, Rossi," he said. "Gotta job in Croton. Two days a week."

"Okay, Joe," said Cutri. "Me, too. Gotta go to work."

But neither man moved. Something held them there—old memories, thoughts from a different time. "Remember, Rossi, how she always made me come inside to consult about the gardens?" Cutri nodded. "I would stand there in the living room until she told me to sit down. 'No, no, Joe, not over there,' she would say. 'Come sit here on the couch, by me. So I can hear you better.' "

"Yeah, Joe, I remember. She was nice 'a lady, Mrs. Wallace." The old Italian shook his head. "But she live too long, Joe. Everything go bad."

Guignardi gave Cutri a consoling pat, then walked away without another word. Cutri watched him go, then grabbed his rake and headed for the rhododendron beds. The bulldozers continued to work, shoving the mutilated bushes into piles for the frontloader. The men operating the machines wore masks against the dust, and guided their vehicles with faceless precision. A breeze freshened from the northwest, sending the swirling clouds high into the air.

Somewhere in those clouds, rising above the faceless men, were the once-living atoms that had composed themselves a century earlier as a squawling baby boy in an upstairs bedroom in a dark and drafty house in St. Paul, Minnesota, and as a queenly girl-child sprung from a blue ornament on Christmas Day in a farmhouse on the bleak plains of southern Manitoba. Now DeWitt and Lila had become atoms of a different sort, lifeless dust disappearing into the blue spaces above the lake, crossing the distant highway, heading south toward the coast and the ocean. The same broad ocean that had brought their ancestors to America three generations before, seeking their own dreams in what they hoped would be a Promised Land.

Author's Note and Acknowledgments

Although I didn't realize it at the time, my involvement with *American Dreamers* began late in 1988, during a ride to John F. Kennedy Airport in Gene Doherty's limousine. I had resigned my position as *Reader's Digest* managing editor the year before, at the height of the turmoil following Black Monday (as described on page 301). Frankly, I was glad to be out of what had become an untenable situation, and looking forward, after twenty-five years at RD, to doing something different with the last third of my life.

But at some point during that ride Doherty began to talk about what had happened up at High Winds during the Wallaces' sad last years. At first, I listened with half an ear. But something in Doherty's voice—his unmistakable anger and frustration—made him hard to ignore. What he was saying seemed far-fetched. Yet Doherty was someone I had known for many years, as reliable as any man I've ever met. And, to tell the truth, his accusations weren't altogether new. There had been rumors after Wally's death in 1981, and again after Lila died in 1984. *Besides,* I remember thinking, *who would make up such stuff? For what purpose?*

During my week on the West Coast, I thought often about what Doherty had told me. When I returned to New York, I arranged to meet him at a diner not far from Digest Headquarters. We talked for three hours. When our conversation ended, I sensed that my involvement with the Wallaces and Reader's Digest wasn't over after all.

I already understood, from personal experience, that a nightmare of sorts had descended on the Wallace's publishing kingdom—a fact that struck me as sad but largely inevitable. In the America of the late eighties, corporate mayhem—buyouts, mergers, mass terminations—was the stuff of daily headlines and fodder for a dozen angry best-sellers. I had no particular desire to add my voice to the growing chorus. But Doherty was indicating that a different kind of nightmare had descended on the Wallaces' personal kingdom. For several decades, this extraordinary couple had rained benevolence on all who came within their orbit: family members, friends, employees, perfect strangers. Their reward for this unparalleled generosity—if Doherty's claims could be confirmed—appeared to have been a descent into hell. And *that*, I told myself, is a story that ought to be told. In the heartbreaking final scene of *King Lear*, as the bodies of Cordelia and Lear are borne away, Edgar speaks these concluding words:

> The weight of this sad time we must obey,
> Speak what we feel, not what we ought to say.

That's how I felt after listening to Doherty. Over the next several weeks, I interviewed others who had worked at High Winds during the Wallace's last years—nurses Dotty Evans and Janine Ardohain, gardener Joe Guignardi, maids Jean Rossi and Adele Bueti, butler Veikko Kotalainen. What these plainspoken servants told me confirmed Doherty's stories and added a wealth of outrageous new details. Evans and Rossi actually cried during our conversations. Evans became so intense—so determined to say what she felt, so afraid of the potential consequences—that she sometimes found it difficult to speak at all. Rossi kept interrupting herself: *"Why, why, why?"* she would demand. *"I still don't understand it!"* Guignardi's memories made him furious. "Is that thing working?" he asked at one point, nodding at my recorder. When I nodded back, his voice rose several decibels: *"I hope you tell the world that Barney McHenry is a son of a bitch!"*

Armed with these new facts, I wrote a proposal outlining the book I had in mind and sent it to agent Sterling Lord. Within a week, Sterling was fielding bids from several publishers. We chose Simon & Schuster primarily because senior editor Chuck Adams seemed to understand right off what I was trying to say. ("This is a *wonderful* story," he told me, "poignant, compelling, all about American dreams and American greed.")

As a longtime Digest employee, I was well acquainted with the principal players in the drama and thus able to interview nearly everyone of importance. In all, I talked with forty-two individuals, many of them on several occasions, and these extensive interviews (along with my own memories) comprise the heart of this book. But the process wasn't as easy as I had imagined it would be. Several of the key players—veteran Digesters who might have made a difference at High Winds had they not aligned themselves instead with the new forces gathering in Pleasantville—were understandably defensive in what they recalled. They were willing, even eager, to discuss the dream years. But the nightmare was a different matter. They had heard stories, sure, but what was the point of going into all that?

Defensiveness was not a problem with Ed Thompson or Jack O'Hara, the two men Wallace picked to lead the Digest into the future. Yet even Thompson and O'Hara were hesitant when it came to the nightmare. They knew bits and pieces of the story, and willingly discussed them. But neither man fully understood how all the pieces fit together, or what they revealed when the puzzle was complete. In my discussions with them, I think both interviewer and interviewee were learning things, clearing cobwebs from painful might-have-beens. I am grateful to both men for their honesty and candor.

I am equally grateful to Judy Thompson, who was anything *but* hesitant. Our talks took place at her country home in the Catskill Mountains, in a dim library crowded with memories and sadness. Several Digesters had warned me about Judy. "Be careful," they said. "She is just like Lila." And so she is, in looks and mannerism. But Judy Thompson is a woman of high good humor and deep personal insight, not really like Lila at all. When I apologized for the intimate nature of certain questions, she laughed out loud. "Don't be silly," she said. "I used to *pay* people to listen to this stuff!"

Only two of the key players refused to see me. Through Digest spokeswoman Carole Howard, chairman George Grune—a man I had known for twenty years—expressed initial willingness to be interviewed on condition that I provide beforehand a sampling of the questions I had in mind. I sent some questions down to Pleasantville, and immediately received a call from Ms. Howard: "Mr. Grune has avoided all discussion of events that occurred prior to his chairmanship," she explained. "He has no intention of changing that policy now. And having seen your sample questions, he sees no reason why he should see you at all."

Laurance Rockefeller was equally wary. Through his assistant, a pleasant man named Fraser Seitel, Mr. Rockefeller explained that he was resting at his summer home in Maine. Perhaps in the fall he might be able to see me. Meanwhile, if I cared to send along some sample questions, that would be helpful.

I sent some questions to Seitel, and to be fair included several that were frank and to the point. ("Who decided which support organizations got how many Digest shares? On whose authority?) Perhaps that was *too* frank. In any case, despite several follow-up letters, I never heard from Seitel or Rockefeller again.

The vast majority of my interviews were tape-recorded. In other cases, I have relied on extensive notes supplemented by backup interviews and phone calls. Wherever there were differing versions of the same event (a not-infrequent occurrence), I have included elements common to all versions and for the rest have selected what seemed most credible to me (with conflicting material included either parenthetically or within the following source notes).

Many people helped along the way. Ed and Susie Thompson offered wise advice and support at several crucial junctures (and frequent hospitality). Eunice Weisensel, archivist at the Macalester College Library in St. Paul, opened the Wallace files to me and provided every assistance. Maggie Lichota was an enthusiastic and wonderfully-able editor, as were Chuck Adams and his assistant Cheryl Weinstein at Simon & Schuster. Thanks also to copy supervisor Gypsy da Silva, and to my agent, Sterling Lord, who provided wise and thoughtful advice from beginning to end.

I am grateful as well to the many individuals who took the time to talk with me. In particular, because our conversations were lengthy, repeated and sometimes painful, I wish to thank: Janine Ardohain, Peggy Cole, Gordon Davies, Gene Doherty, Jack O'Hara, Fulton Oursler, Betty St. John, Fred Stanyer, James Stewart-Gordon and Richard Waters.

After my initial conversations with Doherty, during weekly get-togethers with former Digest colleagues Jerry Dole and Ben Cheever, the subject of this book was given a thorough going-over. For a time, the three of us contemplated writing it together, and during that time Jerry and Ben contributed many valuable insights to what eventually became *American Dreamers*. After considerable thought, Jerry decided to follow a different course. And Ben, no doubt wisely, opted to describe his Digest years (and a great deal more) in fictional form; the result, an exuberant novel called *The Plagiarist* (Atheneum, 1992), is highly recommended.

So, in the end, the "weight" of the Wallaces' sad time was left in my hands. I chose to obey it—to "speak what I feel"—and I believe my decision would please both Lila and DeWitt.

Peter Canning
Westport Point, Massachusetts
January 25, 1996

Notes and Sources

The names of frequently cited sources are abbreviated as follows:

JA	Janine Ardohain
PC	Peggy Cole
GD	Gene Doherty
JOH	Jack O'Hara
BMcH	Barnabas McHenry
FO	Fulton (Tony) Oursler
BS-J	Betty St. John
FS	Fred Stanyer
JS-G	James Stewart-Gordon
ETT	Edward Thompson
JT	Judy Thompson
RW	Richard Waters

Prologue

PAGE

11 *"This is a birthday party!":* Remarks of the major players on the occasion of the Freedom Medal Dinner are taken from a transcript provided by the White House, dated 1/28/72.

14 *Helm had agreed:* "Intrigue Behind the Ivy at Reader's Digest," *Fortune,* 6/25/94.

Chapter One

Material in this chapter, and throughout Part I, is based in large part on the voluminous Wallace Family correspondence (now stored in the University Archives at Macalester College and reprinted here with permission of Wallace executor Barnabas McHenry), and in particular on the following books: Edwin Kagin, *James Wallace of Macalester* (Doubleday, 1957); James Wallace, *Wallace-Bruce and Related Families* (Mohn Printing, 1930); James Playsted Wood, *Of Lasting Interest: The Story of* Reader's Digest (Doubleday, 1958); John Bainbridge, *Little*

Wonder: The Reader's Digest *and How It Grew* (Reynal & Hitchcock, 1945); and Samuel A. Schreiner, Jr., *The Condensed World of* Reader's Digest (Stein & Day, 1977).

PAGE

19   *"He is a baby":* Letter from Janet Wallace to her mother, 12/11/1889.

19   *"The child is a rogue":* Letter from James Wallace to his father-in-law, quoted in Kagin, p. 124.

24   BLEEDING: *May be stopped:* From young DeWitt's *Camping Notes,* written in the same ledger that eventually became his teenage diary.

24   *During meals, James would conduct:* This scene is described in Bainbridge, pp. 31–32.

Chapter Two

PAGE

26   *It is known that he gave:* Details are from DeWitt's letter to James, 5/4/07.

28   *As for that "clean hotel,":* JS-G, 6/4/91, author's interview.

29   *He was initiated:* Schreiner, p. 34.

29   *While shedding their coats:* This scene is described in *Unforgettable DeWitt Wallace,* an unpublished book written by former *Digest* editor Charles Ferguson (a condensation of which appeared in *Reader's Digest,* 2/87).

30   She was talking with several: Several versions of this moment have long been part of RD legend. This version was described by Judy Thompson, 4/18/92, author's interview.

30   *He must have had a fine time:* Based on several letters from DeWitt to James Wallace in January/February 1911.

30   *When exams were over:* Details taken from several letters to his parents.

Chapter Three

PAGE

32   The Apple and How to Grow It: Quoted from *Getting the Most Out of Farming,* published by DeWitt in 1915.

32   *"Oh, that boy could write":* Bainbridge, p. 34.

33   *"White teachers in Florida":* Kagin, p. 209.

33   *"This is an interesting document":* Bainbridge, p. 35.

35   *In the evenings:* From a letter to his parents describing ranch life, July 1917.

36   *What if he took:* This moment, when the idea for *Reader's Digest* burst into full bloom, has been described in several sources, most notably in Playsted Wood, p. 24.

37   *Although this prodigious:* These figures and other details of the historic Meuse-Argonne offensive are cited in Edward M. Coffman, *The War to End All Wars* (University of Wisconsin Press, 1986), pp. 298–312.

37   *By the fifth day:* Jack Heidenry, *Theirs Was the Kingdom* (Norton, 1993), p. 39.

37   *But Wallace seemed able:* JS-G, author's interview, 3/7/91.

37   *Early that evening:* JS-G, author's interview. Additional details provided in DeWitt's letter to Miriam Wallace, 10/6/18.

38   *And one other thing:* Years later, Wallace told several associates he had undergone an early vasectomy. In truth, it was German shrapnel that did the dirty work, as he admitted to his longtime secretary, Betty St. John. Author's interview, 5/2/91.

39   *"People are anxious":* Quoted in Bainbridge, p. 36.

39   *"You can't publish a magazine"* and *"That's too small":* Both from Heidenry, p. 43.

39   *For a few months that spring:* Schreiner, p. 36.

40   *In late September:* This encounter is variously described in all the major RD sourcebooks.

40 *The telegram he dispatched:* The contents of this telegram are described in Schreiner (p. 36), the Ferguson memoir (p. 183 of the version published in *Reader's Digest*), and in several newspaper stories.

Chapter Four

42 *And just then:* The story of the falling ornament has become part of Digest legend, repeated from generation to generation. Perhaps it actually happened. Certainly *Lila* believed it did, and no one ever pressed her on the point.

42 *"There's a sign if I ever saw one!":* Felicia Roosevelt, *Doers and Dowagers* (Doubleday, 1975), p. 187.

42 *Looking back on the Acheson:* Details of the family background were researched by Barclay Acheson in the 1950s (relying on family documents and, in part, on *Burke's Landed Gentry*).

43 What I remember most: Lila related this story to FS. See also Roosevelt, *Doers and Dowagers,* pp. 187–88.

43 *"Daddy was always there":* Roosevelt, p. 189.

44 *"I remember one Sunday":* Lila told this story on numerous occasions. This version recalled by Gene Doherty, 5/4/90, author's interview.

44 *Lila recalled how:* These incidents recalled by Lila during conversations with Fred Stanyer. See also "Her Beliefs Mold Millions," *Asbury Park (NJ) Press,* 7/26/59.

45 *As if to slow the process:* Lila's lifelong anorexia was mentioned by several of those closest to her, including Judy Thompson and Fred Stanyer.

46 *"Daddy was of the Old School":* FS. Also Roosevelt, p. 189.

46 *Lila accepted the position:* For details about Lila's life on Fox Island, see remarks by former New York governor Thomas E. Dewey on the occasion of the Golden Door Award dinner in Lila's honor, May 1970.

46 *During the summer of 1912:* Details from Roosevelt, p. 190. Also JT, author's interview, 4/18/92.

47 *After training in New York City:* Details about Lila's efforts at Pompton Lakes and in New Orleans are found in Playsted Wood, pp. 30–32. Additional details provided during interviews with Fred Stanyer, Gene Doherty and Judy Thompson.

48 I remember standing: Lila related this account to Gene Doherty. Author's interview.

48 *So she began to travel:* Playsted Wood, pp. 32–33.

49 *When you see the immigrants:* Lila's article, entitled "Migrant Work," appeared in the July 1920 issue of *Home Mission Monthly.* It is worth noting that the sentiments she ascribed to these early twentieth-century immigrants ("They come here . . . hoping to educate their children . . .") were precisely those that had brought James and Mary Wallace to America in 1810.

Chapter Five

50 *One week later:* Lila's assignment to Minneapolis is described in Schreiner, p. 36.

50 *The next afternoon, he took:* The meeting in St. Paul is reported in Schreiner (p. 37), Ferguson (p. 183), and Playsted Wood (p. 32). Additional details provided in interviews with Fred Stanyer and Judy Thompson, and in a *Time* cover story dated 12/10/51.

51 *She also felt that she could trust him:* Lila often mentioned the qualities in Dewitt that had initially appealed to her.

52 *He became friendly:* Playsted Wood, p. 33.

53   *"This is the best thing"*: Playsted Wood wrote a second Wallace memoir, never published, in which details of these Pittsburgh events are reported.
53   *Barclay took a photo:* Letter from Barclay Acheson to DeWitt, 10/11/20.
54   *Lila was happy:* Author's interview with FS, 9/16/91.
54   *Back in New York:* Details about the mailing of the first issue of *RD* are found in all the major sourcebooks.
55   When we got back: Lila related this story to Gene Doherty. Author's interview.

Chapter Six

60   *"But then I decided"*: *Time*, 12/10/51.
60   *The next day, over DeWitt's:* Schreiner, p. 38. Additional details provided by JT, 4/18/92, author's interview.
61   *"There was no place to put anything"*: Author's interview with Margaret Sloane Patterson, a longtime Wallace neighbor and friend, 7/31/91.
61   During our first Christmas: Gordon Davies, author's interview, 3/27/91.
62   I watched these changes: Based on author's interview with JT, 4/18/92.
62   *On a bright fall day:* Details of Ralph Henderson's first years at RD are taken from his unpublished memoir, *DeWitt and Lila: Early Days at Reader's Digest*.
64   *The image of that solitary figure:* Ibid., p. 24.

Chapter Seven

PAGE
65   *The circulation of* Reader's Digest: These figures—and much else about the *Digest's* extraordinary rise—were first revealed in the October 1936 issue of *Fortune*.
65   *"It was like making All-American"*: Bainbridge, p. 46.
66   *Payne convinced his fellow: Fortune*, 10/36.
66   *But the real miracle:* Ibid.
68   *"We had a pretty clear sense"*: Playsted Wood, p. 58.
69   Griff and I were chatting: DeWitt related these details to Judy Thompson. Author's interview, 4/18/92.
69   *"I've seen everything"*: The origins and extraordinary success of "... And Sudden Death" are described in all the major RD books.

Chapter Eight

PAGE
72   *"You don't understand"*: Playsted Wood, p. 90.
72   *"He loved those poker games"*: Henderson memoir, p. 11.
73   *In 1934, feeling unwanted:* JT, author's interview, 4/18/92.
74   *But this was all for show:* JS-G, author's interview, 3/7/91.
74   *Sex had never been:* Ibid. Some decades later, while sharing a limousine with Lila and a noted professor of geriatrics, DeWitt suddenly asked the professor how long normal people could expect to enjoy sex. "There's no limit," said the professor. "You can enjoy sex to the day you die." "See, Lila," said DeWitt. "There's hope for us yet!" John Allen, 5/13/91, author's interview. "There was clearly something missing in their sexual relationship," adds Peggy Cole. "It was very complicated—part Greek tragedy, part soap opera. You'd have to be a shrink to figure it out." PC, 6/18/91, author's interview.
74   *"This beautiful creature"*: FS, 9/16/91, author's interview.
75   *(In fact, he had been a test driver):* JS-G, author's interview.

Chapter Nine

PAGE
77   *"He* is *wonderful with figures":* Abbott's background provided by Richard Waters, 1/10/ 91, author's interview.
78   *James's eyes widened:* Lila recounted this story to Gene Doherty on several occasions. Author's interview, 5/20/90.
78   The opening scene: Taken from Lila's "Letter to My Mother," dated 5/38, Macalester Archives.
79   *His problems with brother Ben were worse:* See Heidenry, p. 101.
80   *That it would further free him:* JT, author's interview, 4/18/92.
80   *"I had been dreaming":* Schreiner, p. 102.
81   *"Now that's what God would do":* Playsted Wood, p. 93.
81   *"All those fancy New Yorkers":* BMcH, author's interview, 9/22/93.
82   *"When you walked in there":* FS, 8/12/91, author's interview.
82   *"Very nice," he said:* Schreiner, p. 102.
82   *On more than one occasion:* JT, 6/23/92, author's interview.
83   *"Al took the job":* Details of Cole's early life provided by Peggy Cole, 6/18/91, author's interview.
83   *Impressed, Wallace tried to persuade:* Details from contract between Cole and Wallace signed 12/12/32, and from subsequent correspondence between the two in 1933 and 1934. Also, author's interview with Peggy Cole, 6/18/91.
85   *"Lila's interest in me":* JT, 6/18/92, author's interview.
86   *"I hope you all hear":* Ibid.
86   *"Oh, it was a slippery situation":* Ibid.
86   *Landing on the little High Winds:* RW, 10/15/91, author's interview.

Chapter Ten

PAGE
88   *"A large income":* The Bainbridge *New Yorker* series about RD was later published as *Little Wonder.*
88   *Even the "little people":* Author's interview with Jennie Guignardi, 1/24/90.
89   *When a young editor:* Walter Mahony, 1/14/92, author's interview.
90   *"I'll bet you can't kick":* Heidenry, p. 178.
91   *"There aren't enough people":* Memo from Al Cole to RD staff, 10/41.
92   *In the spring of 1942:* Described by Hobart Lewis, 5/14/91, author's interview. See also Heidenry, pp. 157–59.
92   *Turkey was another key neutral country:* Memo from Fred Thompson to RD staff, 9/43.
93   *The launch of the Japanese edition:* Details taken from Barclay Acheson's year-end report to RDIE executives, 12/31/47. See also Schreiner, pp. 182–86; and Heidenry, pp. 163–67.
93   *By February 1946:* MacArthur later wrote the following message to DeWitt Wallace: "Democracy . . . depends upon an enlightened knowledge which can be acquired only by a general dissemination of the truth. . . . With its wide distribution among the Japanese, no publication has been more helpful along these lines than Reader's Digest. I am grateful for its assistance in this greatest reformation of a people ever attempted in history." Quoted in Acheson report, 12/31/47.
94   *"It is read in foxholes": Time,* 12/10/51.
94   *"We believed the Digest":* Playsted Wood, pp. 169–79.
95   *RD's spread:* Details from interview with Paul W. Thompson, retired RD director of international operations, published in RD *Courier,* 8/94.

95　*In 1947, when Barclay:* Heidenry, pp. 171–72.
95　*The CIA, concerned:* Ibid., pp. 172, 473.
96　*Before long, rumors:* RW, 10/15/91, author's interview.
96　*In fact, Al Cole:* Heidenry, p. 156.
96　*In January 1953, Cole had written:* John Allen, 5/13/91, author's interview.

Chapter Eleven

PAGE
97　*"Wally and I had our happiest time":* GD, author's interview, 3/27/91.
98　*"The problem is not insoluble":* Letter from Norman Cousins to DW, 2/18/44.
99　*Wearing boots, chinos:* Wallace's roadwork was described at length by Veikko Kotalainen, John Tichi, Joe Guignardi and Gene Doherty. Author's interviews, 1991.
101　As I read this manuscript: Kagin, p. 11.

Chapter Twelve

PAGE
103　*On a soft June evening:* Lila described this occasion to Gene Doherty and Gordon Davies. Author's interviews in 1991.
105　*"Wally wants to escape":* JT, 4/18/92, author's interview.
105　*"What he yearned for":* JS-G, 3/7/91, author's interview.
106　*"Our very success":* "He's Too Busy to Die," *Saturday Evening Post,* 3/81.
106　*"We need to place emphasis":* Ibid.
106　*But as time went on:* Gordon Davies, 3/27/91, author's interview.
107　*"All right, you boys":* Gene Doherty, 11/27/90, author's interview.
107　*So Henderson began to dream:* From an undated memo, "How RD Got into the Book Business," written by Al Cole upon retirement in 1965. See also Schreiner, pp. 83–86.
108　*"Al Cole came to me":* The arrival of advertising at RD is described in a 1979 memo written by Cole ("The Story of When, How and Why RD Accepted Advertising"). See also Schreiner, pp. 86–88, and "The Ad That Never Ran," *Advertising Age,* 8/14/72.
108　*"Don't do it!":* JT, 6/23/92, author's interview. It is worth noting that RD's international editions, under Lila's brother Barclay, contained advertising from the beginning, with Lila's complete approval. It was only in the United States, where ads would increase the influence of Cole and Fred Thompson, that she resisted.
110　*In fact, as Lila:* JT, 6/2 3/92, author's interview.
111　*For a number of years:* JT, 6/23/92.
111　*"Fred, why don't you just make love":* Ibid.

Chapter Thirteen

PAGE
111　*One morning during this period:* This entire section was described by JT during a series of interviews in April and June 1992.
112　*"I was wrong!":* Judy Thompson's sturdy sense of humor vanished when she admitted this, and the very real pain she had experienced at her uncle's hands became sadly evident.
114　*"He was at our home":* PC, 6/18/91, author's interview.
114　*"Come on, fellows":* JS-G, 1/25/92, author's interview.
114　*"That's enough!":* Rossario Cutri, 7/31/91, author's interview.
115　*In the fifties, life:* Author's interviews with GD and JT.
115　*"She brought this subject up":* JT, author's interview, 4/18/92.

115   *"Can you imagine the nerve":* GD, 11/27/90.
115   *One evening in 1959:* FO, 3/11/92, author's interview.
116   *He told everyone he was sleeping with Lila:* JT, 4/18/92, author's interview.
116   *Judy had confided:* Ibid.
117   *After they had all gone to bed:* Ibid.
117   After Wally's little trip: Based on what Lila later told JT. Ibid.

Chapter Fourteen

PAGE
117   *In fact, she had suffered:* JT, 6/23/92, author's interview.
119   *Later that summer, on a Monday:* Ibid.
119   *The following Saturday:* Barclay's funeral described by JT, author's interview, 6/23/92.
120   *On a summer afternoon:* FS, 9/16/91, author's interview.
121   *It began in June 1959:* Details of the Morgan/Wallace relationship are provided in the Playsted Wood biography, pp. 168–88; in Schreiner, pp. 209–13; and in Heidenry, pp. 370–82.
123   *Bill Kennedy had entered:* Author's interviews with Judy Thompson and Fred Stanyer.
124   *As the two men entered:* JT, 4/18/92, author's interview.
125   *And from whatever passed:* RW, 10/15/91, author's interview.
125   *"Despite what everyone said":* FS, 8/12/91, author's interview.
126   *Rudick was a senior partner:* RW, 10/15/91.
126   *In 1959, when Cole was:* Ibid.
127   *"But he kept his head down":* BS-J, 5/2/91, author's interview.

Chapter Fifteen

PAGE
127   *In 1962, for the first time: Time,* 2/2/62.
128   *"I got the idea":* Schreiner, p. 82.
128   *"Just tell me where":* ETT, 6/20/91, author's interview.
128   *"But to many of us":* FO, 3/11/92, author's interview.
128   *For as long as he lived:* Tom Bundrick, 5/13/93, author's interview.
129   *In the early years:* GD, author's interview.
129   *The thought of ceding control:* RW, 10/15/91, and PC, 6/18/91, author's interviews.
130   *But Wallace put him off:* JS-G, 6/4/91, author's interview.
130   *But not as elegantly:* FO, 3/11/92, author's interview.
130   *Next came Ken Payne:* Details surrounding Payne's dismissal were provided by Walter Mahony, 1/14/92, and JT, 6/23/92, author's interviews.
131   *"Neither Lewis nor anyone else": Time,* 1/1/65.
132   *"But it was also a way":* PC, 6/22/92, author's interview. "Hobe told Lila and Wally whatever they needed to hear," says Peggy Cole today. "He pretended to be conservative, for example, when in fact he was always a liberal at heart. Al would never do that."

Chapter Sixteen

PAGE
132   *But one day that spring:* JT, 6/23/91, author's interview.
132   *And the physical business ended:* Ibid. At a dinner party in 1985, according to James Stewart-Gordon, Judy suddenly announced that her late uncle "would have made a lousy lover in any case. After all, his *cojones* were shot off in the war!" JS-G, 3/7/91, author's interview.

132   *Wallace's other interest:* Details from Schreiner, Playsted Wood and Heidenry. Also, author's interviews with Fulton Oursler, Cappy Morgan (6/22/92) and Gene Doherty.

134   *"But she was incensed:* JT, 4/18/92, author's interview.

134   *"She took me to the Handball Court":* GD, author's interview.

135   *"After Mrs. Acheson died":* Veikko Kotalainen, 1/11/91, author's interview.

135   *Every year for two decades:* Details of what became known as the Christmas Massacre were provided during author's interviews with Peggy Cole, Hobe Lewis, Dick Waters and Judy Thompson. See also the Playsted Wood biography, pp. 216–18.

137   *When this proved impossible:* Judy's opinion is seconded by Peggy Cole: "Lila's vanity was such that she wanted no one—not even her 'beloved niece'—to inherit what she believed was meant to be hers forever." Author's interview, 6/18/91. Fred Thompson later became vice president of the *New York Times* and assistant to the president of The Times Company.

137   *Indeed, in the spring: Wall Street Journal,* 3/17/66.

Chapter Seventeen

138   *On the evening:* Veikko Kotalainen, 1/11/91, author's interview.

138   *Spying the Nixons:* GD, author's interview.

139   *There was something about Nixon:* Personal knowledge.

139   *According to Maurice Stans:* Stans, *The Terrors of Justice* (Everest House, 1978), pp. 129–35.

140   *Lewis's efforts:* Tom Bundrick, author's interview, 5/13/93.

140   *He ordered a reduction:* Personal knowledge.

140   *Written by former defense secretary:* See Edward S. Herman and Noam Chomsky, *Manufacturing Consent: The Political Economy of the Mass Media* (Pantheon, 1988), pp. 216–17. The Clifford article was not the only victim of Nixon/Lewis pressure. On a Friday afternoon earlier in 1972, Wallace asked the author to prepare a "compilation" of editorial views on the war drawn from publications on both right and left (which would have constituted *RD*'s first deviation from the hawkish Nixon line). When the author arrived at Headquarters the following Monday, bearing what he believed would be an historic breakthrough, he discovered that Lewis had also been busy over the weekend. "The compilation on Vietnam has been cancelled," a note from Lewis informed him. "Mr. Wallace has changed his mind."

141   *Lewis's next target:* Details regarding RD's Hollywood days provided during author's interviews with Fulton Oursler, Dick Waters and Hobe Lewis in 1991. See also *Newsweek,* 6/18/73.

141   *In fact, Lewis's life:* Details regarding the women's suit against RD found in *Mt. Kisco Patent Trader,* 6/15/72; *MS* magazine, 6/73; and the *New York Times,* 11/4/76.

142   *"That lawsuit was my fault":* Hobe Lewis, 5/14/91, author's interview.

142   *"That's no problem":* Nixon's words quoted in Fred Emery, *Watergate* (Times Books, 1994), p. 263.

142   *DeWitt Wallace's name:* Barney McHenry, 9/22/93, author's interview.

143   *Earlier, at Lewis's:* Ibid.

143   *After an IRS:* Ibid. "Hobe is lucky he didn't go to jail," asserts McHenry.

143   *For several weeks:* Personal knowledge. Also, FO, 8/25/92, author's interview.

143   *Only later was it learned:* FO.

143   *While at the clinic:* Ibid.

143   *And inevitably these questions:* Adele Dillingham was not the only source of conflict between Lewis and Wallace during the summer of 1974. With Watergate tapes making daily headlines, Lewis showed up in Tony Oursler's office one morning with an article

from the *Wall Street Journal* that excused Nixon's role in the cover-up. "I want you to run this in your issue," he ordered. "But Hobe," Oursler replied, "by the time this appears in *RD* Nixon may no longer *be* in the White House!" A heated argument ensued, and eventually Lewis left the office, slamming the door behind him. Later that evening, Oursler answered his home phone to hear the familiar reedy voice of DeWitt Wallace. "What's going on, Tony?" Wallace asked. "I could hear your office door slamming all the way up at High Winds." Oursler explained the situation. "You are completely correct," Wallace told him. "That article should not appear in *Reader's Digest.*"

144   *For help in this endeavor:* Cappy Morgan, 6/22/92, author's interview.
145   *"I went to every supplier":* RW, 10/15/91, author's interview.
146   *"It was all a matter of timing":* Lisa Collins, for many years accountant/bookkeeper for the Wallace Funds. Author's interview, 1/22/92.
146   *"Barney knew too much":* FS, 9/16/91, author's interview.

Chapter Eighteen

PAGE
147   *"But then he would start talking":* John Allen, 5/13/91, author's interview.
148   *Now Wallace did draw the line:* JOH, 3/25/91, authors interview.
148   *Nowhere was Wallace's frustration greater:* Wallace's disappointment with Macalester is recorded in the Playsted Wood biography, pp. 240–43. See also Schreiner, pp. 206–207.
149   *At a Guesthouse lunch:* FO, 9/11/92, author's interview.
149   *One Friday that spring:* Personal knowledge (author was one of those phoned).
150   *It was the kind of evening:* FS, 9/16/91, author's interview.
150   *"I had been invited":* Jeremy Dole, 1/31/91, author's interview. Also, personal knowledge.

Chapter Nineteen

PAGE
152   *Rather than slip $10:* GD, author's interview.
152   *He liked his things old and worn:* Veikko Kotalainen, 1/11/91, author's interview.
153   *"It's not right":* Ibid.
153   *Early on, sensing:* Ann Tichi, 1/12/91, author's interview.
154   *"But we came down":* Edward Zeigler, *RD* senior editor, 5/11/93, author's interview.
154   *It wasn't in them to pull rank:* Schreiner, p. 122.
154   *When they reached Montreal:* Edward Zeigler, author's interview.
155   *By the mid-seventies:* The Wallaces were notably secretive about how much and to whom they gave. These estimates are derived from numerous sources and cover the period from the late thirties until the mid-seventies. The actual amount is probably much higher.
155   *When Digest senior editor Andrew Jones:* Andrew Jones, 7/23/93, author's interview.
156   *He kept little lists:* BS-J, 8/26/92, author's interview.
157   *He showed up at Westchester:* Ibid. See also Donald J. Gonzales, *The Rockefellers at Williamsburg* (EPM Publications, 1991), p.70.
157   *In the spring of 1964:* Playsted Wood, pp. 222–24.
158   *Lila was equally happy:* Ibid., pp. 224–25.
159   *In 1972, Pete Kriendler:* Hobe Lewis, 5/14/91, author's interview.
160   *In 1966, Bill Kennedy:* Agnes De Mille, *Martha: The Life and Work of Martha Graham,* pp. 364–67, 378, 380, 398.

160   *"What do you need":* Details provided by Barney McHenry, 9/22/93, author's interview.
160   *Lila was in her limousine:* GD, author's interview.
160   *As it happened:* Details of Lila's involvement with the Met are found in Thomas Hoving, *Making the Mummies Dance: Inside the Metropolitan Museum of Art* (Simon & Schuster, 1993), pp. 181–93, 211–12.
163   *Sipping from the gold cup:* Author's interviews with JT and FS.
163   *"That wonderful Laurance Rockefeller":* "Portrait of A Great Patron," the *New York Times,* 5/12/77.

Chapter Twenty

PAGE
164   *From her earliest years:* JT, 6/23/92, author's interview.
164   *"(Lila could be naive)":* BMcH, 9/22/93, author's interview.
164   *During the bitterest:* Kagin, p. 192.
164   *In 1967, Laurance invited:* John Allen, 5/13/91, author's interview.
164   *"Laurance has always been:* ETT, 11/3/92, author's interview.
165   *"When Laurance Rockefeller went up":* FS, 9/16/91.
165   *"I have had my pleasure":* GD, author's interview.
165   *Early in 1972:* Roy Rowan, "Intrigue Behind the Ivy at Reader's Digest," *Fortune,* 6/25/84.
166   *Laurance Rockefeller is a people person:* RW, 10/15/91, author's interview. Clearly, Laurance saw more in RD than a "public trust." When asked why a man like Laurance Rockefeller would join the board of Reader's Digest, Barney McHenry laughed: *"Because he knew he could get a lot of money!* It's just that simple! Laurance has a *zest* for getting other peoples' money. And, I mean, he *knows* about money. Wake Laurance from a sound sleep and he will come to reciting the relevant sections of the Internal Revenue Code!" BMcH, 9/22/93.
166   *"Making Laurance a trustee":* PC, 6/18/91, author's interview.
166   *On December 4, 1972:* The Wallace wills, and the eleven codicils thereto, are open to the public at the Westchester County Surrogate's Court, White Plains, New York.
167   *"My life has been Zenlike":* Peter Collier and David Horowitz, *The Rockefellers: An American Dynasty* (Holt, Rinehart and Winston, 1977), p. 402.
167   *"When it's raining porridge":* Ibid., p. 11.
167   *Laurance enjoyed a reputation:* Ibid., pp. 213–14.
167   *"He seemed very happy":* RW, 10/15/91.
168   I told the trustees: Ibid.

Chapter Twenty-one

PAGE
169   *"I'm sorry to interrupt":* John Tichi, 1/12/91, author's interview. Also, GD, author's interview.
170   *The story subsequently:* See Bob Woodward, *Washington Post,* 6/27/76.
170   *Partly out of fear:* Emery, pp. 192–93; also, H. R. Haldeman, *The Haldeman Diaries* (Putnam, 1994), p. 475.
171   *What was going on?:* At the time, the corridors at RD Headquarters were rife with these and similar questions.
171   *Lewis's own recollection:* Letter from Hobart Lewis to author, 5/13/94.
171   *H. R. Haldeman: The Haldeman Diaries,* p. 490.
172   *In the summer of 1973:* This incident was described by Jack O'Hara, 3/25/91, author's interview.

172   *"I drove Laurance a lot":* GD, author's interview.
173   *In the summer of 1974:* ETT, 6/20/91, author's interview.
173   *After several years:* Conversation between Hobe Lewis and author, 4/15/75.
174   *"Wouldn't this make a lively":* According to FO, 10/16/91, author's interview.
174   *"Hobe is too old":* John Tichi overheard this conversation while serving dinner to the Wallaces. Tichi, 1/12/91, author's interview.
174   *Two days later:* Lewis later described this occasion to executive editor Walter Mahony. Mahony, 1/14/92, author's interview.
176   *The next morning, Wallace:* ETT, 6/20/91, author's interview.
177   *For a man who hated:* BMcH, 9/22/93, author's interview.
177   *"Dear Ed":* Memo from DW to ETT, 12/8/76.

Chapter Twenty-two

PAGE
177   *"The knives had been out":* FS, 9/16/91, author's interview.
178   *During the winter of 1972:* Details provided by Edie Lewis, 5/14/91, author's interview.
178   *Gene Doherty had driven Lila:* This episode was described during several interviews with Gene Doherty in 1991.
179   *"I would mix":* John Tichi, 1/12/91, author's interview.
179   *"Once his eyesight":* BS-J, 5/2/91, author's interview.
179   *All through cocktails:* Author's own observation.
180   *But the speech he gave:* Reported by John Allen, 5/13/91, author's interview. See also Schreiner, p. 238.
181   *On a sunny afternoon that fall:* This incident was described by John Tichi, 1/12/91, author's interview.
182   *"We let him keep":* BS-J, 5/2/91, author's interview.
182   *"What's he doing here:* John Tichi, author's interview.
182   *"I was their employee":* BMcH, 9/22/93, author's interview.
183   *On a lovely Saturday afternoon:* This incident at Boscobel was described during author's interviews with Fred Stanyer and Gene Doherty, 8/91.
183   *Bill Kennedy's original:* FS, 8/12/91, author's interview. See also "Portrait of a Great Patron," the *New York Times*, 5/12/77.
184   *"He borrowed forty thousand dollars":* This figure was confirmed by Betty St. John, 8/26/92, author's interview. "Mrs. Wallace was furious about that loan," says St. John. " 'Don't ever ask me for another thing!' she told Barney. 'We pay you enough so you should be able to arrange your own mortgage.' " John Tichi, High Winds butler at the time, also remembers hearing the Wallaces discuss the McHenry loan: " 'He wants to pay it back to Boscobel,' Lila complained at dinner one night. DeWitt shrugged. 'Maybe he won't pay it back at all,' Lila said. Then she shrugged as well. So I concluded she just gave it to him." John Tichi, 1/12/91, author's interview.
184   *They ran out of gas:* GD, author's interview.
185   *When she first encountered:* Jean Rossi, 2/12/91, author's interview.
185   *Shortly after his arrival:* GD, author's interview.

Chapter Twenty-three

PAGE
185   *"For the first time":* Memo from Dennis McEvoy to DW, 10/25/76.
186   *During the summer of his second year:* Author's observation.
187   *The Laird/Barron collaborations:* Personal knowledge. See also Heidenry, pp. 478–79.

(Heidenry incorrectly infers that "Jamie" was a reference to James Angleton, the CIA's first and legendary chief of counterintelligence.)

188 *Although Al Cole had always:* "Making billions at RD was always an option," says former CEO O'Hara. "It could have been done at any time. But Wally wouldn't accept the necessary changes." JOH, 11/5/92, author's interview.

188 *"But where is the Digest* going?": Ibid.

188 *"We march to a different drummer":* Quoted in *Business Week,* 3/5/79.

189 *"Look, George":* JOH, author's interview.

189 *"The limitation on using merchandise":* Memo from George Grune to RD sales staff, 6/13/77.

189 *"Take your arguments up there":* JOH, author's interview.

189 People have faith: Memo from DW to ETT, 1 /44/77.

190 *"Would you confirm":* Memo from ETT to DW, 4/8/78.

190 *When Wallace asked him:* Memo from JOH to DW, 4/21/76.

190 *"For the moment":* Memo from ETT to DW, 1/3/77.

191 *While he pondered:* Heidenry, p. 463.

191 *"Laurance wasn't happy":* JOH, 1 1/25/92, author's interview.

192 *"What is meant":* Reader's Digest, 2/76.

Chapter Twenty-four

192 *Even as a child:* Research into Laurance's background, and into the background of the Rockefeller Family itself, is essentially an exercise in good versus evil. The "official" books (authorized by the Family) are replete with praise and glory. The "unofficial" books (based for the most part on news clips and conjecture) present an equally unpersuasive picture of wrongdoing and greed. In the entire literature, the most persuasive and balanced account is found in *The Rockefellers: An American Dynasty* by Peter Collier and David Horowitz, and I have relied heavily on their account in researching chapter 24. Other books that have proved especially useful include: William Manchester, *A Rockefeller Family Portrait,* (Little, Brown, 1959); Myer Kutz, *Rockefeller Power,* (Simon & Schuster, 1974); Ferdinand Lundberg, *The Rockefeller Syndrome,* (Lyle Stuart, 1975); John Ensor Harr, *The Rockefeller Century,* (Scribners, 1988) and John Ensor Harr, *The Rockefeller Conscience,* (Scribners, 1991).

193 *In the late thirties:* Richard Austin Smith, "The Rockefeller Brothers," *Fortune,* 3/55.

193 *Then he set about:* One of Laurance's most successful early efforts, with his friend C. Douglas Dillon, involved the establishment of a textile mill in the Belgian Congo. Labor in the Congo was cheap—5 cents an hour—and cotton could be bought at half the U.S. price. Years later, when the Congolese independence movement began to cause problems, Laurance and Dillon (now serving as undersecretary of state) turned to their friend, CIA director Allen Dulles. Dulles subsequently oversaw several attempts to assassinate rebel leader Patrice Lumumbu. When independence was achieved despite the CIA, Laurance and Dillon quickly sold out.

194 *Brother Nelson backed the plan:* Alan Talbot, *Power Along the Hudson* (Dutton, 1972), p. 88.

194 *Rockefeller Family members:* Robert H. Boyle, *The Hudson River: A Natural and Unnatural History* (Norton, 1979), p. 163.

195 *Two years later:* Myer Kutz, *Rockefeller Power,* p. 189.

196 *There was an enormous:* Author's interviews with Peggy Cole, Fred Stanyer, Ed Thompson and Barney McHenry.

Chapter Twenty-five

PAGE

197 *"Jack and I thought"*: ETT, 11/3/92, author's interview.

197 *"Ed and I were in lockstep"*: JOH, 11/25/92, author's interview.

197 *"Barney had become Laurance's"*: JS-G, 1/25/92, author's interview.

198 *The King and Queen came down:* This occasion was described by JOH and ETT, author's interviews.

198 *Since neither Thompson:* Author's interviews with BS-J and PC.

199 *"He was the only one"*: "They [the Strasburgers and/or McHenry) tried to keep Al away every way they could," says St. John today. "They would tell him Mr. Wallace was sick, or out of town, or that he had visitors. But Al didn't listen. Or else he would bring a memo to me, which I would give to Gene, who would take it directly to Mr. Wallace at High Winds. Barney knew I was doing this and hated me for it. Which is why I was left out of Mr. Wallace's will." BS-J, 8/26/92, author's interview. McHenry sees this issue very differently. "Al was sowing dragon's teeth up at High Winds," he says. "I kept asking him, 'Why are you so worried? There is *nothing* here to steal. It's all going to charity.' But he wouldn't listen." BMcH, 9/22/93, author's interview.

199 *"Barney told Al"*: PC, 6/22/92, author's interview.

199 *On a Sunday evening early:* Gene Doherty, author's interview.

200 *In her altered state:* Ibid.

200 *His rules were simple:* Janine Ardohain, a nurse from Northern Westchester Hospital who worked regular night shifts at High Winds from early in 1979 until Lila Wallace's death in 1984. Author's interview, 8/12/91.

200 *But then he made a foolish error:* McHenry's "foolish error" was described to Betty St. John by Al Cole. BS-J, 8/26/92, author's interview.

201 *"Wally couldn't remember"*: "Intrigue Behind the Ivy at Reader's Digest," *Fortune*, 6/25/84.

201 *Immediately after the lunch:* This memo and other notes and memos created during "the War" (and cited below) were typed by Betty St. John on her special large-type machine. St. John carefully saved copies for her file, and made these copies available to the author. Other memos created by various participants in the War were made available by Ed Thompson and Gordon Davies.

202 *"The appointment"*: Letter from Barney McHenry to author, 6/21/94.

203 *During the course of the luncheon:* ETT, 8/24/92, author's interview.

203 *He will sign anything:* McHenry confirms this. "The Wallaces had complete trust in me and would execute documents without having read them fully because they knew I would not offer anything improper." BMcH, letter to the author, 6/21/94.

204 *I have this tenth codicil:* Ibid.

204 *During this meeting:* Details of this agreement were noted in a memo prepared by Thompson on 6/13/79.

205 *On an earlier date:* Details quoted from the Palmer Baker legal memo of 2/5/79, p. 12.

205 *Thompson and O'Hara insisted:* ETT, 5/13/93, author's interview.

205 *He had labored:* JOH, 11/25/92, author's interview.

206 *Instead, using the "verbal authority":* Following the July 11 meeting, new documents were created (and later made available to the author by Ed Thompson) listing the new directors and outlining guidelines for the dispensation of the Wallaces' cash. Had Thompson and O'Hara remained as directors of the funds, it is likely that one or both would have raised questions about the upcoming stock transfers.

206 *On a Sunday morning:* This incident was described to the author by Robert Patterson, 7/31/91.

Chapter Twenty-six

207 *On occasion, he was asked to witness:* Mary Strasburger, 3/22/92, author's interview. John Strasburger died in 1986, but Mary recalls these signings vividly: "McHenry was always givin' papers to Mr. Wallace. Now, Mister, he can't see anything. So God knows what it was. With Missus, it was worse. He says, 'Just put an X,' and he's helpin' her. Then, downstairs, he gets others to sign as witnesses. I seen that many times." (Mary's daughter, Nancy Swimm, son-in-law Jerry Swimm and John Strasburger's mother Ilse were also present during this interview.) McHenry denies the significance of these "signings." "I don't recall ever asking a nurse to witness anything of real consequence except perhaps an occasional stock power. Letter to the author, 6/21/94.

207 *John's mother moved in:* JA, 9/11/91, author's interview.

207 *"We're going to the Castle in the Sky!":* Jerry Swimm, author's interview.

207 *Food for the Strasburgers:* Details provided by Jean Rossi, author's interview, 2/12/91. Confirmed by nurses Dorothy Evans, Janine Ardohain, Dorothy Schmidt and Julie Waldrun, and by Gene Doherty. Author's interviews.

208 *"But that was all for show":* Lisa Collins, 11/3/92, author's interview.

208 *As John Strasburger's confidence:* GD, author's interview. Also, letter from Tina Hunter, RN, to Barney McHenry, 1/29/80.

208 *"Once, Jack showed me this stack":* Jerry Swimm, author's interview.

208 *But Allen's visits:* GD, author's interview.

208 *But McHenry controlled:* Julie Waldrun, 3/12/92, author's interview.

208 *Over the years, the Wallaces had set up:* Based on documents filed with the Wallaces' wills and available at Surrogate's Court in White Plains, New York.

209 *But the noise:* Author's interview with GD and Julie Waldrun, 3/12/92.

209 *That evening, he called Guignardi:* Author's interview with Joe Guignardi, 1/24/90.

210 *By this time, the Wallaces took supper:* Evenings at High Winds during this period were described by nurses Janine Ardohain and Julie Waldrun. Author's interviews.

Chapter Twenty-seven

211 *In July 1979: Pegasus,* RD newsletter, 7/79.

212 *"He hated the very idea":* JS-G, 1/28/92, author's interview.

212 *"Your pioneering spirit":* Quoted in *Pegasus.*

212 *"The Boss stood there":* GD, author's interview.

212 *"Except for Burger":* Joe Guignardi, 1/24/90, author's interview.

212 *And exactly seventeen months:* Details provided by Robert Gavin, president of Macalester College, author's interview, 6/29/91. "Barney McHenry assured me repeatedly that the Wallaces truly wanted to make this gift," Gavin recalled. "Now, McHenry . . . *there* was an interesting character to deal with!"

212 *Under the bylaws:* "In reality," says McHenry, "RD always controlled the S/O boards." BMcH, author's interview.

213 *"The tax considerations":* JOH, 11/25/92, author's interview.

213 *"In hindsight":* ETT, 5/13/93, author's interview.

213 *The price of the stock:* Personal knowledge. (Author was an RD executive and stockholder at the time.)

214 *"Our fund was meant":* Robert Gavin, author's interview.

215 *After pleasant conversation:* "The Lila and DeWitt Wallace Legacy," reprinted from Colonial Williamsburg *Journal,* Summer 1985, p. 9.

215   *From its beginnings:* Details from Donald J. Gonzales, *The Rockefellers at Williamsburg.*

216   *"The Boss loved that movie":* GD, author's interview.

216   *"As important as Mr. Wallace's gift was":* Humelsine, *The DeWitt and Lila Wallace Legacy,* p. 9.

217   *"I got a call from Wally":* Noel Oursler, 9/11/92, author's interview.

217   *"The S/Os were Laurance Rockefeller's call":* ETT, 11/3/92, author's interview. "In theory," adds Thompson, "I suppose Rockefeller and McHenry could argue that it wasn't just the two of them taking advantage of the Wallaces. Jack O'Hara was included on the board of every S/O. If Jack had had a problem with the process, he could have said something. I'm sure that's how Laurance would defend his actions. Was there a chance in hell that Jack was going to stand in Laurance's path on this? No way. But the point is, he was in a *position* to do so."

217   *"Wally knew he was being sold out":* JOH, 11/25/92.

218   *"Bill Cross was a hothead":* RW, 10/15/91.

219   *Tom Hoving had resigned:* FS, 9/16/91, author's interview.

219   *"Mrs. Wallace had never shown":* Calvin Tompkins, *Merchants and Masterpieces* (Henry Holt, 1989), p. 381.

219   *What she "gave":* Ibid., p. 381.

219   *"To serve on the board":* Hoving, *Making the Mummies Dance* (Simon & Schuster, 1993), p. 14.

220   *In time, those shares:* As of February 1993, the value of the RD shares awarded to the Met was between $500 and $600 million.

220   *This new gift:* In fact, there was a *double* payoff involved in the movement of RD stock from Wallace Funds to Rockefeller S/Os. As *private* foundations, the funds must give away each year an amount equal to 5 percent of total assets. On $2 billion, that's $100 million a year. As funds in support of *public* charities, the S/Os must give away 85 percent of annual *income.* On $2 billion, with dividends kept in the 2 percent range by RD management, that can be as little as $34 million a year.

Chapter Twenty-eight

PAGE

220   *"But by now it was obvious":* Dorothy Evans, 12/10/90, author's interview.

221   *"Jack and I were kept":* ETT, 5/13/93, author's interview.

221   *"But we were under orders":* JA, 9/18/91, author's interview.

221   *"After clearing it":* JS-G, 1/25/92, author's interview.

222   *"Wright then gave him a brief examination":* In defense of Dr. Wright, it should be noted that Wallace was a notoriously reluctant patient, distrusting doctors and preferring to bear his pain in silence. BMcH, letter to the author, 6/21/94.

222   *No one came:* Dorothy Evans, 12/10/90, author's interview.

222   *"I like all my nurses":* JA, 9/18/91, author's interview.

222   *His breathing was raspy:* Dorothy Evans, 12/10/90, author's interview.

223   *After Evans departed, Doherty brooded:* This entire incident was described by Gene Doherty during interviews in 1990 and 1991. Additional details provided by Dorothy Evans, author's interview, 12/10/90. In a letter to the author, McHenry claimed that Doherty was bitter about his termination from RDA and made "some outrageous statements about the last days at 'High Winds.' "

225   *Davies got to the hospital:* Gordon Davies, author's interview, 3/27/91.

226   *Four days later:* ETT, 11/3/92, author's interview.

226   *What the doctors found:* BMcH, 9/22/93, author's interview.

226   *During a meeting:* BS-J, 8/26/92, author's interview.

227   *"There had been a lot":* Dorothy Schmidt, 2/18/91, author's interview.
227   *When Gene Doherty entered:* This episode was described during several author's interviews with Doherty in 1991 and 1992. Also, Dotty Evans, 12/12/90, author's interview.
229   *"I had heard that Wally":* JT, 6/23/92, author's interview.
229   *At five o'clock:* Julie Waldrun, 3/12/92, author's interview.
229   *"Oh!" he cried:* As related to Julie Waldrun.
230   *"Everybody wanted to be the* first: JS-G, 1/25/92, author's interview.
230   *He asked Ilse Doherty:* Ilse Doherty, 5/23/91, author's interview.
230   *"Today has been":* Quoted from diary of Mary Strasburger, 4/2/81.
231   *"Everyone else":* Letter from Gordon Davies to Barney McHenry, 3/26/81.
231   *Curious, Doherty followed:* GD, author's interview.
231   *"I don't suppose we'd say":* Norman Peale eulogy, 4/6/81.
231   *As the Positive Thinker's:* GD, author's interview.
232   *To loyal Gordon:* Gordon Davies, 3/27/91, author's interview.
232   *To angry Betty:* BS-J, 8/26/92, author's interview.
232   *To stubborn Al:* PC, 6/22/92, author's interview.
232   *"I should have done something":* GD, author's interview. Also, PC, 6/22/92.
232   *"Look," he exclaimed:* PC, 6/22/92.
232   *The next morning:* GD, author's interview.

Chapter Twenty-nine

PAGE
235   *Her chief diversion:* GD, author's interviews.
236   *Unlike Thompson:* ETT, 5/13/93, author's interview.
237   *In 1978, he had pleased: New York Times,* 5/9/84. (In all, Lila gave $8 million to Juilliard.)
237   *In 1979, when a fund:* Harr and Johnson, *The Rockefeller Century,* p. 477.
237   *In 1981, he arranged:* Bruce Trachtenberg, director of communications, Wallace/RD Funds. Author's interview, 9/21/93.
237   *Spelman had been:* Collier and Horowitz, p. 98.
237   *In fact, the Spelman gift:* Bruce Trachtenberg, author's interview.
237   *The process that had begun:* Figures are from RD's registration statement filed with the Securities and Exchange Commission upon the initial public sale of its stock, dated 12/89, p. 51 ("Selling Stockholders").
238   *Al Cole had begun to lobby:* PC, 6/22/91, author's interview.
238   *In late April:* GD, author's interview.
238   *"High Winds was incredibly drafty":* Dorothy Schmidt, 2/18/91, author's interview.
239   *Dear Mrs. Little:* Letter from Janine Ardohain to Dorothy Little, 1/15/82.
239   *"No one came":* JA, 8/12/91, author's interview.

Chapter Thirty

PAGE
239   *But the company had earned:* "Intrigue Behind the Ivy at Reader's Digest," *Fortune,* 6/25/84.
240   *At RD, the losses:* Ibid.
240   *"Overall, the company's earnings": New York Times,* 6/1/84.
240   *"They sit there": Business Week,* 3/5/79.
241   *" 'Every book we publish":* The process described by Grune bears an uncanny resemblance to the "Fiction Department" described by George Orwell in his classic novel *1984:* "Julia . . . worked on the novel-writing machines in the Fiction Department. . . .

She could describe the whole process . . . from the general directive issued by the Planning Committee down to the final touching-up by the Rewrite Squad. . . . Books were a commodity that had to be produced, like jam or bootlaces."

241 *"Under George, that began to change":* JOH, 11/25/92, author's interview.

241 *In considering books:* Memo to edit staff from DeWitt Wallace, 7/1/64.

241 *"Our figures showed":* ETT, 11/3/92, author's interview.

242 *"There was always this tremendous pressure":* JOH, 11/25/92, author's interview.

242 *"Readers are well satisfied":* Miriam Lacob, *Columbia Journalism Review,* July/August 1984.

243 *But Stewart-Gordon had turned:* ETT, 8/24/92, author's interview.

243 *Cole had his own complaints:* PC, 6/22/92, author's interview.

243 *"Perhaps I'm wrong":* Memo from Al Cole to Ed Thompson, 10/5/81.

243 *He and Stewart-Gordon met:* JS-G, 1/25/92, author's interview.

244 *For decades, ever since:* Heidenry, p. 172. *RD's* intricate dealings with the CIA and the FBI are further elaborated in the pages that follow.

244 *That dozens of America's:* See Carl Bernstein, "The CIA and the Media: How America's Most Powerful News Media Worked Hand in Glove with the Central Intelligence Agency," *Rolling Stone,* 10/20/77. Joseph Persico addressed this subject in his biography of William Casey: "The press and the CIA are essentially in the same business, gathering intelligence. The only intrinsic difference is that the press reports to a mass audience while the CIA reports to a select few. Otherwise, they have much to tell each other and have always maintained mutually profitable contact." Joseph E. Persico, *Casey* (Viking, 1990), p. 270.

244 *But when Ed Thompson became editor:* Personal knowledge.

244 *In 1977, for example:* See Edward S. Herman and Noam Chomsky, *Manufacturing Consent: The Political Economy of the Mass Media* (Pantheon, 1988), pp. 260–91.

244 *Although scholars would later:* Herman and Chomsky, pp. 280–96.

245 *The origins of the Nosenko:* The Golitsyn defection has been described at length in numerous books, including most prominently the following: Edward Jay Epstein, *Deception,* (Simon & Schuster, 1989), pp. 65–85; David Wise, *Molehunt: The Secret Search for Traitors That Shattered the CIA* (Random House, 1992), pp. 21 ff; John Ranelagh, *The Agency: The Rise and Decline of the CIA,* (Simon & Schuster, 1986), pp. 561 ff; and Tom Mangold, *Cold Warrior* (Simon & Schuster, 1991), pp. 71–117. *Encounter with a Spy,* an unpublished memoir written by former RD deputy editor-in-chief Fulton Oursler, also deals at length with the ramifications of Golitsyn's story.

245 *For two years prior:* See Ranelagh, pp. 336 ff.

245 *Golitsyn's news:* Epstein, pp. 78–80.

245 *"But all of it is nonsense":* During testimony before the Church Committee in 1975, CIA officials admitted that *The Penkovsky Papers* had been "prepared and written by witting Agency assets drawing on actual case material." Edward Epstein, "The Spy Who Came in to Be Sold," *The New Republic,* July 15 and 22, 1985.

246 *Golitsyn also warned:* Mangold, pp. 75 ff.

246 *Then Yuri Nosenko defected:* Wise, pp. 65 ff. Also Ranelagh, Mangold and numerous other books.

246 *Although initially regarded:* According to recently declassified CIA files, in 10/63 the CIA told the FBI that Oswald had met in Mexico City with Soviet consul Valery Kostikov, but failed to explain that it believed Kostikov was a KGB agent who specialized in assassinations. *Had* this belief been communicated, the FBI surely would have had Oswald under surveillance on November 22, 1963, the day JFK was shot. Mark Reibling, "Counterintelligent System," *New York Times,* 3/22/94. In early November, Oswald sent a note to the FBI's Dallas field office threatening to "blow them up" if they didn't stop pestering his wife, Marina. Somehow, this note was ignored. And the agent who received

the note, James Hosty, was later ordered to get rid of it (he flushed it down the toilet). J. Edgar Hoover subsequently lied to the Warren Commission about this event, insisting that the Bureau had had no warning that Oswald might be dangerous. *Time*, 9/6/93. Also, Henry Hurt, *Reasonable Doubt* (Henry Holt, 1985), pp. 250–251.

246 *To deny Nosenko:* Epstein, p. 95.

246 *James Angleton's:* See Mangold, pp. 180, 182, 197; also, Wise, pp. 65–80.

247 *Nosenko was set free:* Mangold, p. 201; Wise, pp. 155–56. Nosenko was "rehabilitated" despite the detailed recommendations of the men who had just spent three years interrogating him. Their report, nine hundred pages long, strongly suggested that Nosenko had been dispatched by the KGB to mislead the Warren Commission about Oswald, to mislead American intelligence about several KGB penetrations, and to devalue the information provided by Anatoli Golitsyn. It recommended further investigation by the FBI. The FBI ignored this recommendation, and the Warren Commission concluded—as J. Edgar Hoover knew it would—that Oswald had acted alone. Oursler, pp. 231–32.

247 *Despite this seeming vindication:* See David C. Martin, *Wilderness of Mirrors* (Harper & Row, 1980), p. 156.

247 *In this role:* Epstein, p. 62. Also, Oursler, "Encounter with a Spy," pp. 1–2, and Heidenry, p. 489.

247 *"You ought to spend some time":* Epstein, p. 12. Also, Oursler, pp. 12–14.

248 *"The Agency is very upset":* FO, author's interview, 3/11/92. Obviously, the CIA already knew what was in the book. Years later, through a Freedom of Information request, the Digest confirmed that copies of the book had been leaked to the FBI. "In a memo classified SECRET on 2/22/78, the Acting Director of the Bureau informed the Washington Field Office that he was enclosing 'one copy each of the drafts of two articles which will appear in the March 1978 and April 1978 issues of Reader's Digest under the title *Legend: The Secret World of Lee Harvey Oswald.*' The stolen drafts themselves (which no doubt contained identifiable editorial markings) were not included, clearly in order to protect the Bureau's source at RD." Oursler, *Encounter with a Spy*, p. 94 of footnotes.

248 *Oursler suggested that:* Epstein's source for Fedora was Bill Sullivan, chief of counterintelligence at the FBI. Like James Angleton at the CIA, Sullivan would eventually be fired for harboring suspicions about KGB penetration. He was later shot and killed in what was billed as a "hunting accident" but which many believe was a KGB murder. Oursler, p. 92 of footnotes.

248 *Oursler was called:* Ibid., p. 296.

248 *Ed Thompson was also called:* ETT, 8/24/92, author's interview. Kalaris and his colleagues genuinely believed that mention of Fedora's name would result in his swift execution. In fact, Fedora later became a Hero of the Soviet Union and died of natural causes in 1990. Wise, p. 153.

248 *"I was prepared":* ETT, 5/13/93, author's interview. When Oursler expressed concern about the growing rift with the Washington bureau and the CIA, Thompson told him not to worry. "Your job is to help Epstein find the truth. As long as you do that, I will back you completely." Oursler, p. 25.

248 *But the stakes:* ETT, author's interview.

248 *But not by the CIA:* In *Encounter with a Spy*, Tony Oursler adds a revealing vignette to the *Legend* controversy. A few weeks after the book's publication, Oursler received from DeWitt Wallace a review of the book clipped from a newsletter called *America's Future*. "The review bore my name in Wally's shaky hand—only that, and an underlining in ink of two phrases in the review. The underlined words were: *'This important book...'* and *'This book is probably the most important written on the subject of the Kennedy assassination.'* It was the last communication I ever received from Wally."

Chapter Thirty-one

PAGE
249   *Early in February:* This incident described by ETT, 3/11/92, author's interview.

250   *"I'm sorry you feel that way":* ETT, author's interview. (Grune declined to answer questions about this meeting.)

250   *For over an hour:* JOH, 11/25/92, author's interview.

250   *He was invited to a luncheon:* This description was provided by James Stewart-Gordon, author's interview.

252   *Lila's diamond:* GD, author's interview.

253   *"You know, Jack":* JOH, 3/25/91, author's interview.

253   *"When we spoke to the Bureau":* FO, 5/12/93, author's interview.

253   *"Good luck":* Oursler, *Encounter with a Spy,* p. 602.

254   *Then Thompson got cold feet:* ETT, 8/24/92, author's interview.

254   *Although distribution of the manuscript:* FO, 9/11/92, author's interview.

254   *During this period:* FO, 9/11/92, author's interview.

254   *"It's true":* ETT, 8/24/92, author's interview.

254   *Cited by the Reagan Administration:* See Herman and Chomsky, *Manufacturing Consent,* pp. 32–33. Also, Michel Brun, *Incident at Sakhalin: The True Mission of KAL Flight 007* (Four Walls Eight Windows, 1995).

254   *That fall, at the height:* Bob Woodward, *Veil: The Secret Wars of the CIA 1981–1987* (Simon & Schuster, 1987), pp. 295–96 (paperback version). A staunch loyalist, Lauder knew without asking what his new job entailed. As he told Woodward, "He would have to establish relationships with reporters, try to determine who could be trusted [so he could] let Casey know when some story that might be trouble was in the pipeline. He would see if he couldn't . . . *recruit* was not exactly the right word, but it was close. Maybe handling reporters might not be too different from his previous work."

255   *"There's something I need to tell you":* ETT, 8/24/92, author's interview.

256   *He felt that Gilmore:* PC, 6/18/91, author's interview. See also Heidenry, p. 557.

256   *In late January:* ETT, 6/20/91, author's interview.

256   *"Mr. President, This Isn't Russia":* After the openness of the Carter years, Reagan and William Casey were seeking by any means to muzzle the media and regain control over information being leaked by congressional staffs. This article was seen as a direct challenge to their efforts. See Ranelagh, pp. 672–75. The *Digest's* insistence that "Directive 84" be recalled was eventually heeded—in part because Secretary of State George Shultz wouldn't go along. "You can polygraph me . . . once," said Shultz. "Then I will resign." Persico, p. 347.

Chapter Thirty-two

PAGE
256   *"In any case":* JOH, 11/25/92, author's interview.

256   March 8: Details of the trip to Mexico provided during author's interviews with Ed Thompson and Jerry Dole, 6/91.

257   *He was interrupted:* Details of Thompson's experiences on March 19 were provided in large part by Thompson himself, with additional input from Jack O'Hara. Author's interviews.

259   *As he studied the older man's hooded eyes:* Thompson's description of Rockefeller on this occasion bears an uncanny similarity to a description of John D., Sr., provided by one of the independent refiners swallowed by Senior during his drive to establish Standard Oil in 1872. "You never *saw* such eyes," the man remembered later. "He took

me all in, measuring just how much fight he could expect from me." Collier and Horowitz, p. 26.

260   *In the hospital's intensive care unit:* Description of Lila's IVs provided by nurses Janine Ardohain and Dorothy Schmidt, author's interviews.

260   *What he saw came:* GD, author's interview.

260   March 21: Details provided by Ed Thompson, author's interview.

260   *"I'll show this to the others":* O'Hara did subsequently show Thompson's memo to Rockefeller. "Interesting idea," said Rockefeller "Perhaps we should consider it in the future." JOH, 11/25/92, author's interview.

261   *"I'll hold on to them":* ETT, author's interview. Cross denies having made this promise.

261   *Rockefeller presented the case:* Board member Dick McLoughlin later described this session to Ed Thompson. ETT, author's interview.

261   *When word of the vote:* ETT, 5/13/93, author's interview. See also Heidenry, p. 561.

262   *He stopped at the office:* David Fuller described this visit to Tony Oursler. FO, 9/11/92, author's interview.

262   *On Monday morning.* Ibid.

263   *CIA director William Casey:* Persico, pp. 458–59.

Chapter Thirty-three

263   *"Every vital organ":* GD, author's interview.

263   *O'Hara was in a terrible:* Details of the Portugal meeting provided by Jeremy Dole, author's interview, 1/30/91.

265   *On their return:* Heidenry, p. 562

265   *Moreover, Cole and Rockefeller:* PC, 6/22/92, author's interview.

266   April 15: Details of this encounter provided by Janine Ardohain, 5/18/91, author's interview.

266   *With time running out:* "Intrigue Behind the Ivy at Reader's Digest," *Fortune,* 6/25/81; Alex S. Jones, "At Reader's Digest, A Fight over Philosophy," *New York Times,* 6/1/84.

266   *Meanwhile, up at High Winds:* JA, 9/11/81, author's interview.

266   *Later that day, McHenry:* Ibid.

266   April 26: *Janine Ardohain called:* Ibid.

267   *By the time Rockefeller:* PC, 6/22/92, author's interview.

267   *After conferring with Strasburger:* GD, author's interview.

267   *In urgent tones:* Ibid. Also, PC, 6/22/92, author's interview.

267   *The four proxy-holders:* As described in the subsequent press release. See below.

267   *Within days, Grune:* PC, author's interview.

268   *Later that afternoon:* JOH, 11/25/92, author's interview.

Chapter Thirty-four

268   *At 9:00 A.M.:* Lila's last moments described in author's interview with JA, 9/18/91.

269   *In the office of the editor-in-chief:* FO, 9/11/92, author's interview.

269   *Later that morning:* This scene was described to author by Gene Doherty, Ross Cutri Joe Guignardi.

270   *"It was purely coincidental":* New York Times, 6/1/84.

270   *"All this speculation":* Ibid.

270   *"I have no comment":* "Reader's Digest: Who's In Charge?" *Columbia Journalism Review,* July/August 1984.

270   *"You could call it that":* "Intrigue Behind the Ivy at Reader's Digest," *Fortune,* 6/25/84.

270   *"I was down there"*: Mary Strasburger, author's interview.
270   *"On this day"*: Peale eulogy, 5/25/84.
271   *The solemn mood dissipated:* FS, 9/16/91, author's interview.
271   *"I was just an ad man"*: Recalled by FO, 8/28/92, author's interview.
271   *"Look at that"*: Ibid.
271   *"You know, Ruth"*: Ibid.

Chapter Thirty-five

PAGE
273   *"I want to show you something"*: Business Week, 6/4/90.
274   *"I am drawn to this room"*: Gannett Westchester Newspapers, 1/25/87.
274   *"We will maintain"*: New York Times, 3/22/86.
274   *It was also true:* Wallace himself was evidently made aware of this problem. "But we convinced him that a way could be devised to get around the deadline," recalls Barney McHenry. "By the time the grace period ended, something else—some new gimmick we hadn't yet figured out—would be in place." Author's interview, 9/22/93.
274   *Each understood that the central issue:* This claim is supported by author's interviews with Ed Thompson, Peggy Cole, Jack O'Hara and Barney McHenry.
275   *Laurance's goal:* Ibid.
275   *Grune's goal:* Ibid.
275   *"We didn't even give them"*: ETT, 11/3/92, author's interview.
276   *"Laurance understood"*: Ibid.
276   *But Digest insiders:* "There was never a time when RD's stock could not have been five or even ten times higher," says Bill Cross. "All we had to do was make basic changes, changes DeWitt Wallace would not allow." Cross, 8/5/93, author's interview. "Hang on to that stock," Dick Waters always advised those he liked. "After Wally goes, someone will push the right buttons and your shares will be worth a fortune." Waters, 10/15/91, author's interview.
276   *The situation at RD:* For a description of the situation at RJR, see Bryan Burrough and John Helyar, *Barbarians at the Gate* (Harper & Row, 1990), pp. 370–71.
277   *"We asked ourselves a simple question"*: Quoted in Adweek, 7/22/85.
278   *"I was named"*: FO, 8/25/92, author's interview.
278   *"I have a question"*: Ibid.
279   *In recent years:* Oursler memo to Management Committee, 1/21/85.

Chapter Thirty-six

PAGE
280   *Bearded and heavyset:* Personal observation. (Author was Tomlinson's supervisor during this period.)
280   *During the fifties:* Tom Bethell, "What the Voice of America Makes of America," Harper's, 5/85.
281   *But in 1980:* Ibid.
281   *Reagan appointed his California:* When a Reagan staff member asked CIA director William Casey about Wick's qualifications, Casey shrugged. "Reagan takes his calls," he said. "That's about it." Persico, p. 204.
281   *"At issue is the credibility:* ABC's *World News Tonight,* 6/17/93.
282   *Pressed for evidence:* Anthony Lewis, "Too Clever by Half," *New York Times,* 6/21/92. Sterling's book became the bible of the Reagan administration and the international right wing and earned her the status of number-one mass-media expert on terrorism. But Sterling's record was far from unblemished. For example, her published claims that

French radical Henry Curiel was "KGB connected" had led to several slander suits (which she lost). When a French court found no support for her charges, she admitted that they were "hypothetical" and not "factual."

282 *Sensing an opportunity:* Woodward, *Veil: The Secret Wars of the CIA,* pp. 126–27.

282 *When the experts were done:* Part of Sterling's information came from a phony story on the so-called "Red Brigade" planted in the Italian press by the CIA. See Woodward, p. 131. Another part was supplied by Czech defector Jan Sejna, whose chief evidence for a Soviet terror network came from a document *forged by the CIA* to test his integrity! When he "recognized" the document, of course, that meant he had failed the test. But this didn't prevent him from showing the document around, or prevent Sterling from citing it in *Reader's Digest.* See Chomsky's *Manufacturing Consent,* pp. 159, 367. Whether Sterling and Gilmore were truly "misled" by these documents—or "misled on purpose"—is another question.

282 *"I paid $13.95":* Woodward, p. 127.

282 *Four months later:* Lewis, *New York Times.*

282 *An intelligence consultant: New York Times,* 1/27/83. In a subsequent letter to the *Times,* Ed Thompson admitted that Henze had been hired by RD's Washington bureau to prepare a background report on Agca. *New York Times,* 2/7/83. See also Heidenry, pp. 493–94, and Paul Henze, *The Plot to Kill the Pope* (Scribners, 1983), pp. 128, 182. Henze had been a staffer at the National Security Council during the Carter administration, and was a protege of Zbigniew Brzezinski—a connection that at least raises the possibility of Laurance Rockefeller's involvement in the affair (since Brzezinski was a close Rockefeller "associate" and a fellow member of the Rockefeller-supported Trilateral Commission, in addition to being Laurance's summer neighbor in Northeast Harbor, Maine). During his CIA years in Turkey, Henze was accused by former president Bulent Ecevit of seeking to "destabilize" the country. See Chomsky, pp. 158 and 160. In 1965, Henze led a supersecret CIA task force on a worldwide tour of facilities run by Radio Liberty, Radio Free Europe and the Voice of America, the purpose being to explore methods of beaming propaganda broadcasts into China. Brzezinski, then a professor at Columbia, was a member of this team, as was *Reader's Digest* roving editor William Griffith. The group recommended that the new broadcast facility be set up under the VOA. Bernstein, "The CIA and the Media," *Rolling Stone,* 10/20/77.

282 *just as Yuri Nosenko:* The symmetry is remarkable: Nosenko had been "made available" because his message absolved the FBI/CIA of malfeasance in the JFK assassination. Now Henze was being "made available" because his message accused the Evil Empire of trying to assassinate the pope.

282 *a specialist in propaganda:* Chomsky, p. 145.

282 *"Take as long as you like":* Quoted in "Solving the Plot to Kill the Pope," *Reader's Digest,* 10/84.

282 *William Safire:* "Cross in the Cross Hairs," *New York Times,* 12/16/82.

283 *Analysts at the CIA:* Woodward, *Veil,* pp. 129–31. As the "most political" director in CIA history, Casey frequently committed the cardinal sin of intelligence: tailoring facts to fit policy. "There was little doubt in his mind as to who was behind the man who had pulled the trigger," writes Joseph Persico. "He pushed his analytical people mercilessly, demanding almost daily to see the latest evidence. 'But our analysis showed that what Sterling claimed didn't stand up,' said John McMahon [Casey's deputy director for operations]. 'It just was not true.'" Persico, pp. 287–88.

283 *Although Casey's deputy:* Lewis, *New York Times.* Casey himself reluctantly delivered the same message to Ronald Reagan. "They claim there's 'insufficient evidence,'" he growled. "Of course, Mr. President, you and I know better." Persico, p. 288. This was *Doublethink* of the highest order. As Orwell expressed it: "To know and not to know, to be conscious of complete truthfulness while telling carefully constructed lies." *1984,* p. 32.

283   *Reagan and Casey:* Woodward, p. 131.

283   *In the summer of 1983:* A detailed account of the Bitov/Panitza/Barron encounters is found in Oursler, *Encounter with a Spy,* pp. 518–20. Oursler points to the "extraordinary parallels" between the Bitov case and the Nosenko case. "The only difference," he writes, "is that in Bitov's case the KGB plan worked. The message was delivered and the defector returned home. What had he said to Barron? How had Barron resolved the contradiction between Bitov's message and the Sterling/RD article? I would never find out. Like the Hurt book, all copies of the Barron article simply disappeared." See also Heidenry, pp. 598–600.

283   *In 1985, alarmed:* Lewis, *New York Times.*

283   *In 1986, the three:* See Chomsky, p. 166. Although there never was a credible case for a Bulgarian Connection, Sterling and *RD* continued to exploit their theory—and reap the publicity rewards—for several years. "The Plot to Murder the Pope" was followed in 1983 by a Sterling/RD book called "The Time of the Assassins," which in turn was followed by an "editorial review" in *RD* called "Solving the Plot to Kill the Pope." Sterling also published three pieces in the *Wall Street Journal,* several in the *New York Times,* and appeared on NBC News, CBS News and the MacNeil-Lehrer NewsHour. For its part, *RD* clearly found articles on KGB terror against important religious figures irresistible. In 12/85, it published "Murder of a Polish Priest," and in 9/91 (five years *after* "The Plot to Murder the Pope" was demolished in court) it published "Murder of a Russian Priest." During these same years, dozens of religious workers, including four U.S. nuns, were murdered in the U.S. client states of Guatemala and El Salvador by right-wing terrorists trained and supported by the CIA. No mention of these deaths ever appeared in *RD.*

284   *"... the U.S. now has a chance...":* Barron, "The Spy Family That Imperiled America," *RD,* 4/87.

284   *"The advantages provided":* Quoted in John Barron, *Breaking the Ring* (Houghton Mifflin, 1987), p. 148. As *RD*'s most-active propagandist for the intelligence services, Barron was given extraordinary access to CIA and FBI activities. In *Breaking the Ring,* he described how FBI agents regularly met with Soviet security officer (and later defector) Vitaly Yurchenko at a Washington drinking establishment. As an "unofficial spokesman" for the Bureau, Barron sometimes sat in on those sessions himself. During the Walker trial, Barron (who admitted to having an FBI security clearance) served as a witness for the prosecution.

284   *"As it happens":* Edward Jay Epstein, *New Republic,* 3/28/94.

284   *This was, in fact, the first question:* Ibid. See also "Deadly Mole," *Newsweek,* 3/7/94.

284   *Yurchenko confirmed:* Newsweek, 3/7/94.

284   *Beyond Howard and Pelton:* Epstein, *New Republic,* 3/28/94.

284   *Director Casey actually bragged:* Epstein, *Deception,* p. 204.

285   *"Yurchenko's redefection":* Persico, pp. 468–70.

285   *But "officials aware":* John Barron, *Breaking the Ring,* p. 25. The CIA simply couldn't believe that Yurchenko might be a plant. "If his defection was a contrived penetration," insisted DDO John McMahon at the time, "then his redefection three months later made no sense." In fact, it made a great deal of sense. In those three months, Vitaly Yurchenko succeeded brilliantly in drawing the scent away from Aldrich Ames— already on his way to becoming the most destructive spy in U.S. history. As a veteran CIA man told Tony Oursler: "For years the KGB served us shit on a dish and told us it was chocolate cake. And the worse part is not that we ate it. The worst part is that we ate it and said, 'Mmm, this is *good!'* " Oursler, p. 571.

285   *Recruited by the KGB:* James Adams, *Sellout: Aldrich Ames and the Corruption of the CIA* (Viking, 1995), pp. 79–106. Oleg Gordievsky was one of the first agents betrayed by Ames. Arrested in Moscow, Gordievsky later managed to escape to England. He was

subsequently debriefed by a CIA team led by . . . Aldrich Ames! See William Shaw-cross, "Notes from the Underground," *Times Literary Supplement*, 5/12/95.

285 *As it happened,* Rick Ames: Epstein, *New Republic.* Also, *Newsweek,* 3/7/94.

285 *So here we have:* See Adams, pp. 100-102. Although Yurchenko knew about Ames, Ames knew nothing about Yurchenko. Thus, on the night before the first interrogation, "he got so drunk he almost overslept."

285 *Rick Ames identified:* New York Times, 9/28/94.

285 *And even when the CIA:* Tim Weiner, *New York Times,* 11/1/95.

286 *"Mind-boggling!":* New York Times, 11/1/95.

286 *"Inconceivable!":* Los Angeles Times, 10/29/95.

286 *"First I will build":* Quoted in *Forbes,* 11/25/91.

286 *Yet it is clear now:* See Richard Ned Lebow and Janice Gross Stern, "Reagan and the Russians," *Atlantic Monthly,* 2/94. The impending collapse of the Soviet Union (the CIA's ominous reports notwithstanding) was evident at the time to several senior U.S. political leaders. "The Marxist ethos is disappearing into a black hole," said Senator Daniel Patrick Moynihan in 1983. "The only people who haven't gotten the word are in Cuba . . . or in the Reagan Administration." Quoted in Persico, p. 336. William Casey himself may have understood the situation. "Casey recognized that Gorbachev was more concerned with saving his country's economy than rescuing the world from capitalism." Persico, p. 576.

287 *"The net effect [of the new reports]":* As quoted in *Time,* 11/13/95. See also: Adams, *Sellout;* David Wise, *Nightmover* (HarperCollins, 1995); and Tim Weimer, David John-ston and Neil A. Lewis, *Betrayal* (Random House, 1995).

Chapter Thirty-seven

PAGE

288 *Indeed, there was a worrisome precedent:* Richard Behar, "A Tempting Target," *Forbes,* 4/18/88.

289 *At the conclusion of the stockholders' meeting:* Author was present on this occasion. Although note-taking was strictly forbidden, he managed to record the basic facts.

290 *In July 1985, combining:* Lisa Collins, 11/3/92, author's interview. "Legally," Collins adds, "this was the right thing to do. The funds are meant by law to be separate from the Digest."

290 *"I had eaten":* BMcH, 9/22/93, author's interview.

290 *But Grune became chairman of the funds:* One wonders why it was a conflict of interest for McHenry to serve RD and the funds if Grune himself could be chairman of both.

290 *Among other things, Stamas:* Lisa Collins, author's interview.

290 *"Everything that has been done":* Quoted in "The Wallace Funds' Dual Identity," *Chron-icle of Philanthropy,* 7/28/92. Bill Cross disagrees with his former boss. "The situation between RD and the funds is totally improper," he says. "Those are the *Wallace* Funds. They should have nothing to do with RD." Author's interview, 8/5/93. "Mr. Wallace would be mad about those name changes," adds Lisa Collins. "But Mrs. Wallace would be *furious!* If the funds were mentioned at all, they were *LAW* Funds. And don't you *dare* mention Reader's Digest!" Author's interview, 11/3/92.

290 *What he failed to understand:* Heidenry, p. 584.

291 *"I didn't want to be part:* Cross, author's interview, 8/5/93.

291 *But the required arm's-length relationship:* Chronicle of Philanthropy, 7/28/92.

291 *"In effect," concluded:* Ibid.

291 *"It so happens":* Ibid.

291 *"The current setup":* Ibid.

291 *"If they have found a loophole":* Quoted in *Forbes,* 4/18/88.

291   *Not satisfied with this answer:* Details of the Cross/Grune legal consultations provided by Bill Cross, author's interview, 8/5/93. In an "affidavit of legal services" dated 4/10/90, Cleary, Gottlieb partner Sandra Weiksner described the problem brought to her by Grune and Cross as "the most interesting and challenging . . . of my career. This affidavit . . . cannot convey the multiplicity and interconnectednes of the issues involved."

292   *Under the Proskauer plan:* As explained in various Digest proxy statements.

292   *"In fact,* nobody *watches":* BMcH, 9/22/93, author's interview. In his latest book, *Who Will Tell the People,* best-selling author William Greider discusses this problem at length: "While the news media focus on the conventional political drama of enacting new laws, another less obvious question preoccupies Washington: Will the government *enforce* the law? Or is there a way to change its terms and dilute its impact on private interests? Lawyers inquire whether exceptions can be arranged for important clients. Major corporations warn . . . of dire economic consequences if legal deadlines are not postponed." See *Who Will Tell the People* (Simon & Schuster, 1992), p. 106.

292   *In private letters: Chronicle of Philanthropy,* 7/28/92.

Chapter Thirty-eight

PAGE

293   *They had discussed:* Letter from BMcH to Jack O'Hara, 3/8/79.

293   *Overnight, feelers from the rich and famous:* Stories about the pending High Winds sale filled local newspapers for months. Even the *New York Daily News* got in on the act.

293   *Never one to miss:* The realtor was Mark Cole of the Vincent and Whittemore agency in Bedford Village. Letter from Barney McHenry to Mark Cole, 9/25/84.

294   *On an afternoon in September:* GD, author's interview.

294   *Six months later: Gannett Westchester Newspapers,* 4/14/85.

294   *In November 1985, it was sold:* Ibid, 3/1/86.

294   *And now Doherty:* GD, author's interview.

295   *"I was after the Digest":* Quoted in *Forbes,* 4/18/88.

296   *When the Digest announced: New York Times,* 3/22/86.

296   *Asked by a reporter: Adweek,* 7/22/85.

296   *Wallace had insisted: Marketing B,* 9/27/85.

297   *When Grune took over:* These figures were routinely supplied during annual meetings of employee stockholders.

Chapter Thirty-nine

PAGE

297   *To participate in the offer:* Language is from the confidential offering statement sent to employee stockholders on 9/15/86.

298   *"Just to be sure":* From "confidential" notes entitled "Stock Part of GVG Speech—Not Included in Official Text," with handwritten emendations by Mr. Grune. Author was present on this occasion.

299   *The One Third Plan:* Cited in a "personal and confidential" letter from Grune to employee stockholders, 6/22/87.

300   *"I saw you on TV":* FO, 9/11/92, author's interview.

301   *"Tell Gilmore to back off":* Dan O'Keefe, 11/22/90, author's interview.

302   *A federal judge later ruled:* Judge Robert Ward ruled that the selling stockholders had every right to sell and that the Digest had then fired them. The author was one of those involved.

Chapter Forty

PAGE

303 *"We tried often enough":* Tom Bundrick, 5/13/93, author's interview.

304 *READER'S DIGEST BREAKS: Wall Street Journal,* 12/29/89.

304 *After a 20-for-1 split:* Details taken from the SEC registration statement.

305 *In 1990, according to:* "The Flap over Executive Pay," *Business Week* cover story, 5/6/91.

305 *"Wally was a humble man": Gannett Westchester Newspapers,* 7/7/85.

306 *In fact, by this point:* Again, echoes of Orwell's *1984* are unmistakable. As the novel's hero Winston Smith explains: "Don't you realize that the past is being abolished? . . . Already we know almost nothing about the Revolution and the years before the Revolution. Every record has been destroyed or falsified, every book has been rewritten, every picture has been repainted."

Chapter Forty-one

PAGE

306 *The average in the industry:* Bill Cross, 8/5/93, author's interview.

306 *Although the gifts:* (See table on p. 307.) These sums were derived by multiplying number of shares awarded to each institution (as reported in the SEC filing statement) times value per share on dates indicated.

308 *In fact, Wallace had given up:* "Wallace wanted to educate kids to be good citizens. That was his real goal. And not at the college level. He felt you had to reach kids at an earlier age. Just look at the record!" PC, 6/22/92, author's interview. A copy of Wallace's guidelines was provided to author by Ed Thompson.

308 *In fact, beyond her sad musings:* FS, 9/16/91, author's interview.

309 *"She always supported* specific *projects":* Lisa Collins, author's interview, 11/3/92.

310 *John was its first:* Harr, *The Rockefeller Conscience,* pp. 120–57.

310 *"Having worked so long with artists":* Ibid., p. 140.

310 *When Lincoln Center:* Ibid., p. 147.

311 *"The days when twenty-five hundred": New York Times,* 12/3/92,

311 *"He just wasn't interested":* ETT, 9/24/92, author's interview.

311 *"Laurance has always hoped":* BMcH, 9/22/93, author's interview.

312 *"They would* never": JOH, 11/25/92, author's interview.

312 *"The Wallaces had nothing to do":* ETT, author's interview.

312 *"Lila provided us":* FS, 9/16/91, author's interview.

313 *And the story at the Wallace Funds:* Figures and examples are from the funds' 1994 annual reports.

314 *"Yet our government":* See Lester Thurow, *The Future of Capitalism* (William Morrow, 1996), p. 16.

314 *AGING AUDIENCES POINT: New York Times,* 12/3/95.

316 *Corporate domination:* Figures are from *The Media Monopoly* by Ben Bagdikian (Beacon Press, 1992).

318 *"Both* Reader's Digest *and* Time *succeeded":* See Bagdikian, p. 112.

321 *"We had research":* Tom Bundrick, recently retired RD sales promotion director, 5/13/93, author's interview.

321 *Then management compounded the problem: New York Times,* 6/18/93.

321 *"It may take us 12 to 24 months": New York Times,* 5/5/93.

322 *"The savings associated":* From C. J. Lawrence stock-analysis report, 11/5/93.

322 *"It is with a deep sense of regret":* Mt. Kisco *Patent Trader,* 6/4/93.

323 *One year later:* From RD's 1994 annual report.

323 *Before joining the Digest: New York Times*, 8/21/91.
323 *In September 1994: Gannett Suburban Newspapers*, 9/8/94.
323 *Eight months later: New York Times*, 4/27/95.
323 Travel Holiday: *Wall Street Journal*, 1/15/96.
323 *In February 1996: New York Times*, 2/1/96.
323 *"We have been a print": Wall Street Journal*, 2/2/96.
323 *Created by the CIA:* Victor Marchetti and John D. Marks, *The CIA and the Cult of Intelligence* (Knopf, 1974), pp. 168–70.

Epilogue

PAGE
327 *Joe Guignardi woke early:* Scenes depicted in the epilogue are based on author's interviews with Joe Guignardi and Rossario Cutri, 6/91.
328 *Peltz had made:* Peltz's past is detailed in (among others) Connie Bruck, *The Predator's Ball* (Simon & Schuster, 1988), pp. 105 ff.
328 *As Guignardi parked:* This would have been Bernard Lafferty, a man whose recent personal troubles provide a fitting ending to the sad last years at High Winds. Fired by Nelson Peltz in 1987 (for being drunk), Lafferty eventually caught on as butler for aging tobacco heiress Doris Duke. After Duke died in 1993 under suspicious circumstances (a nurse has charged that Duke was given a fatal dose of morphine), Lafferty turned out to be a major beneficiary of her estate. But his access to Duke's millions has been challenged in court by Duke's former companion, a young woman named Chandi Heffner, who turns out to be Nelson Peltz's sister-in-law. While the battle over the Duke will continues, Lafferty has returned to heavy drinking, and in June 1994 (according to an account in *Newsweek*) drove his Cadillac through a red light in Hollywood, hitting four parked cars before crashing into the famed *Whisky à Go Go* nightclub. Details from *Vanity Fair*, 3/94, and *Newsweek*, 2/20/95.

Index

About the Author

Peter Canning joined *Reader's Digest* in 1963, after graduation from Harvard College and four years in U.S. Army intelligence. He served as *Digest* managing editor from 1980 until 1988. He lives today in Westport Point, Massachusetts, with his wife Gaelen. This is his first book.